# Custom in Islamic Law and Legal Theory

Palgrave Series in Islamic Theology, Law, and History

This groundbreaking series, edited by one of the most influential scholars and a leading authority on Islamic law, critically examines Islamic theology and law in the historical contexts in which they have developed. The theology ranges from Shi'ism, Sunnism, and Sufism to Wahabism and Muslim Brotherhood, and such wide-ranging topics as terrorism, gender, and human rights are discussed within the field of Islamic law. This series aims to provide cumulative and progressive books that attest to the exacting and demanding methodological and pedagogical standards that are needed in contemporary and future studies of Islam.

*Series Editor:*
**Khaled Abou El Fadl** is the Omar and Azmeralda Alfi Distinguished Professor in Islamic Law at the UCLA School of Law where he teaches International Human Rights, Islamic Jurisprudence, National Security Law, Law and Terrorism, Islam and Human Rights, Political Asylum and Political Crimes, and Legal Systems. He also holds the Chair in Islam and Citizenship at the University of Tilburg, The Netherlands. Dr. El Fadl is one of the world's leading authorities on Islamic law and Islam, and a prominent scholar in the field of human rights.

**Titles:**
*Custom in Islamic Law and Legal Theory: The Development of the Concepts of ʿUrf and ʿĀdah in the Islamic Legal Tradition*
Ayman Shabana

# Custom in Islamic Law and Legal Theory

## The Development of the Concepts of *ʿUrf* and *ʿĀdah* in the Islamic Legal Tradition

*Ayman Shabana*

palgrave
macmillan

CUSTOM IN ISLAMIC LAW AND LEGAL THEORY

Softcover reprint of the hardcover 1st edition 2010 978-0-230-10592-8

First published in 2010 by
PALGRAVE MACMILLAN®
in the United States—a division of St. Martin's Press LLC,
175 Fifth Avenue, New York, NY 10010.

Where this book is distributed in the UK, Europe and the rest of the world, this is by Palgrave Macmillan, a division of Macmillan Publishers Limited, registered in England, company number 785998, of Houndmills, Basingstoke, Hampshire RG21 6XS.

Palgrave Macmillan is the global academic imprint of the above companies and has companies and representatives throughout the world.

Palgrave® and Macmillan® are registered trademarks in the United States, the United Kingdom, Europe and other countries.

ISBN 978-1-349-29022-2 ISBN 978-0-230-11734-1 (eBook)

DOI 10.1057/9780230117341

Library of Congress Cataloging-in-Publication Data

Shabana, Ayman, 1973–
Custom in Islamic law and theory : the development of the concepts of ʿurf and ʿādah in the Islamic legal tradition / by Ayman Shabana.
p. cm.—(Palgrave series in Islamic theology, law, and history)
Includes bibliographical references.
1. Customary law (Islamic law) I. Title.

KBP455.S52 2010
340.5′9—dc22 2010019466

A catalogue record of the book is available from the British Library.

Design by Newgen Imaging Systems (P) Ltd., Chennai, India.

First edition: December 2010

*To Mona, Yusuf, and Maryam*
*with love and gratitude*

# Contents

## Part 3 Development and Expansion

# Series Editor's Preface

This book is the first volume of a new series of original studies on Islamic law and theology that clearly raise the bar for rigorous scholarship in the field of Islamic Studies. The volumes of this series are chosen not only for their disciplined methodology, exhaustive research, or academic authoritativeness, but for their significant insight into the world of Islam as it was, is, and is likely to become. The volumes are selected for their relevance to furthering the understanding of the lived and the living Islam, the realities that have shaped the ways Muslims perceive, represent, and practice their religion. Ayman Shabana initiates the series with his eye-opening study on the role of practice and custom in the development and theory of Islamic law. This is the first systematic study to investigate the extent to which Muslim jurists integrated, rationalized, and normatively legitimated the reliance on both what was thought to be universal or local social norms and practices in the context of a legal system guided by Divine text and will. To date, contemporary scholars, whether Western or non-Western and Muslim or non-Muslim, have assumed that the role of social practice and custom in the normative constructions and theories of Islamic jurisprudence has been very limited. Shabana's original and ground-breaking scholarship not only mandates the re-examination of these inherited perceptions, but, even more, it invites researchers to revisit long-held assumptions about the nature and function of so-called religious legal systems, especially in contrast to the broad and often ambiguous category of secular legal systems. Furthermore, among the profoundly salient issues Shabana's study raises is the dynamic balance between determinism, contingency, and functionalism in a legal system founded on the assumption of a supreme and eternal legislator, and thus, transcendent and universal laws that are perpetually valid, unwaveringly necessary, and always good. These dogmatic assumptions, however, are dynamically and creatively negotiated within the context of other compelling and at times competing assumptions, such as that the laws of God are found not just in texts but also in the nature of creation; the laws of human autonomy, agency, and inheritance of the earth; or the imperative of ending human suffering or avoiding hardship.

Like all solid scholarship, Shabana's work on these critical issues raises as many questions as it answers. But this book will become an indispensable starting point for any person who hopes to understand the nature of Islamic law, and it is bound to become the necessary foundation for any future work on the place of custom, and indeed the role of revelation and determinism, in Islamic jurisprudence. No serious student of Islamic law or theology can afford not to read this original and timely book.

# Acknowledgments

This book started as the dissertation of my PhD degree completed at UCLA in 2009. I would like to start by thanking the members of my dissertation committee for their unfailing support and continued guidance from the beginning of that project until its completion. I owe the chair of the committee, Professor Khaled Abou El-Fadl, such a tremendous debt that I doubt I will ever be able to repay even a portion of it. Professor Abou El-Fadl encouraged me to pursue this topic and graciously provided help along every step of the way. Most importantly, he taught me, by example, that there is neither a royal road to knowledge nor a shortcut to serious scholarship. I am also indebted to Professor Michael Morony for his support, passionate interest in the subject, and probing questions, which incited me to examine the subject from different perspectives. Similarly, I am indebted to Professor Leonard Binder, whose incisive comments challenged me to think deeper and to pay attention to the subtle details. Professor Ivan Strenski has been a wonderful mentor and teacher. I benefited significantly from his feedback and I hope, one day, that I will be able to satisfy his criteria for good writing. Last but not least, I would like to express my gratitude to Professor Scott Bartchy for his overwhelming support and encouragement throughout the period I spent at UCLA. In our frequent discussions on many varied topics, he always impressed upon me the importance of intellectual integrity and its indispensability for any serious scholar.

In the course of writing this book, I have accumulated a huge debt to many teachers, colleagues, and friends. It will be difficult to mention each of them by name, but I would like to express my appreciation for their input, which has, both directly and indirectly, enhanced the quality of this work. I would like, however, to thank Dr. Khalid Masud for his helpful comments and feedback, Dr. Muhammad Shahhat al-Jindi for suggesting useful sources, Dr. Ahmad Atif Ahmad for his comments and for listening patiently, Dr. Kevin Mulroy for his encouragement and for reading parts of the work, and all the fellow members of Professor Abou El-Fadl's Sunday *Halaqah*. I would like also to thank the Islamic Studies Program at UCLA for awarding me scholarships throughout the period of my study for the PhD degree, UCLA Graduate Summer Mentorship Program for awarding me two consecutive summer research scholarships, and UCLA library staff for their dedication and wonderful service. Furthermore, I would like to thank all my colleagues in the Department of Religious Studies of the University of Tennessee at Knoxville for their continuing support and encouragement. Although this work has benefited greatly from the input and contributions of the individuals mentioned here, and many others as well, I alone remain fully responsible for its contents.

Finally, I owe a huge debt to all the members of my family whose love has been a constant source of inspiration. The greatest gratitude, however, I owe to my wife, Mona, and children, Yusuf and Maryam. Their sacrifice has been enormous and the time I spent away from them can never be made up for. I just hope they will understand and that their sacrifice was worthwhile.

# Note on Transliteration and Translation of Arabic Words

Transliteration of Arabic words follows the *ALA-LC Romanization Tables: Transliteration Schemes for Non-Roman Scripts* with the exception of rule 11(b1): the case of (يّة or يّه) representing the combination of long vowel plus consonant where it is written as *īyah* but here it is written as *iyyah* (e.g. *fiqhiyyah*). The Arabic words ḥadīth, muftī, mujtahid, sharīʿah, and sunnah are treated as common English words and therefore are not italicized. As a general rule, the capitalized Sunnah refers exclusively to the sunnah of the Prophet. Translation of Qurʾānic verses either comes from or is a modified version of Abdullah Yusuf Ali's *The Meaning of the Holy Qur'ān*. Unless otherwise indicated, translation of all other passages, including Prophetic reports, is my own.

# Introduction

## Custom in the Islamic Legal Tradition: Past and Present

A quick survey of most modern works of Islamic legal theory reveals the importance of the legal concept of custom. Following the legal reforms that were undertaken in the majority of modern Muslim nation-states, the status of custom as a source of law has been consolidated. Most of these reforms have listed custom as one of the main sources of law, even in some cases before sharīʿah itself. The majority of these legal reforms were inspired by modern Western legal codes and they echoed the theoretical paradigms that shaped these Western legal codes.[1] When we turn to the primary or classical sources of Islamic law, however, we find that custom had traditionally played a more *supportive* role in the construction of sharīʿah-based rulings. Eventually, Muslim jurists recognized custom as one of the sources of Islamic law, though as a secondary source rather than a primary one. This gradual shift in the status of custom is seen mainly as a function of the pressure that was exerted on Muslim jurists to recognize the important role of actual practice in shaping legal theory. According to this view, Muslim jurists initially incorporated custom under other generic concepts such as the tradition (Sunnah) of the Prophet, consensus of the jurists (*ijmāʿ*), or even juristic preference (*istiḥsān*). They, however, had to recognize custom as an independent source of law when such *ad hoc* recognition proved increasingly insufficient.

The shift in the status of custom in the modern period raises the question of whether it was precipitated externally by the modern legal reforms that were imposed on the tradition from without, or internally by other factors from within. Undoubtedly, modern legal reforms have drastically expedited this shift and even pushed it beyond the limits that the legal tradition would allow. Still, however, it would be inaccurate to attribute the causes of this shift solely to the Western-inspired legal reforms.[2] In the following chapters, I argue that the concept of custom underwent an internal, gradual, and incremental process of evolution which, in turn, was a part of a larger process that shaped the entire legal tradition. Moreover, I argue that although on the surface this tradition seemed static, fixed, and immutable, at a deeper level it was subject to constant change and reconstruction depending on the numerous variables that the jurists confronted. Otherwise, how can one explain the extended history of sharīʿah and its various patterns of localization? Despite the apparent rigid structure consisting of the four cardinal sources (Qurʾān, Sunnah of the Prophet, consensus of the jurists, and juristic analogy), the actual construction of the law also relies on a number of secondary sources, built-in mechanisms, and various other nuances that permeate the different stages of the legal process. It is through these multiple sources that the law secures a degree of flexibility that allows it to maintain its currency.

Unmeasured flexibility, however, has the potential of undermining the distinctive identity of a legal system, to the extent that the resultant law becomes completely unpredictable. In the case of Islamic law, it was legal theory that preserved the distinctive identity of the Islamic legal system. Regardless of the particular conclusions that a jurist might reach, these conclusions would be acceptable as long as the jurist remained bound by the main prescriptions of the legal method. These conclusions, however, are not considered final or unquestionable. They remain subject to revision and critique by fellow jurists within a system of peer review that preserves the identity of the tradition . Over time, Islamic law developed within an interpretive legal culture that was governed and bound by its own regulations. Those regulations determined important factors such as criteria for membership, guidelines for lawmaking, and hierarchy within the tradition.

Due to the cumulative and dynamic character of this tradition, it is difficult to study particular concepts in isolation. Because concepts do not exist in a vacuum, they can only be understood in particular contexts. Analyzing the concept of custom in the Islamic legal tradition, therefore, entails the study of other related concepts within the tradition, and ultimately, the study of individual concepts sheds light on the development of the entire tradition.

## Custom and Religion

The relationship between custom and religion is as old as religion itself. One of the primary goals of religion, in the Abrahamic prophetic tradition, is to combat the erroneous practices and customs that conflict with its core principles and teachings. In its constant struggle against later accretions, religion is constantly in need of renewal and reform to regenerate itself and to preserve its pure essence. The famous historian of religion, Friedrich Max Müller, notes:

> If there is one thing which a comparative study of religions places in the clearest light, it is the inevitable decay to which every religion is exposed. It may seem almost like a truism that no religion can continue to be what it was during the lifetime of its founder and its first apostles. Yet it is but seldom borne in mind that without constant reformation, i.e., without a constant return to its fountain-head, every religion, even the most perfect, nay the most perfect on account of its very perfection, more even than others, suffers from its contact with the world, as the purest air suffers from the mere fact of its being breathed.[3]

This dialectical relationship between custom and religion is particularly relevant in the case of Islam. Islam does not consist only of an orthodoxy that defines a certain belief system but—and even to a larger extent—as an orthopraxy that defines normative practice. Custom, by definition, relates more to actions and practices than to thoughts, ideas, or beliefs. If this holds true for the formative period of Islamic history, it also holds true for the subsequent periods, because the encounter between Islam and custom in the different regional contexts never stopped. In a sense, the history of the Islamic legal tradition can be seen as a documentation of the encounter between sharīʿah and the different regional customs. Through renewal and reform, the jurists strove to accommodate agreeable customs and combat disagreeable ones.

The primary focus of this study is the legal concept of custom and the extent to which it influenced the process of lawmaking—or, more particularly, the thinking about lawmaking—as reflected in legal theory. It is important, nonetheless, to keep in mind the distinction between the religious and legal senses of custom. These two senses may appear to be inseparable, but, in fact, their interconnectedness may account for the confusion that the term often evokes. From the religious perspective, custom is perceived as a negative construct that corrupts the original and pure essence of religion. From the legal perspective (as a legal tool), on the other hand, custom is perceived positively as a means that enables the legal system to adapt and adjust to different contexts. By incorporating custom within the larger framework of legal theory, the jurists turned custom from a rival of sharīʿah into a legal instrument that allows the legal tradition to adjust itself to different social and cultural settings. The jurists strove to balance these two considerations. On the one hand, they aimed to purify the law and rid it of the accretions that gradually crept into it over time, and on the other, they sought to incorporate those customary elements that did not clash with the fundamental principles of the law. In other words, the jurists aimed to adjust the law to ensure its applicability, but not at the expense of its normativity.

## Custom and the Problem of Definition

In dealing with a loaded and historically rich concept such as custom, it is important to start by separating its different meanings. Custom as a social norm is probably the most obvious meaning of the term. All societies, past and present, develop common normative systems as well as criteria that govern their interpretations and applications in terms of acceptability and unacceptability. Common values and practices derive either positive or negative connotations from the normative system of the society. This notion of normative system comes close to the concept of *ʿurf* in the Islamic legal tradition. The juristic discussions on the concept of *ʿurf* can be seen as an effort to determine the criteria that characterize a "good" custom within the Islamic legal system. This collective meaning of custom may be contrasted with its individual counterpart. Custom as an individual norm refers to the habits that an individual acquires or develops. Custom in this sense corresponds with the Arabic term *ʿādah*, which is often translated as "habit." As the subsequent discussion explains, the relationship between *ʿādah and ʿurf* cannot always be reduced to the difference between the collective custom and the individual habit.

We can distinguish at least three main domains within which custom was used in the Islamic intellectual tradition: the philosophical domain, the theological domain, and the legal domain. In both the theological and philosophical discussions, custom was used as a universal norm that includes the fixed or semifixed laws governing the entire universe and the human experience of it. In this context, we can distinguish two different meanings of custom. The first refers to a natural or cosmic norm that regulates the relationships between the different components of the physical world. According to the divine plan, the universe is designed to follow regular and recurrent laws that, in turn, account for the order people observe in the different natural phenomena. The second refers to a universal moral code that governs human relationships, in spite of the numerous variations suggesting otherwise. The Qurʾān repeatedly invokes the concept of *sunnat Allah* (God's way), which neither changes nor alters.[4] It includes, for example, provisions that emphasize justice, mercy, and moderation, and guard against injustice, cruelty, and excess. Muslim jurists argue that sharīʿah embodies this universal moral code and seeks to infuse it into the legal rulings on the different substantive issues.

Muslim theologians sought to address the philosophical questions from the Islamic point of view. They employed the concept of custom in their investigation of various questions of metaphysical and natural philosophy. For example, the concept of custom is associated with the concept of nature; accordingly, nature does not function on its own and in accordance with its own independent laws. It is, rather, created by God, and our experience of it is based on the custom that he instituted and that he can break at will. Similarly, custom is used in theological debates on important issues such as divine existence, the need for prophethood, and the scope of religious responsibility (*taklīf*), among many others. I explore this point further in chapter 3.

Within the legal domain, we can distinguish at least three ways in which custom was used. The first is custom in substantive law, used to signify concrete examples of regional and temporal variations. This includes what the jurists used to refer to as linguistic convention (*ʿurf qawlī*) or practical custom (*ʿurf ʿamalī*). The second is also in substantive law, used in comparison with the other two categories of devotional deeds and transactions. The category of custom in this sense, *ʿādāt*, consists of the regular human actions that are not, in themselves, associated with legal prescriptions. Custom here refers to a wide array of activities that the individual undertakes by virtue of being human, such as eating, drinking, or sleeping. In principle, custom in this sense falls under the category of *mubāḥ* (allowed), unless strong evidence proves otherwise. The third, and most important sense, is custom as an abstract tool in legal theory. It is in this sense that the concept was used to educe the numerous examples of customary practices in substantive law. In this study, the term custom is used primarily to refer to this last sense.

## The Purpose of the Study

The treatment of custom in legal theory is particularly important for its direct connection with the critical issue of social change. Jurists used this generic concept to account for different regional practices from the perspective of sharīʿah and its sources. Custom (referred to as *ʿurf* or *ʿādah*) in this sense is a neutral concept; it is not intrinsically antithetical to sharīʿah. It does not, by itself, carry either a positive or negative connotation. This also means that, in principle, sharīʿah neither condones nor condemns custom. In order for such determination to be made, the custom in question needs to be analyzed and scrutinized in the light of the general principles of sharīʿah. Eventually, the jurists developed systems of evaluation that defined the conditions and criteria for such determination. Arguably, customs could be studied as an evaluative measure of the legal system's tolerance for change and flexibility to adapt to different contexts over time.

The study of custom is also important for its rich interpretive potential. Custom offers an illustrative example of a crucial dynamic that connects legal theory (*uṣūl al-fiqh*) and substantive law (*furūʿ al-fiqh*) in the Islamic legal tradition. I refer to it as the "abstraction factor." As the discussion below illustrates, this factor was not limited to the concept of custom but was also critical for the development of other important concepts in legal theory, such as *ijmāʿ* and *istiḥsān*. The abstraction factor governs the development of a certain concept out of countless concrete examples of real-life incidents, questions, or events. When the jurists repeatedly encounter a particular theme either in their own investigations or in similar precedents, they abstract the common features in those questions into principles that can be easily extrapolated without the need to refer to particular examples. The payment of a dowry, for example, is one of the conditions of a valid contract of marriage. Different procedures developed in different places to fulfill that condition. It may be paid at the conclusion of the contract in full or may be paid in two or more installments, depending on the customary practice in a particular region. Similarly, it may be paid in cash, gold, or other valuable items. While the condition (payment of dowry) itself does not change, its application may vary depending on the common custom in particular contexts. These varying practices were incorporated under the abstract legal tool of custom or *ʿurf*.

The concept of custom also serves as an indicator of the different roles that Muslim jurists assumed. As explained in subsequent chapters, Muslim jurists saw their primary task to be adapting their social contexts to the guidelines of sharīʿah. At the most elemental level, sharīʿah stands for God's way, which Muslims believe provides guidance on different aspects of human behavior. The history of the concept of custom offers numerous concrete examples of how the jurists strove to accomplish this goal, both when sharīʿah supplied clear instructions and, even more importantly, when it did not. Tracing the history of the concept of custom can thus reveal the jurists' understanding of both sharīʿah and sharīʿah-based rulings.

Researchers have grappled with the exact definitions of the two terms of sharīʿah and Islamic law and whether they are synonyms. For the purpose of the present context, sharīʿah is used to refer to the divine instructions of legal import that are embodied in divine or divinely inspired texts. Islamic law, on the other hand, is used to refer to the human articulations of these instructions, as expressed by Muslim jurists. Islamic law, therefore, corresponds more to *fiqh* than to sharīʿah; it aims to approximate sharīʿah, but it is never its literal expression. While Muslims believe that sharīʿah is divine, the law remains human because it is the product of a legal theory that is human in every sense of the word. Nonetheless, in view of its connection with sharīʿah, Islamic law is believed to be anchored in divine guidance. As such, it not only aims to regulate human affairs but also to adjust them in accordance with the divine expectations. Divine revelation, as a carrier of religious truth, is perceived as an ultimate source of guidance. Humans, therefore, are expected to submit to its authority even if they fail to understand or rationalize its commands fully. Custom, on the other hand, lacks such unquestionable authority. It is rather an expression of social and cultural norms whose normative value remains always in need of additional validation by either legal or religious sanction. Therefore, the dialectic relationship between custom and sharīʿah, as manifested in different discussions and debates, remained fundamentally marked by one particular tension. This tension had to do with custom's precise role in guiding, constructing, and reconstructing the sharīʿah-based laws.

But if Islamic law, through its emblematic connection with sharīʿah, claims a divine origin, the question of the role and the extent of human agency becomes pertinent. After all, human agency is indispensable for the interpretation, construction, and application of divine commands. Similarly, if Islamic law claims continuity over time, several questions arise about the feasibility of maintaining such continuity on the basis of fixed texts. Religious norms imply fixity, permanence, and immutability. Human law, on the other hand, implies change, flexibility, and temporality. The historical development of the concept of custom is a significant starting point for clarifying several dynamics within the Islamic legal tradition, such as the relationship between the divine and the human, the fixed and the changing, and the goals and means.

This study seeks to trace the evolution and development of the concept of custom in the Islamic legal tradition with a special focus on legal theory (*uṣūl al-fiqh*). The conventional narrative, both by Muslims and Orientalists, indicates that by the fifth century AH (eleventh century CE), the Islamic intellectual tradition in general and the legal tradition in particular had entered into a long phase of *taqlīd* (blind imitation). Building on the findings of recent scholarship, I demonstrate that, although it is true that the main configurations of the Islamic legal tradition in terms of intellectual currents and major schools of thought were developed prior to the fifth century AH, the creative engagement with this tradition did not simply die out after this period. Close examination of the treatment of the concept of custom in the works of major legal theorists, such as al-Shāfiʿī, al-Shirāzī, al-Juwaynī, al-Ghazālī, Ibn ʿAbd al-Salam, al-Qarāfī, and al-Shāṭibī, should reveal that it was used as an important medium through which they negotiated the divide between legal theory and practice as they continued to reconstruct the legal tradition for their own respective contexts. Through their works and careers, these legal theorists, among others, represented major turning points in the history of the legal tradition. They were able to achieve major breakthroughs only after studying, absorbing, and synthesizing the contributions of their predecessors, particularly how these predecessors were able to adjust the law to their own social contexts. The incorporation of the concept of custom within the sharīʿah paradigm reveals that the jurists did not treat sharīʿah as a theoretical enterprise that was meaningful only for the elitist culture of sophisticated scholars. It was rather the cornerstone of the only system of justice that Muslims knew up until at least the eighteenth century. The history of the ideas and theories related to custom should illustrate the interrelationship between theory and practice in the Islamic legal tradition as reflected in the different legal genres.

In studying past ideas, one has to guard against the influence of the present. One has to insure that in studying these ideas, he or she is not projecting modern understanding and sensibilities on the past; one should seek to understand such ideas in their own context and avoid anachronistic constructions. But since history is always written in the present, it seems impossible to escape the influence of the present completely. Nonetheless, one has to be aware of this dilemma and consider the motives that drive one's work. In this vein, one may wonder why we should study the development of the concept of custom in the Islamic legal tradition. In a way, this question applies to the study of historical phenomena in general. Without a deep grasp of history, it would be difficult to understand or explain the present. This is particularly important in the case of literary traditions, where authority is constructed around important texts and the communities of interpretation that produced these texts. Within each tradition there are a number of key ideas on which most of the debates are constructed. The present study seeks to illustrate that custom was one of the concepts that formed the deep structure of the Islamic legal tradition.

But the study of the concept of custom is not only important for understanding the history of the Islamic legal tradition; it is equally important for understanding its reconstruction in the present. For example, the issue of custom offers useful insights about the development of the Islamic legal tradition by illustrating the different phases any legal system undergoes. Once a strong and coherent theoretical framework has been established, the later phases consist mainly of constant adjustment of this theoretical framework to the changing social and historical contexts. The history of the concept of *ʿurf*, therefore, can reveal the different complexities, nuances, and subtleties involved in such adjustments. Similarly, this history points out the significant role of the interpretive communities of the jurists in maintaining and preserving the Muslim juristic idiom and facilitating communication within a single integrated framework. One might refer to this dynamic as a flexible duality; that is, reliance on the fundamental principles at the core of the tradition that gives it its unique identity and openness towards other inductive or deductive methods that address the microlevel changing details.

Studying the issue of custom can also serve as a significant starting point for understanding the impact of Western cultural modernity on the later phases of the Islamic intellectual tradition in general and the legal-jurisprudential tradition in particular. This is mainly exemplified in the modern movements of legal reform and codification that emphasized the role of custom in the process of lawmaking. Through these reform projects, custom not only ceased to function under the auspices of sharīʿah, but it became its competitor. The roots of this paradigm shift go as far back as the roots of Western modernity, where a new understanding of religion began to dominate Western thought and those who came under its influence. According to this new understanding, custom not only impacted religion, but it was the root of religion itself. This explains the approach the early Orientalists took in their works on the Islamic legal tradition. Once again, we see that the concept of custom is inextricably linked with the notion of religion: the attitude toward one would definitely impact the attitude toward the other.[5]

Consequently we may distinguish two main attitudes or "views of the world" towards both religion and custom. On the one hand, we have the materialist, atheist view, which ascribes the controlling powers of this world to the internal and independent natural laws of causality. It does not take any theistic or transcendental considerations into account. According to this view, God is non-existent, dead, or simply disinterested in the micro or even macrolevel details of this world. Here, custom is identified with the concept of nature, in the sense of nature's consistent and recurrent patterns.

On the other hand, we have the theistic view of the world that presumes the existence of an all-knowing and omnipotent creator. According to this view, custom is conditioned by the limitations set by this creator. Of course, these two views represent the extremes of the continuum of faith, with many others in between. Keeping in mind that Islam not only consists of an internal belief system, but also includes regulations that bear on the external sphere, it is easy to understand why Muslim jurists always spoke of custom as a secondary rather than a primary source of law. It also helps explain the tension that Muslim jurists were constantly grappling with between the divine will—as manifested in the founding texts—and the changing sociohistorical contexts. Conscientious jurists have been driven by the motivation to balance fidelity to the ideals of their faith with pressure to accommodate change. The history of the concept of custom in the Islamic legal tradition captures this challenging undertaking like no other.

## The Thesis

The sources of Islamic law consist of two primary sources (the Qur'ān and the Sunnah of the Prophet), two procedural sources (juristic consensus and analogical reasoning), and a number of inductive sources including juristic preference, interest, and custom, among others. These sources are tied together in an ordered and hierarchical relationship. Within this hierarchical order, custom can be a source of law as long as it does not conflict with a higher source. The place of custom in Islamic legal theory, however, is not limited to the question of the sources. Custom permeates the various stages of the legal process. For example, the role of custom is crucial to the interpretation of the textual sources, the determination of their signification, and their scope of application.

In Islamic legal theory, the relationship between reason and revelation is not rigidly linear. It is rather dynamic and two-dimensional with reality (actual practice) as a necessary intermediary element. In inspiring reason, revelation is grounded in reality; in examining revelation, reason is informed by reality. In the former, reality is anchored in the ever significant experience of the Prophet and in the latter, it derives from the particular context of the reader.

The study of the diachronic development of custom as an abstract tool in legal theory reveals that it originated in the two primary sources of the Qur'ān and the Sunnah of the Prophet. Up until the fifth century AH (eleventh century CE), two parallel sources influenced the development of the concept. The first was the many cases in substantive law derived from the normative example set by the Prophet himself as well as the succeeding generations of legal authorities. These normative practices served as models that the following juristic communities of interpretation continued to invoke and reinforce. This is particularly evident in the different classifications of customs that the jurists devised. These were based on the investigation of various substantive issues over time and were documented first in substantive law (*fiqh*) and then, in a more developed manner, in legal maxims (*qawāʿid*). Examples of these classifications include linguistic convention (*ʿurf lughawī*), sharīʿah convention (*ʿurf sharʿī*), general custom (*ʿurf ʿāmm*), and specific custom (*ʿurf khāṣṣ*). Through the abstraction process, custom was incorporated into legal theory as one of the inductive secondary sources of law. Together with this development, custom was concurrently incorporated within the genre of legal maxims. Following these two parallel processes, substantive law was able to reinvigorate legal theory while being constantly shaped by it.

Debates gradually transported from theology into legal theory by the early theologian-jurists constituted the second source. The concept of custom was central to many debates dealing with various theological issues that touched on metaphysics and morality.

These two parallel sources illustrate the efforts of the two major schools of jurisprudence that Ibn Khaldun referred to in his famous historical account of Islamic legal theory: the theoretical school and the applied school. Throughout and apart from these main sources, custom was also used as a built-in mechanism in the various linguistic and hermeneutical debates. In the post fifth/eleventh century period, as the two major schools of jurisprudence gradually blended and expanded, the concept of custom continued to evolve in two main areas. The first was the area of sources: initially through *qiyās* and *istidlāl* before it developed into a secondary source in its own right. The second area was the hermeneutical discussions on *takhṣīṣ* and other related themes. Moreover, the concept was quite instrumental in the development of various emerging subgenres, such as legal maxims, legal objectives, and, of course, substantive law in general and the area of legal application in particular.

## The Scope of the Study

The present study traces the diachronic development of the concept of custom within the Islamic legal tradition. It seeks to highlight the major turning points throughout this development. A study of this nature requires a broader scope than other synchronic studies would normally tolerate. The goal is not to exhaust all uses and applications of the concept; this would necessitate narrowing the scope to a particular timeframe, sociohistorical context, school of thought, or jurist. This study, instead, seeks to highlight the major theoretical constructions and permutations of the concept of custom throughout the course of the premodern Islamic legal tradition.

## The Method

This study uses the inductive-analytical method in surveying representative samples of the writings of major jurists whose works helped shape and transform the Islamic legal tradition. It does not focus on one particular author or school of thought but is rather interested in the major trends and approaches in the treatment of the subject. The study seeks particularly to address the question of continuity and how jurists sought to ensure, through custom, that their ideas and methods were relevant.

The first chapter provides a review of the literature and summarizes the findings of modern scholarship on the issue. As that chapter shows, until very recently, the theme of custom in Islamic legal tradition has hardly been singled out for analysis as an independent subject. Rather, it has often been subsumed within studies of other major aspects of the tradition. The chapter identifies the main trends that influenced how the concept was studied both in Western academia and in the Muslim world.

The second chapter deals with the textual foundations of the concept of custom in the two founding texts of the Islamic legal tradition: the Qur'ān and the Sunnah of the Prophet. It points out the need for more attention to not only the direct references to the concept in those textual sources but, more importantly, to the indirect and implicit ones as well. A thorough study of the relevant passages in these sources would reveal the strong connection of the concept with both the notion of social custom and the notion of the good (*maʿrūf*).

The third chapter deals with the theological foundations of the concept of custom. It focuses on the use of the concept of *ʿādah* in the theological debates over the issue of causality, which was, in turn, connected with many other debates on important issues such as human freedom, responsibility, generation, and the veracity of Prophetic miracles. The chapter argues that the transportation of the theological concept of *ʿādah* into the main works of jurisprudence, through the works of the theologian-jurists, was instrumental in the development of the legal concept of *ʿurf*.

The fourth chapter traces the development of the concept up until the fifth century AH (eleventh century CE). It explores the treatment of the concept by the two main schools that shaped Islamic jurisprudence during this period: the theoretical school and the applied school. The proponents of the theoretical school utilized the concept of *ʿurf* to provide rational and non-textual grounds for important principles such as *tawātur* and *ijmāʿ*. On the other hand, the proponents of the applied school appealed to *ʿurf* in their treatment of the two closely related concepts of *qiyās* and *istiḥsān*.

The fifth chapter deals with the development of the concept of custom in legal theory in the post fifth/eleventh century period. It demonstrates that during this period, the concept continued to evolve in two main areas: sources and legal hermeneutics. In the area of sources, the concept was repeatedly invoked within the framework of *qiyās* and later, *istidlāl*. In the area of legal hermeneutics, it was invoked in the debates over particularization (*takhṣīṣ*).

The sixth chapter deals with the concept of custom within the genre of legal maxims. As classical legal theory gradually expanded, new genres emerged within the larger domain of jurisprudence; legal maxims (*al-qawāʿid al-fiqhiyyah*) was one of the important examples of these genres. It was the result of the jurists' efforts to abstract the general foundational principles underlying the myriad issues in the different chapters of substantive law. By extracting these fundamental principles, the jurists aimed to extrapolate them to other comparable situations in what became commonly known as *takhrīj*. The chapter examines how the concept was used within the genre and how this genre contributed to the general development of the concept of custom.

The other important genre that developed within the larger framework of jurisprudence was the objectives of sharīʿah (*maqāṣid al-sharīʿah*). The seventh chapter explores the use of the concept of custom within this genre of legal objectives. It represents an approach or a method that contemplates the purpose of the law rather than focusing on law in and of itself; it sees law as a means rather than a goal. In constructing legal rulings, the jurist seeks to realize the objectives that the Lawgiver intended for the institution of sharīʿah. The chapter focuses on the contribution of Abū Isḥāq al-Shāṭibī, who is credited with formally founding this genre.

The eighth chapter deals with the concept of custom within the sphere of legal application. Legal application has traditionally been associated with *ijtihād* (independent reasoning)—both as a concept and as a process—and it was carried out in two distinct modes: legal responses (*fatāwā*) and judicial verdicts (*aḥkām*). The chapter seeks to highlight the role of custom in the development of these important institutions.

These chapters are viewed as modules within a larger framework that aims to account for the different constructions and applications of the concept of custom in the Islamic legal tradition. Admittedly, each of these modules merits separate and independent treatment, but the main objective here is to focus on the general contours of the framework rather than the specific details of its individual modules. Focusing on the place of custom in the Islamic legal tradition should improve our understanding of how this tradition developed over time and how the jurists negotiated the localization of sharīʿah in the different regional and sociohistorical contexts.

# Part 1

# Custom and the Major Debates in the Field of Islamic Studies

# Chapter 1

# Custom and Islamic Law in Modern Scholarship

The relationship between custom and Islamic law has been one of the most contested issues in modern scholarship on the Islamic legal tradition. This subject has been closely connected with two major debates that have largely shaped the modern field of Islamic studies in Western academia, namely, the debates on the origins and nature of Islamic law. It is not the goal of this chapter to give a full account of these two debates,[1] but rather to illustrate how this issue influenced the development of major positions on the continuums of these debates. Moreover, the subject of custom arises in many disciplines, such as history, law, sociology, and anthropology, though each field has its own methodologies and research strategies. Studies on Islamic law within all these disciplines, however, were heavily influenced by Orientalist scholarship[2] and its reconstruction of Islamic legal history, particularly from the late nineteenth to the first half of the twentieth century.[3] Generally speaking, modern Orientalist studies on the place, status, and role of custom in Islamic law fall into two main categories. The first includes philological or text-based studies, and the second includes ethnographic or field studies. While the former seeks to determine the impact of customs on the formal construction of Islamic law as documented in its written sources, the latter attempts to determine the degree of agreement or disagreement between customs and Islamic law on the one hand and Islamic law and particular social practices on the other.[4] To these, another category may be added, which includes normative juristic studies by Muslim scholars who approach the issue from within the Islamic tradition, building on successive generations of Muslim jurists since the formative period. Admittedly, this classification is neither precise nor exhaustive, but it should help identify and account for most of the studies that have shaped the different discourses on this subject. Moreover, this classification does not suggest that these approaches have been completely separate or independent from each other. This chapter demonstrates that the distinctions are sometimes blurred, or at least are less clear than they initially appear.

## The Beginnings and the Emergence of a Dominant Paradigm

The debate on the origins of Islamic law has occupied Western scholars for more than a century. It has revolved around the origin, transmission, and authenticity of Islam's primary sources, namely the Qur'ān and Ḥadīth (or Sunnah of the Prophet).[5] The sizable literature devoted to the origins of Islam in general and Islamic law in particular has to be placed within the context of the Western philological studies. Many Islamicists sought to subject Islam's primary sources to the same methods that were applied to the Bible. They debated the origins of Islam and argued that Islamic law was derived from foreign sources such as the earlier Abrahamic religions, the earlier Arab tribal traditions, other foreign traditions (Roman, Aramaic), or a mixture of all of the above.[6]

The issue of custom is of great relevance to this debate because most scholars who favored the borrowing thesis invoked foreign customary influences to support their argument.[7] This is more evident in the works of early Islamicists such as Goldziher and Hurgronje, who drew on the various evolutionary theories within the humanities and social sciences as these fields developed during the late nineteenth and early twentieth centuries. This was the golden time of science, doubt, and discovery. As the newly emerging disciplines of the social sciences were taking shape, scholars were inspired by the scientific method and the wonderful discoveries it enabled in the natural and applied sciences. In linguistics, sociology, anthropology, psychology, and literature, evolution was a common theme. The evolutionists were convinced that their primary task was to "discover" and "explain" the origins, the roots, or the beginnings of the phenomena they were studying. The early Orientalists undertook their research within this academic and cultural environment, which could explain their near obsession with the origins of Islam, among other religious and cultural traditions.[8]

It was not uncommon during this period to identify the non-European with the backward, a sentiment that applied not only to peoples but also to their cultural systems. Human history was seen through the prism of progress, advancement, and civilization, on which the European represented the pinnacle. In legal thought, modern state law was seen as the ideal, the ultimate goal of legal evolution.[9] Historically, customary law—often identified as unwritten law (*lex non scripta*)—was characterized as oral, flexible, anonymous, old, primitive, folkish, peasant-like, and rural. In contrast, the modern European written law (*lex scripta*) was characterized as fixed, of known author(s), new, civilized, elite, aristocratic, and urban.[10] Within this framework of European dominance, Islamic law was studied in its indigenous contexts, in which it often mixed with the local cultures of the African and Asian colonies.

In the following section I trace the emergence of the dominant paradigm in the field of Islamic legal history. Two complementary types of studies—ethnographic and textual—informed this paradigm. For each of these two types, I highlight the work of two major figures: William Robertson Smith and Christiaan Snouck Hurgronje for the early ethnographic studies, and Ignaz Goldziher and Joseph Schacht for the textual studies. Within this paradigm, scholarly treatment of Islamic sharīʿah vacillated between the realms of law and custom, with which sharīʿah was often confused.[11] Only casual reference was made to *ʿurf* as an abstract juristic method, and it was often subsumed under overarching themes such as sunnah or *ijmāʿ*. *ʿUrf*, in this sense, was believed to be a very late development or invention.

## Ethnographic Studies

Most of the early studies on the origins of the Islamic legal tradition were based on primary literary sources and the eighteenth- and nineteenth-century ethnographic studies of Muslim societies by European scholars and travelers. Most of these works were less interested in the theoretical constructions of the law than in the way these constructions related to reality in the contemporary Muslim societies. Both Smith and Hurgronje were among the early European scholars who undertook fieldwork in Muslim societies; their works left a lasting impact on the way Islam and Islamic law have been studied in Western academia.

William Robertson Smith (1846–1894) was born in Aberdeenshire, Scotland, where he received his early education under his father, who was an ordained minister in the Free Church of Scotland. His excellent preliminary education enabled him to join Aberdeen University when he was only 15. He pursued diverse interests, including science, mathematics, and languages (especially Hebrew). Emulating his father, he pursued a career in ministry along with his academic profession.[12] He was later accused of heresy, however, and the university consequently prevented him from teaching (1878) and dismissed him (1880). During this period he traveled widely in Europe, as well as North Africa, Egypt, and Arabia. In addition to his work as editor of the ninth edition of the *Encyclopedia Britannica*, Smith was one of the founders of the project to compile the *Encyclopedia of Islam*.[13]

Smith studied under Julius Wellhausen and was influenced by the school of the Higher Criticism, which espoused, among other things, the approach of *Sitz im Leben*. According to this approach, religion is to be studied in its wider social and cultural context, not merely theoretically as a detached or abstract phenomenon.[14] Smith believed that by studying the contemporary Arab tribes, he would enhance the understanding of the ancient Hebrew tribes because of the similar conditions under which they both lived. Although he stayed only six months in Arabia, he was convinced that what he saw there closely resembled the Hebrew Old Testament reality. Through his travels in Arabia, disguised as Abdullah Effendi,[15] he gained a wealth of information on the Arab socioreligious customs and institutions. His two main works, *Lectures on the Religion of the Semites* and *Marriage and Kinship in Arabia*, examine the various religious and cultural institutions of the ancient Arab tribes.[16]

Smith argued that behind the religions of Judaism, Christianity, and Islam existed an ancient religious tradition, which had survived through countless successive generations. By combining history, his fieldwork in Arabia, and comparative philology, he developed an interpretive model for uncovering the mysteries of the Hebrew Bible. From his studies of Arab tribal history he developed a theory of social and cultural evolution. According to this theory, religious practices and institutions—such as sacrifice—grew out of other, much older ones. These practices stood in contrast to the core of the biblical prophetic message, which placed stronger emphasis on spiritual and moral teachings.[17] Although Smith's comparison of the ancient Hebrews to the Bedouin Arabs was widely challenged, his analysis of the origins of sacrifice was quite influential.[18]

Smith's work left a lasting impression both on his contemporaries and later generations. He is credited for important ideas and methods, such as the creative application of the comparative method and the idea of social and religious evolution.[19] Smith's influence on other notable figures in social sciences, including Malinowski, Durkheim, and Freud, is evident and often recognized.[20] Similarly, his influence on the early Islamicists is unmistakable, especially in works on pre-Islamic or early Islamic Arab history. Goldziher later used Smith's model in his studies on the history of the Sunnah, which Joseph Schacht further expanded.[21]

Another influential figure who based his studies of Islamic legal history on ethnographic fieldwork was the Dutch Islamicist Christiaan Snouck

Hurgronje (1857–1936). He held the chair of Arabic Studies at Leiden University from 1906 to 1927. He started his career with a book on Arabia, followed by a similar work on the Dutch Indies (Indonesia) during his service in the Dutch colonial administration and which documents his observations about the indigenous population. Hurgronje emphasized the role of custom in the development of the Islamic tradition in general and Islamic law in particular. This was evident, for example, in his study on the rituals of Ḥajj, which he attributed to pre-Islamic customs.[22] In his view, Islam's development can only be explained in terms of foreign influences, especially those of Judeo-Christian origin. For him, evolution was an extremely powerful force that could transform any set of rules, even one claiming divine origin.

Hurgronje's study on Makkah and the pilgrimage was the beginning of his lifelong interest in Muslim peoples, traditions, customs, and cultures. His goal was not to study the theoretical rulings or rituals of pilgrimage, but rather the daily life of the Makkans and the other Muslims who gathered from all over the world during the annual religious festival. Due to the Dutch involvement in the East-Indian colonies, he was particularly interested in the experiences of the East-Indian pilgrims and the impact their extended sojourns in Ḥijāz had on their worship and religious education. Hurgronje provided detailed descriptions of daily life in Makkah and his encounters with pilgrims from different backgrounds.[23] His account covers the customs practiced throughout the year according to the Hijrī calendar. Many of these customs are associated with festivities or major life events such as birth, marriage, and death. Clearly addressed to a Western audience, his account is replete with trenchant remarks and cynical gestures.[24] Hurgronje's work is divided into four main parts, each of which focuses on an important dimension in the life of the Makkans: the daily life in Makkah, family life in Makkah, learning in Makkah, and the Jawah Indians in Makkah. This last part was the beginning of a lengthier, more detailed study on the Indonesian society as observed when he was serving in the Dutch colonial administration.[25]

Hurgronje's interest in Muslim peoples and societies in general and the Indonesian Muslims in particular is reflected in his two-volume study, *The Achehnese,* first published in 1893–1894 in Dutch and in English in 1906. In the introduction, he noted that his goal was "to study the religious element in the political condition of that country." Due to the shortage of literature on Indonesian culture, he aimed to complete a comprehensive study of the life of the Indonesian people. Following the approach that he adopted in his previous study on Makkah, he describes the daily life of the Achehnese people. In the section on "domestic life and law," the reader finds a detailed account of the arrangements, ceremonies, and formalities related to marriage, divorce, and death. Throughout his discussions, he focuses primarily on the actual practices and customs rather than on the theoretical details of Islamic law. He is particularly interested in cases where actual practice diverges from Islamic law.[26]

Hurgronje devoted a sizable part of this study to the influence of *ʿurf* and *adat* (*ʿādāt*) on the Indonesian people and society and to the relationship between *adat* law and Islamic law. The main thesis of the book, as repeatedly reiterated, is that the Achehnese were for the most part following unwritten customary law rather than Islamic law, and that the former was in conflict with the latter on many occasions. Furthermore, he notes that both systems—*adat* law and Islamic law—have existed side by side without either gaining precendence over the other. He also denied that the translated foreign (Arabic) sharīʿah books had any significant influence on Achehnese daily life. He criticizes the then common identification among many Europeans of *adat* law with Islamic law without any distinction between the two, ascribing this error to insufficient knowledge of the natives and their systems.[27]

Hurgronje did not limit his observations to Indonesia. For him, the failure of Muslims to live up to the demands of their religion, whether in Indonesia or elsewhere, was not a new phenomenon, but one that started very early in Islam's history. He argued that the law's demand for full obedience in all spheres of life was met with indifference by its followers who fell short of acquiring comprehensive knowledge of it, let alone observing it. Using the then nascent Wahābī movement as an example, he went on to emphasize that those who claimed full observance of the law were always in the minority.[28] In his view, the contrast between the religious law and human practice was both vast and widespread. Instead of following the letter of the law, people resorted to other more practical measures that could often be cast as following one of the schools of thought, but in reality rested on an entirely different basis. Such foundations, according to Hurgronje, could easily be found in pre-Islamic traditions and institutions.[29] Writing at the end of the nineteenth century, Hurgronje concluded his study with an overall evaluation of the place of Islam in the world as well as a prediction of its future. In light of the dwindling power of the Ottoman Empire against the ascending European influence on Muslim peoples, he expected that the growing encroachment of popular customs on Islamic law would only increase with time. Islam, he argued, was doomed to be reduced to a set of rituals that would not have any impact on public life.[30]

Hurgronje expressed his fully developed ideas on Islamic law and society in lectures that he delivered in 1914 (published in 1916) under the auspices of the American Committee for Lectures on the History of Religion.[31] Through these lectures, Hurgronje attempted to explain the origin of Islam, the religious and political development of Islam, and the relationship between Islam and modern thought. His extensive field research in both Arabia and Indonesia enabled him to speak with unchallenged authority. He ascribed the initial appeal and success of Islam to the Prophet's ability to combine pre-Islamic customs and traditions with elements from the Judeo-Christian tradition (e.g., Abraham and pilgrimages).[32]

In fact, the beginnings of the long and controversial discussions on the origins of Islamic law, especially the Sunnah, are found in Hurgronje's treatment of this subject. He refers to the Prophet's ability to incorporate the foreign systems—pre-Islamic and Judeo-Christian—in the form of ḥadīth, which he considered a method the early followers of Islam used to remove all traces of borrowed material.[33] He did deal with the legal concepts of *ʿurf* and *ʿādah* as treated by Muslim jurists, but he thought that the jurists limited their scope in such a way that these concepts were of little practical significance. He preferred instead to speak about the impact of customs in general (divergent practice) on sharīʿah (theoretical optimal model) in terms of two conflicting forces usually at war with each other. He not only thought that sharīʿah had to concede to custom, but he expected that the latter would eventually replace the former.[34]

Hurgronje's evolutionary approach is most evident in his assertion that many of Islam's laws and institutions were bound to be treated as obsolete survivals of the past. He notes "the irresistible power of the evolution of human society is merciless to laws even of divine origin (which will) transfer them, when their time is come, from treasury of everlasting goods to a museum of antiquity."[35] Hurgronje ascribed Islam's dysfunctional modern state to its lack of a mystical core and its perpetual reliance on political authority. When the political authority weakened, Islam was unable to sustain its vitality.[36] Therefore, he projected that Islam's lack of flexibility and its failure to consider the practical needs of its adherents would seriously impact its future.

## Literary Textual Studies

The second type of discourse that informed what I identified as the dominant Western paradigm consists mainly of literary or text-based studies. In this section I focus on the works of Ignaz Goldziher and Joseph Schacht, who are unanimously considered the leading figures in the field of Islamic legal history.

Ignaz Goldziher (1850–1921) is most famous for his studies on the origins of the Sunnah of the Prophet.[37] His account of the development of Islamic law reveals an understanding similar to Hurgronje's. Their diaries show that they corresponded with each other regularly and that they were well acquainted with each other's work.[38] Goldziher argued that the Prophet was unaware of the impact his religion would have on history because "Muhammad's thought was always occupied, first and foremost, with the immediate conditions of the moment."[39] He dismissed the argument that "Islam entered the world as a rounded system"; instead, he noted, "the Islam of Muhammad and the Quran is unfinished, awaiting its completion in the work of the generations to come."[40] One of his main theses was that "legal development commensurate with public need" did not occur in Islam until "after the prophet's death."[41]

For Goldziher, the foreign origins of Islam was a settled issue. In his two-volume study *Muhammedanische Studien,* he presented his main arguments regarding the origins and development of Islamic law. The reader of both Hurgronje and Goldziher would easily identify the views that both authors shared. Goldziher's study is organized like Hurgronje's earlier framework: the pre-Islamic origins, the Judeo-Christian origins, theory and practice in the Islamic tradition, and finally, examples based on ethnographic studies. Goldziher credits the Prophet for imposing on the Arabs foreign principles that had failed to capture their attention previously. According to Goldziher, part of the Prophet's success was due to his ability to combine both these Judeo-Christian elements with original Arabic traits such as *murūwwa* (magnanimity), and eventually these two contributed to the development of the Prophets's *dīn* (religion).[42]

Smith's influence on Goldziher is evident in the latter's treatment of the evolution of Islam,[43] particularly in his characterization of the Arabs as a group with a high regard for ancestral customs and a low level of religious development. Ancestral customs incorporated into Islam included tomb visitation and saint worship cults.[44] On the more pertinent issue of the history of ḥadīth literature, Goldziher notes that the concept of sunnah was not an Islamic invention.[45] Pre-Islamic Arabs had used it and held on to it during the first two centuries of Islam as the traditions, customs, and habits of the ancestors. It was only in the second century,[46] especially under the influence of the Abbasids,[47] that the concept of the Islamic sunnah started to take shape. Goldziher traces the different ḥadīth reports either to pre-Islamic Arab or Judeo-Christian origins. Regarding the development of Islamic law (*fiqh*) and the early two legal schools—School of Opinion (*ra'y*) and School of Tradition (ḥadīth)—he traces the first to the Roman tradition and the latter to the spurious reports fabricated for the purpose of supporting certain legal opinions.[48]

Goldziher argues that sunnah alone was not sufficient to bring cultural attitudes in line with the scheme of Islam, which is why the early jurists introduced the concept of consensus (*ijmāʿ*).[49] If a certain custom could not be incorporated through sunnah, it could still be subsumed under *ijmāʿ*. When the latter needed to be based on a sunnah, it was not difficult to invent it.[50] After all, for Goldziher, not only was the sunnah's support of the authenticity of *ijmāʿ* questioned, but the legitimacy of the sunnah itself was in doubt. Goldziher recognizes early Muslims' efforts to sift out the original Prophetic reports from the fabricated ones, but, in his view, these early efforts fell short of scrutinizing the growing literature.[51] He concluded that "legal literature proper, which represents the result of comprehensive thinking, is chronologically prior to the literature of ḥadīth."[52]

It was Joseph Schacht (1902–1969) who developed the views of this earlier generation of scholars into a coherent synthesis. He is considered the true heir of the ideas the early Islamicists, Goldziher and Hurgronje in particular, put forward.[53] Schacht started his studies in Germany and traveled extensively throughout Europe and the Middle East. He taught Arabic at Leiden University and later accepted a position at Columbia University, where he stayed until his death. His work on Islamic law in general and on ḥadīth and sunnah in particular is usually seen as an extension to the work of Goldziher and Hurgronje. Although he revised some of their ideas, especially on the sources of Islamic law, he adopted their general conclusions. His last and most influential book, *An Introduction to Islamic Law*, remains—in the opinion of many Islamicists—the unchallenged authority in the field.

In the introduction to this book, Schacht observes that Islamic law represents the "epitome of Islamic thought, the most typical manifestation of the Islamic way of life, the core and kernel of Islam itself." At first glance, Schacht's presentation seems radically different from that of Hurgronje and Goldziher. Right from the beginning, he contradicts one of the main arguments tirelessly maintained by his predecessors: the foreign origins of Islamic law. He observes instead that Islamic law not only is dissimilar from both Jewish law and Canon law, but is also radically different from pre-Islamic Arab paganism.[54]

Upon closer examination, Schacht does not entirely dismiss the argument of Hurgronje and Goldziher, but he modifies it. According to Schacht, "Islamic law is the result of a scrutiny, from a religious angle, of legal subject matter which was far from uniform, comprising as it did the various components of the laws of Arabia and numerous elements taken over from the peoples of the conquered territories."[55] On the issue of pre-Islamic Arabian customary law, he disagrees with the view that it survived under Islam. If it did, in his view, it was a matter of legal terminology, which should not mean that Islamic legal terms go back to the pre-Islamic Arab customary law. In other words, some words and terms did survive from the pre-Islamic period but these words either acquired new meanings or were completely rejected by the new system.[56]

Although Schacht goes to great lengths to prove that the legal system that the Prophet introduced was "innovation in the law of Arabia,"[57] he argues that the Prophet's goal was not to create a new legal system. He tries to remove this apparent contradiction by suggesting that the Prophet's intention was to establish an ethical system to help Muslims pass the test of the Day of Judgment. In other words, the Prophet originally created a moral system without any legal implications. Later, and due to the changed circumstances, the Prophet started applying moral principles to legal institutions. Schacht tries to prove his point by referring to the moral injunctions in the Qur'ān on several issues. Schacht's examples, however, remain far from extensive and his assertion flies in the face of an extended historical reality.

Schacht notes that during the first century of Islam, customary law was the standard in the legal and administrative fields. The old concept of the sunnah was accepted and smoothly assimilated. Furthermore, Islamic law, in the technical sense of the word, had not yet come into existence.[58] Consequently, Schacht links the development of Islamic law to the widespread adoption of the legal and administrative institutions of the conquered lands, which was not limited to institutions and practices, but also included legal concepts and maxims. Some of the examples he uses are the "consensus of scholars" and the "five qualifications."[59] To a large extent, educated new converts (*mawālī*) facilitated this process of adoption, assimilation, and borrowing.[60] Schacht refers to this as the "period of incubation,"a time that allowed the easy assimilation of concepts, ideas, and principles from the ancient traditions of the conquered lands. Only in the second century of Islam did these ideas take the form of ripe, fully developed, integrated Islamic legal theory.[61] In the meantime, the early judges based their rulings and judgments mainly on the customary practices and, as much as possible, on the general principles of the Qur'ān and the new Islamic norms. Still, while Schacht refers earlier to Islamic law as an extreme case of the "kadi system," he denies that this early *kadi* (judge) tradition had any impact on the second-century development of the legal tradition.[62] This development, he maintains, was influenced by circumstances that detached Islamic law from the living reality because Islamic law served more as an "expression of a religious ideal in opposition to it (reality)."[63] The emergence of the early schools of thought (*madhāhib*)[64]—was a major development that would change the historical course of Islamic law—with the introduction of the "living tradition of the school" Slowly the general customary practice changed into the customary practice of the school, which was the basis for the concept of *ijmāʿ*.

Schacht argued that from the early decades of the second century, this living tradition of the early schools was projected backwards on some of the great figures of the past. Given the normative authority with which the prominent figures of the earlier generations were endowed, later jurists aimed to ascribe their legal constructions to earlier authorities to secure juristic legitimacy. Schacht, therefore, differentiates between these early figures as they appear in the literature and their historical reality, the difference between the literary Ibn Masʿūd, for example, and the historical Ibn Masʿūd. The notion of backward projection was one of the major theses that Schacht developed to explain the early development of the Islamic legal tradition.[65] Schacht's denial of the historical reality of figures such as the seven lawyers of Madinah[66] was a necessary step to support his overall thesis that Islamic law did not develop in Ḥijāz in the Islamic first century, as the Islamic sources indicate, but rather in Iraq during the second century, due to the influence of foreign (non-Ḥijāzī) factors.[67]

Schacht's main thesis is that the literary period of Islam begins in about AH 150 (767 CE), and it is possible to trace its development from that time onward. The period before that point represents the incubation period that lacked any distinct identity. Like his predecessors, he views the legal *ʿurf* or *ʿādah* as restrictive elements that played marginal roles in the classical legal theory. With the beginning of the fourth century, the gate of *ijtihād* was closed, and this in turn ushered in the beginning of a new stage in the Islamic legal tradition.[68] Although *taqlīd* (blind following) preserved the basic structure of Islamic legal theory, the latter gradually grew out of touch with daily life.

This sketch outlines the treatment by the Western Islamicists (until Schacht) of the role of custom in the development of the early Islamic tradition. It reveals how they understood not only the genesis of Islamic law but that of Islam itself. Their works, however, have to be read as products of their own political and intellectual time. In fact, it would be difficult to study the works of the Islamicists independent of the major intellectual currents that influenced modern European thought, especially during the eighteenth and nineteenth centuries. The work of Smith inspired not only the Islamicists, but also many other scholars in different fields such as history, sociology, and anthropology. His studies on the history of the Semites, particularly his attempt to reconstruct and reinterpret many of their institutions as the basis of his research on the contemporary Arab tribes, have had an enduring impact. Smith, as an evolutionary thinker much like Edward B. Tylor and James Frazer, aimed to discover and explain the origins of religious thought and practices. Tylor traced the origin of religion to the theory of Animism, and Frazer traced it to magic. Both Tylor and Frazer thought that at a later stage of social evolution, people should be able to replace religion with science and technology. Smith, however, thought that the evolution of religion would lead to emphasis on morality and ethics, rather than on rituals and institutions.[69]

The Islamicists' obsession with discovering the origins of Islam fits perfectly within this evolutionary paradigm. The subjugation of many Muslim countries under European colonization not only facilitated their work but, indeed, justified it. These Muslim subjects were still at an earlier stage of evolution (intellectually, socially, and politically), and the colonization experience would help them attain civilization.[70] This attitude is unmistakable, for example, in the ethnographic studies of Hurgronje, who occasionally presents himself as the expert who understands the indigenous populations better than they understand themselves. His travels in Arabia and Indonesia, as a colonial officer, enabled him to speak with unquestioned authority. While Goldziher was Hurgronje's intellectual mentor, Goldziher benefited from Hurgronje's travels and practical experience. Schacht drew on the theoretical knowledge and practical experience of both these scholars and took their preliminary ideas to their logical conclusion.

The debates on the origins of Islamic law have spurred numerous other debates, including that on the nature of Islamic law. Some have argued that Islamic law is a highly idealized system and therefore unlikely to adapt to social change. Noel Coulson was probably the most prominent representative of this view. He notes that "Islamic jurisprudence had in fact been essentially idealistic from the outset. Law had not grown out of the practice but had originated as the academic formulation of a scheme alternative to that practice."[71] He also notes, "Jurisprudence, divorced from actual legal practice, had become an introspective science, wherein law was studied and elaborated for its own sake."[72] When seen as a system steeped in fixed religious norms, Islamic law becomes a static system that defies social reality, demanding that society conform to its dictates rather than being shaped by society. It is easy to see the relationship between this tension thesis and the earlier picture drawn by Hurgronje. According to Hurgronje, legal theory and social praxis in Islam are constantly clashing with each other, and ultimately the former has to give in to the latter.[73] One of the other important sources of this tension thesis was Max Weber's treatment of Islamic law within his grand legal typology.

## *Qāḍī* Justice and Max Weber's Influence

There is a near consensus that Max Weber was the first to coin the Qāḍī-justice notion in the context of his famous comparative legal typology.[74] Weber distinguished four types of legal systems. The first is irrational substantive law in which legal decisions follow the emotional feelings of the judge instead of any normative criteria. Weber cites the Islamic Qāḍī-justice system as the prime example of this type of law, which "knows no rational rules of decision (*Urteilsgründe*) whatever."[75] The second type is formally irrational law guided not by reason, but rather by oracles and divination. The third type is substantive rational law, which is based on judgments derived from sacred scripture or ideology. The fourth type is formal rational law, which is based on abstract thoughts without recourse to non-legal sources.[76]

The standard view of how the Islamic legal tradition developed over time does not support this Weberian characterization. Islamic law is described as an ideal case of a jurist-law developed by private scholars, independent of government influence. Through a long and uninterrupted chain of trained jurists, Islamic law remained theoretically free from government interference. The jurists' success was manifested in the creation of a legal tradition and a legal method to which everyone, including the rulers, adhered—even if sometimes only in theory. Contrary to this view and following Weber's typology, some have held the opinion that Islamic law was the product of a Qāḍī-justice culture. The exact nature of this culture is best captured in this quote by Lord Justice Goddard: "The court is really put very much in the position of a Cadi under the palm tree, there are no principles on which he is directed to act. He has to do the best he can in the circumstances, having no rules of law to guide him."[77] In this quote, Goddard depicts Islamic law as an ad-hoc subjective enterprise devoid of any disciplined or logical legal method.

This view of the nature of Islamic law not only overlooks the fact that the primary sources of Islamic law are derived from a body of normative texts that Muslims consider sacred, but, more importantly, it reveals striking unfamiliarity with Islamic legal methodology.[78] Here, too, focus is placed on the tension between rigid legal theory and overpowering customary practices. Little attention, if any, is given to the built-in mechanisms, such as *ʿurf*, within Islamic legal theory that examine such customary practices before they can be incorporated into Islamic substantive law or *fiqh*. This Weberian framework, however, reconciles the seemingly contradictory views of Islamic legal development that one encounters in the literature. On the one hand, it is argued that Islamic law is an idealized theoretical system, and, therefore, it is static and immutable. On the other hand, it is argued that Islamic law lacks any substantive core, and that it reflects, over time, an appropriation of local customs. In Weber's view, as Islamic legal theory gradually lost touch with reality, the Qāḍī-justice method gave in to customary practices, sometimes at the expense of this rigid legal theory. Such a simplified conclusion, however, ignores the extended historical development of Islamic law as reflected in Muslim sources. I deal with this point in more detail in the chapter on legal application.

## Reactions to the Dominant Paradigm

Stephen Humphreys reports that Schacht's work generated three distinct reactions. The first is that Schacht did not properly understand the processes of ḥadīth transmission in early Islam. Proponents of this view include Nabia Abbott,[79] Fuat Sezgin, and M. Azami.[80] The second is that he might have overestimated his case. Proponents of this view include W. M. Watt and Juynboll.[81] The third is that he was right, and, therefore, his conclusions should be developed further.[82]

A careful review of the literature from the time of the publication of the works of Schacht up to the present would support Humphreys's evaluation. The Islamic first century remains the decisive period around which the larger part of the debate centers. Muslims have always accepted oral transmission of, Prophetic reports during that early period, not only because it was considered a standard method of imparting knowledge, but also because of the initial Prophetic command forbidding the writing of any religious text other than the Qur'ān. This last point, however, has recently been debated in the light of the view that there were written texts other than the Qur'ān in existence at the time of the Prophet himself.[83]

Unsurprisingly, the general Muslim reaction to the Islamicists' theses was not a favorable one. The majority of Muslim scholars have disregarded their conclusions. A few Muslim scholars, however, sought to engage these arguments and take part in the debate. There are three main attitudes among Muslim scholars in response to the Islamicists. The first is that of the radical critics. Focusing on issues of methodology, they sought to reveal the flaws in the Orientalist scholarship, which they attributed to lack of training, lack of understanding, or failure to systematically uphold a consistent method. Azami is considered the main representative of this trend.[84] The second trend refers to those who accept the conclusions of the Orientalists without reservation. The third trend refers to those who may be described as liberal critics. Although they generally support the adoption of a more critical approach, they don't agree with *all* of the Orientalists' conclusions.

Fazlu Rahman is considered the main representative of this third trend. His main argument is that sunnah was a *behavioral* concept used to refer to the *sum* of the verbal teachings as well as the normative example of the Prophet, even in the absence of an exact text to that effect. Rahman argued that while the Orientalists were debating the *content* of the sunnah, they extended their conclusion to the *concept* of the sunnah. For Rahman, although the content of the sunnah had undergone significant modification and even fabrication, the concept of the sunnah was clear from the beginning.[85] The concept of the Sunnah of the Prophet was not completely divorced from the practice of early Muslims. The early Muslim community was keen on following not only the word of the Prophet but, more importantly, his practical example. Therefore, the Sunnah of the Prophet was transmitted more through practice rather than either verbally or literally. Rahman presents his reading of the Sunnah of the Prophet (in the early period prior to al-Shāfiʿī) as the collective *ijmāʿ* of Muslims based on *ijtihād* and not the other way around (*ijtihād-ijmāʿ*, not *ijmāʿ-ijtihād*). In other words, the concept of sunnah in the early period was synonymous with the concept of *ijmāʿ* which was the result of the collective *ijtihād* of the Muslim community. Rahman notes that it was al-Shāfiʿī who reversed this order, not only by severing this organic relationship between *ijtihād* and *ijmāʿ*, but also by relegating them to a secondary position after a more fixed ḥadīth-based sunnah.[86] Rahman's explanation of the concept of *ijmāʿ*, however, brings it closer to the concept of *ʿurf*, which ultimately blurs the distinction between concepts such as sunnah, *ijmāʿ*, and *ʿurf*.[87]

## Revisions and Paradigm Shifts

As this quick review shows, until very recently, most of the studies focused on the first two centuries of Islam. With the beginning of the 1980s, however, a series of new studies started to challenge the main outlines of this dominant paradigm. Focus gradually shifted away from the beginnings to the later periods of the Islamic legal tradition.[88] First, scholars criticized the thesis of the closure of the gate of *ijtihād*.[89] Second, more scholarly attention was devoted to the theme of change within legal schools (*madhāhib*) by tracing the juristic treatment of certain legal issues over time.[90] Gradually, a more nuanced understanding of the development of the Islamic legal tradition started to emerge. This understanding was based on a deeper appreciation of the roles of the different legal genres and how these genres negotiated the divide between legal theory and social practice.

Legal texts are no longer viewed as monolithic. They are rather classified into distinct genres, each serving a well-defined goal, and together these genres seek the ultimate goal of bridging the gap between theory and practice.[91] In particular, the legal genres of legal opinions (*fatāwā*)[92] and court judgments (*aḥkām*)[93] have recently received increasing attention due to their role in uncovering the extent to which sharīʿah shaped Muslims' social practice over time.

## Studies Devoted to ʿ*Urf*

The historical development of the concept of *ʿurf* acquires added significance due to its close connections with the origins of the Sunnah of the Prophet. In its literal sense, sunnah means custom, and in the technical sense it is reserved to the custom approved by the Prophet. As the foregoing review shows, the connection between these two terms was at the heart of the debates that have occupied the field of Islamic studies for the last two centuries. These debates, however, focused more on the role of custom as a social or ethnographic concept. Only random reference was made to *ʿurf* as an abstract tool in Islamic legal methodology.

Several recent studies have attempted to fill this vacuum, but closer examination reveals that the dominant Orientalist paradigm continues to heavily influence modern scholarship. Gideon Libson's study is a good illustrative example. Despite his careful review of the sources, Libson ultimately reproduces many generalized statements not only about the Ḥanafi school, the main focus of his study, but about Islamic law in general. For example, although he cites Shāfiʿī's *al-Umm* and *al-Risālah,* he notes that "one finds almost no references to custom in the works of al-Shāfiʿī, although such references appear frequently in later Shāfiʿī law books."[94] Libson probably means that al-Shāfiʿī did not use the word *ʿurf* in the sense that it acquired in the later legal works. Closer examination of al-Shāfiʿī's writings, however, indicates that the concept of *ʿurf* is implicit in his legal methodology. For example, al-Shāfiʿī employs this concept in his analysis of several substantive examples.[95] What is interesting to note about these examples is that, while al-Shāfiʿī used them in his treatment of issues such as the status of Sunnah, its authority, and its abrogation, later jurists used them (the same examples) in their treatment of other mature principles such as *istiḥsān* and *ʿurf*.[96]

This shift obviously reflects a more developed stage in the tradition. In other words, what one finds in the works of al-Shāfiʿī is the concept of *ʿurf*—or at least its roots—while the later juristic works articulate a more developed legal principle.[97] These examples should illustrate two important points. First, they reflect different stages of development in a legal tradition that was constantly evolving and expanding. Second, they indicate the nature of *ʿurf* as an interpretive tool in Islamic legal theory. The interpretive activity, by definition, requires development and scrutinization before it matures and gets distilled into disparate views, opinions, or theories. A careful review of the slow, yet steady development of *ʿurf* is a clear testimony to this process. It is easy to confuse this slow development with the otherwise common explanation that it was only in the later stages of the Islamic legal tradition that *ʿurf* reached such a prominent status and received full legal recognition.

This was exactly one of Libson's conclusions. He observed that Muslim jurists "granted *de facto* recognition to certain customs by resorting to other, 'legitimate' sources of law."[98] He argued that *ʿurf* in this sense was considered a material as opposed to formal source of law. Moreover, he listed three means through which *ʿurf* attained legal recognition: sunnah, *ijmāʿ*, and written stipulation. His ultimate conclusion is that although custom was denied formal recognition, it was admitted in the early period under sunnah and *ijmāʿ*. After the codification of sunnah, it was admitted under *istiḥsān*. Although Libson's theory seems appealing and may present a plausible reconstruction of the development of *ʿurf* in the later period after the fifth—eleventh centuries, it remains lacking overall on a number of counts. First, it is clear that it still feeds off the old Orientalist paradigm, with all its limitations, regarding the origins of the Sunnah. Second, Libson's thesis not only tries to confirm the thesis of Schacht and Goldziher, which was limited to the early period, but it also tries to extrapolate their results to the subsequent periods of Islamic history. Within this framework, the main focus is placed on uncovering the "true" origins, meanings, or concepts, and therefore suggests that classical sources are always suspect. Third, Libson's study involves a great deal of generalization that recent historical research does not seem to support.

It is true that in the later period, more frequent references were made to *ʿurf* than in the early period. But this does not necessarily mean that the jurists had to admit it ipso facto because they could no longer subsume it under sunnah or *ijmāʿ*. It simply indicates a normal development of a legal tradition that increasingly required more adjustments to cope with the ever changing social practice. After all, legal traditions do not develop in a vacuum; they dialectically interact with the social realities that constantly challenge them to evolve and accommodate change.[99]

In fact, the examples found in the writings of the early formative period, such as those of al-Shāfiʿī and Mālik, are almost direct references to substantive issues covered either by the Qurʾān or the Sunnah. The efforts of the later jurists concentrated on deeper analysis and higher levels of abstraction, which is how concepts such as *istiḥsān* and *ʿurf* emerged and were incorporated within legal theory. In other words, the relatively late appearance and use of custom as a legal abstract tool was the result of nothing more than a slow development beginning with the founding texts themselves. The fact that the jurists continued to use the same examples and references to a small number of Qur'ānic verses and Prophetic precedents further proves this point. We shall have a closer look at these examples and references in the following chapters.

On the relationship between custom and texts (*naṣṣ*), either the Qur'ān or the Sunnah, Libson's treatment requires some qualifications. First, he does not deal with the concept of custom in the Qur'ān; he focuses exclusively on the Sunnah. Most modern studies on the issue generally overlook this point, but one of the goals of the present study is to draw attention to the Qur'ānic concept of *'urf.* Second, on the issue of conflict between sunnah and custom, Libson cites the famous disagreement within the Ḥanafī school between Abū Yūsuf and the majority of jurists. Libson interprets Abū Yūsuf's view as giving precedence to custom in cases of conflict with the Sunnah.[100] This issue, however, pertains to a particular type of Sunnah, which itself was based on custom at the time of the Prophet, such as the case of the means of measurements (weight or volume). Abū Yūsuf's reasoning suggested that since Sunnah in this case was based on the common custom at the time of the Prophet, the ruling based on this Sunnah would change if the originating custom changed.[101] The majority view, on the other hand, held that since custom in this case was confirmed by the Sunnah of the Prophet, it would remain as such and would not change even if the originating custom changed. It is, therefore, evident that Abū Yūsuf's view pertains to a specific type of Sunnah, not Sunnah in general as Libson would have us believe.[102]

This classical example pertains to the famous ḥadīth in which the Prophet delineated the occurrence of usury in six items: gold, silver, wheat, barley, dates, and salt. The Ḥanafī school held that the operative cause (*'illah*) for the prohibition of these items was the means of measurement, namely weight (gold and silver) and volume (the rest). There was a disagreement, however, on the criteria for determining the measurement of these items either by weight or by volume. The majority opinion within the Ḥanafī school held that the criteria is the ḥadīth itself; these six items shall remain forever traded in the same way that the Prophet stipulated. Abū Yūsuf, on the other hand, held that the Prophet was merely citing the custom of his time. Thus, if such a custom were to change, so would the ruling. Therefore, the criterion in this case should be custom rather than Sunnah.

However, since for Libson, all sunnah is based on custom, this distinction is of little material significance.[103] This almost complete identification of custom with sunnah is both tenuous and misleading: tenuous because it is not borne out by conclusive evidence and misleading because of the circularity of the argument. On the one hand, Libson maintains that sunnah originated in custom but, on the other, that custom is disguised as sunnah. The following chapters should show that the distinction between sunnah and custom was not so contested. The repeated references to custom in classical sources not only as a semi-independent source, but also as a built-in mechanism in many legal processes, contradict the argument that the jurists were keen on disguising their use of custom by incorporating it through various stratagems into more acceptable sources such as sunnah or *ijmāʿ*.[104]

Libson's study of custom in Islamic law is meant to provide a contextual background to his larger comparative study of the place of custom in the Islamic and Jewish laws during the Geonic period. Libson concludes that while Jewish law recognizes custom as a formal source of law, Islamic law recognizes custom only as a material source, often under the guise of other concepts. He attributes this to the fact that:

> For Muslim legal scholars, everything comes from God, and human beings have no authority to legislate new laws on the basis of custom or through the use of enactment. Their function is limited to revealing the true law. In order to meet the pressing needs of the times, they must seek other stratagems. Even consensus (*ijmāʿ*), which is recognized in Islamic law as a formal source, was intended solely to reveal the validity of a particular law and to maintain the unity of Islamic law, not as is sometimes thought, to serve as a means in the creation of new laws.[105]

Exploring and examining the full implications of this quotation shall occupy us throughout this entire study. For now, suffice it to mention that it confuses the famous distinction between sharīʿah and *fiqh*; it obscures the role and function of legal theory; and it mystifies the meaning of *ijmāʿ* and its relationship with the other sources of Islamic law. Despite its limitations, Libson's study is useful because it breaks away, although partially, from the dominant paradigm, even if only by focusing on the issue of *ʿurf* as an independent subject in its own right.

In his study on the issue of legal change in Islamic law, Wael Hallaq explored the inner dynamics that influenced such change. In his study, Hallaq does not ask whether change occurred but rather how it occurred.[106] After examining several legal genres, the different roles various legal actors assumed, and the processes involved in the construction of legal authority, he rightly concluded that:

> Legal change did not occur only in an *ad hoc* manner, as it were, but was rather embedded in processes built into the very structure of the law. And

> since it was a structural feature, the jurists effected it as a matter of course. This inevitably suggests that the much-debated issue of whether change ever occurred in Islamic law is a product of our own imagination.[107]

It is precisely this structural feature, embedded in the very constitution of Islamic law, that is so important to emphasize in connection with the issue of custom. *ʿUrf* has, in fact, been used as a prime example of such structural features or built-in mechanisms that have negotiated legal change over time.[108] Through the examination of several issues in substantive law, Hallaq traces the process of legal change by uncovering the numerous factors on which such a process depends.[109] Hallaq focuses on the *fatāwā* genre by investigating not only how they served the immediate goal of providing legal advice but also how they articulated the current position of a legal school on a given issue. Legal responses, therefore, often were not limited to their immediate context; they eventually ended up in the school's standard substantive law books through the hermeneutical efforts of the jurists.[110] In this context, Hallaq explored the role of custom in the process of legal change within the legal corpus of the later Ḥanafī tradition. Hallaq's argument is so important that it is worthwhile to quote it in full:

> Custom presented a major problem for later Ḥanafī jurists, since the school tradition of positive law and legal theory left little latitude for customary practices to establish themselves readily as authoritative entities. The difficulty is apparent in the fact that legal doctrine never succeeded in recognizing custom as an independent and formal legal source. Indeed, even when compared with the so-called supplementary sources—*istiḥsān*, *istiṣlāḥ*, etc—custom never managed to occupy a place equal to that which these latter had attained in the hierarchy of legal sources. As a formal entity, it remained marginal to the legal arsenal of the four schools, although the Ḥanafites and the Mālikites seem to have given it, at least outwardly, more recognition than did the other two schools, however informal this recognition might have been.
>
> The failure of custom to occupy a place among the formal sources of the law becomes all the more striking since Abū Yūsuf, a foremost Ḥanafite authority and second only to Abū Ḥanifah himself, seems to have recognized it as a source. But for reasons that still await further research, Abū Yūsuf's position failed to gain majority support and was in effect abandoned. Instead, throughout the five or six centuries subsequent to Abū Yūsuf, the Ḥanafī school upheld the fundamental proposition that the textual sources unquestionably overrode custom.[111]

This long quotation is reproduced here because it may safely be said to represent the current state of scholarship on the issue. It summarizes many of the views that are otherwise scattered in the literature. In this quotation, Hallaq's observation about the failure of legal doctrine to recognize custom as an independent formal legal source completely accords with Libson's earlier conclusion. It is important to spell out precisely what that means: classical jurists have based their analysis of customs on two main criteria: its scope (general [*ʿāmm*] or specific [*khāṣṣ*]) and textual authority (presence or absence thereof). After the verification of its scope, custom was to be dismissed only when it contravened definitive textual sources. Custom, therefore, was analyzed within a hierarchical system of legal sources, in which it was treated as a source as long as it did not conflict with a higher source of the law.

Careful analysis of the role of custom in the Islamic legal tradition reveals the inadequacy of the binary classifications of sources into formal/material or dependent/independent.[112] Custom clearly shows that there is a need for another analytical tool that will enable us to take full cognizance of all the nuances that the subject involves. Instead of the binary classification, a contextual hierarchical framework may be more useful in reconstructing the juristic treatment of custom. Within this framework, the specific legal context would mainly determine the admissible types of proofs or legal sources, which may, at times, be custom itself. As noted earlier, within the Islamic legal structure, custom per se is not necessarily antithetical to sharīʿah as long as the custom in question does not conflict with a higher source or a fundamental principle of sharīʿah. In fact, as the following chapter will show in more detail, the concept of *ʿurf* in the Qurʾān is closely tied to the concept of the good (*maʿrūf*), and that is why some exegetes argued that *ʿurf* can serve as a source of not only legal but also moral prescription.[113]

The main problem with most of the studies that examine the role of custom in Islamic law is that they view custom almost exclusively through the prism of the sources; that is, whether or not custom is treated as a source of Islamic law. Consequently, they overlook the other ways in which the concept was used and the numerous factors that contributed to its slow development over time. Apart from the textual references in both the Qurʾān and the Sunnah of the Prophet, these factors included important legal precedents from the time of the companions of the Prophet onwards, the theological foundations as reflected in the debates of scholastic theology (*kalam*), and the wide array of applications in the different legal genres. It is only through the careful and balanced examination of all these relevant factors that we may gain a fresh insight into how custom influenced the construction of rulings within the Islamic legal tradition.

In the quotation, Hallaq also reinforces the common view that the Ḥanafī and the Mālikī schools have accorded more importance to custom than have the other two schools—Shafiʿī and Ḥanbalī. As the following chapters will illustrate, however, in the process of their historical development, legal schools not only borrowed from each other but they constantly influenced each other within the larger shared framework of Islamic jurisprudence.

The reference to Abū Yūsuf's disagreement with Abu Ḥanifah may suggest that Abū Yūsuf opted for full recognition of custom even against clear textual indication. As pointed out earlier, Abū Yūsuf's reasoning pertains to a specific type of Sunnah that was initially based on custom, in which case the ruling will follow custom whenever such a custom changes.[114] It is inconceivable that Abū Yūsuf believed that customs should always take precedence over texts in cases of conflict. Such a conclusion would have immediately placed him outside the boundaries of Islamic legal norms. It was, therefore, a disagreement on the interpretation of the Sunnah and its proper application rather than a disagreement on the hierarchy of legal sources.

## Normative Juristic Approach

Ever since the early modern efforts to update the sharīʿah system and bring it in line with modern legal standards, *ʿurf* has been one of the important tools employed to facilitate this task. The majority of modern Muslim legal reformers were convinced that in order for such reform to succeed, it had to arise from within the system rather than be imposed from without. The underlying assumption was that if the sharīʿah-based system was able to endure for such a long period of time, it must have possessed certain mechanisms that enabled it to update itself, confront challenges, and accommodate change. A cursory look at the major works of legal scholarship in the Muslim world over the past century should confirm this observation. In the remaining part of this chapter, I point out some prominent examples of modern legal works and examine how they treated the issue of custom. Most of these works were written in Arabic by Arab authors but they may serve as a representative sample for other works written elsewhere in the Muslim world.[115]

The work of the famous Syrian Ḥanafī jurist Muhammad Amīn Ibn ʿĀbidīn (d. AH 1252–1836 CE)[116] represents a major turning point in the long history of the development of *ʿurf* in the Islamic legal tradition. His work is an important transition between the pre-modern and modern legal landscapes. The Damascene jurist was the leading authority of the Ḥanafī school of his time. He is well-known for writing one of the most authoritative commentaries on the Ḥanafī substantive law.[117] He is equally famous for writing a number of legal treatises that became increasingly influential thereafter.[118] One of these treatises was exclusively devoted to the role and significance of *ʿurf* in the construction of legal rulings.[119] His treatment of custom is not limited to this particular treatise but permeates 16 other treatises as well.

What is significant about his *ʿurf* treatise is the method he followed in its composition. He started out with a short introduction, elaborating on the definition of *ʿurf* and its textual foundations. He then proceeded to place it within the historical context of the Ḥanafī school. He cited the major jurists who used it, together with several examples of rulings that were built on it. It is clear from his exposition that Ibn ʿĀbidīn's goal was not to introduce any new configurations to the classical theory of *ʿurf* but rather to highlight its importance and to point out how significant it was in the works of his predecessors. His frequent coded references and numerous citations from the reliable works of the Ḥanafī school testify to his deep knowledge of the Ḥanafī legal tradition. This also shows that Ibn ʿĀbidīn was addressing his fellow expert jurists, not novices or a lay audience.

Some researchers credit Ibn ʿĀbidīn with ushering in a new phase in the Islamic legal tradition in which more focus was placed on non-revelatory elements in lawmaking.[120] A closer examination of the text, however, reveals that the author is careful to remain within the boundaries of his school even when he adopts the more liberal views. He is clearly well-versed in the linguistic practice and legal tradition of the Ḥanafī school.[121] Ibn ʿĀbidīn's mastery of the school's authoritative texts enabled him to locate and bring together all the relevant references involving *ʿurf* from the otherwise scattered passages in the various substantive law texts. One reason his work is so important is that it was the first time *ʿurf* received separate or independent treatment. As the following chapters illustrate, *ʿurf* was traditionally treated within the framework of numerous subjects that cut across the different legal genres. Ibn ʿĀbidīn's contribution was a major step in the long development of *ʿurf*, and it paved the way for more daring efforts by his successors who struggled not only to defend the sharīʾah system but even to justify it. Ibn ʿĀbidīn's work is arguably the last pre-modern contribution before the advent of new challenges that would force the later jurists to deal with a sociopolitical reality in which sharīʾah was no longer the unchallenged source of the legal system.

Another major turning point in the modern history of *ʿurf* was the composition of *Majallat al-Aḥkām al-ʿAdliyyah*. A committee of experts on Ḥanafī law wrote it with the goal of providing easy reference to the legal corpus of this school in imitation of modern European codes.[122] The *Majallah* is considered the first attempt to establish a modern civil code based on Islamic law. It served for a short period of time as the civil code of the Ottoman Empire and many Arab countries in the post-Ottoman era before different national civil codes replaced it.[123] Despite the criticism to which it was subjected, which eventually resulted in its annulment, the *Majallah* remains an important turning point in the long history of Islamic law in general and its relationship with modern legislation in particular.[124] The *Majallah* is particularly significant for the issue at hand. Building on the rich genre of legal maxims, it opens with 99 examples of these maxims, which are presented as the core of the Ḥanafī legal corpus. Out of these maxims, at least ten deal directly with the issue of custom and its different applications in substantive law.[125]

Following the example of the *Majallah*, many other projects ensued in the newly formed Arab nation-states after the collapse of the Ottoman Empire. Each of these projects merits separate study, but what is important to note here is the prominent role that was assigned to *ʿurf* in almost all of them.[126] The prominent Egyptian jurist ʿAbd al-Razzāq al-Sanhūrī, the author of the civil code of Egypt and many other Arab countries, observed that among the sources of the Egyptian civil code, *ʿurf* took precedence to sharīʿah, second only to legislation.[127] Although he was keen on ensuring the compatibility of this code with the rules of sharīʿah, al-Sanhūrī explained that the process had to be undertaken gradually rather than abruptly. This was one of the reasons other countries refused to adopt the Egyptian civil code; it was not seen as fully compatible with sharīʿah.[128] The objection, however, was not to the inclusion of *ʿurf* but rather the order it occupied. A careful review of the modern writings on the issue reveals that the overwhelming majority of modern Muslim legal scholars consider *ʿurf* a structural component of Islamic jurisprudence. Therefore, disagreements on *ʿurf* are often a matter of degree or scope rather than of principle.

The question of the role and status of *ʿurf* in modern times places us right in the middle of the debates on reform and renewal that occupied scholars from the late nineteenth century through the entire twentieth century. *ʿUrf*, as well as similar legal principles such as *maṣlaḥah*, was an important legal tool that Muslim reformers invoked in their efforts to work out a comprehensive methodology to bridge the gap between the past and the present on the one hand and legal theory and practice on the other.[129] In no other place was that clearer than in *al-Manār* of Rashīd Riḍā, the faithful disciple of Muḥamad ʿAbdū, who strove to continue his master's mission of religious reform and renewal. In the *fatāwā* that he gave in answer to questions from Muslims all over the world, addressing every possible aspect of Islamic law, references to *ʿurf* and *maṣlaḥah* are numerous.[130] For Riḍā there is a clear distinction between rulings on matters of belief and worship on the one hand and practical worldly affairs on the other. The former are fixed and unchangeable while the latter are to be considered in the light of the changing times, places, and customs. This theme runs throughout his *fatāwā* and also his interpretation of the Qur'ān.[131] He emphasizes the importance of exercising *ijtihād*, especially on new issues for which the classical law books give no answer.[132] To a large extent, the issues that Riḍā was grappling with remained the subject of legal and intellectual debate long after him, as the numerous subsequent *fatāwā* collections clearly indicate.

Part of the reason for the increased skepticism towards Western modernity in the Muslim world has been the fact that it was introduced within the framework of domination and colonization. The challenges that the Muslim world had to face during the period of European colonization were multifaceted.[133] In fact, the impact of colonization was nowhere more felt than in the legal and judicial domains. The challenges posed by the colonizers were not limited to military subjugation; the introduction of modern legal codes proved to have a more lasting impact. Modern Muslim jurists felt that it was their duty to defend the sharīʿah-based legal system against the Western legal codes, which were seen as another form of occupation. Renewal and reform within the framework of sharīʿah were seen as necessary means to free the Muslim world from this legal occupation.

Gradually, and with the recurrent calls for breaking the shackles of blind following (*taqlīd*), similar calls were made to engage in free independent examination of the primary sources (*ijtihād*). The practice of *ijtihād* during this time, however, consisted largely of careful perusal and selection from among the considered opinions of the eminent jurists on the various substantive issues, without any restrictions on school affiliation, a practice that became known as free and creative selection, or *talfīq*.[134] Moreover, comparative juristic discussions extended beyond the usual inter-*madhhab* comparisons to include modern European legal systems.[135] Major legal principles were extracted from the major compendia and studied separately along with their applications, often in comparison with their counterparts in modern (Western-inspired) legislation. Principles such as public interest (*maslaḥah*), rights (*ḥuqūq*), and custom (*ʿurf*) were among the most famous ones.

It is within this context that the modern discussions on *ʿurf* are situated. Following the earlier efforts of Ibn ʿĀbidīn and the authors of the *Majallah*, hardly any book on Islamic legal theory written thereafter overlooked the subject of custom and its role in the Islamic legal system. These later treatments consisted largely of abstracts and summaries of classical works but, unlike Ibn ʿĀbidīn's work and the *Majallah*, they were not restricted to a single legal school. Discussions on *ʿurf* in the modern period can be located in at least four main genres: works of *uṣūl* (jurisprudence/legal theory), which are largely either summaries of classical works or reproductions of these works in new annotated editions;[136] works on Islamic substantive law (*fiqh*);[137] comparative studies between sharīʿah-based rulings and positive laws;[138] and finally, probably most importantly, works in the *fatāwā* collections.[139]

## Concluding Remarks

Scholarly studies both in the West and in the Muslim world have undergone their own developments. Early treatments in the West were locked into the debates of the origins of Islamic law and were heavily influenced by the dominant Orientalist paradigm in its two main philological and ethnographic subdisciplines. Later efforts started to break away from this typical Orientalist paradigm by producing more historically nuanced studies that focused more on the sociohistorical context than on generalized theses such as the foreign origins or conflict between theory and practice. In the Muslim world, studies on *ʿurf* were precipitated by the modern codification movement, although significant precursors predated the codification period, as evident from the different genres of legal scholarship. Overall, in the Muslim world, studies were normative in approach and juristic in method. Historical reconstructions have been rare or nonexistent.

The survey of the literature indicates a growing interest in the subject of *ʿurf*, especially in the Muslim world where there is a felt need to vindicate sharīʿah and prove its ability to survive the successive onslaughts of modernity. The prominent status assigned to *ʿurf* in the later periods of the tradition has led some commentators to conclude that under compelling exigencies, Muslim jurists were forced to finally recognize custom as a source of law in its own right rather than—following a long-held practice—subsuming it under other more "legitimate" sources such as sunnah or *ijmāʿ*. This conclusion, however, overlooks the slow process of development that the concept of custom underwent and also the many factors (purely legal and otherwise) that contributed to the development and consolidation of this concept.

# Part 2

# Beginning and Early History

# Chapter 2

# Normative Foundations of the Concept of Custom in the Islamic Legal Tradition

This chapter seeks to highlight the normative, mainly textual, foundations of the concept of custom in the Islamic legal tradition. After a brief general overview of the Islamic legal method, the chapter discusses the definition of custom and the different terms that have been associated with it. This is followed by a survey of the different contexts that address the concept of custom in the two primary sources of Islamic law: the Qur'ān and the Sunnah of the Prophet. It is important, however, to start with a word about the juritic interpretive framework.

Muslim jurists have understood their primary objective to be finding God's will as manifested or embodied in his revelation to the Prophet. For Muslims, God's revelation is used mainly to refer to the text of the Qur'ān, which they believe to be God's literal word. Divine revelation, however, is not limited to the text of the Qur'ān. It also includes divine inspiration to the Prophet who communicated it, in his own words, in the form of ḥadīth or sunnah. These two terms are occasionally used as synonyms. Technically, however, ḥadīth refers to the Prophet's verbal expressions and sunnah refers to his example, which is set as a normative model to be emulated by his followers. Sunnah, therefore, is a comprehensive concept which includes the Prophet's statements (*aqwāl*), actions (*af^cāl*), and tacit approvals (*taqrirāt*). The Qur'ān and the Sunnah represent the two primary foundations on which the entire juristic tradition is built.

This explains the ubiquitous citations from these two sources in almost every legal discussion. Within the juristic culture, the degree to which any answer or conclusion is held authoritative is measured by its correspondence with the general principles enshrined in these two sources. God's will, as contained in the divine revelation, is referred to as the supreme criterion against which human actions are to be evaluated. No jurist, however, can claim absolute knowledge of God's will in every case, especially cases for which the primary sources do not give clear direction. This may sound like a conundrum; while the law is supposed to be grounded in God's will, there is no guarantee that God's will can be objectively located or determined on every occasion.

The jurist's search for God's will can, therefore, result in two equally unsettling results. It can, on the one hand, result in an elusive sense of certainty regarding the divine will and how it should impact the construction of the law. In this case, one has to guard against mistaking God's will for one's own. On the other hand, it can result in a relaxed flexibility, which may turn into legal relativity.[1] The jurist is constantly occupied with the perennial question of how to search for God's will without falling into either of these two traps. There is no ready or easy answer to this question, but the search for one was the main impetus behind the development of the entire juristic enterprise in general, and legal theory (*uṣūl al-fiqh*) in particular.

Two main objectives drove this juristic enterprise. The first was insuring that the legal process was free from political abuse, appropriation, or co-optation. Because the legal process, by its nature, is subject to political manipulation, the jurists sought to redress this vulnerability by developing a theoretical system that maintains the independence, consistency, and coherence of the process. Throughout the course of the Islamic legal tradition, there have been many examples illustrating the struggle between the jurists and the rulers over this point. The relationship between the political and juristic authority in Islamic history has been shaped by a great deal of manipulation, exploitation, and occasionally serious confrontation.[2] Whenever the jurists dared to challenge the political authority, they were often punished, imprisoned, or even killed. Ultimately, the jurists' triumph was clearly manifested in the development of a sophisticated legal system to which the political structure was subjected, even if sometimes only in theory.[3]

The second objective of the jurists was ensuring the objectivity of the law. The jurists sought to develop methods that would enable them to locate and interpret the divine will as objectively as humanly possible. These methods involved four main areas: types of indicators (*adillah),* guidelines for their interpretation(*ṭuruq al-dalālah*), rulings (*aḥkām*) deduced from the indicators, and finally the qualifications of a jurist competent to undertake the task.[4] The indicators on which the law can be based fall into three main categories: textual, derived, and rational. The textual indicators (*adillah sharʿiyyah*) consist of the two primary sources, the Qur'ān and the Sunnah of the Prophet. The derived indicators (*adillah istinbāṭiyyah*) are based on the primary sources, such as the consensus of the jurists (*ijmāʿ*) and analogical reasoning (*qiyās*). Rational indicators (*adillah ʿaqliyyah*) were admitted as long as they did not contradict the other textual or derived indicators.[5]

Two factors determine the interpretation of the textual indicators: their reliability (*thubūt*), which can be definitive (*qaṭʿī*) or speculative (*ẓannī*), and their signification (*dalālah*), which can also be definitive or speculative.[6] There is no disagreement among Muslim jurists on the divine origin of the Qur'ānic text. They disagree, however, on the signification of particular passages thereof; that is, whether the meaning deduced from these passages can be established definitively. The situation in the case of sunnah is different because the scope of the definitive is more limited both in terms of reliability and signification. The majority of aḥādith fall in the category of singular (*āḥād*). Although a singular report is considered a valid proof in itself, it remains incomparable to the Qur'ānic text. The word *āḥād* literally means "singular" and technically refers to the category of ḥadīth that is neither successive (*mutawātir*) nor famous (*mashhūr*). The successive report is narrated by such a large number of transmitters in every stage of its chain of transmission (*isnād*) that it is inconceivable to assume that they all agreed to fabricate it. The famous report is the one that follows the successive report in order. A great deal of the disagreement among the jurists is attributable to differences on the evaluation of particular indicators. In the case of the Qur'ān, the jurists investigate the means and degree of signification, whether it is definitive or speculative. For example, this includes the interpretation of certain imperative forms and whether they denote obligation or mere commendation. In the case of sunnah, the jurists investigate the Prophetic traditions in terms of both reliability and signification, whether they are definitive or speculative.[7] In other words, they start by verifying whether a particular report can be safely ascribed to the Prophet. Once the reliability of the report has been established, they turn to the question of signification and how it can be confirmed.

The rulings that are deduced from the indicators can be either determinate (*taklifiyyah*) or correlative (*waḍʿiyyah*). The determinate rulings fall into five categories commonly known as the five rulings (*al-aḥkām al-khamsah*). The actions of the legally competent individual (*mukallaf*) can be classified as mandatory (*wājib*), recommended (*mustaḥabb*), allowed (*mubāḥ*), abominable (*makrūh*), or forbidden (*ḥaram*). The correlative rulings are the ones that are determined in the light of certain considerations that include, for example, a cause (*sabab*), a condition (*sharṭ*), or an impediment (*māniʿ*).[8] These considerations determine the evaluation of certain actions in terms of validity (*ṣiḥḥah*) or invalidity (*buṭlān*). For example, every legally competent individual is required to establish regular prayer. The validity of prayer, however, is dependent on the fulfillment of certain conditions (e.g., timeframe) and the absence of certain impediments (e.g., impurity of body or garments) that may violate such validity.

Early on, the jurists realized that the texts of sharīʿah are finite. The changing social contexts, however, constantly give rise to infinite novel questions. In the light of the Muslim belief that sharīʿah constitutes the final divine revelation that should serve the needs of the Muslim community until the end of time, the jurists reasoned that the means of constructing legal rulings cannot be limited to textual sources.[9] With the exception of the Ẓāhirī school, this view was upheld by almost all juristic schools.[10] There is ample evidence that support for this view goes back as early as the time of the Prophet, who himself encouraged his companions to exercise *ijtihād* in the absence of clear textual indication.[11] Therefore, in addition to the textual sources of the Qurʾān and the Sunnah, the jurists have also relied on a number of other derived and rational sources such as consensus, analogical reasoning, juristic preference (*istiḥsān*), public interest (*maṣlaḥah*), and custom (*ʿurf* or *ʿādah*). The following discussion is devoted to the treatment of *ʿurf* within the framework of legal sources.

Over the long course of its development, *ʿurf* was closely connected with other similar sources such as sunnah, *ijmāʿ*, and *ʿamal* (literally, practice). The origin of this connection is rooted in the linguistic definitions of these concepts. Etymologically, all these terms share certain elements that are common to the English equivalent of practice or custom. It is important, however, to note that each one of these terms has acquired a distinctive technical meaning (*maʿnā iṣṭilāḥī*) that eventually separated and distinguished it from the others. *Ijmāʿ*, for example, has gradually come to refer to the consensus of the qualified and competent jurists respectively. Similarly, *ʿamal* has become associated particularly with the practice of the people of Madinah. In addition to this distinctive juristic meaning, and with the exception of the term sunnah, each of these terms—*ijmāʿ*, *ʿamal*, and *ʿurf*—acquired a more nuanced meaning within the legal corpus of the different legal schools. This, in turn, added another layer of complexity, which helps explain many of the juristic disagreements. We shall have a chance to deal with this point in more detail in the subsequent chapters.

The close relationship among these three terms reveals the nexus between concepts and the terms that are used to refer to them. Throughout intellectual history, abstract systems of analysis and classification often follow, in order, the concepts or the phenomena that they seek to analyze or classify. Logic and grammar are two cases in point. These two examples are understood to be abstract systems that seek to illustrate the latent patterns within the subjects of their inquiry, namely, thinking and language.[12] This, of course, does not mean that people cannot think without prior formal knowledge of logic or that they cannot speak a language without prior formal knowledge of its grammar. To a large extent these abstract systems mimic the natural processes of thinking and speaking, and provide a map of the functions of the two faculties.

This important link between terms and concepts is inherent in the human capacity for language that facilitates reference and communication.[13] This still does not suggest that studying certain phenomena by focusing on the terms that have been associated with them, as well as their development over time, is unimportant or unhelpful. What is suggested here, rather, is that exclusive focus on terms, to the exclusion of concepts, can be limiting and elusive.

How does that relate to the issue of *ʿurf*? Highlighting this connection can help us understand the evolution of the concept of *ʿurf* as well as the expressions or terms that became associated with it. These expressions and terms, in turn, can serve as indicators of the turning points in the development of this concept. For example, if systematic use of *ʿurf* appeared only in the post-classical period (after the fifth century AH/eleventh century CE), does this mean that the history of *ʿurf* as a legal principle started only during this period? Modern Muslim studies on Islamic legal theory do not deal with this question. The approach adopted by most Muslim studies is normative and non-historical. As we saw in the previous chapter, some Western commentators, based on this observation, reached the conclusion that this was actually the case. A conclusive answer to this question, however, would require a closer examination of the early stages of the Islamic legal tradition in order to trace the foundations of the concept and how it evolved over time. We shall start our inquiry by exploring the meaning of the terms of *ʿurf* and *ʿādah*, as well as their place, meaning, and use in the two primary sources of Islam, the Qurʾān and the Sunnah. As mentioned earlier, these textual sources have always provided the normative foundations on which legal discourses were constructed, reconstructed, or even deconstructed.

## The Definition of *ʿUrf*

Etymologically, the word *ʿurf* is derived from the root of the verb "to know." The word *ʿurf* has many senses but it is usually used in two main senses: "what is known" as opposed to "what is unknown" and "what is good, wholesome, or commendable."[14] The two words *ʿurf* and *maʿrūf* are used as synonyms and both were mentioned in the Qurʾān, as will be shown shortly.[15] Linguistically, *ʿurf* refers to any common practice, whether good or bad. Juristically, it refers exclusively to the common practice that has been established as good by the testimony of reason and has become acceptable to people's disposition (*ma istaqarrat al-nufus ʿalayhi bi shahadat al-ʿuqūl wa talaqqathu al-ṭabāʾiʿ bi al-qabūl*).[16] The word *ʿādah* is derived from the root that means "to return" or "to repeat." It refers to a habit or a continuous practice (*daydan*).[17] Juristically, it refers to a continuous practice whose repetition cannot be explained rationally (*al-amr al-mutakarir min ghayr ʿalāqah ʿaqliyyah*).[18]

While some jurists used the two terms *ʿurf* and *ʿādah* interchangeably,[19] others distinguished between them. The latter disagreed about which of the two terms is more general than the other,[20] but the majority of researchers held that *ʿādah* is more general than *ʿurf*. While *ʿādah* can be either individual or collective, *ʿurf* refers only to collective habits. In other words, every *ʿurf* is *ʿādah*, but not every *ʿādah* is *ʿurf*. Moreover, while *ʿādah* includes naturally induced phenomena, such as reaching the age of maturity—which depends largely on average temperatures or geographical locations—*ʿurf* does not. The distinction between the two terms is based also on material and formal considerations. While *ʿurf* involves a material aspect (the actual occurrence or repetition of the action) as well as a formal aspect (the recognition of its status as a common accepted practice), *ʿādah* involves only the former. In other words, while the recognition of *ʿurf* is intuitive, the recognition of *ʿādah* requires further ascertainment.[21]

## Textual Foundations of *ʿUrf* in the Qurʾān

The word *ʿādah* itself is not mentioned in the Qurʾān. Instead, several derivatives of the root, mostly in the verb form, are used to denote repetition or recurrence.[22] The Qurʾān mentions *ʿurf* several times, however. In one verse (77:1), it refers to one of its linguistic senses, which is "following each other."[23] Two other verses (7:46 and 7:48) use the word in the plural form in the sense of a "high or elevated place."[24] It is verse 7:199 that is occasionally referred to as a possible foundation for the legal concept of *ʿurf*.[25] Three main interpretations are given to the word *ʿurf* in this verse. The first and most famous one is "what is good and commendable." In this sense, it denotes all good deeds commended by sharīʿah that involve, for example, forgiveness, generosity, and obligations toward one's family.[26] The second interpretation is "what is known and accepted as a good common practice."[27] The third interpretation is "what is known to be important and necessary."[28]

The word *maʿrūf* occurs 38 times in the Qurʾān.[29] In most of these contexts the word stands for kindness, goodness, and benevolence. In some instances it is understood as the common standard or criterion according to which divine commands are to be interpreted. In verse 2:233, for example, the Qurʾān instructs husbands to provide for their nursing wives and babies "*bil maʿrūf*."[30] Al-Tabarī (d. AH 310/922 CE) notes that this phrase means, "according to common standards in comparable situations" (*bima yajibu limithlihā ʿalā mithlihi*).[31]

In a similar verse[32] that deals with the divorcee's right to alimony, it is asserted that payment should be determined based on the financial ability of the payer and in accordance with the common practice.[33] A careful review of the contexts in which the word occurs in the Qurʾān demonstrates that there is a great deal of overlap between the different meanings of *maʿrūf*. These meanings are not, after all, completely unrelated. As evident from the linguistic meanings of the word, it indicates both what is known and what is commendable. Things could be well-known either for positive or negative reasons, but when the reason is not specified, it is generally assumed to be a positive one. This could mean, for example, that because things are praiseworthy, they become well-known or they become well-known for their praiseworthiness.

*Maʿrūf* is often contrasted with the word *munkar,* which denotes not only what is unknown but also what is detestable, deniable, or condemnable. Within the framework of sharīʿah, it stands for what is condemned by the Lawgiver. Out of the 38 references to *maʿrūf* in the Qurʾān, it was used nine times in contrast to *munkar.*[34] The command to enjoin the good—*maʿrūf*—and condemn the evil—*munkar*—is one of the most fundamental tenets of faith. Both the Qurʾān and the Sunnah of the Prophet are replete with references to this principle, which has always had a strong connotation in juristic, theological, and even political discourses. In most of the other contexts, the word *maʿrūf* is used in the sense of "what is good or commendable." In several instances, it is used to denote "what is known" or "according to the common practice."[35]

Apart from these direct and indirect references to *ʿurf* and *maʿrūf*, it is also important to note the implied references to the concept of *ʿurf* in the Qurʾān, especially in the context of the verses that deal with legal issues. These verses are seen as closely linked to the social realities they address. Whenever a command is given without further details on the mode of application, it is considered applicable to any relevant context. Part of the jurist's task is to relate Qur'ānic instructions to particular contexts. The Qur'ān repeatedly reiterates the notion that duties and obligations fall within human capacity.[36] In other words, in stipulating the different legal enactments, the Lawgiver has already taken into account the different psychological, social, and economic dimensions of the human condition. For example in verse 57:7, which refers to non-obligatory charitable donation, Muslims are invited to spend from what they are entrusted with.[37] The verse promises great reward for those who respond to the invitation, but it specifies neither the item nor the amount. These details are left to the various individual and collective conditions, which are measured in the light of common customs or *ʿurf.* The common standards determine what is deemed valuable in a given society, whether knowledge, wealth, or other types of items. Whenever the amount is not specified, it is generally understood to be the average, as expressly indicated in several instances. In verse 5:89, for example, the expiation for a broken oath can be one of three alternatives: feeding ten needy individuals, setting a slave free, or fasting for three days. The feeding of the needy individuals is to be determined according to the average staple food of the expiator's family and region.

The concept of moderation is an important principle often reiterated in the Qur'ān. In several verses, Muslims are advised to avoid drifting into extremes. For example, verse 7:31 explains that people are permitted to enjoy God's bounties but they should avoid overindulgence and wasteful consumption.[38] Similarly, verse 17:29 sets the perfect model for personal finances and spending habits.[39] This perfect model is neither stinginess nor extravagance. It is the balanced degree of moderation. Again, the Qur'ān does not spell out the exact degree of moderation; it is to be determined, rather, in light of the relevant common practice.

In conclusion, reference to *ʿurf* in the Qur'ān is not only direct or indirect but it is also—more frequently so—implied. The Qur'ān considers the human context, both at the individual as well as the collective level. This is more evident in verses that address legal issues because these verses often do not provide for the small or specific details. As the examples above illustrate, these details are to be supplied in light of the common, and accepted, agreed upon practices, or *ʿurf.*

## *ʿUrf* in the Sunnah of the Prophet[40]

In tracing the foundations for *ʿurf* in the Sunnah of the Prophet, the jurists often refer to the concluding portion of a ḥadīth narrated by the companion Ibn Masʿūd that states: "Whatever Muslims deem good, it is good in the sight of God, and whatever they deem bad, it is bad in the sight of God."[41] This report has been classified as *mawqūf*, a report whose chain of transmitters reaches only to a companion, and the link between the companion and the Prophet is unverified.[42] Therefore, the report is considered, in all probability, a saying of Ibn Masʿūd himself rather than of the Prophet.[43] The same report is also used to prove the authority of *ijmāʿ*, which further explains the close connection between the two concepts.[44] Hadīth commentators gave three different interpretations to the word Muslims in the report: companions of the Prophet, qualified jurists, and Muslims in general. The first interpretation takes the immediate context of the report into considerationas it was addressed to the companions of the Prophet. Such interpretation refers to the view of *ijmāʿ* as the consensus of the companions exclusively. According to the second interpretation, *ijmāʿ* is not limited to the consensus of the companions but is extended to include that of qualified jurists of any period of time. The third interpretation refers to the collective agreement of Muslims both learned and lay; here it will refer to *ʿurf* or common custom. Regardless of the authenticity of this report, it remains important because of the prominent role it played in the development of an extensive juristic discourse on both *ijmāʿ* and *ʿurf*.

Apart from this contested report, a strong case for the concept of *ʿurf* can be made on the basis of the other indirect and implied references to it in the Sunnah of the Prophet, as we noted earler in the case of the Qur'ān as well. In the books of *ṣaḥiḥ*,[45] there are several examples that cover the previously mentioned triple classification of sunnah: the verbal, the practical, and the tacit. While some aḥādīth include the word *ʿurf* or *maʿruf*, others refer to the concept rather than the term itself. For example, in the famous *Muwaṭṭa'* of Mālik (d. AH 179/795 CE), one of the earliest books of collected written aḥādith, the Prophet is reported to have indicated to his wife ʿĀ'ishah that when the Makkans were renovating the Kaʿbah, they failed to rebuild it on the foundations laid by Prophet Ibrāhim.[46] ʿĀ'ishah wondered why he (Prophet Muhammad) declined to rebuild the Kaʿbah on these original foundations. The Prophet indicated that he had to take the Makkans' recent acceptance of Islam into account.[47] For the Makkans, Kaʿbah was the most sacred place and the Prophet Muhammad felt that they would not be able to tolerate the shock of seeing it being desecrated. In his commentary on this ḥadīth, Al-Bāji (d. AH 474/1081 CE) noted that the attitude of the Prophet indicated that what was more important was insuring the proper performance of the circumambulation around the (whole) Kaʿbah, which could be done without rebuilding it.[48] In other words, the practice of the Prophet indicated that acknowledging people's sensibilities or common practices is important as long as doing so does not violate the rules of sharīʿah.

In a famous ḥadīth narrated both by al-Bukhārī (d. AH 256/869 CE) and Muslim (d. AH 261/874 CE), it is reported that the Prophet was asked whether a wife could spend on household needs from her husband's money without his knowledge or permission.[49] The Prophet indicated approvingly that it was permissible as long as it was done according to the common practice (*bil maʿrūf*). The word *maʿruf* here clearly indicates the accepted common standard, practice, or custom. Al-Bukhārī, who is known for his thematic classification of the aḥādīth in his collection, listed this ḥadīth in a chapter titled "On the consideration of the common customs of the different regions."[50] The commentator on al-Bukhārī's book, Ibn Ḥajar al-ʿAsqalānī (d. AH 852/1448 CE), provided further explanation for the words *ʿurf* and *maʿrūf*. He also listed numerous other examples of its different applications in the chapters of substantive law.[51]

There are many other Prophetic reports that deal with the concept of *ʿurf*, particularly in the area of transactions. These reports were often cited in the juristic discourses on legal concepts such as analogical reasoning (*qiyās*), juristic preference (*istiḥsān*), and public interest (*maṣlaḥah mursalah*). These aḥādīth served as the raw material that the jurists utilized to construct not only particular substantive rulings but also general legal principles from which these rulings can be deduced. For example, there is a group of aḥādīth that address the issue of *ʿarāyā* (palm trees whose crops were intended for charity). In one ḥadīth, the Prophet is reported to have forbidden the sale of unripe fruits on trees (prior to harvest time).[52] This type of transaction was prohibited because it involves a great deal of uncertainty (*gharar*), which can lead to exploitation.

In another ḥadīth, however, the Prophet permitted this type of sale only in the case of *ʿarāyā* within the limit of five *awsuq* (about 321 pounds).[53] Based on the commentary of al-ʿAsqalānī, the word *ʿarāyā* has more than one meaning. The first refers to the case in which a person asks the owner (of palm trees) to sell him the crops of one or more palm trees in return for their estimated future measure in dried dates. This person does not own palm trees and otherwise would not have access to the fresh dates of the new season for his family's personal consumption.[54] The Prophet permitted this type of transaction because it was commonly known and popular. The second meaning refers to the case in which the owner donates the crop of several palm trees to another (needy) person and later tries to avoid the inconvenience of the latter's entrance into his property by estimating the value of this crop and paying it in advance in the form of dried dates.[55] The third meaning refers to the case in which the designated beneficiary, due to extreme need, cannot wait until the harvest time (or when the fresh dates turn into dried dates), so he estimates the measure of the future dried dates of the designated crop and sells it either back to the donor or to someone else. In all these examples, *ʿarāyā* is a type of transaction that was excepted from the general prohibition to sell unripe fruit on trees prior to harvest time. The exception was given in consideration of the common practice of people, to obviate the hardship that would result if these common practices were not accommodated.

Another important example is the *salam* (advance payment) sale, which again was an exception of the Prophetic command prohibiting the sale of the unowned property. In one ḥadīth, the prophet is reported to have instructed a companion not to sell what he did not own.[56] This ḥadīth pertains to what the juristic discourses refer to as the sale of the nonexistent (*bayʿ al-maʿdūm*), such as birds in the air and fish in the water. Yet, on the other hand, in a number of other aḥādith, the Prophet is reported to have said that "whoever engages in *salam* transaction, let him specify the measure, the weight, and the term."[57] According to the narration of al-Bukhārī, this ḥadīth is prefaced by the remark of its narrator, the companion Ibn ʿAbbās (d. AH 68/687 CE): "When the Prophet came to Madinah, he found people dealing in *salam* transactions for terms up to three years."[58] As evident from these reports, the Prophet again gave a concession after an initial prohibitive command in view of the common practice of the people of Madinah.[59]

In a particularly significant incident, which was recorded in a number of aḥādīth, the Prophet is reported to have accorded great importance to common customs. As the Prophet was once passing by a group of people who were pollinating their palm trees, he suggested that it might be more useful if the palm trees were left unpollinated. They followed the advice and, as a result, the harvest did not turn out as good as it used to. When he was told about the harvest, the Prophet noted, "If this practice (pollination) is useful, let them do it. That was just a thought (of mine), so let them not hold on to it. But, when I convey to you something from God, hold on to it for I will never lie to you about God."[60] According to another narration, he said, "I am but a human. If I order you to do something concerning religion, hold on to it. If, however, I order you to do something on the basis of my personal opinion, know that I am but a human."[61] In yet another famous narration, he is reported to have said, "You know better about your areas of experience in the affairs of this world."[62]

This ḥadīth has been used to delineate the different roles that the Prophet assumed and consequently, the type and scope of authority that is associated with each of them. The jurists distinguished three distinct roles that the Prophet held. The first was his role as the political leader of the community and in this capacity he conducted the affairs of the Muslim state. The second was his role as a judge and arbiter and in this capacity he settled different types of disputes and disagreements. The third was his role as a carrier and communicator of the divine revelation to the Muslim community. Only in this last capacity is he considered infallible.[63]

This distinction among the different roles of the Prophet is extremely important for understanding the relationship between sunnah and *ʿurf.* A careful survey of the vast scope of the Prophetic Sunnah would support the observation that the Prophet gave attention to the *ʿurf* of the community within the capacity of his first two roles, i.e., as a political leader and also as a judge or arbiter. However, if *ʿurf* stood in contrast to his role as a carrier and communicator of revelation, it would be subjected to the demands and guidelines of revelation.

Moreover, in terms of the relationship between the Sunnah of the Prophet (in his role as a carrier and communicator of revelation) and pre-Islamic customs, there are three types of Sunnah: affirmative, reformative, and prohibitive. The first category involves the pre-Islamic customs that were approved and transported into the Islamic system with slight or no modification. The adoption of these customs could have been negotiated through express commands or tacit approval of the Prophet. As a general rule, all the pre-Islamic customs that did not contradict any of the tenets of sharīʿah were automatically approved and allowed to continue. This was probably the theoretical foundation of the legal principle of original permissibility (*istiṣḥāb*). Within juristic discourses, *istiṣḥāb,* or *istiṣḥāb al-barāʾah al-aṣliyyah,* meant that unless otherwise indicated, the rule is always permissibility or innocence rather than impermissibility or guilt. In one ḥadīth, for example, it is reported that the companion Ḥakīm Ibn Ḥizām asked the Prophet about some of the charitable activities he used to do before he accepted Islam and whether he would still be rewarded for them. The Prophet's answer indicated that he approved of these practices and also encouraged him to continue to do them.[64] In another report, the Prophet alluded to a pre-Islamic pact among the Makkans in which they agreed to help the weak and redress injustice. He emphasized that he would join such a pact if he was called to it after Islam.[65]

The second category of Sunnah involves the customs that were adopted, but only after amendment or adjustment. This category includes all the practices that were amended and reformed in the light of the dictates of sharīʿah, which included a wide range of issues of legal import. In a famous report, for example, ʿĀʾishah narrated that before Islam, the Arabs knew four types of marriage, of which only one type was approved and allowed to continue. All the other three were condemned and discontinued.[66] Along with the regulation of the marital relationship came the rulings regarding relationships of lineage as well as the other social configurations. For example, the pre-Islamic methods of kinship verification based on resemblance of bodily features (*qiyāfah*) were replaced by reference to the existence of a valid marital bond or lack thereof.[67]

The third category involves the customs and practices that were condemned and therefore discontinued. This category applies, again, to a wide range of issues of legal and semi-legal import. The prohibition of usury (*ribā*) and other questionable transactions that involved uncertainty, deceit, and exploitation are prominent examples of this category.[68] Also included are the other rulings that pertain to dietary and drinking regulations.[69] It also addresses customs pertaining to different aspects of social life such as clothing,[70] mourning and celebration arrangements, and other customs associated with different rites of passage.

Therefore, in his role as a communicator of divine revelation and in his articulation of the three types of Sunnah (affirmative, reformative, and prohibitive), the Prophet transformed what Toshihiko Izutsu referred to as the evaluative ethical terms of the pre-Islamic Arabian environment. These are the terms that are infused with social and cultural meaning and serve as measures for evaluating activities within a certain culture. The terms *maʿrūf* and *munkar* were examples of the new evaluative ethical terms that served as indicators of the Islamic ethical structure. With the advent of Islam, all the pre-Islamic customs and practices had to be reexamined in light of the guidelines enshrined in the Qurʾān and its worldview.[71]

In conclusion, similar to the case with the Qurʾān, the relationship between sunnah and *ʿurf* is not limited to the report of Ibn Masʿūd on "the consensus of Muslims," as it is sometimes suggested in the literature. A more comprehensive approach that focuses more on the concept, rather than on the terms of *ʿurf* and its derivatives or synonyms, will be more useful. The examples cited show that the concept of *ʿurf* permeates the entire landscape of the Sunnah of the Prophet. The word *sunnah*—which literally means way, path, or pattern—was juristically restricted to the normative example of the Prophet, which is meant to provide elaboration on the primary Qurʾānic revelation. *Ijmaʿ*, as a legal principle, referred only to the consensus of the qualified jurists, whose considered opinions were essential for establishing legal normativity in case a clear indication was missing in either the Qurʿān or the Sunnah. *ʿAmal,* which literally denotes practice and juristically indicates the practice of the people of Madinah is probably the closest to the concept of *ʿurf.* While *ʿurf* refers to common custom or practice in general, *ʿamal* was mainly used to refer to the practice of the people of Madīnah exclusively. Traditionally, *ʿamal* was one of the main sources of the Mālikī school of thought.

As seen in the previous chapter, most of the Western studies on Islamic legal history focused on the question of the origins of Islamic law and, more particularly, on the origins of the Sunnah during the first two or three centuries. According to these studies, there is a great deal of confusion between sunnah and custom because sunnah was seen as a by-product of custom. Later studies continued to feed on this account and presented a view of the development of legal custom as having been disguised as sunnah. According to these later studies, the jurists denied custom formal recognition, but they admitted it under other formal sources such as Sunnah or *ijmāʿ*. Ultimately, this leads to the concept of Sunnah based on custom and custom disguised as sunnah without the slightest attention to the circularity of this argument.

In the following two chapters, I look closer at the development of *ʿurf* from the early formative period until the fifth century AH (eleventh century CE), when the basic configurations of the Islamic legal tradition were established and consolidated. I investigate when and how the concept emerged and how it was distinguished from the other legal sources.

# Chapter 3

# From *ʿĀdah* to *ʿUrf*

## Theological Foundations of the Concept of Custom as reflected in the Debate over Causality

During his lifetime, the Prophet represented the supreme authority for the Muslim community; his presence guaranteed the resolution of any disagreement that may have arisen. Soon after his death, differences and disagreements started to emerge. His absence was immediately felt in the inability of the Muslim community to concur on a number of important issues. In the beginning, most of the disagreements were related to political questions such as the appointment of a successor to the Prophet and the grounds for such appointment, whether it was textual authority or the community's choice.[1] Competing groups sought to support their positions with strong proofs. Eventually, these views developed into a multitude of disparate theological schools.[2]

At a later stage and subsequent to the Islamic conquests, Muslims came into contact with new systems of thought and felt the need to defend their religion against the onslaughts of foreign religious and cultural influences. As evident from the extant works on *kalam* (theology) and *firaq* (sects), most of the debates centered around some key issues such as divine attributes, the relationship between divine will and human freedom, the reality and purpose of human existence, the nature and goal of Prophethood, and the reality of afterlife, in addition to the question of imamate or caliphate.[3]

Since these issues pertain to the fundamentals of religion, they must be founded on strong rational proofs. Such proofs should not appeal merely to textual authority, because this would result in circularity. In other words, these proofs aim to establish the veracity of the textual authority, which cannot be used to prove itself. *ʿĀdah*, in the sense of a recurrent custom, was one of the tools that the theologians appealed to in many of their theological debates.[4] Custom in this sense represented the sum total of the theologians' understanding of the world and the natural laws that govern its functions, borne out by the shared human experience. In this chapter, I focus on the theological foundations of the concept of custom by exploring the way it was invoked in the debate over causality.

## *The Muʿtazilī and the Ashʿarī Schools on Causality*

The Muʿtazilī theologians are known in Islamic history as the champions of rational thought. Their vehement defense of divine justice and inimitableness against the anthropomorphic and deterministic tendencies of other groups was one of their most distinctive characteristics. In one of the early extant works of the Muʿtazilī school, the famous theologian Abu al-Ḥasan ʿAbd al-Jabbār (d. AH 415/1024 CE) has given full exposition to their five founding principles.[5] Abu al-Ḥasan al-Ashʿarī who was originally a Muʿtazilī, founded a new school, which sought to reconcile the extreme rational tendencies of the Muʿtazilī school with the literal tendencies of the traditionists, *Ahl al-Ḥadith*.[6] Eventually, this Ashʿarī school along with its close associate, the Maturīdī school, came to represent the mainstream in Islamic theology since the beginning of the fifth century AH (eleventh century CE), as they acquired the title of *ahl al-sunnah wa al-jamāʿah*.[7] The rise of the Ashʿarī school coincided with the gradual decline of the Muʿtazilī school.[8]

It is in the theological debates and counterdebates between the Muʿtazilī and the Ashʿarī schools that we can trace the birth of the concept of custom as an abstract tool that they both used to bolster their views. It was, however, the Ashʿarī school that relied extensively on this principle in their critique of the Muʿtazilites' almost exclusive reliance on rational reasoning, particularly in their metaphysical debates.[9] The Ashʿarī theologians used the concept of custom to reconcile the Qurʾānic passages that imply deterministic tendencies based on God's absolute will with those passages that imply human freedom of choice. Accordingly, some events occur *when* other particular events occur, but not necessarily *because* of them. The Ashʿarī theologians sought to prove that what their Muʿtazilī counterparts referred to as purely causal relationships were nothing more than customary relationships established by God who can, at will, set them apart. The divine miracles that were mediated through the agency of the Prophets were the clearest manifestation of how these customary relationships can be disconnected in the physical world. This concept of custom was important for the Ashʿarī theologians because it enabled them to defend their view of divine omnipotence, unrestricted by the human understanding of rigid causality.

The theological roots of the concept of custom, therefore, can be traced to the larger debate over causality, particularly among the Muʿtazilī and Ashʿarī theologians. As will be shown in more detail, causality was a central question that had significant implications on many important debates, the most prominent of which was the reason versus revelation debate. In no other work is the exchange between Muʿtazilī and Ashʿarī theologians clearer than in the theological encyclopedia of ʿAbd al-Jabbār, *al-Mughnī fī Abwāb al-Tawḥid wa al-ʿAdl*.[10] In this multivolume work, ʿAbd al-Jabbār set out to clarify the views of his Muʿtazilī school and refute those of its opponents in general and the Ashʿarī theologians in particular. In ʿAbd al-Jabbār's work, most of the Muʿtazilī theologians are presented as defending a theory of causality that interprets the different physical and metaphysical phenomena in terms of consistent causal relationships, as opposed to the Ashʿarī theologians' advocacy of a theory of custom. It is not the goal of this chapter to undertake a comprehensive analysis of *al-Mughnī* but rather to look into the question of causality as used in the Muʿtazilī—Ashʿarī encounter and how, in the process, a competing theory of custom was developed to avoid the theological problems that a strict theory of causality leads to.

In his account of the debate on the possibility of seeing God, ʿAbd al-Jabbār confirms the Muʿtazilī view that denies such possibility. Based on the premise of divine inimitableness and incomparability, the Muʿtazilī theologians argued that God cannot be confined to a place. Since he cannot be confined to a place, it is impossible for humans to see him.[11] However, according to the Ashʿarī school, humans see by a special power that God placed in their eyes. If humans are not endowed with the power to perceive God in this world, God can change this "custom" by enabling them to see him in the hereafter.[12] ʿAbd al-Jabbār, on the other hand, argued that humans simply see by their eyes and that, in the absence of any deficiencies or obstructions, they must see observable objects. ʿAbd al-Jabbār invokes causality and argues that absolute contingencies (*mūjibāt*) are different from customs (*ʿādāt*) in that the former are always consistent while the latter are not necessarily so.[13] He gives several examples to illustrate his argument that confusing causes with customs inevitably leads to erroneous conclusions.[14] This debate is significant because it reveals the epistemological foundations on which both the Muʿtazilī and the Ashʿarī theologians based their arguments. According to ʿAbd al-Jabbār, the use of the senses, in the absence of deficiencies and obstructions, leads to reliable perception which, in turn, generates knowledge.[15] The Ashʿarī theologians, on the other hand, argued that the use of senses leads to a kind of perception that is based on the customary association between senses and objects. Although this perception results in certain knowledge (*ʿilm ḍarūrī*), it remains subject to the habit that God instituted in the world, which he can change at will.[16]

The famous Ashaʿrī theologian-jurist Imām al-Ḥaramayn al-Juwaynī (d. AH 478/1085 CE) used the word *ittiṣalāt* (connections) rather than *idrākāt* (perceptions) to refer to this sense-object relationship. Accordingly, this connection between a sense and an object does not necessarily amount to (an absolute) perception, although it is customary to think of it as such.[17] ʿAbd al-Jabbār vehemently opposed this custom-based sense perception; if perception was based on custom, logic would not rule out—either in the past or in other places—the possibility of other modes of sense perception such as smelling colors or seeing odors.[18] This distinction between the *fixed* nature and the *changing* custom is one of the main arguments that he used consistently in his refutation of the Ashʿarī theory of custom, not only in this particular debate but in many others as well.[19] The Ashʿarī theologians, on the other hand, by promoting the theory of custom in their discussions on the sources of knowledge, sought to remove all limitations on divine omnipotence either within or beyond the realm of the senses. They sought also to allow for divine intervention pursuant to God's will, which is not constrained by the human condition or experience.[20]

Similarly, this concept of custom was important for the debate on human freedom and accountability. The Muʿtazilī school argued that human responsibility stems from the individual's capacity to create his or her own actions.[21] The Ashʿarī school, on the other hand, adopted the famous theory of *kasb* (acquisition), according to which human voluntary actions are created by God but acquired by humans.[22] This is in line with their view that God is the sole creator of everything in the world including human actions.[23] The Ash'arī school argued that the verb *create* should be reserved for God's exclusive power to bring things or beings out of nonexistence into existence. The Muʿtazilī school argued that there is no material difference between "creation" and "acquisition" and consequently accused the Ashʿarī theologians of failing to produce a convincing argument to differentiate the two terms.[24] Eventually, the creation versus acquisition debate remained one of the unresolved issues in the history of the Muʿtazilī–Ashʿarī encounter as it continued to shape their views on many other theological questions.[25]

The debates on causality and human freedom were closely related to the debate on generation (*tawlīd*) or the indirect or unintended effects of direct or intended actions.[26] The question that the theologians debated was whether the actor is responsible for the indirect or unintended effects of his action in the same way that he is responsible for the direct or intended ones. The Muʿtazilī theologians held that the doer of a voluntary action is responsible for the effects, both direct and indirect, of his action. ʿAbd al-Jabbār links the responsibility for such indirect effects to the actual intent (*qaṣd* or *irādah*) that initiates the cause of the action. Because, according to the Muʿtazilī view, humans create their voluntary actions, they are accountable for all the effects of these actions.[27] The Ashʿarī theologians, on the other hand, argued that generated effects are ascribed to God rather than to humans.[28] They link these generated effects to the ability (*qudrah*) to create these effects, which they see as belonging to the exclusive domain of God.

As mentioned earlier, the Ashʿarī theologians held that God is the true originator of all actions, including human voluntary actions, which humans only acquire rather than create. Here, too, the Ashʿarī theologians rely on the concept of custom to prove that what the Muʿtazilī theologians refer to as generated effects, ensuing from direct actions, are nothing more than customary associations that are not impossible to change. According to the famous Ashʿarī theologian Abū Bakr al-Baqillānī (d. AH 403/1013 CE), the Muʿtazilī theologians would associate the downward movement of a stone after it has been pushed down a slope with the act of pushing (itself), while there is really nothing more than a customary relationship present, which God can change at will.[29] ʿAbd al-Jabbār used the same logic whenever the theory of custom was invoked; he drew a distinction between the *fixed* nature and the *changing* custom.[30] He argued that confusing these two terms could undermine the most fundamental means of verification available to humans; that is, direct observation of causal relationships. In other words, when direct sense-based perception is in doubt, it becomes even more difficult to trust any other types of perception.

Like the debate on human freedom and accountability, the debate between the Muʿtazilī and the Ashʿarī theologians on generated effects remained unsettled. Each group reduced the arguments of its opponents to mere unverified claims. The Muʿtazilī theologians, in their quest for a consistent rational method, accused their Ashʿarī counterparts of logical inconsistency. Conversely, the Ashʿarī theologians, in their quest for reconciling religious texts with rational proofs, accused their Muʿtazilī counterparts of overstepping the boundaries set by the revealed texts.

It was, however, in their treatment of the themes of prophethood and miracles that the Muʿtazilī and Ashʿarī theologians made the strongest appeal to the concept of custom. By definition, a miracle indicates departure from common norms and defiance of the usual order of things.

Although the theologians admitted that accepting the claims of prophethood or the occurrence of miraculous events relies to a great extent on faith, they still referred to the concept of custom to justify them, especially in debates with groups that denied such supernatural events. A prerequisite for the verification of a miracle is the condition that it must entail elements that break with what is customary or what is ordinary. Another prerequisite is the ability of its agent or producer to effect it at will in order to support his claims and challenge his opponents. Citing the normal, the ordinary, or the customary as a proof for a supernatural claim does not carry any evidentiary weight.[31] In order for prophets to support their supernatural and metaphysical claims, they need miracles that transcend the common norms of the physical world.[32]

## *Al-Ghazālī and Ibn Rushd between Occasionalism and Determinism*

In tracing the theological foundations of the concept of custom in the Islamic legal tradition, it is important to point out the role of Abū Ḥāmid al-Ghazālī (d. AH 505/1111 CE) in the slow, yet steady development of this concept.[33] Al-Ghazālī was not merely a prominent theologian but was also an outstanding jurist. Following the example of his master, al-Juwaynī, he was one of the theologian-jurists who facilitated the merger between the two domains of theology and jurisprudence. His attack on the philosophers ushered in a new era of thought that would change the theological landscape forever.

Al-Ghazālī is known as the heir of the Ashʿarī theological tradition and its spokesperson par excellence. Despite the radical changes that marked his scholarly career, he consistently defended the Ashʿarī views against the other theological schools. He is most well-known, however, for his scathing critique of the philosophical tradition—particularly as developed by the two famous Muslim philosophers, al-Fārābī and Ibn Sīnā. Al-Ghazālī was not only well-versed in the theological discourses, but he was also well-acquainted with the philosophical debates and methods. In his famous book *Tahāfut al-Falāsifah*, he set out to deconstruct the arguments of Muslim philosophers and prove their inconsistencies purely on philosophical grounds.[34] For this particular reason, al-Ghazālī has been both credited and blamed for the demise of philosophical thinking in the Islamic tradition. Conventional wisdom has it that philosophy never survived the fatal blow dealt by al-Ghazālī, in spite of the repeated attempts of many scholars—the earliest and most famous of which was undertaken by Abū al-Walīd Ibn Rushd (d. AH 595/1198 CE)[35] in his celebrated *Tahāfut al-Tahāfut*.

Historians of the Islamic intellectual tradition note that al-Ghāzalī inaugurated a new phase in which theological and philosophical debates were unwittingly merged rather than distinctly separated.[36] As evident from his autobiography, al-Ghazālī's own thought underwent sharp successive transformations that make it quite difficult to speak of a single distinct Ghazalian paradigm.[37] Given his diverse and extensive works on more than one branch of the Islamic sciences, interpreting his views on a particular issue must be done within the broader context of his intellectual development.

For the purpose of the present context, we will focus on the development of the debate over causality and the place of custom in this debate, first, as expounded by al-Ghazālī in his tirade against philosophy and, second, as defended by Ibn Rushd. Al-Ghazālī's *Tahāfut* is divided into two main parts. The first part involves 16 questions that pertain to metaphysical philosophy. The second part includes four questions that deal with natural philosophy. For the purpose of this chapter, we will focus on the seventeenth question in the second part, which elucidates al-Ghazālī's understanding and use of the theological concept of custom. In this section, al-Ghazālī develops his argument against a strict theory of natural causality. His argument, which resonates with the views of his Ash'arī predecessors, reiterates the interpretation of the common association between causes and effects in terms of recurrent customs rather than intrinsic characteristics in objects that automatically and independently trigger certain effects.[38] Al-Ghazālī's goal in addressing these questions of natural philosophy is to prove God's free will and absolute power.[39] He opens the section with a forceful statement indicating that the common conjunction of causes and effects is not inseparable.[40] He goes on to cite several chains of events commonly linked together as causes and effects such as "the quenching of thirst and drinking, satiety and eating, burning and contact with fire, light and the appearance of the sun, death and decapitation, healing and the drinking of medicine."[41]

Al-Ghazālī denotes that these interrelationships have been primordially linked by the decree of God (*fī taqdīrillah*), which in itself does not limit his absolute power (*fī al-maqdūr*) to sever these relationships and allow satiety without eating, death without decapitation, or decapitation without death, and so on.[42] This argument of al-Ghazālī represents the foundation of the theory of contingency (*tajwīz*), which became one of the distinctive characteristics of the Ashʿarī school of theology. Although, as we saw above, it was developed by earlier Ashʿarī theologians, al-Ghazālī is credited for providing its clearest and most eloquent expression.[43]

Al-Ghazālī's adoption of the theory of contingency enabled him to deny the intrinsic properties in things. According to al-Ghazālī, therefore, a piece of cotton can touch the fire without burning, or it may burn without coming into contact with the fire.[44] Al-Ghazālī supports his thesis with two different arguments. First, he disputes the claim that fire burns by its nature. He claims that our judgment that the piece of cotton must burn when it touches the fire is based on the recurrent habit that we observe (the burning *at* the contact with fire) but there is no proof that the burning happens *because* of the fire. The only evidence we have for this judgment is our own observation. The mere fact that we do not see any other causes does not mean that they do not exist. The real agent of burning, therefore, is not the inanimate fire but God, either directly or indirectly through angels.

Second, he disputes the claim that the effect depends on the nature of the recipient (*al-maḥall*). In other words, some theologians maintained that the same causes could lead to different effects depending of the nature of the recipient, such as the case of the sun, which whitens clothes but darkens the skin.[45] Al-Ghazālī's main objective here is to justify and defend not only the concept of a miracle but also its historicity. The Qur'ān, for example, mentions that Prophet Ibrāhīm was thrown into fire without being burned. The natures of both the fire and the human body are such that if they come into contact with each other, the former must cause the burning in the latter. In order for al-Ghazālī to preserve the authenticity of the Qur'ānic miracle, he not only denied the intrinsic nature of the cause but also of the recipient. For al-Ghazālī, God is the only real agent who sometimes acts directly but may, at other times, act indirectly through causes.

Expecting that some might find this argument implausible, al-Ghazālī goes on to posit some absurd hypothetical examples that a critic may produce to refute his thesis.[46] Al-Ghazālī grants that these irrational hypothetical situations are far-fetched and unlikely to ever occur. He contends, however, that being extremely unlikely does not mean that they are impossible. They are, in fact, as possible as their more likely counterparts. Our judgment of a given chain of events is based entirely on past recurrent habits that confirm our belief in their consistency, since they continue to follow the same pattern invariably.[47] That things are set by God's decree to follow a certain order or sequence does not limit God's power to reverse this order or upset that sequence whenever he wishes. God created in humans the knowledge that certain possibilities are more likely to occur than others; thus humans continue to believe that other possibilities are extremely unlikely, although, in themselves, they are not impossible.[48]

Ibn Rushd takes al-Ghazālī to task precisely over this point. Contrary to al-Ghazālī, Ibn Rushd not only confirms the intrinsic properties (*dhawāt*) of objects, but he also confirms the efficacy of particular causes to produce particular effects.[49] The mere fact, he contends, that certain causes are not yet known should not cast doubt on the causes that are already known. Moreover, he maintained, denying the intrinsic properties of things removes immediately all distinctions between them, which is rather nonsensical. Ibn Rushd questions the concept of custom that al-Ghazālī repeatedly invokes by asking: Whose custom is it? Is it the agent's (God), the object's, or the people's custom in issuing judgments? He notes that God cannot be said to have a custom because custom refers to that which is occasional, while the Qur'ān declares that God's way (sunnah) "in doing things" does not change.[50] Direct observation of the different natural phenomena shows the consistent order that these phenomena follow. Such order cannot be the result of mere "custom" because the very notion of custom allows for a certain degree of irregularity.

Similarly, objects cannot be said to have customs because customs are conceivable only with reference to animate beings. Inanimate things do not have customs; they have distinctive natures or realities. Their intrinsic properties do not change; if they do, they will turn into other things and consequently they will cease to have the same names.[51] Thirdly, if custom refers to individuals' custom in issuing judgments, it is nothing more than the human reasoning faculty.[52]

In his critique of the Ghazalian concept of custom, Ibn Rushd highlights the need to determine the contextual meaning of this ambiguous term, *lafẓ mumawwah*.[53] According to Ibn Rushd, the word custom that al-Ghazālī reiterates is nothing more than the basic elemental or distinctive characteristics of objects; he describes al-Ghazālī's attempt to prove otherwise as sheer sophistry.[54] As far as the exact relationship between causes and effects is concerned, Ibn Rushd grants that causes lead to effects, but the former are neither self-sufficient nor independent. They (the effects) rely for their efficacy on one or more outside agents, although the philosophers disagreed on the reality of this outside agent.[55] Ibn Rushd links the causal relationships between causes and effects to the "inalterable" sunnah of God. Moreover, proof of God's absolute power is not dependant on a "weak" theory of contingency that itself threatens to eliminate all sense of wisdom behind the order instituted by God in the universe.

It is evident from al-Ghazālī's discussion that the impetus behind his theory of contingency was to provide a rational justification for the concept of miracles. For example, when he was arguing against the intrinsic properties and the causal relationships, he argued for an alternative theory that recognizes both the intrinsic properties and the causal relationships, but which also allows for the suspension of the latter by a change in either the agent or the recipient.[56] Moreover, al-Ghazālī does not deny the existence of a causal nexus between causes and effects, but he rather interprets the latter in a manner that does not imply complete independence from the will of the supreme agent.[57] Al-Ghazālī uses the example of the talcum powder that prevents burning to indicate that human intellect often judges on the basis of past known experiences but it fails to perceive the full extent of God's knowledge or power.[58] Al-Ghazālī's goal was to develop a general interpretive framework within which both reason and revelation could be reconciled. He repeatedly refers to the perennial tension between these two domains and how different groups sought to resolve it.[59] He chooses the view that reason and revelation corroborate each other. His argument is that, while revelation encourages the use of reason, it is on the basis of reason that the truth of revelation is verified.[60] Al-Ghazālī, however, warns against absolute reliance on reason when it conflicts with revelation.[61] It is precisely on the basis of this caveat that al-Ghazālī has often been accused of compromising reason in favor of revelation.

Ibn Rushd, on the other hand, notes that the concept of miracles is one of the fundamentals of religion that, similar to the fundamentals in every field, has to be taken for granted. These fundamentals are to be accepted as givens without dispute because they fall beyond the capacity of the human intellect, and consequently they are not subject to philosophical inquiry.[62] In other words, while al-Ghazālī sought to rationalize the concept of miracles, Ibn Rushd sought to remove it entirely from the domain of philosophical inquiry and thereby establish a clear division between these two distinct spheres. As often as al-Ghazālī is accused of having sacrificed reason in order to preserve faith,[63] Ibn Rushd is accused of having conceded religious principles to his strong Aristotelian convictions.[64]

Over the course of Islamic intellectual history, al-Ghazālī and Ibn Rushd have been identified with the two extreme positions on the continuum of reason and revelation. Throughout their scholarly careers, both sought to provide a conclusive answer to this critical question. Interestingly enough, their answers were determined on the basis of their attitudes vis-à-vis the concept of custom.

## *Al-Juwaynī and the Link between the Theological ʿĀdah and the Juristic ʿĀdah?*

The foregoing discussion was devoted to the concept of *ʿādah* within the theological discourses, especially as developed by the Ashʿarī theologians first against the Muʿtazilites and later, with al-Ghazālī, against the philosophers. The question that needs to be clarified at this point is how closely, if at all, this theological concept was related to the juristic concept of *ʿādah* or *ʿurf* especially in its later constructions. How feasible is it to argue that the jurisprudential (*uṣūlī*) concept originates in the theological concept?

We can begin the inquiry by exploring the juristic works of al-Juwaynī, a significant choice for many reasons. As much as it was in the scholarly character and career of al-Ghazālī that both theology and philosophy were merged, it was in the scholarly character and career of his master, al-Juwaynī, that theology and jurisprudence were merged. Although other theologians preceded al-Juwaynī in bridging the divide between these two disciplines, he remains one of the pioneers in this respect; he is credited for preserving and rejuvenating both the Ashʿarī school in theology and the Shafiʿī school in law. Moreover, he was one of the founders of the rational or theoretical juristic school, which carried over many of the theological discussions into jurisprudence and sought to develop the juristic discourse along theological lines.[65] His *magnum opus*, *al-Burhān fī Uṣūl al-Fiqh*, is considered one of the four founding books of this school.[66] It is, therefore, important to note that he carries on many of his theological discussions in his juristic works. This accords with the tendency of the jurists within the theoretical school to begin their works with discussions on general epistemological issues in order to provide a theoretical background for the subsequent juristic questions.

In his juristic works, al-Juwaynī established a strong nexus between theology and jurisprudence, and this, in turn, facilitated the reception of many theological concepts within the mainstream juristic discourse. In *al-Burhān*, al-Juwaynī observes that the field of jurisprudence (*uṣūl al-fiqh*), is derived from the disciplines of theology (*kalām*), Arabic language (*al-ʿarabiyyah*), and substantive law (*fiqh*).[67] He opens his book with three issues that belong more to theology than to jurisprudence: the status of rulings in terms of beauty (*ḥusn*) and ugliness (*qubḥ*), religious responsibility (*taklīf*), and the sources of knowledge (*madārik al-ʿulūm*).[68] On the sources of knowledge, al-Juwaynī specifies three: reason, miracles, and textual sources (the Qurʾān, the sunnah, and *ijmāʿ*).[69] His Ashʿarī theological framework inspires his explanation of the second source.[70] According to al-Juwaynī, the order of these three sources is important. While reason establishes intuitive perceptions, miracles establish the authenticity of the prophets and, consequently, the texts. As shown earlier, the ultimate verification of miracles is dependent on their power to break with the normal, the recurrent, or the customary.

*Al-Burhān*, like purely theological works, is replete with references to *ʿurf* and *ʿādah*, usually indicated by phrases such as "according to recurrent habits" (*fī iṭṭirād al-ʿādah*), "according to established habits" (*fī mustaqarr al-ʿādah*), and "according to common custom" (*fī ʿurf al-nās*) but here in the course of his treatment of purely juristic questions. The transition from theology to jurisprudence seems not only natural but also logical. Can this be said to represent a significant turning point in the history of the concept of *'urf*? A thorough examination of al-Juwaynī's purely juristic works as well as the works of *uṣūl* after him is likely to support an affirmative answer to this question. Al-Juwaynī's treatment facilitated the transformation of both the perception and the use of the concept of *'ādah* from purely theological debates into the mainstream Sunni juristic discourse. The following chapters include many examples that illustrate this transformation.

# Chapter 4

# Custom between the Theoretical School and the Applied School

## The Beginnings and the Origins

As shown in the second chapter, the foundations of the legal concept of custom can be traced back to the two primary sources of Islamic law, the Qur'ān and the Sunnah of the Prophet. In addition to these two sources, the early development of the concept prior to the development of legal theory in the second century was particularly connected with the practice of the people of Madinah (*ʿamal ahl al-madīnah*) as articulated and constructed by the founder of the Mālikī school, Mālik Ibn Anas (d. AH 179/795 CE). The concept of *ʿamal* itself was closely tied to the Sunnah of the Prophet. It was understood as the practical expression of the Sunnah. In fact, Mālik thought of *ʿamal* as the most authoritative form of sunnah because it was not limited to what the Prophet said but, more importantly, what he did. More precisely, it was not simply what the Prophet did, but what was commonly understood and accepted as the established practice first instituted by the Prophet and handed down to succeeding generations in the form of continued practice. The early development of the concept of *ʿurf*, therefore, goes back to these two important concepts: the Sunnah of the Prophet and the *ʿamal* of the people of Madinah.

Conventional wisdom in Western studies on early Islamic legal history holds that during the first Islamic century, the Sunnah of the Prophet did not acquire the unique, independent, or distinctive status that it assumed at a much later point, with much disagreement on this exact historical point. The Sunnah of the Prophet was one among many sunan (plural of sunnah) of other prominent historical figures, particularly the companions of the Prophet. In other words, for the entire first Islamic century, sunnah was still used in its linguistic generic sense, as used in the pre-Islamic Arabian culture.[1] This generic concept of sunnah was then replaced by the newly emerging formal ḥadīth traditions. The early concept of sunnah embodied the teachings of the Prophet as transmitted, internalized, and practiced in the different local contexts through the agency of the different companions of the Prophet who emigrated from Madinah after his death. The ḥadīth traditions emerged only as a later development by a new class of scholars who came largely from provinces where the concept of sunnah was not well-developed.[2]

According to the classical Muslim position, however, during much of the first Islamic century, ḥadīth was preserved and communicated orally. Although the term sunnah was not a new Islamic invention, it was eventually reserved for the normative example of the Prophet. Ḥadīth and sunnah were almost synonyms. Technically, however, ḥadīth, which stood for the Prophet's statements, was only one type of sunnah, which also included the Prophet's practices and tacit approvals. The Prophetic traditions were committed to memory and transmitted orally until they were collected and recorded in major compendia such as the six authentic (*ṣaḥīḥ*) books.[3]

The modern Western obsession with the origins of Islam's primary sources has inspired a great deal of scholarly interest in the earlier ḥadīth collections, those written before the third Islamic century (ninth century CE). One of the earliest collections of the Prophetic traditions is the famous *Muwaṭṭa'* of Mālik.[4] Technically, the *Muwaṭṭa'* is not exclusively a collection of aḥādīth; it includes Qur'anic verses, Prophetic aḥādīth, reports from the companions and the successors, as well as Mālik's own opinions. Mālik intended his book to be a compendium of the most agreed-upon legal practices (*'amal*) among the people of Madinah. For him, *'amal* was the most authentic and reliable representation of the entire range of the Sunnah of the Prophet. Madinah was the abode of the Prophet and his companions, who not only heard what the Prophet taught but, more importantly, *lived* his teachings. If the people of Madinah agreed upon a certain practice, it must have been based on a continuous authoritative proof that went back to the Prophet himself. This was why the scholars considered Mālik's *mursal* ḥadīth[5] to be even more reliable than the *musnad* ḥadīth.[6] The underlying assumption was that if Mālik, well-known for his meticulousness,[7] did not care to mention the full chain of transmitters (*isnād*) of a report, it must have been unanimously considered authoritative.[8]

Mālik's *Muwaṭṭa'* has proven to be a unique resource of invaluable information about the critical period of the first two Islamic centuries. The sources that originate in this critical period are particularly important because they precede the theoretical framework of Islamic legal theory (*uṣūl al-fiqh*), which was first articulated by Mālik's student and the founder of the Shāfiʿī school, Muḥammad Ibn Idrīs al-Shāfiʿī (d. AH 204/820 CE). Within this framework, the status of the Sunnah of the Prophet was *formally* consolidated as a legal source second only to the Qurʾān.[9] This does not mean that al-Shāfiʿī was the first to recognize the Sunnah as the second source of law. It simply means that prior to al-Shāfiʿī there was no clear structure of legal sources, or at least it was not as clear as the one that al-Shāfiʿī developed. Since the time of its compilation, the *Muwaṭṭaʾ* has been a constant subject of scholarly research.[10] Apart from being the primary source of the Mālikī legal school, it has enjoyed a similar prestige among the scholars of ḥadīth as well.[11]

## The Works of Jurisprudence (*Uṣūl*): The Early Structure of the Sources

In order to understand the early development of the concept of *ʿurf* and how it later became recognized as a source, we have to start with the formative structure of the legal sources. Prior to the development of legal theory, Islamic legal thinking consisted mainly of direct reference to relevant passages in the two primary sources. Systematic legal thinking emerged with the provincial schools founded on the teachings of the eminent companions of the Prophet, the most famous of which were the two schools of Madinah and Iraq. With the development of legal theory, a new chapter in the Islamic legal tradition began. Muslim sources trace the beginning of this legal theory to al-Shafiʿī's *Risālah*.

*Al-Risālah* opens with an introductory discussion on the concept of *bayān* (explanation/demonstration). Al-Shafiʿī cites several Qurʾānic verses that stipulate that the goal of revelation is providing *bayān* for every possible event or occasion.[12] Al-Shafiʿī elaborates on the definition of *bayān* and the different means through which it is communicated. *Bayān*, he notes, is the aggregate of what God provides in his book and holds the believers accountable for as a matter of faith. He refers to four different types of *bayān*. The first is conveyed by an unambiguous text. This is the case, for example, of the pillars of religion, which include prayer, fasting, alms, and pilgrimage. The second type takes the form of a general command in the Qurʾān, which is explained by the Prophet in his Sunnah. This, for example, is a description of the exact manner in which these pillars should be performed. The third is transmitted by a clear command from the Prophet, yet without a clear provision in the Qur'ān. Al-Shāfiʿī explains that in following the command of the Prophet, the believer is automatically following the command of God, who repeatedly predicated obedience to him on obedience to his Prophet.[13] The fourth is the command to exercise *ijtihād* to reach the proper *bayān* for a given issue or question. The example given is the case of turning towards the direction of Kaʿbah in prayer.[14] The believers are asked to *seek* the proper direction, although this proper direction cannot always be ascertained. In case of uncertainty, prayer will still be valid provided that the believer has tried his utmost to find the proper direction. In other words, as far as this category is concerned, all that the individual is asked to do is exercise due diligence in seeking the proper direction, even though he may never know for certain whether the direction he faced was in fact correct.[15]

Al-Shāfiʿī argues that it is not permissible for anyone to make a determination of permission or prohibition without a sound basis of knowledge. Such basis could only come from one of four sources: the Qur'ān, the Sunnah of the Prophet, *ijmāʿ* (consensus), or *qiyās* (analogical reasoning).[16] (For al-Shāfiʿī, *ijtihād* and *qiyās* are synonyms.)[17] These sources are arranged hierarchically, following the order mentioned in the ḥadīth of Muʿādh.[18] In the search for the *bayān* in a given case, the qualified jurist must start with the text of the Qur'ān, and if he finds a relevant reference therein, it will serve as the basis for the ruling (*ḥukm*). If such reference is not found, the jurist should turn to the Sunnah of the Prophet. If still no reference is found therein, he should turn to the precedents of the earlier jurists and investigate whether a juristic consensus was reached. After exhausting these three possibilities, the jurist would be entitled to start his own *ijtihād*, reasoning on the basis of a clearer precedent with which the new case shares a common operative cause (*ʿillah*).[19] Al-Shāfiʿī did not use the word *ʿillah* but he instead used the word *maʿnā* (meaning) in his elaboration on this process.[20] Later jurists characterized this *ijtihād* as *qiyās*.

This basic structure of *bayān* articulated by al-Shāfiʿī in his *Risālah* represented the birth of Islamic legal theory and ushered in a distinctive juristic discourse that would last for centuries.[21] This should explain al-Shāfiʿī's significant role in the development of the Islamic legal tradition, a role that was often likened to that of Aristotle in the development of Greek logic.[22] Most importantly, al-Shāfiʿī's framework not only elevated the status of the Sunnah of the Prophet and placed it next to the Qur'ān,[23] but also achieved a synthesis of the schools of ḥadīth and *ra'y* .

As with the word *ʿillah*, there is no direct mention of the word *ʿurf* in *al-Risālah*. Al-Shafiʿī deals with the concept of *ʿurf* in his analyses of the Qur'ānic verses and the different categories of the Sunnah of the Prophet.

As indicated earlier, he refers to *bayān* as a process that seeks to relate the rulings embodied in revelation or the foundational texts to every possible event (*ḥāditbah*), either directly or indirectly.[24] This *bayān*, therefore, has to account for *ʿurf*, since the latter is often inseparable from these real-life events.[25]

Some examples should illustrate this point. In his discussion on the possibility of abrogation (*naskh*) of one ḥadīth by another ḥadīth, he cites several reports concerning the meat of sacrificial animals. He first cites a ḥadīth in which the Prophet forbade Muslims to save this meat for more than three days. When, later, some companions complained that they could not benefit from the sacrificial animals as much as they used to, the Prophet was reported to have noted that the prohibition was made on account of the (unexpected) arrival of many pilgrims on that particular occasion. The Prophet's prohibition, therefore, was meant to address this situation by instructing the pilgrims to save only what was enough for three days and offer the remaining part to those who were in need. The companions understood this to be a general permanent rule, but actually, they continued to have the choice to eat, offer in charity, or save with no restriction.[26]

Several narrations of this report mention only the initial prohibition (to save beyond three days), such as the reports of ʿAlī and ʿAbd Allah Ibn Wāqid. Other narrations mention only the later permission to benefit from the meat of sacrificial animals even after three days, such as the report of Anas. There are several possibilities that could explain why Anas did not mention the Prophet's prohibition. It is possible, for example, that he did not know about this particular incident. It is also possible that he knew about it but, in view of the understanding that the later permission abrogates the former prohibition, he chose not to refer to the initial prohibitive command. There is another narration—that of ʿĀʾishah—that refers to both incidents.

Al-Shāfiʿī comments that each of these narrators communicated what he or she knew about the issue. Such cases, he observes, illustrate the attitude of the companions and subsequent generations towards the Sunnah of the Prophet. They used to share whatever knowledge they had of it so that all reports recounting a particular event could be compared.[27] Al-Shāfiʿī concludes that these reports could be reconciled in two different ways. The first is that the later permission would be determined on the basis of the given circumstances (customary practice). Accordingly, in the case of dire need, such as the existence of many deserving people in the example, the prohibition to save for extended periods of time would apply. Conversely, in the absence of such need, the later permission would apply. The second way of reconciling the two is for the later permission to apply indefinitely, based on the principle that a later ruling repeals a former one.[28]

What is important to point out here is not the examples themselves, but rather the ways in which they have been used and the methods employed in their analysis. While al-Shāfiʿī cited the different narrations to illustrate the issue of abrogation (*naskh*) or particularization (*takhṣīṣ*) of one type of sunnah by another, later scholars invoked the same examples as cases of abrogation or particularization on the basis of certain legal principles or methods such as *ʿurf*, *istiḥsān* or *maṣlaḥah*. In other words, the jurists would look into these normative examples for the underlying causes that resulted in the particular ruling and would attempt to extrapolate them to other cases that shared this common element, and therefore were qualified for the same ruling. So, the case of *salam* was cited by the later jurists as a precedent to allow the contract of manufacture (*istiṣnāʿ*). In the contract of manufacture, the customer agrees with an artisan to manufacture something for him. The jurists debated the permissibility of this contract because the object does not technically exist at the time of contract. Although this contract, similar to the case of *salam*, violated the ḥadīth of the Prophet forbidding the sale of the non-existent, it was still permitted as an exception because of common practice and was referred to as an example of a ruling that was based on *istiḥsān*, *maṣlaḥah*, or *ʿurf*. We shall have a chance to deal with this point in more detail in the subsequent chapters.[29]

Following the preliminary foundations that al-Shāfiʿī established, later jurists started adding the different building blocks of Islamic legal theory, which was fully developed by the fifth century AH (eleventh century CE). Historians observe that after al-Shāfiʿī, two main approaches influenced the development of *uṣūl al-fiqh*: the theoretical approach and the applied approach.[30] The Shāfiʿī jurists and theologians represented the former, while the Ḥanafī jurists represented the latter. Moreover, while some jurists sought to synthesize these two approaches, others sought to develop their own distinctive methodologies.

## The Theoretical Approach (*Ṭariqat al-Mutakallimīn*)

The early jurists did not deal with *ʿurf* as an independent legal source. They treated it within other main themes, such as definitions (*ḥudūd*), juristic consensus (*ijmāʿ*), particularization of the general ruling (*takhṣīṣ al-ḥukm al-ʿāmm*), and independent reasoning (*ijtihād*).

## *Conventional Signification (al-dalālah al-ʿurfiyyah)*

Linguistic analysis has always been considered one of the main concerns of *uṣūl al-fiqh*. Al-Shāfiʿī repeatedly emphasized the importance of mastering the Arabic language (*al-lisān al-ʿarabī*) as a prerequisite for the proper understanding of the founding texts of Islam.[31] The major works of *uṣūl* often start with an introductory chapter that discusses themes such as definitions (*ḥudūd*) and significations (*dalālāt*). More particularly, they address the relationship between legal stipulations, texts embodying such stipulations, contexts in which these texts originated, and the possible contexts in which these texts apply.

In the introductory chapter of his *al-Muʿtamad fī Uṣūl al-Fiqh*, Abū al-Ḥusayn al-Baṣrī (d. AH 436/1044 CE) distinguishes between two modes of speech: real and metaphoric.[32] Real speech is further divided into three types: literal (*lughawī*), conventional (*ʿurfī*), and religious (*sharʿī*). If a word is used in a manner different from the one for which it was coined, the context will change from the real mode into the metaphoric mode.[33] The jurists debated the role of *ʿurf* in creating, sustaining, or changing meanings. A conventional meaning is marked by certain characteristics that are obtained from the common practice or custom that, in turn, will either specify or change the literal meaning.[34] Al-Baṣrī was of the opinion that both *ʿurf* and sharīʿah can change the literal meaning of words. The former changes it into a conventional meaning, and the latter changes it into a religious one. For example, a word such as *ṣalāh* (prayer) literally means *duʿāʾ* (supplication), but according to the convention of sharīʿah, it refers to the Muslim prayer according to the rules set in sharīʿah.

The example that was often used for the conventional meaning is the word *dābbah,* which literally refers to "any living being that walks or steps" (*mā yadubb*).[35] Conventionally, however, it refers exclusively to the horse. Several factors may lead to the emergence or the transformation of a certain conventional meaning. In the case of the horse, for example, it was singled out because of its importance and fame among the Arabs. Al-Baṣrī uses this example to show that the horse's fame in the Arab culture constituted a "conventional signification" which changed or specified the literal meaning of the word *dābbah.* On the question of the primacy of the conventional meaning over the literal, al-Baṣrī refers to the criterion of recognition. A conventional meaning will be superior to a literal meaning if the listener or the reader is able to recognize the former before (or even to the exclusion of) the latter. If, however, one has to rely on the context to distinguish the intended meaning of a word, the meaning in question will be common or equivocal. (*maʿnā mushtarak*).[36]

Abū Isḥāq Ibrāhīm al-Shirāzī (d. AH 476/1083 CE) stipulates that conventional meanings in legal texts must be interpreted according to the conventional contexts of these texts, particularly in the case of the Sunnah of the Prophet.[37] In other words, the convention in question must have been in place at or before the time the text was written, but not after. This is for the obvious reason that conventional meanings identify or clarify the intent of the author. Al-Shāfiʿī, for example, observed that if a person from Egypt leaves a will stating that a particular individual be given a *dābbah*, it means that person receives a horse, a mule, or a donkey. Al-Shāfiʿī explains that, although in the general conventional usage, the word *dābbah* refers specifically to the horse, in the particular conventional usage of the people of Egypt, it refer to any of these three animals.[38]

## *Particularization of the General (Takhṣīṣ al-ʿĀmm)*

In his *Risālah*, al-Shāfiʿī highlighted the question of signification (*dalālah*) and the ways to determine it from texts. He distinguished between two main categories: general (*ʿāmm*) and particular (*khāṣṣ*).[39] Much of his analysis of the different verses and aḥādīth was undertaken in the light of this binary classification of signification. Since the time of al-Shāfiʿī, this type of analysis has become a standard element in every major work of legal theory. It investigates, among other things, the different factors that determine the scope of the context in question. Whether a word, a statement, or a command in a text is general or particular ultimately affects the scope of the resultant ruling. In other words, it determines whether the ruling is universal (beyond the immediate context), particular to the immediate context (either in full or in part), or contingent on contextual factors.[40]

The jurists debated the possibility of limiting the scope of the general ruling by means of the customary practice. For example, if people developed the habit of drinking a certain type of blood in spite of a general stipulation against drinking blood, can an argument be made in this case for the general meaning of the text to be particularized in view of this customary practice? Al-Baṣrī categorically states that custom in this case is not a valid proof, because people develop both good and bad habits.[41] The underlying assumption is that custom cannot trump a clear textual injunction; otherwise, it will defeat the purpose of sharīʿah. This example illustrates the allowed scope of custom within a sharīʿah-based system. Within such a system, custom is not denied altogether, but it is not given absolute power either. For example, al-Baṣrī seems to distinguish this case from the earlier mentioned possibility of a linguistic convention modifying a literal meaning (such as the example of *dābbah*). While it is possible to accept the role of *ʿurf* in changing the literal meaning, it is not acceptable to give precedence to *ʿurf* in cases of conflict between a customary practice and a general textual stipulation.[42] Similarly, al-Shirāzī denies the possibility that customary practices can particularize the general textual stipulations. He links this point to the ultimate objective of sharīʿah and the will of the Legislator. Sharīʿah aims to achieve people's benefits, which are not always dependent on agreement with common customs.

Although it is not always possible to identify or determine God's will in every occasion, the clear rules of sharīʿah serve as important indicators of God's will. These two considerations emphasize the transcendental dimensions of a sharīʿah-based system. These dimensions require the believer to rely on faith and submit to the will of God even if it requires departure from a customary practice. As we will see repeatedly, this question is not always as simple or straightforward as it may appear.[43] The role of *ʿurf* in the various hermeneutical debates was not intended for its own sake. It had a direct impact on the outcome of the juristic process; that is, on the final rulings on the various substantive questions. Moreover, the interpretive activity was not limited to the primary sources of the Qurʾān and the Sunnah of the Prophet, but it also extended to earlier authoritative opinions and precedents.

## *ʿUrf and the Verification of Reports (Tawātur and Ijmā)ʿ*

During the formative period of *uṣul*, the jurists devoted a great deal of attention to the verification of the Prophetic reports. The criteria they developed for evaluating the soundness, and therefore the admissibility, of the different reports pertained to two main considerations: the chain of transmitters (*isnād*) and the text of the report (*matn*). The analysis of *isnād* involved examining the narrators of a given report based on their number, competence, propriety, and moral rectitude. In terms of the number of narrators, reports are divided into two main categories: successive and singular. The successive (*mutawātir*) report is one narrated by many individuals in every stage of its transmission. The singular (*āḥād*) report is the one that falls short of the successive.[44] The former could be verbal (*mutawātir lafẓī*), repeated verbatim by all the narrators, or semantic (*mutawātir maʿnawī*), conveying the same meaning but not necessarily word for word. A successive report represents the most authoritative type of report, and consequently the knowledge that it conveys is considered certain (*ʿilm qatʿī/yaqīnī*). Given the collective mode of their transmission, successive reports are hardly questioned. In addition to the Qurʾān, a small number of aḥādīth satisfy the criteria for an acceptable successive report. The authenticity of a singular report, on the other hand, depends on the outcome of the verification process. Such a process involves the examination of both the chain of transmission and the text of the report. Conventionally, the analysis of reports relied mainly on the former. If the chain of narrators proved trustworthy, the report would be automatically accepted.

What is important to emphasize here is the approach adopted by some jurists for establishing the authenticity of successive reports. Their approach depended entirely on rational grounds rather than on appeal to other reports, revelatory or otherwise. A successive report is defined as a report that is known by necessity (*darūratan*). Such a large number of people have communicated it that, pursuant to the common customary practice, it is impossible to have been concocted (*istiḥālat al-tawāṭu' ʿalā al-kadhib*).[45] The jurists debated the various requirements that a report must satisfy in order to qualify as successive. These requirements address, for example, the exact number of narrators, the type of issues that can be transmitted, and the different types of contextual evidence needed to support it.

Al-Juwaynī singles out custom as the main criterion for the establishment of succession (*tawātur*). Custom indicates that intuitive knowledge is transmitted across generations. This includes, for example, knowledge about famous individuals, places, and events.[46] Obviously, not every person knows about these things through direct experience. No one, however, doubts the veracity of this type of knowledge. Given the speculative character of theoretical reasoning (*naẓar*), some jurists limited the scope of succession to the domain of sensory cognition.[47] In other words, to be classified as successive, knowledge must have been originally acquired through sensory perception and communicated successively by a large number of individuals without any disagreement that could undermine its veracity. Al-Juwayní does not rule out the possibility of succession for all types of intuitive knowledge, however, whether sensory or rational.[48]

Similarly, in the domain of sharīʿah, there are several elements that have been known through succession. These elements constitute its core because they have been established by means of necessary knowledge (*maʿlūm min al-dīn bi al-ḍarūrah*). They have been acquired through direct experience and subsequently communicated by multitudes of individuals, both lay and learned, from one generation to the next. This knowledge includes, for example, the historical reality of the Prophet and his companions, the five pillars of Islam, and the text of the Qur'ān. These elements represent the constitutive structure of sharīʿah, recognized as such by every Muslim.

Rather than focusing on a specific number of narrators as a prerequisite for succession, al-Juwaynī provides that the sole criterion is the establishment of knowledge (*al-ʿilm wa ḥuṣuluh*).[49] Al-Juwaynī implies that knowledge is a state of mind in which the knower becomes not only aware of what he knows, but also certain about it. Such a state of mind depends on clues that are extracted from customary practices and various types of circumstantial evidence (*qarāʾin al-aḥwāl*) in place at the occurrence of the event in question. Al-Juwaynī predicates this characterization of knowledge on matters of custom, practice, or experience (*ḥukm al-ʿādāt*).[50] In general, people can refer to the shared human experience and various contextual clues to establish the veracity of a report. Such clues are difficult to specify because they are so numerous and highly contingent. In other words, different reports may require different types of proofs and circumstantial evidence pursuant to the issues in question.

Al-Juwaynī seeks to establish the principle of tawātur on purely rational grounds. By linking the category of *mutawātir* in sharīʿah with the category of practical or experiential knowledge, he tries to steer clear of all types of speculative or conjectural proofs and therefore remove, or at least minimize, the scope of disagreement on the fundamentals of religion. It is important to emphasize the rational approach that al-Juwaynī adopted in justifying the issue of *tawātur*. As mentioned earlier, the traditional approach in dealing with succession, or the analysis of reports in general, focused on the verification of the chain of transmitters in addition to support from other reports. Because he considered succession the strongest type of evidence for any substantive legal issue, al-Juwaynī sought to head off any charges of potential circularity that might be invoked against it. He appealed to another source of verification independent of other reports, including even revelation. He identified custom as the locus on which rational justification is to be based.[51] Al-Juwaynī's characterization of the role of custom on this point accords with his overall rational juristic approach based on three main epistemological foundations: reason, custom, and revelation.[52]

Another source used to verify Prophetic reports, in addition to the chain of transmitters, is the text of the report itself. The soundness of the text is determined by examining its compatibility with the fundamental principles of sharīʿah and, according to some jurists, reason.[53] Al-Shirāzī enumerates several criteria for the evaluation of the text of a report. One of these is the inconceivability test. If a report contains elements that contradict intuitive knowledge, experience, or common sense, the report shall be rejected as inauthentic. So also is the case of a report that contradicts a clear text either in the Qurʾān or the authentic Sunnah of the Prophet. Similarly, if a report contradicts a ruling or a principle that has been established through a verified consensus of the jurists (*ijmāʿ*), it must be rejected. Al-Shirāzī adds two more significant stipulations that function as contextual criteria.

The first is the case of a singular report that denotes a certain compulsory requirement that is not substantiated by other pieces of authentic evidence. Compulsory requirements are usually indicated by multiple sources of authentic proofs, rather than by a singular report. The second is the case of a report that denotes a type of information that is customarily communicated by a multitude of people rather than a single individual. If, for example, a report recounts a public event or a collective activity, it must be reported by a group of witnesses rather than a single narrator. In these two cases, if the report fails to satisfy important contextual criteria for authenticity, it shall be rejected as inauthentic.[54] Some jurists placed particularly heavy emphasis on the role of custom in the verification of reports. Al-Juwaynī, for example, went so far as to argue that "any report that contradicts the common customary practice should be considered inauthentic."[55]

Al-Juwaynī's rational vindication of the concept of *tawātur* serves as a preliminary step for his treatment of *ijmāʿ*. As much as *tawātur* is the strongest type of reports, *ijmāʿ* is the strongest type of proofs. Each of them, however, derives its authenticity from particular textual references, both in the Qurʾān and the Sunnah of the Prophet. Al-Juwaynī aims to confirm the rational foundations of *tawātur* and *ijmāʿ* in order to head off any charge of circularity that may be leveled against them.[56] He begins his treatment of *ijmāʿ* by downplaying the textual grounds that the jurists consistently invoke for its support. Alternatively, he highlights a number of rational arguments as the true foundations of the concept of consensus.[57] Once again, as with the principle of *tawātur*, the concept of custom is at the heart of his argument.[58]

The debate over *ijmāʿ* has been one of the most contentious debates in the history of Islamic legal theory.[59] The roots of the debate go back to the Mālikī concept of the consensus of the people of Madinah, which al-Shāfiʿī extended to qualified jurists in general. Over time, the jurists debated important questions concerning *ijmaʿ*, such as its feasibility, its conditions, and its authority. Ultimately, *ijmāʿ*as the consensus of jurists during a particular generation on a given issue has become the third source of Islamic law, after the Qurʾān and the authentic Sunnah of the Prophet. And according to some jurists, it even ranks higher than these two sources.[60]

*Ijmāʿ*, like *qiyās*, is a procedural or derivative source of Islamic law rather than a formal source such as the Qurʾān or the Sunnah of the Prophet.[61] The procedural sources themselves are based on the formal sources, and this is what is meant by the view that *ijmāʿ* takes precedence over the Qurʾān or the Sunnah of the Prophet. The different significations derived from both the Qurʾānic or the Prophetic texts are classified hierarchically in terms of clarity and authority in denoting legal prescriptions. This analytical examination of textual references occurs both independently and in comparison with other relevant pieces of evidence. Once a ruling (*ḥukm*) on a given issue has been reached, the process of *ijmāʿ* commences. If all the qualified jurists in a given generation agree not only on the *ḥukm* but also on the analytic process through which this *ḥukm* came into being, the ruling in question acquires the status of *ijmāʿ*, which means that it will remain binding permanently. *Ijmaʿ* involves considerable complexity, with potential for disagreement in each stage leading up to it, which has led some jurists to question many of the cases claimed to have attained unanimous, undisputable *ijmaʿ*.[62]

This has been the traditional form of *ijmāʿ* and the way in which the constitutive core of sharīʿah acquired its status as necessary knowledge(*maʿlūm min al-dīn bi al-ḍarūrah*). This form of *ijmāʿ* was the mechanism used to *fix* the meanings of the founding texts. In other words, the meanings that were derived from the texts, especially those with legal content, were communicated within the framework of *ijmāʿ*-governed texts rather than neutral or fluid ones. This allowed Islamic law to sustain its distinctive structure over extended periods of time in different social contexts. This form of *ijmāʿ* has also been referred to as the "sanctioning" or "retrospective *ijmāʿ*."[63]

For the purpose of the present context, what is important is how custom was used to justify and vindicate the principle of *ijmāʿ* itself. Once again, it was al-Juwaynī who gave such *ʿurf*-based justification its clearest exposition.[64] Generally speaking, the jurists were divided into a minority that denied the feasibility of *ijmāʿ* and a majority that approved it. The latter group was again divided into a majority that established its argument on the textual foundations supporting the infallibility of collective opinion[65] and a minority that based its position on rational—almost non-textual—grounds. Al-Juwaynī, the chief representative of this last group, engaged both those who denied the feasibility of *ijmāʿ* and those who sought to establish it solely on textual grounds.

The critics of *ijmāʿ* argued that people may agree on error as often as they agree on truth. Moreover, they maintained, the textual foundations invoked by the supporters of *ijmāʿ* are by no means definitive (*qaṭʿiyyah*) either in terms of reliability of transmission (*thubūt*)—in the case of the Sunnah—or signification (*dalālah*)—in the case of both the Qurʾān and the Sunnah. Al-Juwaynī retorted with two counter arguments. First, he explained that on the basis of customary practices, it is well-known that opinions on speculative matters tend to diverge rather than conform. When there is a consensus among agents who are more likely to disagree than to agree, it is logical to conclude that their agreement must have been founded on a source external to the issue in question. This source must have had such definitive authority that it commanded the agreement of those rationally independent agents. This authoritative source could even be a previously unknown textual reference.[66] Second, al-Juwaynī refers to a conventional practice of rebuking those who break the consensus. Such collective rebuke can itself serve as sufficient evidence for the desirability of *ijmāʿ* and the undesirability of breaking it. In other words, *ijmāʿ* has been consistently considered such a morally binding principle that its violators have been seen as deserving of the severest reproach. But, even more importantly, this collective condemnation against the consensus breakers could have been founded on a textual references which has been communicated by the Prophet along with circumstantial evidence that implied the Prophet's intent, even if the actual Prophetic report did not reach us.[67] In either case, consensus must have been built on a definitive foundation, whether such a foundation can be conclusively identified or not. The fact that a collective agreement was achieved and recognized over the generations is, in itself and following the customary practice, an indication that it must have been founded on strong evidence, although later generations might not have direct access to this evidence.

## *ʿUrf, Ijtihād, Istiftāʾ*

As mentioned earlier, major works of legal theory usually include a chapter on the process of *ijtihād* and the proper qualifications of a competent *mujtahid* or muftī. The list of qualifications includes thorough knowledge of the primary sources and mastery of the tools—linguistic, interpretive, and rational—required to understand these sources. *Ijtihād* stands for the ability to relate the rulings embedded in the founding texts to a particular question or issue. The process of *ijtihād* starts from the particular question or issue for which the answer is needed. These questions or issues are rooted in real-life events and, consequently, are usually connected with social customs. *Ijtihād*, therefore, cannot be a rigid process that follows a fixed formula, because customs change according to sociohistorical contexts. Some jurists, therefore, have argued that regardless of whether an answer for a question already exists or not, the process of *ijtihād* has to start anew every time the same question is raised. The answer to a particular question may vary depending on each sociohistorical context; different contexts require different analyses. The *mujtahid*, therefore, is advised to reexamine the issue in its new context rather than automatically apply the ruling of an earlier precedent.[68]

After enumerating the proper qualifications of the *mujtahid* in terms of the required knowledge base, al-Juwaynī singles out one skill that he describes as indispensable. He refers to it as "understanding of the self" *(fiqh al-nafs),* the ability to understand the distinctive characteristics in different personalities and how to deal with each of them effectively. The jurists' discussion implies that it is a type of wisdom that is partly inborn and partly acquired through the experience of dealing with people of different characters in different situations.[69] Ideally, therefore, the competent *mujtahid* seeks not only to understand the proper sources, texts, and methods, but also—equally importantly—seeks to understand the particular issue in its own context.[70] We shall have a chance to deal with this point in more detail in chapter 8, which is devoted to the issue of legal application.

## *Al-Juwaynī's Theory of ʿUrf and the Discourse on Political Contingencies*

In addition to his important contributions in the fields of theology and jurisprudence, Al-Juwaynī also made a significant contribution in the field of political thought. He discussed the relationship between sharīʿah and political rule in a book that he wrote solely for this purpose. In this book, he advocated the primacy of sharīʿah as the sole foundation of the political system in Islam.[71] The book presents rulers and their deputies as servants of sharīʿah whose legitimacy is predicated on their obedience to its rules. Al-Juwaynī's mastery of Islamic theology, substantive law, and jurisprudence enabled him to develop a skeletal prototype of sharīʿah that he adopted in almost all of his writings. Such a skeletal prototype consists of a set of fundamental principles that inspire the myriad rulings that apply to every possible question or issue.[72] Al-Juwaynī offers a number of penetrating insights as to how this sharīʿah-based prototype can be applied, even in the absence of a fully qualified caliph or competent jurists. Al-Juwaynī envisions his prototype as applying on two different levels: collectively, in the form of a political system, and individually, in the form of a model to be internalized by individual Muslims. In both cases, the role that he assigns to *ʿurf* is substantial.

Al-Juwaynī starts out by investigating the question of the caliphate, its justification, and its normative foundations. He argues against the text-based theory advocated by the Shīʿī jurists, which maintains that the Prophet did name ʿAlī as his successor. His reasoning is quite similar to al-Shīrāzi's criteria for textual criticism: important events and questions pertaining to public affairs are usually communicated successively by multitudes of people rather than individually by means of singular reports.[73] Caliphate is one of the most important issues of public concern; if the Prophet were to nominate a successor, it would have been known by means of succession (*tawātur*). In the absence of the latter, the only viable foundation is *ijmāʿ*.[74] Here, once again, al-Juwaynī reiterates his non-textual justification for *ijmāʿ*: "I say that the vindication of consensus depends on custom and its recurrence because it is impossible for consensus to contradict known and recurrent customs." His main argument is that the authority of *ijmāʿ* does not exclusively depend on the texts that have consistently been associated with it. The fact that the jurists developed a consensus on a given issue, despite all the factors that customarily could have otherwise prevented such consensus from emerging, is in itself an indication that such consensus is based on a definitive proof.[75] In other words, the mere fact that the jurists across generations were able to reach such consensus is a proof of its authenticity.

Al-Juwaynī concludes that *ijmāʿ* is based mainly on *ʿurf*.[76] Because of people's different propensities, aptitudes, and idiosyncrasies, they can only agree if there is a definitive proof. Reason does not rule out the possibility that knowledge of such a proof could gradually fade in view of the growing interest in the consensus itself rather than its foundation.[77] Therefore, according to al-Juwaynī's argument, caliphate cannot be based on a definitive text. It is based rather on *ijmāʿ*, as the example of the rightly guided caliphs indicates.

Al-Juwaynī emphasized the role of actual practice over purely theoretical formulas.[78] For example, long before Ibn Khaldun and his views on the caliphate and the importance of political power (*shawkah*),[79] al-Juwaynī takes a more realistic approach in recognizing the validity of the caliphate of the individual who is able to earn people's support and possesses other prerequisites summarized in two main conditions: Qurayshī-descent and sufficiency.[80] Under sufficiency, he lists several qualities such as independence, knowledge, freedom, masculinity, and—above all—piety. Al-Juwaynī speaks of these conditions more as normative ideals than prescriptive or indispensable tenets . Along with these normative ideals, he speaks about exceptional contingencies in which one or more of these conditions are missing. For example, he addresses two different possibilities: the caliphate of the less qualified individual (*imamat al-mafḍūl*)[81] and the difficulty of meeting all the proper requirements (*inkhirām al-ṣifāt al-muʿtabarah fi al-aʾimmah*).[82]

According to al-Juwaynī, the main objective of the legal system is to serve people's needs according to the fundamental prototype of shariʿah; within such a prototype, *ʿurf* is a structural component. For example, in his discussion on the factors that should result in the removal (*khalʿ/inkhilāʿ*)

of officials, he emphasized the importance of taking the different circumstances into consideration.[83] He does not provide a fixed formula or prescription, but rather implies that each case should be studied individually in order to enable calculated decisions taken on the basis of potential risks and benefits. This is clearly demonstrated in cases such as the deposition of officials,[84] the proper application of the principle of commanding the good and forbidding the evil,[85] and the choice of relevant *fatwas*.[86] In these examples, sharīʿah is depicted less as a fixed structure than as a dynamic framework seeking to address the different needs of society in a creative manner that takes various contextual variables into consideration.

## The Applied Approach (*Tarīqat al-Fuqahāʾ*)

In contrast to the theoretical approach adopted mainly by the Shāfiʿī jurists, their Ḥanafī counterparts adopted a more applied approach that focused on the particular details of substantive law. This method involved a three-stage process that aimed to analyze the rulings of particular cases, abstract the founding principles underlying these rulings, and extrapolate these founding principles to other similar cases. This reverse analytical process initially focused on the works of recognized authorities such as the school's founder, Abū Ḥanīfah (d. AH 150/767 CE), and his most prominent disciples, Abū Yūsuf (d. AH 182/798 CE) and Muḥammad Ibn al-Ḥasan al-Shaybānī (d. AH 189/805 CE). These founding principles, *uṣūl*, are usually by-products of a retrospective analysis of the different substantive rulings. Given the close relationship within this Ḥanafī approach of these *uṣūl* and the different substantive issues, reference to and use of *ʿurf* was pervasive.

In his famous treatise on the founding principles of the Ḥanafī school, Abū al-Ḥasan al-Karkhī (d. AH 340/951 CE) pointed out the importance of *ʿurf* in the different stages of the juristic process. For example, he highlighted the role of *ʿurf* for the proper interpretation of oaths, contracts, and different contractual procedures, especially in cases of dispute.[87] Moreover, in his view, rulings are to be analyzed in the light of the common practices rather than rare or exceptional ones. Commenting on this treatise, al-Nasafī (d. AH 537/1142 CE) gives the example that if someone swears not to eat eggs, it will be understood as chicken eggs rather than, say, fish eggs, unless otherwise indicated. This is because eggs,as food, usually refer to chicken eggs rather than any other type of eggs.

The famous early Ḥanafī jurist ʿUbayd Allah Ibn ʿUmar al-Dabbūsī (d. AH 430/1038 CE) refers to the disagreement between Abū Ḥanīfah and his two disciples, Abū Yūsuf and al-Shaybānī, on the difference between real and metaphorical meanings. For example, if a statement has both a used real meaning (*ḥaqīqah must'malah*) and a common metaphorical meaning (*majāz muta'āraf*), the former takes precedence according to Abū Ḥanīfah, but according to his two disciples, the latter.[88] The import of this disagreement comes to effect in the interpretation of oaths. If, for example, a person swears not to eat wheat, but eats wheat bread instead, has the person violated the oath? According to Abū Ḥanīfah, this action does not break the oath, but according to his disciples it will.

In his collection of the different founding principles employed by the authorities of the Ḥanafī school, al-Dabbūsī cites many cases that are built on these principles. For example, according to Abū Ḥanīfah, in cases of doubt or disagreement, one should presume the surest possibility, based on the principle of necessary precaution (*wājib al-iḥtiyāṭ*).[89] Abū Ḥanīfah consistently upheld this founding principle (*aṣl*) in different cases of substantive law. For example, in cases involving a missing individual, a maximum speculative term of 120 years from the date of the person's birth is set for the declaration of this person's legal death. Because people do not normally live beyond this age, it is presumed as the surest possibility.[90] The question of whether the individual actually lives until reaching that age is of little significance. Similarly, the maximum age at which menopause occurs is presumed to be 60. Although it is known that menopause normally occurs before this age, this limit is presumed as the maximum point or the surest possibility.[91] The question that concerns us here, however, is what the qualifier "normally" actually means. When we say that people do not *normally* live beyond 120 years or that women *normally* reach menopause before the age of 60, what are the actual parameters on which these presumptions are built? It can be experience, successive knowledge, or expert opinions. Whatever the case maybe, it is safe to argue that the common customary practice is an integral part of all these possibilities.

The concept of *'urf* as the common practice permeates the founding principles that the early Ḥanafī jurists extracted from the works of the school's pioneering authorities. The concept is invoked in a number of ways to explain factual details in different legal contexts. For example, the common currency (*al-naqd al-ghālib*) is held to be the implied payment method unless otherwise explicitly indicated.[92] So also is the concept of the equal (estimated) price (*ajr al-mithl*), especially in cases of doubt or disagreement.[93] This concept was extensively invoked in chapters dealing with financial transactions such as alms, blood money, and slavery, as well as marriage-related expenditures like dowries, alimony, and child support. The evaluation of the exact values of these different types of payments was to be determined by recourse to the common custom.

Al-Dabbūsī also refers to the famous disagreement on the question of the units of measurements mentioned in the founding texts, especially the Prophetic traditions. This question pertains specifically to the ḥadīth on the usurious items (*al-amwāl al-ribawiyyah*). While al-Shaybānī held that the textually indicated units of measurement shall remain unchanged, Abū Yūsuf held that the determination of such units follows the common practice. If, for example, people develop the practice of selling wheat by weight instead of volume, as indicated in the Prophetic report, would it be possible to recognize this practice? According to al-Shaybānī, the text takes precedence and, consequently, the practice should be rejected. Abū Yūsuf, on the other hand, argued that the Prophet merely *cited* the common practice in his time, and if that practice changes, so does the ruling.[94]

## *The Debate on Juristic Preference (Istiḥsān)*

Since most of the early Ḥanafī treatment of *ʿurf* was undertaken within the framework of *istiḥsān*, we shall examine how these two concepts were tied together. In his treatise on the nullification of juristic preference, *Ibṭāl al-Istiḥsān*, al-Shāfiʿī launched severe criticism against this Ḥanafī principle. As mentioned earlier, al-Shāfiʿī held that a legal ruling is to be determined exclusively by means of one of four sources: the Qur'ān, the Sunnah of the Prophet, consensus of the learned, or analogy to one of these three.[95] So, according to al-Shāfiʿī, *istiḥsān* is an unwarranted addition to the only four legitimate sources. The Ḥanafī jurists, however, characterized *istiḥsān* not as an additional source, but rather as a mere method for analyzing the sources.[96] In this context, *istiḥsān* is simply understood in its literal sense, as choosing the proper source or interpretation (*mustaḥsan*). It can also mean choosing the best *qiyās*.

Abū Bakr al-Jaṣāṣ (d. AH 370/980 CE), for example, distinguishes between two main types of *istiḥsān*. The first involves the exertion of effort (*ijtihād*) to determine the different values mentioned in the texts precisely.[97] For example, the proper evaluation of "common expenditure" mentioned in some texts would be a form of *istiḥsān*. Similarly, the proper evaluation of the amounts that are not textually determined, such as those in the area of compensations, would fall under this type of *istiḥsān*. The second is the supersession of a *qiyās* by more forceful evidence.[98] This latter form of *istiḥsān* is again divided into two main types. The first is a form of *qiyās* in which a derivative (*farʿ*) can be attached to more than one source (*aṣl*), and it is attached to the one with which it shares a stronger relationship.[99] Al-Jaṣāṣ holds that this is the most subtle type of evidence because it requires a great deal of scrutiny to decide which of the viable sources is closer to the derivative in question. The example given is the case of collective thievery: a group of thieves breaks into a protected property but only one of them carries the stolen items out of the premises. The question debated was whether all of them are liable to the *ḥadd* punishment or only the carrier of the stolen items. According to *qiyās*, only the latter is liable to the *ḥadd* punishment. The *qiyās* in question is the case of abduction when a group of individuals kidnap a woman but only one of them assaults her sexually. In this case, while all of them would be liable to some form of punishment, only the sexual assaulter would be liable to the full *ḥadd* punishment. According to *istiḥsān*, however, all the individuals would receive the *ḥadd* punishment for theft. Another analogy using the case of brigandage or banditry—collective collaboration in premeditated highway robbery (*ḥirābah*)—justifies this interpretation. All the bandits are held responsible for the action even if they did not participate individually in the different crimes perpetrated. Therefore, the case of the collective thievery would be compared to the case of highway robbery by means of *istiḥsān* rather than to the case of abduction by means of simple analogy.[100]

The second and more controversial form of *istiḥsān*, which is closely related to the issue of *ʿurf*, was also known as "particularization of the operative cause" (*takhṣīṣ al-ʿillah*).[101] The standard procedure in a valid *qiyās* relies on the mutual interdependence between the operative cause and the resultant ruling; whenever a certain operative cause (e.g., intoxication) deserving of a certain ruling (e.g., prohibition) exists, the ruling automatically applies. Here, however, although the operative cause exists, it is superseded by *istiḥsān* on account of another (more deserving) consideration. This supersession of the operative cause is called "particularization" in the sense that the existence of the operative cause is rendered ineffective. Al-Jaṣāṣ argues that the operative cause can be particularized by means of a textual reference, a juristic consensus, or a commonly known practice—*ʿurf*.[102] The examples that he gives for a particularization by means of *ʿurf* include the undetermined fees for admission into public bathhouses. In a lease contract, the benefits (of using the leased item) are thought of as the equivalent of the sold item in a sale contract. In the lease contract, the term and the payment have to be clearly indicated. In case of the use of public bathhouses, however, neither the payment (admission fee) nor the duration (time to be spent) is indicated. Rather, they are determined on the basis of the common practice; therefore, a case like this is considered as an exception to the rule. Al-Jaṣāṣ also lists the case of manufacture (*istiṣnāʿ*) as an example of this type of *istiḥsān*.[103]

Some Ḥanafī jurists, such as al-Bazdawī (d. AH 483/1046 CE) and al-Sarakhsī (d. AH 490/1096 CE), severely criticized the argument favoring particularization.[104] They argued that the main criterion for a valid operative cause is its recurrence (*iṭṭirād*). If a given operative cause exists and does not produce the expected ruling, it is not actually a valid operative cause, which, in turn, renders it void (*mulghāh*) rather than particularized (*makhṣūṣah*). In line with the Ḥanafī school's approach towards *qiyās* and *istiḥsān*, these jurists distinguish between these two categories based on the efficacy of the operative cause in question. If it is weak, it will be called *qiyās*; if it is strong, it will be called *istiḥsān* or *qiyās mustaḥsan* (preferred juristic analogy).[105] Apart from the *istiḥsān* in the determination and evaluation of the measurements,[106] they speak of two main types of *istiḥsān*. The first is a *qiyās* which is superseded by a textual reference, a juristic consensus, or necessity.[107] The second is the case of the hidden *qiyās*, such as the case of disagreement between the buyer and the seller before the payment of the price. According to Islamic rules of adjudication, the plaintiff is required to produce evidence to support his claim. If the defendant denies the charge, he is required to take an oath averring this denial. While according to *qiyās*, the seller in this case does not take the oath because he is the plaintiff (he is claiming a higher price), according to *istiḥsān*, both of them take the oath because each of them has a different claim: the seller is claiming a different price while the buyer is claiming the denial of the seller to produce the item.[108] The main difference between these two types of *istiḥsān* is that the first one (by text, consensus, or necessity) cannot be extended to other cases, while the second type (the hidden juristic analogy) can be extended because it relies on the operative cause—which is, by definition, extendable (*muṭṭaridah*).[109]

For the purpose of the present context, it is important to point out how pervasive the concept of *ʿurf* was within the Ḥanafī discourse on *qiyās* and *istiḥsān*. Despite their disagreements on the operative cause and the classification of *istiḥsān*, the examples used were similar and references to *ʿurf* in these different classifications were numerous. In the following chapters, we will see how this treatment of *ʿurf* through *istihsān* developed within the framework of the different legal genres.

# Part 3

# Development and Expansion

# Chapter 5

# The Expansion of Legal Theory

## Custom in Mainstream Legal Theory and Emerging Legal Genres

By the end of the fifth Islamic century (eleventh century CE), a consensus over the theoretical synthesis that al-Shāfiʿī systematically developed in his *Risālah* was achieved. The majority of jurists in later generations accepted al-Shāfiʿī's articulation of the sources of the law as a blueprint for Islamic legal theory. His quadruple classification of Islamic legal sources into the Qur'ān, the Sunnah, *ijmāʿ*, and *qiyās* became the keystone of the Sunnī legal methodology. Those who did not subscribe to this framework remained a minority that was often criticized by the overwhelming majority.[1] Although the methodology that was built on this basic structure continued to evolve over time, al-Shāfiʿī's initial imprints were always recognizable and he was often credited as its original founder. Gradually, more items were added to the list of legal sources with much disagreement on their order and authority relative to the basic four sources.

As noted earlier, the initial discussions over the legal concept of *ʿurf* started with the direct and indirect references in both the Qur'ān and the Sunnah of the Prophet. With the goal of constructing a legal system guided by the will of God, Muslim jurists grounded their system in the texts that they believed embodied the divine will. Multiple factors influenced the early development of the formal concept of *ʿurf*. Besides the textual references in both the Qur'ān and the Sunnah of the Prophet, it was shaped by the early juristic foundations first developed by the leading authorities of the different regional schools and later articulated by the founders of the main surviving schools: Abu Ḥanīfah, Mālik ibn Anas, al-Shāfiʿī, and Aḥmad ibn Ḥanbal. Moreover, the early theological debates on the concept of *ʿādah* contributed to the development of the legal concept of *ʿurf.* The theological influences were manifested in the transportation of key concepts into the juristic discourse through the works of eminent theologian-jurists such as al-Baqillānī, al-Juwaynī, and al-Ghazālī. Many Muslim theologians, particularly from the Ashʿarī school, relied on the concept of custom in their treatment of many issues from causality to human freedom to legal responsibility. In the works of these theologian-jurists, custom provided rational justification for important legal concepts that were mostly conceived as solely text based, such as *tawātur* and *ijmāʿ*.

Likewise, the Ḥanafī jurists incorporated the concept of custom in their treatment of the two closely related concepts of *qiyās* and *istihsān*; this was in keeping with the tradition developed by earlier jurists in the school, among them al-Karkhī and al-Dabbusī, and later al-Jaṣāṣ, al-Rāzī, al-Bazdawī, and al-Sarakhsī. Similarly, the Mālikī jurists drew on the well-established concept of the *ʿamal* of the people of Madinah as first articulated in the *Muwaṭṭaʾ* of Mālik and the subsequent body of texts based on it. The Ḥanbalī jurists also adopted the formal structure of legal theory as we can see from the work of Ibn ʿAqīl and later authorities of the school.

In this second part of the book, I explore the history of the concept of *ʿurf* after the fifth Islamic century (eleventh century CE). Two main developments characterized this period. The first was the blurring of the lines that traditionally separated the different schools of jurisprudence (*uṣūl*). Unlike substantive law (*furūʿ*), which continued to develop along distinct school lines, purely juristic discussions in *uṣūl al-fiqh* literature developed into a shared, interschool theoretical framework; interschool disagreements were recognized but often overcome. The second main development was the emergence of disparate genres and subgenres within the larger framework of legal theory. Two main examples of such genres are legal maxims and the objectives of sharīʿah. These two genres are discussed in the following chapters. This chapter focuses on the treatment of *ʿurf* within the main juristic framework as it continued to evolve during this period, particularly within the framework of *qiyās*, *istidlāl*, and *takhṣīṣ*.

## Custom within the Four Sources: *ʿUrf* and *Qiyās*

Al-Shāfiʿī's legal template was so influential that later modifications had to be introduced within his basic juristic structure of the four main sources.

The texts of the Qur'ān and the Sunnah of the Prophet were recognized as authoritative in themselves, while their interpretations were determined through the mechanism of *ijmāʿ*. The Sunnah of the Prophet, as well as the precedents of the early companions and successors, provided a historical interpretive framework for the system. Under the concept of *ijmāʿ*, these founding texts were assigned specific interpretations based on their historical contexts, which were communicated along with the texts themselves. This linkage between the texts and their contexts was not limited to the occasions within which the texts originated, known in the Islamic tradition (in the case of the Qur'ān) as *asbāb al-nuzūl*, but it also extended to the subsequent occasions in which the texts provided authoritative foundations for particular rulings (*aḥkām*). Throughout the history of the Islamic legal tradition, these juristic precedents were invoked along with the texts themselves to indicate how the texts should be understood and, more importantly, how they should relate to daily life.

But, how was this fixity, brought about by *ijmāʿ*, balanced against the incessant pressure for change by the lived reality? This is a well-known challenge, by no means unique to the Islamic legal tradition. Every legal tradition seeks to accommodate change without compromising its basic philosophical or epistemological principles. In the case of the Islamic legal tradition, *qiyās* facilitated such evolution. By relying on *qiyās*, the Muslim jurists were not only able to provide a solution to new questions, but they were able to do so while remaining faithful to the basic structure of the system. This was the reason why al-Shāfiʿī equated *qiyās* with *ijtihād* in his *Risālah*. Eventually, however, as they underwent their own developments, these two categories became increasingly differentiated. This explains why chapters about *qiyās* in major works of legal theory during the post-classical period were the longest and most thorough.[2] It was in these chapters that new ideas were debated and propositions for modifications were made. Moreover, many of the so-called contested sources (*al-adillah al-mukhtalaf fīhā*) originated in the debates over *qiyās*. The most prominent example of this dynamic is the case of public interest (*al-maṣlahah al-mursalah*) which originated in the discussions on the operative cause of legal analogy, before it became an independent source. This was the same dynamic that transformed *istiḥsān* from a subcategory of *qiyās* into an independent source in its own right. We shall have a chance to treat this point in more detail below. What is important to emphasize here is that the same dynamic was, in some measure, repeated in the case of custom.

To begin with, the jurists debated the question of the applicability of *qiyās* to habitual or customary practices. For example, they questioned whether the rulings founded on habitual events or practices can be extended to other similar situations. It is evident from the examples cited that the habitual events here are induced by nature, such as the age of puberty and the duration of the menstrual period, rather than human volitional interference. Given the changing nature of such events, which depend on variables like geographical location or average temperature, the jurists reasoned that *qiyās* cannot be used to extrapolate these rulings to comparable situations. In other words, the rulings on such habits are to be based on the opinion of a reliable expert witness (*qawl al-ṣādiq*), not analogical reasoning.[3] This conclusion reflects the jurists' understanding of the proper function of *qiyās:* it is a means of extending the ruling of an already existing text to a new situation rather than creating such a ruling *ab initio*. The ruling in question is discovered in the existing text-based legal treasury rather than instituted by the novel circumstance. In other words, the ruling needs to be anchored in a text either directly or indirectly. In cases of habitual situations such as the ones cited here, *ʿādah* indicates a certain legal status rather than justifying such a status. Because *ʿādah* here does not function as a source, it cannot be treated as an *aṣl* in a valid *qiyās*.

Reference to custom within the *qiyās*-related debates was mainly connected with the question of the operative cause (*ʿillah*). For example, while enumerating the different types of operative causes, al-Qarāfī included the operative cause that is based on a customary indication, such as one's social status.[4] Based on this consideration, some jurists observed that a well-to-do woman is not obligated to breastfeed her own baby because it was customary for well-to-do families to hire wet-nurses to breastfeed their babies.[5]

Another important use of custom within the *qiyās*-related debates was in determining the operative cause (*ithbāt masālik al-ʿillah*). Regardless of the different classifications of *qiyās*,[6] the jurists were in agreement about its four pillars: the original case (*aṣl*), the new case (*farʿ*), the ruling (*ḥukm*), and the operative cause (*ʿillah/manāṭ*). In order to ensure that the ruling of the original case could be extended to the new case, the operative cause of the original ruling had to be verified. The jurists used three different types of verification. The first, which is referred to as *tanqīḥ al-manāṭ*, is used to examine the scope of the original case and ensure that its ruling is not limited to its specific context. In other words, if a verse or ḥadīth refers to a particular individual or incident, the jurist investigates whether the ruling in question can be applied to other similar situations after suppressing the particular details of the original incident.[7] The second type of verification, which is referred to as *taḥqīq al-manāṭ*, identifies the relevant attributes of the operative cause and their presence in the example under investigation (new case). For example, the law stipulates that the acceptance of a testimony is dependent on the uprightness of witnesses. The verification of the uprightness of particular witnesses, however, depends on the common standards as indicated by *ʿurf*, reason, or other types of circumstantial evidence. In the case of the wine, for example, the jurist would first verify the ruling (prohibition) of the original case (wine), which is based on textual evidence. Second, he would verify that the operative cause of the original case (intoxication) is present in the second case (e.g., alcohol). This can be determined by the common custom. In other words, if it is known through *ʿurf* that X shares the operative cause of Y, then X will automatically share the ruling of Y.[8]

The third and most famous type of verification is referred to as *takhrīj al-manāṭ*. It ensures that the particular operative cause in the original case, is *the raison d'etre* of the given ruling. The ruling is then extrapolated to all similar cases that share this particular operative cause. Again, the most famous example is the prohibition of wine. Other beverages such as alcohol, for example, receive the same ruling (prohibition) because they share the same operative cause (intoxication). The main difference between the second and the third types of verification is that, while *taḥqīq al-manāt* focuses on the new case, *farʿ*, *takhrīj al-manāṭ* focuses on the original case, *aṣl*. These examples indicate that custom is used mostly in the second type of verification, *taḥqīq al-manāt*, but it can also be used, with varying degrees, in the other two types, *tanqīḥ* and *takhrīj al-manaṭ*.

Another important method for ascertaining the operative cause was the establishment of its relevance (*munāsabah*). In order for the jurist to verify that a given ruling is linked to a given operative cause, he would seek to prove that the latter is the real cause of the former. For example, concerning the famous ḥadīth "let no judge decide on a case while in a state of anger," the jurists argued that anger was the operative cause of the prohibitive command. The question of the relevance of the operative cause was closely connected to the question of the rational justification of legal rulings (*taʿlīl al-aḥkām*) and whether such justification is always possible. This latter issue, in turn, was built on the fundamental question of the moral epistemology of the rulings in the Islamic legal tradition known as *ḥusn* (beauty) and *qubḥ* (ugliness). The epistemological debates were primarily focused on the proper role of both reason and revelation, not only on purely theological issues, but on jurisprudential and substantive issues as well.[9] In juristic parlance, *ḥusn* and *qubḥ* are used in three different senses. The first is the sense of "what is known by nature or intuition to be either good or detestable," such as the difference between sweetness and bitterness. The second sense is "what is considered either a positive attribute, which is a sign of perfection, or a negative attribute, which is a sign of imperfection," such as the difference between knowledge and ignorance. The third sense, the subject of disagreement among theologians, is "what is commended and rewarded by God and what is condemned and punished by him." While the Ashʿarī theologians held that this can be known only by sharīʿah, the Muʿtazilī theologians held that it can be known by reason.

The jurists disagreed over the rational justification of legal rulings. Some argued that God's rulings are not in need of any justification, for the simple reason that the divine will itself provides such justification. Others argued that legal rulings are rationally justifiable although, according to some, such justification is not always accessible. The jurists pointed out the connection between *ʿurf* and the relevance of the operative cause (*munāsabat al-ʿillah*) in their attempt to precisely characterize the concept. According to the advocates of justifiability (of rulings), *relevance* refers to the means of achieving good or removing harm. On the other hand, according to the advocates of unjustifiability, *relevance* signifies suitability to the habitual conduct of rational individuals.[10] This disagreement over the characterization of the concept of relevance (*munāsabah*) is similar to the disagreement over the concept of the operative cause itself and whether it is considered a basis (*bāʿith*) for the ruling or a mere sign (*ʿalāmah*) of it.[11] What is of more concern for us here is to indicate how the concept of *ʿurf* was invoked in these debates to determine the understanding of the concept of relevance, which was one of the foundations of the concept of *maqāṣid* (objectives) of sharīʿah.[12]

In most of the *ʿillah*-related debates, the invoked concept of custom was closer to the rational concept of *ʿādah* in theological discourses than to the concrete examples of *ʿurf* in legal or juristic discourses. The predominance of the theological concept of custom over the legal concept in most of the operative cause discussions helps explain the influence of the different theological schools in the early juristic debates. The inclusion of the theological views in juristic debates marked a significant turning point in which legal theory became more differentiated from substantive law, drawing as heavily from theology as it did from pure *fiqh*.[13]

## Beyond the Four Sources: *ʿUrf* and *Istidlāl*

The development of the concept of *istidlāl* represented another significant turning point in the history of *ʿurf* in general and its relationship with legal sources in particular. Prior to the consolidation of *istidlāl* as a source, the role of *ʿurf* was mainly substantive; it was used in the interpretation of texts or employed within the microdebates of *ijmaʿ* and *qiyās*, but hardly singled out as an independent source in its own right. To a large extent, the consolidation of *istidlāl* was in itself a consolidation of *ʿurf* because the latter was eventually recognized as a subset of the former. But, what does *istidlāl* mean precisely, and how did it develop?

Literally, *istidlāl* means "seeking evidence." Whenever a jurist is confronted with a question, he seeks to find an answer for it in the founding sources of the Islamic legal system (*yastadill*). The history of *istidlāl*, therefore, is the history of legal theory itself because it refers more to a process than to a particular concept or principle. Like the other major concepts in Islamic legal theory, *istidlāl* was also a subject of heated debate among jurists throughout its long course of development. I will highlight some of the examples that reveal how *istidlāl* was discussed.

Al-Juwaynī was the first to undertake a systematic treatment of the concept. Before him, it was used either in its general linguistic sense (to seek evidence) or as a synonym of *qiyās*.[14] He defined it as an investigation to find a "meaning which is appropriate for a certain ruling and conducive to it based on rational reasoning, even in the absence of a definitive textual basis, which entails an effective justification."[15] In other words, the jurist's search for the ruling does not have to be limited to mere textual references in the main sources. He should seek to *abstract* meanings from these sources and these meanings should serve as viable bases for rulings. Therefore, while in *qiyās*, the presence of an original case—which serves as an *aṣl*—is important, in *istidlāl* it is unnecessary. For the latter, the jurist seeks to relate the given ruling to a meaning that is congruent with the fundamental principles of sharīʿah (*al-uṣūl al-thābitah*).

These fundamental principles represent the aggregate of the rules and objectives that the Lawgiver intends to achieve when sharīʿah is enforced, whether they are expressed verbally or extracted deductively. *Istidlāl* in this sense comes very close to the concept of *istiṣlāḥ* or *maṣlaḥah mursalah*, which the Malikī school was famous for adopting and this is the reason why some later jurists equated al-Juwaynī's definition of *istidlāl* with *maṣlaḥah*.[16] Al-Juwaynī, however, criticized the Mālikī approach towards *maṣlaḥah* because, according to him, they turned it into a source in its own right, independent of the texts.

Al-Juwaynī qualified his definition of *istidlāl* to distinguish it from the Mālikī school's unrestricted use of *maṣlaḥah* on the one hand, and from those who rejected it altogether on the other—thereby restricting the scope of *istidlāl* to the area of conventional *qiyās*.[17] While the former sought to achieve the objective of the Lawgiver—the best interest of people—the latter sought to guard against the possibility of reducing sharīʿah to a pragmatic self-serving undertaking, which could possibly undermine its ultimate objectives.[18] In other words, al-Juwaynī sought to reconcile what he in fact saw as two irreconcilable extremes. While seeking to incorporate the concept of *maṣlahah*, it has to be pursued in a manner that is compatible with the textual indicators of sharīʿah.

Although al-Juwaynī, following al-Shāfiʿī, allowed for the possibility of constructing a ruling on the basis of *maṣlaḥah* in the absence of a textual foundation, he maintained that the fundamental principles structurally ingrained (*qārratin*) in sharīʿah should guide such *maṣlaḥah*.[19] Al-Juwaynī bases his opinion on two premises: first, rulings are to be based on the divine will and second, the texts are limited while events are limitless.[20] This understanding of *istidlāl* fits perfectly with al-Juwaynī's characterization of sharīʿah not as a body of texts but rather as a skeletal framework of the basic fundamental principles deductively extracted from the texts. Moreover, it also accords with his repeated emphasis on the quality of *fiqh al-nafs* (sound judgment as predicated on the proper understanding of the self), which he deemed a prerequisite for a competent jurist.[21] Such a quality comes not only through extensive knowledge of the rulings of sharīʿah but also—equally importantly—through extensive knowledge of the contexts in which these rulings should apply.

Some jurists counted *istidlāl* as the fifth source of law, after the four main ones.[22] This was an important turning point in the history of *istidlāl* which started to be viewed as a general category that included the contested sources (*al-adillah al-mukhtalaf fīhā*), other than the four main ones. It is important to trace this development of the concept of *istidlāl* because of its close connection with the development of *ʿurf*. The latter was subsumed under the former before they were both treated as secondary sources. For example, al-Āmidī (d. AH 631/1233 CE) spoke of two main types of *istidlāl*. The first entails a set of rational or logical principles that help the jurist construct legal rulings such as, "the ruling applies whenever its cause exists."[23] Although these principles are not derived directly or literally from texts, the jurist can still find strong support for them in the texts. The second type of *istidlāl* that al-Āmidī mentioned was the presumption of continuity (*istiṣḥāb al-ḥāl*). At the most elemental level, it means that once a certain rule is established, it is presumed to continue until the opposite is proven.[24] This principle, similar to the others in the first type, is used as a procedural measure that the jurist relies on during the various stages of the juristic process. Al-Āmidī, who was famous for his extensive use of logic in legal theory, went to great length to describe the details of these principles, using illustrative examples from substantive law. Thus, *istidlāl* emerged as a comprehensive category that included a set of rational or logical principles tied to the concept of *ʿurf*, if not dependent on it.[25]

Following the example of al-Āmidī, many later jurists treated *istidlāl* as a generic category that included different juristic or legal principles extracted from the different rulings of substantive law. For example, Ibn al-Ḥājib (d. AH 681/1282 CE)[26] spoke of three types of *istidlāl*: the logical correlation between two rulings without a common operative cause (to distinguish it from conventional *qiyās*),[27] the presumption of continuity (*istiṣḥāb*), and the laws of monotheistic religions before Islam (*sharʿman qablanā*).[28] Ibn al-Subkī (d. AH 771/1369 CE) went one step further and used *istidlāl* to refer to all the sources other than the four main ones. In his commentary on Ibn al-Ḥājib's text, al Subkī expanded al-Juwaynī's definition and argued that the differences between the early jurists could be reconciled in terms of *istidlāl*; that is, while all jurists recognized the existence of another source beyond the four main ones, different schools gave different expressions to this "additional" source. The Ḥanafī jurists called it *istiḥsān*, the Shāfiʿī jurists called it *istiṣḥāb*, and the Mālikī jurists called it *maṣlaḥah*. According to Ibn al-Subkī, all these different terms ultimately refer to the same process of constructing rulings on the basis of a source other than the four main ones.[29]

This quick overview reveals that the concept of *istidlāl* passed through several stages. First, it was used in its literal meaning to refer to the process of seeking evidence primarily in the four main sources. Second, it was used as a generic category to refer to a set of rational/logical and then juristic/legal principles that the jurist relies on during the different steps of the legal process. Third, it was used as a generic category to refer to all the sources other than the four main ones. Finally, it was referred to as an example of the secondary or contested sources.[30]

Apart from the inclusion of *ʿurf* as a subcategory of *istidlāl*, the last phase in the development of *ʿurf* as related to the four main sources was its treatment as a secondary source in its own right. For example, the Mālikī jurist al-Qarāfī (d. AH 684/1285 CE) spoke of two main types of sources: textual sources (*adillat mashrūʿiyyah*) and contextual or confirmatory indicators (*adillat wuqūʿ*). The former refer to the four main sources in addition to fifteen other secondary sources, custom among them.[31] The latter refer to contextual or circumstantial evidence that indicates the occurrence of a given event or action such as the efficacy of causes, the fulfillment of conditions, or the absence of impediments. According to al-Qarāfī, these contextual sources are countless since they differ from one case to another.[32] Al-Qarāfī argues that in order for a ruling to apply to a certain event or incident, the latter (event or incident) needs to be established beyond any doubt. The establishment or the materialization (*taḥaquq/wuqūʿ*) of an incident depends on the verification of the attendant circumstantial evidence.

For example, in order for someone to receive an entitled share of inheritance, the (actual) death of the relative must be established and the exact relationship between the deceased and the recipient must be verified. These material or factual details have to be established within their social and cultural settings. After the jurist verifies them, he examines the relevant legal sources to construct his ruling. Within this binary framework of sources (textual and contextual), custom figured prominently both as a normative abstract principle and a contextual or circumstantial indicator for establishing the factual details related to a given event or incident. Similarly to al-Qarafī's approach, Ibn Juzayy (d. AH 741/1340 CE) counted 20 sources, which he divided into three main types: textual, transmissional, and deductive.[33] The first refers to the Qur'ān and the Sunnah. The second refers to the consensus and the opinions of the companions. The third refers to the rest of the sources, including custom.[34]

It should be noted that the order of these contested sources was flexible; this is how interschool differences were often reflected. For example, while the Ḥanafī school emphasized *istiḥsān* and the Mālikī school *maṣlaḥah*, the Shāfiʿī and the Ḥanbalī schools emphasized *istiṣḥāb*. Moreover, while some jurists expanded the list by combining famous sources such as *istiḥsān* or *istiṣlāḥ* with general rational or juristic principles that were often treated under *istidlāl*, other jurists narrowed down the list to just four or five items. For instance, while both al-Āmidī and Ibn al-Ḥājib treated *istiṣḥāb* as a subcategory of *istidlāl*, al-Ṭūfī (d. AH 716/1316 CE), in his commentary on Ibn Qudāmah's text, referred to it as one of the original sources along with the Qur'ān, Sunnah, and *ijmāʿ*.[35] Al-Ṭūfī's example is important for our purposes because his argument for *istiṣḥāb*, whether rational or juristic, was made by strong appeal to the rational concept of custom.[36]

Although, as noted earlier, Ibn al-Subkī sought to reconcile these apparent disagreements over the concept of *istidlāl*, it is evident that it continued to acquire different semantic and juristic connotations, which influenced the way it was constructed and reconstructed over time. The case of *istidlāl* is instructive because it illustrates the complexity of any attempt to analyze such historically and juristically loaded concepts. Al-Zarakshī captured this complexity in his frequent allusions to the different constructions and uses of *istidlāl* by the different jurists or schools.[37] These examples indicate that any meaningful analysis of these concepts and terms has to start by placing them in their wider historical and juristic contexts. Therefore, it is inaccurate and even misleading to speak of them as if they were static, monolithic, or uniform.

The jurists in the post-classical period devoted much of their efforts to preserving the legacy of their predecessors and building on the foundations that were bequeathed to them. Although these efforts primarily took the form of abridgments, glosses, and super-glosses of major texts within each of the recognized schools, recent scholarship indicates that these activities were not always redundant.[38] Through them, the jurists were able to consolidate the authority of the older texts and integrate the necessary changes that their particular contexts dictated. The concept of custom was one of the main tools used to integrate these changes into the body of Islamic law and legal theory. The jurists' engagement with the classical texts often involved higher levels of abstraction as well as novel forms of classification and reclassification. The two examples of legal maxims (*al-qawāʿid al-fiqhiyyah*) and objectives (*maqāṣid*) of sharīʿah are two cases in point, as the following two chapters demonstrate.

## The Scope of the Sources: *ʿUrf* and *Takhṣīṣ*

In the post-classical period, the jurists continued to debate the role of custom in determining the signification (*dalālah*) of texts and the extent to which it may effect, change, or rule out a particular meaning of a text. They examined this function of custom within the framework of other larger themes such as particularization (*takhṣīṣ*) and limitation (*taqyīd*). The question debated was to what extent a general text can be particularized or limited by a customary practice. The jurists differentiated between a linguistic convention (*ʿurf qawlī*) and a practical custom (*ʿurf ʿamalī*). The majority of the jurists held the view that linguistic conventions can particularize the general meanings of texts.[39] Sharīʿah, they argued, was meant to be intelligible and accessible; texts have to be interpreted according to people's common conventions, not limited to strict literal meanings. This is the case, for example, with terms in contracts. The question that comes to mind here is whether the conventions used as reference points to textual expressions should be those common at the time of the original text or those common at the time of the contemporary reader of the text. In order to decide between these two possibilities, the jurists devised yet another classification: antecedent and subsequent customs. As far as linguistic conventions are concerned, the jurists—almost unanimously—held the view that the interpretation of textual expressions should be determined according to the conventions common at the time of the original text.[40]

This attitude towards linguistic conventions is based on the view that a speech or a text can only be understood in the light of its social and cultural context; conventions usually alter or even abrogate literal meanings. The criterion for the determination of such common conventions is precedence of recognition. Once a conventional signification (*dalālah ʿurfiyyah*) becomes widely recognized as superseding the literal meaning, even in the absence of contextual or circumstantial evidence, it acquires the status of an accepted conventional meaning of the word in question.[41] The examples that are commonly used in the *uṣūl* literature are *dābbah* for either a horse or a donkey as well as words such as *ghā'iṭ* and *khalā'* for a toilet.[42] Although the literal meanings of these words are much broader, common convention restricted their meanings to those indicated. Similarly, technical terms within the texts of sharīʿah should be understood in light of the conventional signification of sharīʿah. For example, words such as *ṣalah* (prayer), *Ḥajj* (pilgrimage), and *ṣawm* (fasting) are to be interpreted as the specific prayer, pilgrimage, and fasting of Muslims according to the regulations of sharʿīah.

Al-Qarāfī distinguished two more types of linguistic conventions: singular and compound. The singular expressions refer to singular words such as *dābbah* and *ghā'iṭ*. Compound expressions refer to the specific semantic relationships inherent in certain linguistic structures. When the Qur'ān declares, for example, in verse 4:23, "prohibited on you are your mothers," it does not refer to the prohibition of the person of the mothers, but to the prohibition of the marital relationship between children and their parents.[43]

While the jurists were unanimous in their agreement on the applicability of linguistic conventions, they disagreed on practical customs. Contrary to the majority opinion, the Ḥanafī jurists held the view that practical customs can particularize the general meaning of texts or statements.[44] The most famous example cited is the word *ṭaʿām* (food) in the ḥadīth that prohibits usurious food transactions. The question that was raised was whether the word *food* in this ḥadīth refers to a specific type of food. The Ḥanafī jurists argued that it refers exclusively to wheat, since it was the common referent of the word in Ḥijāz at the time of the Prophet. The majority view, however, was that the word food in the ḥadīth is not limited to wheat but covers any other foodstuff.[45] The jurists differentiated between antecedent and concurrent customary practices on the one hand and subsequent customary practices on the other.[46] The former are practices that were known and common before or at the time of the general text (the Prophet), and the latter are the ones that emerged after the time of the text. In the case of the former, if the customary practice was not in agreement with the general text but was not condemned by the Prophet, it received his tacit approval. Although some jurists held that antecedent or concurrent customary practices in this case are valid examples of practical *ʿurf*, others argued that the sanctioning of such cases is based on the tacit approval of the Prophet (*taqrīr*), not the influence of the practical custom.[47] The subsequent customary practice, on the other hand, is considered ineffective for altering the general meaning of a text. The general text institutes a ruling that embodies the will of the legislator, and if subsequent practices were permitted to change or amend general texts, it would eventually change the legislative intent of sharīʿah. The jurists often use the example of currencies in contractual agreements, which are customarily taken to refer to the currencies in circulation at the time of the contract in question. Similarly, in matters related to sharīʿah, only the antecedent or concurrent practices have to be considered.

Al-Rāzī (d. AH 606/1209 CE) differentiates between three types of customary practices relative to a general text. The first includes the practices that were known to the Prophet and although they might not have been in agreement with a general text, the Prophet did not condemn them. These practices are to be upheld on the basis of the Prophet's tacit approval. The second category comprises the practices that were not known to the Prophet because they developed after his death. These practices are to be upheld only by means of a juristic consensus. Their approval would be founded on the juristic consensus rather than the practical custom. The third type includes the practices about which it is not definitively known whether the Prophet knew about them or not. This type of custom should be subjected to extensive juristic scrutiny until its status is verified; consequently, its capacity to particularize the general text remains questionable at best. Al-Rāzī's classification indicates that customary practices cannot particularize the general texts of sharīʿah on their own. Such practices would need to be supported by other stronger types of evidence such as a sunnah that denotes the approval of the Prophet or a juristic consensus that ensures that the practice in question does not conflict with the other rulings of sharīʿah.[48] Al-Rāzī's sceptical attitude towards the role of custom in the particularization of texts is indicated by his inclusion of *ʿādāt* among the conjectural means of particularization.[49]

Generally speaking, the jurists divided the particularizing proofs into two main types: connected and disconnected.[50] The former refers mainly to the particles that denote either an exception (*istithnāʾ*) or a condition (*sharṭ*). They are described as connected because they are usually attached to the ruling or statement in question. The latter type refers to the independent proofs that are external to the ruling or statement. This latter type is further divided into textual and nontextual proofs. The textual proofs refer to the Qurʾān and ḥadīth. The nontextual proofs include reason (*ʿaql*) and sense-based knowledge (*ḥiss*).[51] While some jurists, such as al-Rāzī, separated these two categories, others included the sense-based knowledge in the category of reason. The examples given occasionally make it difficult to determine the category to which they belong.[52] Al-Qarāfī referred to them (*ʿaql* and *ḥiss*) as two separate categories and added three more: reality (*wāqiʿ*), circumstantial evidences (*qarāʾin al-aḥwāl*), and customary practices (*ʿawāʾid*). Al-Qarāfī used these three categories to refer to the range of possible "implied" information of a text. Although this type of information is not explicitly stated in the text, it is clearly understood from the person's knowledge of the context. Such knowledge is usually assumed to fill gaps and indicate necessary unsupplied details.

What is interesting to note here is that while al-Qarāfī included customary practices among the disconnected particularizing proofs,[53] he—following al-Rāzī's typology—counted them among the conjectural means of particularization.[54] He used the plural form *ʿawāʾid* in the former case and the other plural form *ʿādāt* in the latter case. Al-Qarāfī's treatment of the issue reveals that in order for customary practices to function as valid particularizing proofs, they need to satisfy two main conditions. First, they have to be concurrent with the text in question. Antecedent, discontinued, and subsequent customs cannot particularize general statements. He repeatedly uses the examples of contracts, wills, and endowment documents—which have to be interpreted according to concurrent customary practices only. Similarly, sharīʿah texts are to be interpreted according to concurrent practices commonly known at the time of the Prophet only.[55] The second condition is that it has to be a linguistic convention, not a practical custom. He goes to great length on this point and even cites some earlier sources indicating that this point was decided by means of a juristic consensus.[56]

Some later commentators[57] differentiated between two cases of custom relative to the founding texts. The first refers to a custom that remained in existence although it was in conflict with a text embodying a general ruling. Example of this type include the cases of *salam* and *ʿarāyā*.[58] These transactions are considered exceptions to general rulings conveyed by general texts. The questions debated among these later commentators were: Would custom in this case particularize the general text? Would this particular customary practice be considered an exception to the general ruling? Would that ruling remain applicable to other cases (excluding the excepted case[s])? Or, conversely, would the general ruling remain effective even as far as the custom in question is concerned? Generally speaking, answers to these questions relied on al-Rāzī's triple classification of custom relative to the founding texts.

The second case refers specifically to the antecedent customary practice that may qualify the meaning or scope of the text. For example, the people of Madinah at the time of the Prophet considered wheat, which was commonly referred to as *ṭaʿām* (food), as the common foodstuff. In the analysis of the ḥadīth prohibiting usurious food transactions, the question that was debated was whether the prohibitive command referred to all types of food (the literal meaning) or to wheat only (the meaning according to the customary practice). It is on this precise point that the Ḥanafī jurists disagreed with the majority view. They chose to interpret the word food as referring to wheat only, according to the common usage of the people of Madinah. The majority of jurists, on the other hand, held that the word refers to any type of food because limiting its meaning to wheat would amount to forcing an arbitrary restriction on the legislative intent of the Lawgiver.

These two cases pertain mostly to the practices that preceded the founding texts. The subsequent practices are generally considered ineffective and therefore cannot particularize the general rulings embodied in those texts, in cases of conflict between the two. Some jurists argued that if a certain ruling was originally founded on a customary practice, such ruling would change if these practices changed. This view finds its strongest support in the famous opinion of Abū Yūsuf on the six items mentioned in the ḥadīth of usury (gold, silver, wheat, barley, dates, and salt). The majority view was that since the text indicated the units of measurement for these items were weight for both gold and silver and volume for the four remaining items, such means of measurement shall remain effective indefinitely. Abū Yūsuf, on the other hand, argued that in this ḥadīth the Prophet merely cited the units of measurement that were commonly known and used in Madinah; therefore, they may change if such customary practice changes.[59] Abū Yūsuf's opinion is meant to apply solely in cases where the original ruling was based on a customary practice, as indicated in the example. The jurists usually emphasize this qualification to rule out the possibility that customs turn into loopholes to circumvent textually based laws.

Contrary to the dominant view of the distinction between linguistic conventions and practical customs, al-Qarāfī strongly argued that only linguistic conventions can particularize the general ruling. He noted that the examples that many jurists gave for practical customs are essentially examples of linguistic conventions. His argument is based on the view that only linguistic conventions can turn literal meanings into conventional meanings, without the need for circumstantial or contextual evidence (*qarīnah*).[60] This particular feature is missing in the practical custom, which does not affect the literal meaning of texts.[61] As noted earlier, this view of al-Qarāfī echoes the famous disagreement on the role of customs in the particularization of texts or rulings. While the majority of jurists accepted only linguistic conventions, the Ḥanafī jurists, and some Mālikī jurists, upheld practical customs as well.[62] Al-Qarāfī, however, goes one step further by contesting the status of what many jurists identified as practical customs, which, for him, were nothing but linguistic conventions.

## Conclusion

The treatment of the concept of custom within the main framework of legal theory as it developed in the post-classical period can be located in three main areas: *qiyās*, *istidlāl*, and *takhṣīṣ*. Undoubtedly, these are broad themes; within each of them there are many school-specific details. The goal of this chapter was to identify the general development of the concept within the general theory of sources rather than underscore particular treatments or interschool variations.

*Qiyās* has traditionally been the most comprehensive module within the mainstream legal theory. It was the main channel through which new ideas were introduced and many *ʿurf*-related discussions were undertaken within its framework . For example, the jurists examined the question of whether determinations based on custom can be extrapolated to comparable cases through *qiyās*. Most of the *ʿurf*-related discussions, however, were associated with the verification of the operative cause, the most subtle among the pillars of *qiyās*. Prior to its emergence as one of the secondary sources, *ʿurf* was used as one of the means for the evaluation of the operative cause, which connects the two major parts of *qiyās*: the source and the derivative.

Similarly, in the cases of *istidlāl* and *takhṣīṣ*, *ʿurf* was invoked repeatedly to ensure that legal methods and procedures remain tied to actual practice. The constructions of *istidlāl* ranged from treating it as a process (seeking evidence) to treating it as an independent category (fifth source). In both cases, the development of *istidlāl* was an important turning point in the development of the concept of *ʿurf*. *Takhṣīṣ* was one of the important hermeneutical procedures that were important for determining the proper scope of texts, whether it should be tied exclusively to its original context or, conversely, it could be extended to comparable contexts. The jurists used *ʿurf*, among several other mechanisms, to answer this question. They distinguished between antecedent and concurrent *ʿurf* on the one hand, and subsequent *ʿurf* on the other. They also distinguished between linguistic conventions and practical customs. While concurrent linguistic conventions were unanimously approved as possible particularizers, antecedent and subsequent linguistic conventions—as well as practical customs—were subjects of a great deal of disagreement. In the following chapters, I focus on the development of *ʿurf* within particular genres, both juristic and substantive, that arose during the post-classical period. Chapters 6 and 7 deal with legal maxims and objectives of sharīʿah and chapter 8 deals with the literature on *fatāwā* and *qaḍāʾ*.

# Chapter 6

# Custom and Legal Maxims
## *al-Qawāʿid al-Fiqhiyyah*

Legal maxims constitute one of the main genres that illustrate the prominent role of custom in both legal theory and practice in the post-classical period. That this genre started to take shape and assume independent existence during this period does not mean that it did not exist prior to this point in time. As noted earlier, the emergence of new ideas and classification systems within any field of knowledge often represents a new development rather than a sudden or isolated eruption. New ideas and classifications come as extensions or reactions to or substitutes for earlier ones. The development of legal maxims, therefore, highlights one of the important features of the Islamic legal tradition, which is its cumulative growth.

In this chapter I give a brief overview of the history of this genre with a special focus on the different ways in which the concept of custom was treated. The chapter aims to underscore the dynamic relationship between custom and legal maxims in the Islamic legal tradition by showing how the concept of *ʿurf* facilitated the consolidation of *qawāʿid*, and how *qawāʿid*, in turn, was an important turning point in the general development of *ʿurf*.

## The Development of the Genre

In the modern period, the genre of legal maxims has received increased attention since the composition of *Majallat al-Ahkām al-ʿAdliyyah*. It was written in 1286 (1870 CE) by a committee of leading Ḥanafī jurists under the auspices of the Ottoman authority. It was meant to update the applicable sharīʿah law according to the Ḥanafī school along the lines of modern European codes. The authors of the *Majallah* sifted through the major texts, glosses, and super glosses of the Ḥanafī legal corpus and formulated its rulings, mainly in the areas of personal law and transactions, in the form of general principles. The *Majallah* aimed to facilitate reference during court adjudications and, consequently, to ensure standard application of the law. Closer examination of the *Majallah* reveals that the authors sought to update the applicable Ḥanafī law in terms of form rather than content. The *Majallah* was the formal civil code in most of the Ottoman Empire and even remained as such in Palestine, Jordan, Syria, Iraq, and Libya long after the fall of the empire in 1924, until it was finally replaced by different national codes.[1] The *Majallah* opens with a list of 99 legal maxims, the guiding or constitutional principles on which the text is founded. About ten of the foundational principles deal directly with the different uses and applications of custom in Islamic law.[2] Several works were written as commentaries either on the entire text of the *Majallah*[3] or only on the introductory part that comprises these legal maxims.[4]

Although the goal of this chapter is not to trace the development of the genre of legal maxims, but rather to study how it impacted the evolution of the legal concept of *ʿurf*, it is important to outline this field's development because it in itself represents a major turning point in the history of *ʿurf* as an abstract legal tool. Recent studies on legal maxims point out three main stages of development that this genre underwent: rudimentary beginning, incremental growth, and finally, maturity and full-blown development.[5] This last stage is usually associated with the composition of the *Majallah*.[6]

The first stage started at the time of the Prophet and extended until the end of the third Islamic century (ninth century CE). The two founding texts of Islam, the Qur'ān and the Prophetic reports, are replete with concise statements that were often invoked in the different sections of Islamic law. While the texts of the Qur'ān and the Prophetic reports inspired many of the legal maxims, some maxims were even taken verbatim from these sources. Examples from the Qur'ān include, for instance: "Allah intends every facility for you; He does not want to put you to difficulty";[7] "If one is forced by necessity, without willful disobedience, nor transgressing due limits, then he is guiltless";[8] "On no soul does Allah place a burden greater than it can bear";[9] "He (God) has imposed no difficulties on you in religion";[10] and "Nor can a bearer of burdens bear another's burden."[11] Similarly, examples from the Prophetic reports include: "Deeds are judged by intentions (of the doers)";[12] "Leave what is doubtful for what is doubtless";[13] "Harm shall neither be inflicted nor reciprocated";[14] and "Muslims are bound to fulfill their conditions."[15]

The second and most important stage of development of the field of legal maxims—incremental growth—started in the fourth century AH (tenth century CE). In chapter 4 we referred to the two main approaches that influenced the development of Islamic jurisprudence during the formative period: the theoretical approach and the applied approach. The latter approach focused mainly on abstracting the underlying general principles that the early jurists used, mostly implicitly, while constructing the different substantive rulings. This method proved to be extremely useful, as it enabled later jurists to relate the myriad substantive details to a few general principles (*uṣūl/qawāʿid*) that can be applied in the different chapters of substantive law. This method, commonly known as *takhrīj* (extrapolation), gained increasing popularity with the gradual consolidation of the major schools of law. Gradually, each of them developed its own legal identity characterized by the methods developed by its founder. Major commentaries were written to elaborate on the considered opinions within each school, often in comparison with those of the other schools.[16] In the process, legal maxims were treated most notably under the title of *takhrīj*, but also under different other titles such as *ashbāh wa naẓā'ir*, *furūq*, *uṣūl*, and, of course, *qawāʿid*.

The earliest text that has reached us from this period is the treatise of Abū al-Ḥasan al-Karkhī (d. AH 340/951 CE), followed by the treatise of ʿUbayd Allah Ibn ʿUmar al-Dabbūsī (d. AH 430/1038 CE). Although legal historians often trace the *takhrīj* method to the early Ḥanafī school, because of the writings of these two jurists, closer examination of the early history of the other schools reveals striking parallels. The similarities became more evident during the post-classical period. For example, while al-Karkhī summed up the fundamentals of the Ḥanafī school in 38 general principles,[17] the Shāfiʿī jurist Ḥusayn al-Marwarrūdhī (d. AH 462/1069 CE) summed up the fundamentals of the Shāfiʿī school in four general principles[18] (others added yet a fifth one[19]). As legal maxims gradually developed into a well-established genre in all the major legal schools, their construction reflected both inter- and intraschool differences, though these differences remained a matter of detail—never of principle.

There is near consensus that al-ʿIzz Ibn ʿAbd al-Salām (d. AH 660/1261 CE) wrote the first fully developed work entirely devoted to the theme of legal maxims.[20] Most succeeding jurists consider him the founder of the genre.[21] In his text, Ibn ʿAbd al-Salām set the tone and established the template that later jurists followed and developed further. His treatment shifted the structure of these maxims, one that was formally legalistic into one that was more objective-oriented. We deal with this point in more detail in the next chapter.[22]

## *ʿUrf* and the Criteria for the Evaluation of Benefits

The main goal that Ibn ʿAbd al-Salām set for his book was highlighting the benefits of following the commands of sharīʿah, as well as the consequences of violating them. He holds that sharīʿah seeks either to achieve a benefit or to circumvent a harm, both of which could either be direct or indirect, of this world or the next.[23] He uses different criteria to evaluate and distinguish the benefits and harms of this world from those of the afterlife. The benefits and harms of the afterlife should be evaluated solely on the basis of the clear textual indicators (a reference in the Qurʾān, authentic Sunnah, valid consensus, or sound analogy).

The benefits and harms of this world, on the other hand, should be evaluated on the basis of human judgment. That includes necessary knowledge, experience, customs, and considered probabilities (*al-ẓunūn al-muʿtabarāt*).[24] Ibn ʿAbd al-Salām's emphasis on considered probabilities accords completely with the jurists' general juristic assertion that most of the substantive rulings are based on them.[25] People trust these probabilities because they have ordinarily been validated by the well-established norms and recurrent events (habits) in this world.[26] For example, communal trust is based on the principle that people are presumed honest until the opposite is proven. Overlooking this general principle would significantly undermine the social capital that is indispensable for effective social interaction.[27]

Ibn ʿAbd al-Salām constantly draws a distinction between the domain of the absolute (God), which includes such things as the afterlife (*ākhirah*) and the unknown (*ghayb*), and the domain of the relative (human), which includes this world and the human experience of it.[28] He does not suggest a complete divorce between these two domains; there are areas that belong, concurrently, to both of them.[29] He suggests, however, that a distinction can normally be made between them and that their respective benefits and harms require different types of evaluation criteria.

There is a close connection between this issue and the debate over the proper scope of both reason and revelation on the question of moral epistemology (commonly discussed in terms known as *ḥusn* and *qubḥ* [beauty and ugliness]).[30] Ibn ʿAbd al-Salām emphasized the role of reason not only in evaluating the benefits and harms of this world but in evaluating the veracity of religion itself, let alone the benefits and harms prior to the advent of religion in general.[31] For him, there is a clearly recognizable affinity between the commands of sharīʿah and rational reasoning, unless the religious command pertains to the limited area of devotional deeds that aims to achieve full and unquestionable compliance with the divine commands (*taʿabbud*).

Ibn ʿAbd al-Salām closes this difficult question by arguing that moral judgments based on rational reasoning are applicable only to human action, which is conditioned by the human experience. This is borne out by the efficacy of causes (*asbāb*),[32] which God has consistently and recurrently linked to their expected effects. Such moral judgments are inapplicable, however, to the domain of divine action, which is governed solely by God's absolute will and power.[33] In other words, although it is perfectly valid to apply descriptions of justice, injustice, beauty, and ugliness to human action according to rational reasoning as tested and verified by the established norms and the recurrent habits in this world, it would be inappropriate to apply the same standards to the domain of divine action, for God is neither bound nor limited by the boundaries of this world.

## Types of Indicators

Ibn ʿAbd al-Salām divides the indicators into two main types: textual (*sharʿiyyah*) and contextual (*wuqūʿ*).[34] The first refers to the legal sources of sharīʿah: the Qur'ān, authentic Sunnah of the Prophet, consensus of the jurists, legal analogy, and *istidlāl*. The second type refers to the fulfillment of the conditions (*shurūṭ*) on which rulings are dependant. The fulfillment of these conditions can be known with certainty or at least with varying degrees of probability. One example of certain fulfillment is the proper timing of the five daily prayers. The valid performance of a prayer depends on it being performed within its proper timeframe. Examples of probable fulfillment of conditions are numerous and most of them depend on the common customary practice. For example, acceptance of the testimony of witnesses requires the verification of their uprightness. The verification of such uprightness can be evaluated in light of the common standards or practices.[35]

Al-ʿAlā'ī (d. AH 761/1359 CE) expanded the typology of Ibn ʿAbd al-Salām by adding a third type, evidentiary indicators of proper disposition (*taṣarruf*).[36] This third type deals with the ways and means of establishing proper evidence, especially before a judge. These indicators are again divided into "agreed upon" and "disputed." The first entails either admission (*iqrār*) the testimony of two upright male witnesses or one male witness with two female witnesses. The second includes a witness with an oath (of the claimant), the oath of the claimant together with the defendant's refusal to take an oath, or four female witnesses.[37] The textual indicators are to be used by competent jurists who can extract the rulings from the different sources of sharīʿah. Individual Muslims can use the contextual indicators to verify the fulfillment of the conditions (of the different rulings). The evidentiary indicators are mostly for the use of judges when analyzing claims and settling disputes.[38]

## Scattered Implications of *ʿUrf* in Substantive Law

The jurists often emphasize that the ability to extract or abstract legal maxims comes only after thorough examination of the entire corpus of substantive law. Only through extensive study of the different aspects of the legal corpus can a jurist develop the skill to detect the latent foundational principles that permeate the entire system.

In their search for the underlying foundational principles of Islamic law, the jurists collected the different cases that share common features, regardless of the actual sections to which these cases belong. As mentioned earlier, this approach emerged after the major unabridged commentaries within each school were written and a new method was needed to navigate through the ever expanding legal corpus. The two works of Ibn ʿAbd al-Salām and Ibn al-Wakīl (d. AH 716/1316 CE) in particular offer examples of how this method started.[39] Although their successors credited Ibn ʿAbd al-Salām and Ibn al-Wakīl with being pioneering figures in this area,[40] their works lack the well-organized format that characterize the subsequent works on legal maxims.

Ibn ʿAbd al-Salām gave many examples of how to relate a general principle to many different cases of substantive law. One of the important principles that he singled out was the equivalence of customary implication to explicit indication.[41] The extent to which this principle pertained to many different areas of the legal system is borne out by the extended list of cases to which this principle was said to apply. Many of the cases that he used were connected to transactions. For example, the general rule in a sale or lease transaction is that unless otherwise explicitly specified, the value of a commodity or a service is presumed to be an equal (fair) price, which is to be paid in the common currency. Similarly, in a sale or lease transaction, unless otherwise explicitly specified, the inclusion or exclusion of different amenities follows the common practice.[42] By the same token, if a crop is sold or bought prematurely, it is understood, pursuant to the customary practice, that the transaction concludes only at the harvest time. Prior to this term, the maintenance of the crop remains the responsibility of the seller.[43]

Ibn ʿAbd al-Salām emphasizes the role of the customary practice in determining the proper kind and value of the different weights and measures. This is often expressed by phrases such as "equal price" (*thaman al-mithl*), "equal dowry" (*mahr*), "equal measure" (*miqdār*), and "equal compensation" (*ujrah*).[44] Similarly, the average (*ghālib*) measure, amount, size, or foodstuff (*qūt*) is known by reference to the common customary practice. This is particularly important in questions that pertain to the payment of different kinds of alms and other types of monetary transactions.[45]

Apart from the different cases of transactions, Ibn ʿAbd al-Salām uses the common customary practice as an indicator of accepted social behavior. For example, it is acceptable for a Muslim to enter public premises or a place such as a mosque or a school without permission, on the basis of the implicit customary indication that such permission is not needed. On the other hand, it is not acceptable for a Muslim to enter a non-Islamic place of worship such as a church or a synagogue without permission, again on the basis of the implicit customary indication that prior permission would be required.[46] Recourse to such tangible indicators is important in many cases that depend on personal judgment. For example, while there are several texts in sharīʿah that urge hospitality towards guests, the application of such instruction ultimately remains a matter of personal judgment. Ibn ʿAbd al-Salām goes to great length to explain what constitutes a socially acceptable behavior, either as a host or as a guest, on the basis of the common customary practice.[47]

## Customary Permission and Customary Condition

As a general rule, each individual enjoys full and complete freedom of action in what pertains to his or her property. However, such freedom ends or becomes subject to clear legal stipulation as soon as another person's rights are involved. In order for a person to act on behalf of another, legal authorization must be secured, either in the form of explicit permission indicating consent or by proxy—as is the case with minors. The jurists, however, spoke about certain cases in which a person can act on behalf of another person even without the latter's permission. These cases depend on the implicit customary permission (*al-idhn al-ʿurfī*). The implicit customary permission is predicated on the premise that people are presumed to cooperate with each other in good faith and preserve each other's rights and interests, especially in cases of emergency. For example, if a person breaks into his neighbor's house to put out a fire or to save a life, he will not be legally liable for the damages that he causes in order to fulfill such a goal.[48] Similarly, in every valid contract, certain conditions are presumed to apply on the basis of implicit customary practices (*sharṭ ʿurfī*). For example, a sale contract assumes that unless otherwise indicated, the parties agree that the price is to be paid according to the common currency. It also assumes that both the payment of the price and the handing over of the sold item occur at the conclusion of the agreement.[49]

Despite the importance of the implicit customary indication and its extensive use in the different areas of substantive law, Ibn ʿAbd al-Salām asserts that it remains weaker than the explicit indication. In other words, the explicit indication trumps the implicit customary indication, especially in cases of conflict. This is, however, subject to an important qualification. Implicit customary indication falls into two main categories. The first is what is deemed indispensable either by sharīʿah or intuition, and the second is its opposite. The first is treated as a necessary condition even if it is not expressly indicated. For example, an agreement that involves a violation of an obligatory requirement, such as the five daily prayers, would be considered invalid. Similarly, an agreement that includes a condition that is impossible to fulfil, such as a provision to work continuously without sleep for two months, would be invalid. Both these cases involve violations of strong implicit conditions within a valid contract. The first violates the implicit condition of non-contradiction of shariʿah (*al-sharṭ al-sharʿī*), and the second violates the implicit condition of non-contradiction with accepted social norms (*al-sharṭ al-ʿurfī*).

Conversely, a contract that includes a condition of the non-performance of a supererogatory devotional deed would be valid. Unlike a religious duty, a supererogatory deed is merely recommended; therefore, failure to observe such a deed would not amount to a major violation of sharīʿah. So also is a contract that involves a difficult condition, such as continuous work for one or two consecutive days. According to the common customary practice, although such a condition is difficult, it would not be impossible to abide by.[50]

## Jurisprudential Maxims and Substantive Maxims

Ibn ʿAbd al-Salām's book comprised both jurisprudential (*uṣūliyyah*) and substantive, (*fiqhiyyah*) maxims. The former address different aspects that pertain to the sources and the way they should be interpreted and applied. In other words, they deal with issues that belong to Islamic legal theory proper. The latter, on the other hand, deal with patterns that recur in the different areas of substantive law, on the basis of which generalizations can be made. Clear distinctions between these two types of maxims were stressed only in the later stages of the history of the genre.[51]

The famous Mālikī jurist Shihāb al-Dīn al-Qarāfī (d. AH 648/1250 CE) was probably the first to emphasize this distinction.[52] The treatment of custom within the legal maxims genre varies, therefore, depending on the particular focus of the maxims in question. Jurisprudential maxims, for example, highlight the relationship between custom as a source of law and other sources. They also focus on a host of linguistic and hermeneutical issues that are traditionally treated within the jurisprudential literature. Substantive maxims, on the other hand, focus on the different applications of custom and the general principles underlying these applications.

Like Ibn ʿAbd al-Salām, Ibn al-Wakīl mixed both the jurisprudential and the substantive maxims. He started with a general principle that governs the interpretation of the founding texts. Such interpretation should follow a four-step hierarchical scheme that starts with the sharʿī convention, followed by the customary convention, then the linguistic convention, and finally, the allegorical convention. In other words, upon examining a founding text, the jurist should begin by investigating whether sharīʿah has an idiosyncratic meaning for the context in question. If the context involves terms with specific sharʿī connotations, such as prayer, fasting, and pilgrimage, they should be interpreted according to the idiom of sharīʿah. Ibn al-Wakīl here reiterates the juristic discussion over the question of signification (*dalālah*), which the jurists divided into the four categories. The choice of any of these categories follows a hierarchical order of precedence beginning with the sharʿī connotation and ending with the allegorical connotation. Customary interpretation, however, has to be further analyzed in order to determine the type and the scope of the custom. This includes, for example, whether it is the current custom at the time of the Prophet or the current (contemporary) custom and whether it is a general custom or a specific custom.[53] The application of the allegorical connotation depends on contextual evidence (*qarīnah*) that justifies choosing it over the other three (real) connotations.[54]

From the many cases that Ibn al-Wakīl listed as examples involving reference to the customary practice, he singled out the issue of oaths. The jurists have consistently highlighted the role of custom in the interpretation of oaths to such extent that the interpretation of oaths is generally considered solely based on custom.[55] In sharīʿah, oaths are not merely an issue of pure religious import but they can also have serious civil consequences, as is often the case with oaths associated with divorce statements.[56] Therefore, the utterance of certain phrases socially identified as synonymous with the divorce formula can have the same effect as the divorce formula within this social context, but not in others.[57]

Ibn al-Wakīl underscores the importance of the common customary practice as a tangible criterion in the absence of a clear indication in sharīʿah. One case, for example, is the definition of the concept of "separation" (*tafarruq*) at the conclusion of an agreement. With minor interschool differences, the classical jurists observed that an agreement cannot be finalized as long as its parties remained in the session, without separation. Many scholars interpreted separation according to the common customary practice which could be physical departure or a symbolic gesture such as shaking hands or uttering certain phrases. Determining the exact time of separation, therefore, is significant because of the ensuing consequences. As long as the parties remain in the session before separation, they have the freedom to revoke the transaction according to *khiyār al-majlis*.[58] By the same token, the common customary practice is considered the criterion to determine the defects that validate a claim to revoke a transaction and return the defective (sold) item according to *khiyār al-ʿayb*.[59] In other words, in order for *khiyār al-ʿayb* to be invoked, it has to be proven that pursuant to the common customary practice, the item in question is presumed to be free from such defects, which means that these defects are customarily recognized as justifying the revocation of the transaction.

Similarly, Ibn al-Wakīl refers to the use of the common customary practice as a criterion to specify the limit of the small quantities or amounts that people often share freely (*muḥaqqirāt*). While some scholars held that such amounts are measured by the limit at which the punishment for theft (*niṣāb al-sariqah*) becomes applicable, others held that it is set according to the common customary practice. This is also the case with determining the limit of the insignificant impurity, the frequency of movement that would nullify prayer, and the average of solvency and insolvency in matters related to payments and expenditures, among many others.[60]

The jurists often refer to a long list of the substantive cases that depend on the common customary practice. We can group these cases into four main categories. The first includes cases that involve estimating the proper age, time, length, or measure. Examples would include the age of menstruation and its duration as well as the terms of pregnancy and confinement.[61] As a general rule, unless otherwise clearly specified in sharīʿah, the jurists would refer to the common custom as an important factor in estimating these variables.[62] The second category includes cases that pertain to financial transactions, such as the means of payment, the proper amount (fee, wage, compensation), signs indicating transfer of ownership (hand, movement, evacuation), and the inclusion or exclusion of certain amenities. The third category includes cases pertaining to proper social manners such as times of visitation and the etiquette governing exchange of gifts. The fourth category pertains to the interpretation of linguistic expressions, including contracts, wills, endowment deeds, and oaths.

Based on their analysis of these and other similar cases, the jurists laid down some rules to guide the investigation into some key questions. The discussions over these questions in the later works can be seen as a refined restatement of earlier discussions in the two most important genres in the Islamic legal tradition, namely, substantive law and legal theory. For example, one of these questions was about the relationship between custom, repetition, and recurrence. The word *custom* by itself denotes the notion of repetition, but the question that was raised was about the criterion for differentiating between a merely repeated action and a consistent recurrent custom. The rule they established was that a particular custom can be considered as an implicit condition only when it becomes acknowledged as recurrent. In other words, the recognition of a custom depends not only on the *existence* of recurrence, but also on the *common recognition* of such recurrence. If proven recurrent, a custom will be accepted as valid; otherwise, it will be subject to further qualification. For example, if a contract does not specify the currency, it will be interpreted as referring to the common currency, if there is only one currency commonly accepted as the standard means of payments. If, however, there is more than one currency in circulation, the agreement must explicitly specify the intended currency.[63]

## Legal Maxims and the Deep Structure

We noted earlier that the development of the genre of legal maxims followed the consolidation of the famous legal schools. This consolidation was marked by the emergence of a clear sense of school identity, shaped by the unique ideological structure of each of them. The school's ideological structure comprised a set of key components such as a body of founding texts ascribed to the founder of the school or his immediate disciples, detailed and exhaustive commentaries on these texts written by the school's recognized authorities, and finally, a successive chain of jurists that facilitated the uninterrupted transmission of the school's teachings to the succeeding generations. This general pattern can be easily found in each of the four major Sunnī schools. In fact, the survival of these particular schools was, to a large extent, a function of this pattern. Other schools that failed to develop this pattern could not compete and eventually disappeared.

The example of the Mālikī jurist Shihāb al-Dīn al-Qarāfī is instructive. After writing one of the most acclaimed commentaries on the Mālikī substantive law, *al-Dhakhīrah*, he noted that the scattered cases of the law are linked to a set of foundational principles that together constitute the underlying structure of the legal system.[64] In a pioneering work, he collected these foundational principles and sought to explain the subtle distinctions and differences among them. Al-Qarāfī highlighted the role of the common customary practice in charging certain linguistic expressions with specific legal connotations.[65] As mentioned earlier, this is particularly critical in cases such as sale transactions and divorce statements. In general, the jurists adopted the linguistic distinction between a non-initiating statement (*khabar*) and an initiating statement (*inshā'*). Al-Qarāfī argued that to a large extent the distinction between these two categories is customary; custom transforms a certain expression from the domain of *khabar* to the domain of *inshā'* in what is known as "customary transformation" (*naql 'urfī*).[66]

*Khabar* statements can be described as either true or false. *Inshā'* statements, on the other hand, cannot be described as either true or false: whether the statement is a command (both affirmative and negative), an expression denoting hope (*tarajjī*), or an interjection. There was disagreement on other categories such as oaths and certain contractual expressions that denoted sale or purchase. Al-Qarāfī argued that these contested categories were originally non-initiating statements that common practice transformed into initiating statements. The most important distinction between these two types is that while a non-initiating statement simply conveys a meaning, the initiating statement creates such meaning.

The criterion that al-Qarāfī uses to prove this customary transformation is not limited to mere frequency of use. As noted earlier, the repeated use of a certain expression in a certain sense does not by itself indicate a permanent change of the meaning, unless it is customarily recognized as such.[67] Al-Qarāfī concludes that rulings pertaining to these customary expressions follow the social context within which they acquired their meanings.[68] If these expressions change their customary connotations, the rulings associated with them would consequently change to reflect that.

The most prominent examples that al-Qarāfī uses are the oaths associated with different divorce expressions and how these expressions or their interpretations differ from one place to another.[69]

## The Five Cardinal Maxims

Most of the sources agree that the origin of what has become known as the "five cardinal maxims" can be traced back to a quote from the famous Shāfiʿī jurist Ḥusayn al-Marwarrūdhī (d. AH 462/1069 CE).[70] Many jurists took issue with limiting the foundational principles to five, arguing that this means that they are the most important ones. The Shāfiʿī jurist Ṣalāḥ al-Dīn Khalīl Kikaldī al-ʿAlāʾī was probably the one who devised the famous classification scheme that later works on legal maxims adopted and extended. This scheme consisted of a few cardinal maxims and other more general ones.[71] What is of most interest to us here is that custom has consistently been counted as one (usually the fifth) of those cardinal maxims.[72]

Al-ʿAlāʾī starts his treatment of the fifth maxim by underscoring the Qurʾānic foundations of the concept of custom. Interestingly, these citations refer to passages that do not include direct reference to the words *ʿurf* and *maʿrūf*. For example, in verse 13:38, the Qurʾān refutes the disbelievers' argument that a true Prophet should not be human.[73] The verse points out that all earlier prophets were human, and, except for Jesus, they got married and had families. Al-ʿAlāʾī's point is that the Qurʾān referred to a recurrent custom to support an argument. By the same token, in verse 28:58 the Qurʾān instructs adults to teach children and minors about the importance of seeking permission before entering private chambers at the times when people are accustomed to take rest. The Qurʾān specifies three times: before dawn, at noon, and after the night prayer. Al-ʿAlāʾī comments that by citing these three time periods, which were identified as regular rest times, the Qurʾān is pointing out the importance of acknowledging the common customary practice.

Similarly, Al-ʿAlāʾī investigated the foundations of the concept of custom in the Sunnah of the Prophet. For example, in one report the Prophet explained that people should use the weight units common in Makkah and the volume measures common in Madinah.[74] The reason given was that Makkah was a famous trading center, and its weight units were quite well-known across most trading circles. Madinah, on the other hand, was famous as a major agricultural center whose volume measuring units were also quite well-known in Arabia. Similarly, in another report, the Prophet drew the limits of responsibility in cases involving animal trespassing. He explained that landlords should safeguard their properties during daytime and animal owners should safeguard their animals during the night.[75] Therefore, the establishment of guilt or negligence would be based on this principle. Al-ʿAlāʾī explained that in these two reports the Prophet based his decisions on well-known customary practices and thereby set an important precedent to be followed in similar cases.[76]

After al-ʿAlāʾī, most of the succeeding jurists followed the same approach in their treatment of legal maxims within the framework of their respective schools. From that moment on, maxims were classified into two main categories. The first included a few overarching maxims that permeate the deep structure of the entire legal corpus and the second included many minor maxims that address particular details in the different chapters of substantive law.[77]

The gradual evolution of the concept of custom within the genre of legal maxims began with the scattered applications in substantive law. The numerous references to a number of foundational principles in the different substantive discussions inspired efforts to abstract these underlying foundational principles, which can be easily extrapolated to other comparable situations. It was particularly in this last phase that *ʿurf* emerged as an independent analytical tool that, together with the other foundational principles, informed the legal system and enabled it to address the changing needs of social reality.

# Chapter 7

# Custom and the Objectives of Sharīʿah

## *Maqāṣid al-Sharīʿah*

The word *maqāṣid* is the Arabic plural form of *maqṣid* and means "objective, intent, or goal." As a legal genre, the objectives of sharīʿah refer to a body of literature that explores the goals sharīʿah seeks to achieve. The roots of this genre originated in the primary sources of Islamic law, which comprised statements indicating the purposes behind certain commands or stipulations. The Qur'an, for example, states that the purpose behind the obligation of fasting is the achievement of righteousness.[1] It also states that the purpose behind retribution is the achievement of deterrence, which in turn leads to the protection of life.[2] Because the purposes that the lawgiver intended for the different rulings are not always stated explicitly in the texts, the jurists seek to uncover these purposes and ensure their incorporation in legal constructions. In looking for clues and signs of such implicit purposes, the jurists are guided by the other explicit ones.

In this chapter, I use the term *legal objectives* not only to refer to a specific legal genre but also to a specific approach within legal theory that sought to view, and even reconstruct, the entire legal process from the perspective of its purported objectives. It assumes that behind the letter of a law there is a higher purpose that this law aims to achieve. Accordingly, legal theory should not be exclusively devoted to the formal deduction or construction of rulings from the sources. Deep within the diverse textual indicators, there is a uniform legal structure that the jurist should reflect in the individual rulings that he constructs. This approach started within the various legal genres before it gradually developed into a subfield within Islamic legal theory. For our purposes, focusing on this genre is important because of its connection with the question of legal philosophy. It was in this genre that Muslim jurists examined the rationale behind the law as well as its relationship with other social institutions. In particular, they investigated the relationship of mutual influence between law and custom.

In keeping with the main subject of this research, I focus on how the concept of custom was used in the debates over the objectives of sharīʿah and how these debates contributed to the consolidation of the concept of custom. As noted earlier, although the early precursors of the genre of legal objectives existed in the early stages of the Islamic legal tradition, it started to take independent shape in its later stages. The famous Andalusian jurist Abū Isḥāq al-Shāṭibī (d. AH 790/1388 CE) is unanimously recognized as the formal founder of the genre. Historians of the Islamic legal tradition recognize that many legal theorists such as al-Juwaynī, al-Ghazālī, Ibn ʿAbd al-Salām, and al-Qarāfī preceded al-Shāṭibī in calling for a more objective-oriented approach within legal theory. Still, al-Shāṭibī is generally considered the main figure who, almost single-handedly, synthesized the contributions of his predecessors and formulated a fully developed theory of the objectives of sharīʿah in his famous work *al-Muwafaqāt*.[3] This chapter focuses primarily on al-Shāṭibī's treatment of *maqāṣid al-sharīʿah* and demonstrates how deeply ingrained the concept of custom is within his legal framework. Before examining al-Shāṭibī's synthesis in more detail, I give a brief outline of the genre prior to al-Shāṭibī and examine how the concept of custom figured in the pre-Shāṭibī treatment of the objectives of sharīʿah.

## *Maqāṣid* in Legal Theory

One of the main concerns that occupied Muslim jurists throughout the extended history of the Islamic legal tradition was the search for the definitive principles of sharīʿah. From the very beginning they were aware that they could not completely eliminate disagreements and differences on most of the substantive law issues simply because the rulings pertaining to these issues are often based on preponderant probability rather than absolute certainty.[4] The underlying assumption behind this constant search for definitive principles was that such principles, if found, could potentially eliminate or at least minimize disagreement. In fact, that was the impetus behind the development of Islamic legal theory as a field of research completely independent from substantive law. It was meant to provide the competent jurist with the necessary tools and guidelines to facilitate the analysis of the texts and consequently the development of a uniform method for the construction of substantive rulings. Although the goal was not achieved completely, the search for these definitive principles never stopped. In the previous chapters we saw many of the efforts to reach this goal through the example of legal maxims (*qawāʿid fiqhiyyah*).

If the genre of legal maxims aimed to abstract the foundational principles that underlie the countless questions of substantive law, the objectives (*maqāṣid*) of sharīʿah genre aimed to justify these foundational principles by investigating the wisdom behind them and by relating them to the intent of the lawgiver. More particularly, it aimed to uncover the universal principles (*kulliyāt*) that the lawgiver intended to emphasize by instituting sharīʿah. Both these genres, maxims and objectives, represent the efforts of Muslim legal theorists to systematically abstract the main principles that constitute the *spirit* of the Islamic legal system. Ultimately, a *maqāṣid*-based approach sought to approximate the universal principles as embodied in the fundamentals of sharīʿah and ensure that the different substantive rulings are in harmony with them.

Before al-Shāṭibī, several legal theorists discussed the notion of objectives as embodied in the fundamentals of sharīʿah with varying degrees of detail. One of the earliest attempts was by al-Juwaynī, who spoke of the three fundamental categories of sharīʿah: necessities, needs, and embellishments.[5] From the time of al-Juwaynī onwards, the subject underwent several developments. Because the ultimate purpose of sharīʿah was perceived to be the achievement of the benefits of people, the jurists applied the same classification of the fundamentals to the benefits. Al-Ghazālī, for example, spoke of three types of benefits: necessary, complementary, and embellishing.[6] The necessary benefits amount to the protection of five fundamental categories, *al-ḍarūriyyāt al-khams*, (religion, life, intellect, progeny, and wealth) and the complementary and embellishing benefits, supplement them.[7] The juristic treatment of the concept of benefits or interests (*maṣāliḥ*) continued to evolve in two main contexts. The first was the verification of the operative cause in analogical reasoning (*qiyās*), especially under the concept of relevance (*munāsabah*).[8] The second was the disputed secondary source of public interest (*istiṣlāḥ* or *maṣlaḥah mursalah*).[9] Al-Shāṭibī collated the different treatments of the concept of public interest and reformulated it within the general framework of a theory of sharīʿah objectives.

## *Custom in al-Shāṭibī's Theory of Objectives*

Al-Shāṭibī called for the restriction of the field of jurisprudence to the definitive foundations of sharīʿah (*uṣūl qatʿiyyah*) that are supported by the strongest types of evidence. His emphasis on and vindication of the definitiveness of these fundamental principles were meant to prove the divine origin of sharīʿah.[10] Although this conclusion is by no means new to Muslims in general and Muslim jurists in particular, what distinguishes al-Shāṭibī's approach is the method he used rather than the conclusions he reached. Other jurists argued that because sharīʿah is divine, its foundations are definitive. Al-Shāṭibī, however, reversed the argument and observed that because the foundations of sharīʿah are definitive they must be divine. But how can the definitiveness of these foundations be verified in the first place?

Al-Shāṭibī set out to survey the cardinal principles that sharīʿah strongly emphasized, placing them within a general framework of divine objectives. If sharīʿah emphasized these principles so strongly, they must reflect the purposes that the lawgiver intended. According to al-Shāṭibī, the definitiveness of the foundations of sharīʿah is anchored in multiple rational, customary, and textual indicators.[11] These foundations acquired their status and derived their authority from the collective body of evidence that supports them. Because each of these universal principles is supported by multiple types of indicators, they together constitute inductive evidence that is sufficient to denote definitiveness. It was al-Shāṭibī's championing of this inductive method that earned him the unique position he assumed in the history of the Islamic legal tradition.

Although al-Shāṭibī frequently invokes rational indicators, he does not endorse absolute reliance on rational reasoning. He supports reasoning in as much as it is needed to substantiate the textual indicators of sharīʿah.[12] He repeatedly affirms the view that in legal matters (that is, sharīʿah legal matters) reasoning is used primarily to ascertain the law, but not to prove its rationality. The law is posited on the authority of revelation, which needs no justification or rationalization. Al-Shāṭibī conceded that the argument for the definitiveness of the foundations of sharīʿah remains a religious claim. While the establishment of religious claims is based on rational verification in the first place (the domain of theology), the establishment of sharīʿah-based legal stipulations depends on definitive textual indicators (the domain of jurisprudence). In other words, while rational evidence can verify legal stipulations, the definitive textual indicators of sharīʿah must guide and inform such evidence.

It is interesting to note that al-Shāṭibī's strongest argument against unrestrained rational inference in sharīʿah matters, or even in general, is based on custom. He uses the word *custom* here to refer to practical wisdom or experiential knowledge. This knowledge is based on thorough examination of earlier nations' customs and ways of life throughout history, particularly prior to the advent of religion. He argued that this practical knowledge indicates that absolute rational deduction, independent of divine guidance, does not guarantee the attainment of sound opinions. After all, reasoning can be misused and, therefore, cannot rule out wrong conclusions. Reason alone did not protect earlier nations from erroneous opinions or improper practices. Revelation, therefore, remains the ultimate source of guidance, even when reason fails to fully understand the logic behind some of its injunctions.[13]

But if absolute reliance on reason is insufficient or questionable, textual indicators, even if successive, are based on premises that do not necessarily result in definitive knowledge. The veracity of these textual indicators is based mainly on the authority-criticism method. Here al-Shāṭibī echoes earlier legal theorists' efforts to link these successive reports to first-hand experience, which is based on sense perception, in order to eliminate all doubt about their authenticity. If it was proven that a large number of people witnessed the initial event in which the report in question originated and if a comparable number of witnesses was sustained throughout generations by multiple chains of transmitters, little doubt, if any, would remain regarding the authenticity of these reports. In fact, the authenticity of the successive report as a type of legal evidence has hardly been in doubt. Once a report was proven to have satisfied the criteria of succession (*tawātur*), it automatically ranked among the most reliable indicators (which is the case with the Qur'ān and a smaller number Prophetic reports). The real challenge, however, was determining whether particular singular reports (*āḥād*) qualified as successive or not.

The jurists managed to overcome this perennial problem through the medium of the secondary sources. In the earlier chapters we saw that the fundamental structure of Islamic legal methodology was based on four main sources and many other secondary sources. These secondary sources were largely inductive sources that were founded on a number of scattered indicators, textual and otherwise, supporting a certain principle such as equity (in the case of *istiḥsān)* or public interest (in the case of *maṣlaḥah*). The same inductive feature is clearly identifiable in blocking the means (*sadd al-dharāʾiʿ*), custom (*ʿurf*) as well as the rest of the secondary sources, although with much interschool disagreement on their order and the grounds for such order. The common denominator between these different secondary sources was the originating principle (equity, interest, etc.). If this principle was based on a non-successive report or a certain interpretation of a successive report that did not convey definitiveness, the resulting inconclusive indicator could still be supported by other similar indicators, which together would achieve definitiveness. Al-Shāṭibī resorts to this same medium—textual induction supported by rational reasoning—in formulating his theory of legal objectives. On this particular point, he comes very close to al-Juwaynī's earlier argument on the authority of juristic consensus.[14] If individual pieces of textual evidence alone do not reach the level of succession (*tawātur*) that would automatically yield definitiveness, then, in combination with other types of non-textual indicators, they will.[15]

### *The Objectives of Sharīʿah*

Al-Shāṭibī echoes Ibn ʿAbd al-Salām's argument that the ultimate objective of sharīʿah is to achieve the benefits of people both in this life and in the afterlife.[16] In order to ensure the realization of this ultimate objective, al- Shāṭibī posits several other subsidiary objectives. These subsidiary objectives include the intelligible constitution of sharīʿah, its entailment of legal injunctions (*taklīf*), and the subjection of individuals to the rule of sharīʿah to liberate them from the rule of their own desires. Closer analysis of al-Shāṭibī's elucidation of these objectives reveals that custom is central to each of these objectives.

## The Ultimate Objective: Achieving People's Benefits

Because the ultimate objective of sharīʿah is conjoined with the concept of benefits, I will start with al-Shāṭibī's characterization of the benefits and the measure he uses to evaluate them. He begins by contrasting the definitions of worldly benefits and harms with their otherworldly counterparts. While the former are relative, mixed, and impure,[17] the latter are absolute, unmixed, and pure.[18] All worldly benefits are inextricably associated with various degrees of discomfort that significantly diminish the individual's enjoyment of these benefits. This includes, for example, the effort needed not only to procure a certain benefit, but also to preserve it. The same applies to worldly harms which are often associated with various appealing temptations. This constant paradoxical association of benefits and harms, even within the same entity, often results in confusion, distraction, and misjudgment.

Consequently, this state of affairs can obscure any clear distinction between real benefits and harms. But, if worldly benefits and harms are so mixed up, what would be the ultimate evaluation criteria for these two opposite poles? Al-Shāṭibī indicates that these two categories are to be evaluated on the basis of custom. He uses *custom* here to refer to the collective wisdom, knowledge, or experience. Worldly benefits and harms are to be categorized in accordance with people's understanding of the customary benefits and harms (*al-mafhūmah ʿurfan*).[19] More particularly, in cases of uncertainty about mixed benefits or harms, the deciding factors should be determined in light of the common custom. If the beneficial considerations outweigh the harmful ones, they should assume a higher priority and vice versa. Al-Shāṭibī goes one step further by emphasizing that this characterization of both benefits and harms according to custom does not (always) conflict with sharīʿah. In stipulating the different legal injunctions, sharīʿah not only condones the customary definitions of benefits and harms, but it also often acknowledges them. Disregarding these customary benefits and harms would only diminish the applicability of legal injunctions.

Worldly benefits and harms are intrinsically mixed and confounded; but the law can make them less so. When the law upholds a benefit, it purports to achieve the beneficial elements within such a benefit. Any incidental discomfort that it may entail is not intended for its own sake. It is rather an expression of the trial factor embedded in the law. Such a factor is meant to test the individual's degree of deference to the law and sense of compliance even when it goes against his own liking.[20] But this incidental discomfort does not often exceed the customary limit that determines the difference between customary benefits and harms. Upholding the injunctions of sharīʿah is considered a benefit in view of the resultant consequences, even if these injunctions involve some elements of discomfort or inconvenience. The uncomfortable or inconvenient elements are trumped because they conflict with a superior benefit known from sharīʿah and considered, therefore, a superior and worthier objective. This clearly shows that sharīʿah's acknowledgement of customary benefits and harms is not absolute. Customary evaluation of benefits and harms is upheld as long as such evaluation does not conflict with the higher evaluation of sharīʿah.[21] Sharīʿah not only seeks to ensure the comfort and convenience borne out by the acknowledgement of the customary benefits and harms, but it seeks to balance them with the other benefits and harms of the everlasting afterlife, to which this life is only a prelude.[22]

Al-Shāṭibī's cautious attitude towards the customary definition of benefits and harms, like his reserved endorsement of reason, coincides with the Ashʿarī underpinnings of his legal methodology.[23] Therefore, he felt compelled to qualify Ibn ʿAbd al-Salām's more liberal characterization of benefits. As mentioned earlier, Ibn ʿAbd al-Salām observed that while the otherworldly benefits are exclusively known by revelation, worldly benefits can be known entirely by reason.[24] Al-Shāṭibī's point is that if sharīʿah enunciates only the otherworldly benefits, the many injunctions in sharīʿah pertaining to worldly benefits would be superfluous. Thus he takes Ibn ʿAbd al-Salām's view to mean that worldly benefits are substantiated and confirmed by reason, after they have been established by revelation.[25]

This clearly shows that the concept of custom itself is not static or fixed. It is, rather, more often flexible and fluid. For example, Ibn ʿAbd al-Salām's characterization of worldly benefits reveals that the concept of custom is very similar to—even synonymous with—the concept of reason. Al-Shāṭibī, on the other hand, uses *custom* in two main senses: practical/experiential knowledge and collective/communal knowledge. According to al-Shāṭibī, custom in the former sense results in a superior type of knowledge according to which rational conclusions must be adjusted. Following the hitherto famous three-tier classification of benefits into necessary, complementary, and embellishing, al-Shāṭibī developed a general framework of sharīʿah objectives which comprises these three types of benefits.[26] Al-Shāṭibī organized the three famous types of benefits hierarchically in terms of importance and precedence. The necessary benefits pertain to people's basic necessities that are important for their survival. All legal systems, religious or secular, strive to secure and preserve them.[27] They aim to safeguard the so-called five fundamentals: religion, life, intellect, progeny, and wealth.[28] The complementary benefits are meant to expand the scope of the necessary benefits and to redress the hardships that may incidentally ensue in particular circumstances. The embellishing benefits are meant to augment both the necessary and the complementary benefits and address luxuries that enhance the quality of life beyond the scope of the necessary and ordinary needs.

In order to connect this abstract typology of benefits to the various aspects of human life, al-Shāṭibī distinguished three main domains of activity. The first is the domain of rituals (*ʿibādāt*), which involves the various devotional deeds that the individual performs in compliance with a religious command, such as prayer, fasting, and pilgrimage. The second is the domain of customs (*ʿādāt*), which covers a vast array of activities that the individual undertakes simply as a human being such as eating, drinking, and communicating with others.[29] The third is the domain of transactions, which covers all formal agreements that people conclude in order to exchange benefits such as sales, leases, and other types of lawful contracts.

While the difference between rituals and customs is easy to identify, the difference between customs and transactions is not always as clear-cut.

After all, transactions can be viewed as a subcategory of customs in the sense just specified. On several occasions, al-Shāṭibī seems to treat it as such. The most important factor that distinguishes rituals from customs and transactions is the intention of the agent.[30] Rituals serve primarily a pure religious or transcendental objective, such as serving God, fulfilling a religious duty, or securing a heavenly reward. Ultimately, they seek to achieve full and unquestioning obedience to God (*taʿabbud*).[31] Customs and transactions, on the other hand, serve primarily an immediate or worldly objective.

Since the ultimate objective of rituals is full and unquestioning compliance with the divine command, they should not be subjected to rationalization (*taʿlīl*) or, consequently, analogical reasoning (*qiyās*).[32] The individual should not strive to uncover their goals because that, in itself, would defeat their purpose. Customs and transactions, however, are meant primarily to achieve worldly benefits. Therefore, they should be subjected to rationalization and analogical reasoning. This is particularly important in the absence of a clear stipulation in sharīʿah. In this case, the jurist embarks on the task of finding or constructing the relevant ruling while keeping in mind the ultimate objective that such a ruling should serve.[33]

This does not mean that rituals do not involve a worldly objective or that customs or transactions do not have a transcendental or an otherworldly purpose. It does mean there is a distinction between what al-Shāṭibī calls the original objective (*aṣlī*) and the ancillary objective (*tabaʿī*).[34] The original objectives of rituals are otherworldly, but they can also incidentally have worldly objectives. In fasting, for example, the individual intends to serve God but he might also fast in order to lose weight or for other health-related purposes.[35] Conversely, the original objectives of customs and transactions are immediate or worldly but they could also incidentally involve otherworldly considerations. For example, by concluding a proper sale agreement the individual seeks primarily to make a profit, but he could also seek to help others or to serve other philanthropic purposes.

Speaking of the objectives of sharīʿah in general and its connection with their rationalization or justification in particular relates to the important question of the will of the divine lawgiver and whether this will is accessible to humans.[36] Al-Shāṭibī's treatment of the objectives of sharīʿah is predicated on the view that the will of the legislator can be accessible. The most important clues as to the will of the legislator are his explicit commands and prohibitions.[37] Such clear directives express the intent behind particular legislations. Similarly, contemplating the operative causes and rationales of rulings can also reveal the legislative intent and consequently the will of the lawgiver.[38] This characterization of both the will of the legislator and the objectives of sharīʿah allows al-Shāṭibī to extract these objectives directly, when provided, and inductively, when implied, by exploring all likely indicators, textual and otherwise. This inductive process occurs within the general framework of both the ultimate and the subsidiary objectives.

The triple classification of rituals, customs, and transactions is extremely important for al-Shāṭibī. It bears not only on his treatment of the objectives of sharīʿah but of many other issues as well. For example, the famous distinction between the rights of God and the rights of human beings is based mainly on this classification.[39] Al-Shāṭibī divides rights in general into three main categories. The first is the pure right of God, which consists mainly of the devotional deeds and is based on full compliance with the divine commands. The second is the mixed right of God and the individual, in which God's share is greater. This is the case with sharīʿah-based retributions. The third is the mixed right of God and the individual, in which the individual's share is greater. This is the case with most types of transactions.[40]

Similarly, the distinction between rituals and customs bears on the two important concepts of validity (*ṣiḥḥah*) and invalidity (*buṭlān*). The meaning of validity in rituals is not the same as validity in customs or transactions. The validity of a ritual deed, for example, is dependent on the proper performance of this deed according to the sharīʿah-based instructions. Since these devotional deeds often contemplate transcendent objectives, the ultimate verification of their validity rests only with God. The validity in customs, on the other hand, requires compliance with the teachings of sharīʿah if the sharīʿah provides specific instructions for the custom in question. In transactions, validity means the fulfillment of the attendant conditions and stipulations. Because most transactions purport to achieve a worldly objective (such as transfer of ownership), the verification of their validity rests with the designated civil authority.[41]

The triple classification of benefits (necessary, complementary, and embellishing) cuts across the three domains of rituals, customs, and transactions. Necessary benefits seek to preserve the existence of the five fundamentals: religion, life, intellect, progeny, and wealth. In the area of rituals, necessary benefits include the protection of religion through stipulations of proper and improper performance of the obligatory rituals. In the area of customs, they include the protection of life and intellect through different stipulations of dietary rules as well as other basic necessities. In the area of transactions, necessary benefits include the protection of progeny and wealth through stipulations of valid and invalid contracts and agreements. Complementary benefits seek to insure the proper fulfillment of the necessary objectives both in ordinary and extraordinary circumstances.

Examples in the area of rituals include religious concessions in cases of sickness. Examples in the area of customs include the enjoyment of permissible items beyond the basic necessities. Lastly, examples in the area of transactions include cases of agreements that are considered exceptions to general rules, such as *salam*. The embellishing objectives seek to maximize ease and comfort in people's lives. In the area of rituals, embellishing objectives include the removal of impurities as well as emphasis on cleanliness and beautification. In the area of customs, they include the proper manners of eating and drinking. In the area of transactions, they include different types of dealings that fall outside the scope of both the necessary and the complementary objectives, such as the free sharing of water and basic foodstuffs.[42]

Al-Shāṭibī's theoretical model illustrates the close connection between the benefits that sharīʿah seeks to achieve (necessary, complementary, and embellishing) and the various aspects of human activity (rituals, customs, and transactions), taking into account both worldly and transcendental considerations. Each type of the benefits corresponds with a particular sphere of action and, collectively, they are meant to serve people's interests both in this world and the next—the ultimate objective behind the enforcement of sharīʿah.

## The Subsidiary Objectives

In order for the ultimate objective of sharīʿah to materialize, several other subsidiary objectives have to be realized. These subsidiary objectives support and facilitate the actualization of the ultimate objective that the lawgiver intended. Al-Shāṭibī enumerated three distinct subsidiary objectives. The first is the intelligible constitution of sharīʿah. What this means is that the legislator structured sharīʿah in such a way that it is accessible and comprehensible to the average individual. For example, sharīʿah was addressed to its immediate audience, the Arabs, not only in a language that they could understand but in a style that was familiar to them.[43] Moreover, the accessibility of the revelation meant that the average individual could understand it even without any prior formal training.

This has been the reason Islamic knowledge remained emblematically connected with the Arabic language and linguistic competency has been considered an indispensable prerequisite for Islamic education.[44]

Al-Shāṭibī goes to great length to demonstrate that the Qurʾān was addressed mainly to the general public not to the select few.[45] It is true that the learned jurists are expected, and even encouraged, to search for the deeper meanings in the text. But at the level of the obligatory requirements, all believers stand equal before the law, and all share the same responsibility to uphold it.[46] Al-Shāṭibī intended to undermine all claims of esoteric knowledge, especially those made by the Gnostic Sufis, who taught that revelation consists of an external surface addressed to the general public and a deeper core addressed to the few chosen initiates.[47] The Arabs were not seen as completely lacking in knowledge and morality.[48] Pre-Islamic Arabic culture entailed many elements that were seen as remnants of past revelation and wisdom preached by earlier prophets and wise men; the new revelation did not intend to uproot this culture, but instead incorporated commendable existing elements into the new sytem.[49] In fact, there are several legal rulings that originated in pre-Islamic Arabic customs, such as the evaluation of blood money (*diyyah*), some of the rules of inheritance, and the rituals of pilgrimage.[50]

Sharīʿah sought to amend or change the elements that were inconsistent with its moral and legal spirit. Al-Shāṭibī highlights the psychological dimension that must be contemplated in the process of introducing a new legislation. In order for such legislation to achieve its intended goals, it has to be framed in a manner consonant with the cultural milieu of the society for which it is designed.[51] Obviously, al-Shāṭibī did not intend his discussion of this point to be a mere history lesson. He included it in his book on legal theory to intimate that studying the early history of sharīʿah offers useful insights on how abstract legal principles can be translated into concrete rulings. If this was the attitude of the Prophet towards the culture and customs of his society, it is the duty of his inheritors, the learned in general and the jurists in particular, to imitate his example. Because the legal process is not a detached enterprise to be undertaken by the jurist in a remote ivory tower, because it is organically linked with the culture of the society, and because it is addressed to the general public, al-Shāṭibī argues that intelligibility of the law was an objective that the lawgiver aimed to achieve.

The second subsidiary objective that al-Shāṭibī deduced is that sharīʿah by its constitution is meant to entail legal injunctions. These injunctions are considered direct expressions of the will of the Legislator. The primary goal of individual agents, therefore, is to uphold the will of the Legislator by implementing these sharīʿah-based legal injunctions. Al-Shāṭibī strives to balance this objective of sharīʿah (imposition of legal injunctions) with the numerous other indications that imply the alleviatory purposes of sharīʿah.The Qurʾān and the Prophetic reports are replete with passages that assert the mitigatory goals of sharīʿah. These passages assert that the law is instituted primarily to achieve the benefits of people (*taḥqīq maṣāliḥ al-ʿibād*), to redress harms (*darʾ al-mafāsid*), and to remove hardship (*rafʿ al-ḥaraj*). But, if the law is designed to remove hardship, does not legal enforcement amount to hardship in the first place? Obviously, the mere notion of enforcement or obligation involves a certain degree of discomfort or inconvenience, but what is the limit at which such difficulty turns into a hardship that impedes the achievement of the higher objective(s) of the Lawgiver?

Sharīʿah seeks to enforce certain obligations, but it does not purport to impose hardship on people. Al-Shāṭibī seeks to reconcile this apparent conflict between these two implications of legal injunction in sharīʿah by appealing to the concept of custom. In this context, al-Shāṭibī uses the term *custom* in the sense of common or collective knowledge that determines the customarily accepted measure, limit, or degree. Since the idea of legal obligation by itself denotes an element of hardship, he differentiates between bearable and unbearable hardship. Unbearable hardship falls entirely beyond the capacity of the individual. For example, the denial of a basic human instinct, such as the need for food, drink, or shelter, would amount to an unbearable hardship. Sharīʿah does not involve this type of hardship for it would be inconceivable to ask people to do things that they cannot possibly do. Texts, reason, and even common sense dictate the impossibility of an injunction that involves an unbearable hardship simply because an unbearable legal obligation (*taklīf ma lā yuṭāq*) would be a contradiction in terms.[52]

Bearable hardship, on the other hand, can be undertaken, but with varying degrees of difficulty.[53] Reference to custom is made with respect to this type of hardship, which may derive from a certain action which is intrinsically difficult, especially when combined with another action. Fasting, for example, is difficult alone, but when combined with travel (or sickness), the difficulty is doubled. Sharīʿah redresses this type of hardship through the granting of concessions. In these two cases (combination of fasting with travel or sickness) the individual is permitted to forgo this injunction and compensate for it with another bearable substitution. Hardship may come not merely from an intrinsically difficult action but also from the (over)repetition of a normal action. This would be like the case of an individual who takes upon himself an intensive course of non-obligatory deeds of devotion. In these situations, sharīʿah advises moderation because it is much more likely to support sustainability over the long term. Finally, hardship can even be present in the performance of one's regular duties. Sharīʿah definitively admits this type of hardship and people are expected to endure it as they must endure the difficulty involved in discharging their responsibilities in general. Failure to carry out one's responsibilities is considered intolerable and often associated with the stigma of laziness.[54] The criterion for measuring this "normal" hardship is that it should not result in an injury that would lead to the disruption or discontinuation of the action in question. This is often the distinction between a customarily acceptable hardship (*mashaqqah ʿādiyyah*) and a customarily unacceptable hardship (*khārijah ʿan al-muʿtād*).[55] In sharīʿah, the notion of legal obligation (*taklīf*) is often coupled with the concept of trial. The believer has to be tested in order to verify his commitment to the law. The customary hardship inherent in legal obligation, however, is hardly intended for its own sake. Its purpose is to instill in the individual a sense of self-discipline, which is in itself part of another objective of sharīʿah.

The third subsidiary objective of sharīʿah is the subjection of the individual to the rule of sharīʿah rather than personal desires or the egoistic lower self. This means that the individual feels religiously obligated to comply with its rulings. Compliance with the rulings of sharīʿah amounts to a practical testimony to one's commitment even when it conflicts with one's own desires. By adhering to the obligations of sharīʿah, the human agent achieves voluntary servitude to the divine. In principle, all creatures share a degree of servitude to the divine simply by means of being his creation. Sharīʿah seeks to instill and reinforce this awareness in the human consciousness. By recognizing the divine, agents are transformed from involuntary servants of God into voluntary ones.[56] By becoming a voluntary servant to the divine, the individual automatically achieves self-discipline. Here, again, al-Shāṭibī makes another appeal to the concept of custom in the sense of practical wisdom. Knowledge derived from custom in this sense confirms the interconnectedness between suppression of personal desires and achievement of self-discipline.[57] He uses the experiential knowledge derived from the thorough examination of people's customary practices as corroborative evidence to support the sharīʿah-based stipulations. By adding this third subsidiary objective, al-Shāṭibī seeks to add an important qualification to the ultimate objective that he deduced earlier. Sharīʿah aims to achieve people's benefits not in an absolute sense or as they deem appropriate. Instead, benefits are seen as intrinsically embodied in the sharīʿah-based injunctions and stipulations, considering the demands of the afterlife, the trial factor, and the purpose of religious obligation (*taklīf*).[58]

## *Classifications of Customs*

So far we explored two main uses of custom in al-Shāṭibī's treatment: custom as a category and custom as a measure. Al-Shāṭibī uses custom as a category to refer to a wide array of practices that are not necessarily regulated by sharīʿah. This is the reason he contrasted it with rituals, which clearly are regulated by sharīʿah. This is not a general rule, however, because some of the customs are regulated by sharīʿah but not in the same manner that the rituals are. Custom as a measure, on the other hand, is used as a scale or a means of evaluation. I will explore this point further.

## Custom as a Category

Al-Shāṭibī classified customs, from the perspective of their relationship with sharīʿah, into two main types.[59] The first involves the customs that have been subject to a definitive stipulation. It includes customs that have been enforced, such as the ones pertaining to personal hygiene or the covering of the private parts (*ʿawrah*). It also includes customs that have been disapproved, such as most pre-Islamic Arabian customs (e.g., naked circumambulation around the Kaʿbah, mourning rites, and female infanticide). Sharīʿah rulings concerning these customs are fixed. Given the clear stipulations on these customs, changing them would result in the unwarranted consequence of abrogating sharīʿah after the death of the Prophet.[60]

The second main type includes the customs concerning which there are no definitive stipulations in sharīʿah. This type is further divided into two subcategories of customs. The first refers to customs that are based on instinctive drives such as eating, drinking, and speaking. These customs are not subject to any legal stipulation in themselves unless they pertain to a legal injunction, in which case they follow the injunction in question. For example, eating and drinking are not in themselves described as either permissible or impermissible, but with reference to the injunction of fasting they can be either.[61] The second subcategory includes a wide array of changing customs that vary widely depending on many different considerations. These considerations may include people's perception or judgment—which can change from time to time or from place to place. Al-Shāṭibī gives the example of the headgear which is considered important in some regions and unimportant in others. They may include linguistic expressions or conventions that change over time or across different regions. Rulings involving such linguistic conventions would change accordingly. They may also include customary practices associated with certain agreements or transactions, such as means and methods of paying prices, dowries, or other expenditures. They may include natural factors such as temperature or geographical location, which may affect the attainment of the age of maturity. Finally, they may even include extraordinary or exceptional situations. This is the case, for example, of an individual who, due to a urinary malfunction, undergoes a surgery to have an artificial urinary passage. In this case, the new artificial passage "inherits" the same rulings that apply to the normal one (for religious purification purposes).[62]

Al-Shāṭibī argues that these changing customs do not affect the definitive stipulations of sharīʿah per se. The change of rulings in the case of these evolving customs reflects a difference in circumstances rather than in the legal stipulation itself. In other words, each condition or state of affairs requires a certain ruling; any change in these conditions may subsequently result in a change in the applicable rulings. For example, in some places children may attain maturity before or after their counterparts in other places. Legal responsibility (*taklīf*) is not linked to a specific age but rather to the attainment of maturity, which may differ from one place to another. Also, in some places the payment of the full dowry is expected at the conclusion of the marriage contract, while in others only half of it is paid and the other half is deferred. In this case, a definitive injunction in sharīʿah demands the payment of the dowry, but custom determines the method of its payment. While the former is immutable, the latter is changeable. What these examples show is that custom itself is not the *basis* of the law but it serves a supportive role in legal application. The jurists have traditionally studied this function of custom in their discussions on the three-step process of the verification of the operative cause, especially the second one, *taḥqīq al-manāṭ*.[63]

In addition to the classification of customs on the basis of their relationship with sharīʿah, al-Shāṭibī introduced another classification of customs with reference to their actual occurrence. From this perspective, customs are again divided into two main types. The first includes customs that are based either on instinctive human drives (such as the need for food or sleep) or basic human characteristics (such as causes of happiness or sadness). This type of basic existential customs cannot change. They are presumed to have always existed and to continue to exist as long as humans themselves exist. The second type includes all types of qualitative customs that pertain, for example, to the way people dress or how they live. These customs cannot be taken for granted but they have to be verified and analyzed as far as the actualization of particular legal injunctions is concerned. Al-Shāṭibī argues that while the first type is presumed, fixed, and to a large extent indifferent to the legal process, the second type is changing, flexible, and may affect the legal process.

Therefore, the jurist should not be solely concerned with the formal construction of the law, but he should also contemplate its objective as it is actualized and contextualized. This last step cannot be achieved without thorough knowledge of the common customs in the context for which the law is said to apply. Overlooking, ignoring, or disregarding people's customs that do not conflict with the fundamental principles of sharīʿah would undoubtedly run counter to the objectives that the Lawgiver intended for the sharīʿah-based rulings.

## Custom as a Measure

The other important use of custom that al-Shāṭibī employed in his treatment is that of custom as a measure. I noted earlier the two main connotations of custom: practical/experiential knowledge and communal/collective knowledge. The former constitutes a corroborative evidence that, together with reason, supports the claims of sharīʿah. In this sense, custom represents the sum total of human knowledge and wisdom, especially as taught and communicated by earlier prophets and wise men. The latter represents the collective knowledge and wisdom, especially as shared by people in particular social or historical contexts. It is used to provide factual details associated with the application of particular rulings in these contexts.

As the earlier discussion on hardship illustrates, custom in either of these two senses can be used as an evaluative measure, especially in the absence of explicit normative criteria in sharīʿah. Custom as an evaluative measure is one of the most important tools that the jurist uses to adjust a general rule to a particular context. When sharīʿah, for example, admonishes moderation in expenditure without providing any further specifications, it is understood that the law leaves it to common custom to determine the two extremes of excess and parsimony.[64] Custom as an evaluative measure is important for the process of legal adjustment (*takiyīf*) and legal actualization (*tanzīl*). Although sharīʿah advises moderation, the exact meaning of that term would definitely differ from one sociohistorical context to another. It is not surprising, therefore, to see that chapters on transactions in substantive law are replete with references to common custom for the determination of the exact quantitative measures (weight, volume, length, area, etc.) since these would certainly differ from one place to another and from one time to another.

Al-Shāṭibī also uses the evaluative measure of custom as an indicator of the natural or cosmic order. He employs this sense of custom in his discussion over the question of causality. According to the Ashʿarī doctrine of contingency (*tajwīz*), God is the true agent who links causes with their effects. The relationship between causes and effects is neither necessary nor independent (unmediated). The regular connection between them is based on God's recurrent custom in creation (*al-ʿādah al-jāriyah fī al-khalq*)[65] that he can break or disrupt at will. Al-Shāṭibī refers to this concept of custom in his treatment of the correlative rulings (*al-aḥkām al-waḍʿiyyah*), which have traditionally been contrasted with the charging rulings (*al-aḥkām al-taklīfiyyah*).[66] These correlative rulings usually entail three main elements: causes, conditions, and impediments (of rulings). According to al-Shāṭibī, there is a fundamental difference between causes and effects. God is the true creator of causes but the individual possesses the capacity to acquire them. Effects, however, are solely created and controlled by God. Because humans are unable to control effects, human responsibility is associated with causes only.[67] In other words, when a ruling is made that depends on a certain cause, the individual is responsible for this very cause but not for the materialization of its effect. Al-Shāṭibī's frequent references to al-Ghazālī remind us of the latter's distinction between contact with fire and burning or between drinking and satiety. For al-Shāṭibī, an argument in favor of human responsibility for effects would amount to impossible obligation (*taklīf mā lā yuṭāq*), which is negated in sharīʿah.[68] Al-Shāṭibī's discussion reveals his tireless vindication of the Ashʿarī theory of contingency, according to which the divine power is not constrained by limited human understanding of strict and automatic causal relationships.

But to speak about the human inability to control effects might seem contradictory to al-Shāṭibī's entire legal approach, which is mainly devoted to contemplating the intents and objectives of the legal process. Al-Shāṭibī's answer to this objection is twofold. First, he again points to the cosmic custom to indicate that the individual may seek to achieve a certain effect when he knows, inductively, that it does not contradict the divine intent (the effect). So, the individual may seek to support his family (the effect) by pursuing a lawful job (the cause). The individual is never sure that the effect will necessarily follow the cause. But, given that the effect is worthwhile and the cause is legitimate, and based on the indication of the cosmic custom that in such cases effects are likely to follow their (expected) causes, the individual may seek to achieve this effect by initiating the cause. Second, al-Shāṭibī again distinguishes between the two categories of ritual deeds and customs. Because ritual deeds are based on strict compliance without consideration of the objectives, effects should not be pursued. Because customs, on the other hand, are based on justification and rationalization, effects may be investigated, especially by competent jurists.[69]

Al-Shāṭibī differentiates among three views on the interpretation of the causal relationship. The first is the view that the individual can independently control effects. According to this view, the relationship between causes and effects is necessary, independent, and inevitable. For al-Shāṭibī, this view would be tantamount to admitting that the individual is a partner with God since God is the true creator of effects. The second is the view that the individual seeks to achieve the effect by pursuing its most likely cause. It is based on the cosmic custom that combines the two, but here the effect occurs *at* the materialization of the cause not *because* of it. Although according to this view the relationship between causes and effects is not necessary, it is quite likely, because it is based on the cosmic custom established by God. The third is the view that God is the sole creator of both causes and effects in a direct sense. This view is possible only for the individuals who achieved the highest degrees of religious conviction which results in complete faith and reliance on God.[70]

These differences over the interpretation of the causal relationship might seem like theoretical hairsplitting with no practical implications. Nonetheless, al-Shāṭibī reveals that these distinctions may result in notable differences in the legal process, especially between the holders of the first and the second views on the one hand and the holders of the third view on the other. Because the former see effects as dependent on causes, they don't visualize the possibility that effects could occur without their causes (satiety is dependent on drinking and burning is dependent on contact with fire). We have to keep in mind, of course, the fundamental difference between the first view and the second view (causality being necessary or likely). While they disagree on the characterization of the causal relationship, they at least share a view of the interconnectedness of causes and effects. The latter (the third view), however, see God as the sole creator of effects, with or without causes. In other words, one's degree of attachment to the causes is an indicator of the level of his religious conviction. For example, if a sick person believes that fasting will increase sickness, he or she should forgo fasting (fasting as the cause of the worsening of the condition). Conversely, if the person believes that healing (the effect) is not dependent on breaking the fast (the cause), he or she can uphold the fasting. In short, in such conjectural cases, one's view of the nature of causal relationships may result in different interpretations of the law.[71]

By differentiating among these views of causality, al-Shāṭibī seeks to reconcile the various textual indications on the issue. While some texts advocate God's absolute command over the universe, human action included,[72] others advocate human responsibility and freedom.[73] Al-Shāṭibī's discussion suggests a distinction between two frames: theological and legal.

Within the theological frame, one's view of causality will determine one's attitude towards the issue of human freedom and responsibility, which, as we saw earlier, may incidentally impact the way one approaches legal issues (more particularly, devotional issues). Within the legal frame, however, al-Shāṭibī seems to assume the second view as the general norm. (According to the cosmic custom, causes and effects are joined.) Effects occur *at* the materialization of causes, not *because* of them. Through this view of causality, al-Shāṭibī—following al-Ghazālī—upholds divine omnipotence without negating human responsibility. The first view, which advocates the complete independence of the causal relationship, runs the risk of denying divine omnipotence. Conversely, the third view could result in the elimination of human freedom, a prerequisite for human responsibility without which any discussion of legal stipulations would be meaningless.

Therefore, al-Shāṭibī argues that within the legal frame, one's responsibility for a certain cause entails one's responsibility for its effect. This is because the cosmic custom indicates that the connection between causes and effects is recurrent.[74] Consequently, once a person initiates a cause, he or she is responsible not only for the cuase but also for its (known and expected) effect. The connection between cutting a person's throat and that person's death is axiomatic; it would be implausible to argue otherwise. This principle is important when evaluating cases of negligence. The responsibility of physicians, cooks, or artisans in general for their mistakes is determined based on the attending causes and whether the individual was not merely aware of the causal connection but also did everything possible to avoid the occurrence of these mistakes.[75] Al-Shāṭibī argues that in the legal sphere the connection between causes and effects is presumed. The repeated references to this connection in the various founding texts indicate that legal stipulations already take it into account.[76] By recognizing this causal relationship, the agent acts according to the objectives of the Lawgiver, which in itself is a primary objective of sharīʿah. Al-Shāṭibī's treatment of this theme not only reveals the theological but also the mystical underpinnings of his approach. He emphasizes devoting one's attention to causes rather than effects in order to achieve a higher degree of sincerity. When the individual focuses all his attention to effects (results), he may be driven (even unconsciously) towards personal goals rather than compliance with the commands and prohibitions of sharīʿah. This is especially true in the case of ritual deeds, which are intended to increase one's righteousness. If a person undertakes any of the ritual deeds with a personal goal (fame, respect, social status) in mind, it may lead to hypocrisy. Again, speaking about disregarding effects within a general framework that asserts objectives may seem problematic. It is important, however, to separate the different underlying frames that al-Shāṭibī sometimes employs concurrently.

For example, we can refer to the theological frame, the legal frame, the mystical frame, the jurist's frame, and finally the agent's frame.

A full exploration of al-Shāṭibī's treatment of the issue of causality is beyond the scope of the present context.[77] Our goal here is to indicate how al-Shāṭibī built on the classical Ashʿarī theory of contingency to explain the causal connection as it pertains to the correlative rulings. As we saw in chapter 3, this has been one of the themes that reveals the close relationship between Islamic law and theology. Sharīʿah-based law by definition cannot violate its theological principles. But as we learn from history, we can hardly speak about a single theology—or rather, a single approach—within Islamic theology. Al-Shāṭibī's treatment offers a useful example of how Muslim jurists had to argue their cases in purely legal terms but also accommodate their legal views to the larger framework of Islamic theology.

To conclude, this chapter aimed to explore the treatment of custom within the genre of legal objectives mainly through the work of Abū Isḥāq al-Shāṭibī. His treatment demonstrates that the concept of custom had multiple applications in the legal process. We differentiated between the two main ways in which he used the concept: as a category and as a measure. Al-Shāṭibī used the concept of custom as a category in contrast with the other two categories of rituals and transactions. He used it as a measure to evaluate abstract ideas and principles.

Al-Shāṭibī used custom, in the sense of practical or experiential knowledge, to support revelation and to argue against total reliance on reason. Ultimate guidance comes from revelation; historical knowledge proves the viability of the divine teachings. He also used custom as an indicator of collective knowledge or wisdom. Custom in this sense is used to measure abstract notions such as moderation, hardship, or convenience. Finally, he uses custom to refer to the natural or cosmic order, which includes the rules that regulate the various relationships among different entities within the created universe. Custom here is synonymous with the theological concept of *ʿādah*, the cornerstone of the theory of contingency.[78] In these three senses, custom is used as a criterion or a measure to evaluate, support, or refute particular arguments. One important feature that surfaced in al-Shāṭibī's treatment of the question of causality is his employment of two distinct frames: theological and legal. Overlooking this important point seriously diminishes the appreciation of al-Shāṭibī's argument.

Al-Shāṭibī is particularly known for his work on the objectives of sharīʿah. He is unanimously considered the formal founder of the genre. The concept of custom is deeply ingrained within the structure of these objectives. The ultimate objective of sharīʿah is the achievement of the benefits of people, but the realization of this ultimate objective requires three subsidiary objectives: sharīʿah was meant to be accessible and intelligible; it was meant to entail religious stipulations; and finally, these stipulations are not meant to burden the individual but rather to free one from the influence of the lower self. Al-Shāṭibī's treatment of the concept of custom (in its various senses) shows that sharīʿah acknowledges custom when it does not conflict with its teachings, an attitude that has allowed sharīʿah to maintain its accessibility, comprehensibility, applicability, and adjustability over time.

# Chapter 8

# Custom, Legal Application, and the Construction of Reality

In the preceding chapters, we examined the historical development of the concept of custom within the wider framework of Islamic legal theory. As these chapters illustrate, the concept of custom underwent several permutations that were organically linked with the core ideas that gave this field its distinctive identity. Custom in its various senses and applications played a significant role in the development of important concepts such as *ijmāʿ*, *istiḥsān,* and *istidlāl.* It also was effective at implementing several juristic procedures such as particularization (*takhṣīṣ*) and restriction (*taqyīd*).With the gradual development of the field and the emergence of legal genres and subgenres, custom was one of the most important mainstays, figuring prominently in legal maxims (*al-qawāʿid al-fiqhiyyah*) and sharīʿah objectives (*maqāṣid al-sharīʿah*), as it had earlier with juristic concepts and procedures. Custom was one of the important tools that the jurists utilized to construct their opinions and to ensure they were applicable to real-life circumstances. Ideally, the primary goal of a legal theory is to spell out the guidelines that inform and regulate the legal process. It is, therefore, necessary for this theory to explain the relationship between the law and the social reality to which it applies.

In the case of Islamic law, the general rule provides that legislation supersedes custom. Legislation constitutes the supreme form of authority to which everyone must defer, not only for fear of indictment in a judge's court but, more importantly, in God's court. This characterizing feature of Islamic law has always presented the most challenging task for both ruler and ruled. The ruler has to guard against mixing his own interests with those of the Lawgiver. The ruled have to be aware of the difference between the two and strive to keep them separated.

In theory, it is easy to speak about law and custom as two separate entities. In reality, however, law and custom are intrinsically linked to each other. Custom can be thought of as the pre-law condition (in the sense of a less institutional kind of law). Each human society is governed by a set of principles that define and regulate the different relationships among its members. In the absence of a deliberate legal code, custom becomes the norm. If we speak of custom as social norms in the pre-law stage and law as a deliberate set of principles that purport to organize and regulate relationships within society, then law has to contend with these social norms. Law does not operate in a vacuum and if it ignores the dominant social norms in a given society, it risks being irrelevant. Therefore, instead of looking at law and custom as two irreconcilable competitors, custom can be seen as the social context within which law is framed, constructed, and continuously being reconstructed. Moreover, custom is not limited to the social norms in the pre-law stage but it also includes the ones that survive, accompany, and coexist with law. Because society is continuously evolving, so also is law. In the process of construction and reconstruction, law relies on custom to achieve some of its main goals, which include, for example, maintaining order and serving justice.[1] The viability of law, however, depends on two main conditions: intelligibility and applicability. Custom, as the previous chapters illustrate, is indispensable for the fulfillment of these two conditions.

So far we have seen the role of custom in the formal theoretical construction of rulings. We have yet to see the extent to which custom was used in the actual application of these rulings. The relationship between legal theory and legal application is usually mediated through the process of *ijtihād*. By the time Islamic legal theory assumed its archetypal format, the discussion about the question of *ijtihād* became one of its major components.[2] In these discussions the jurists investigated the questions pertaining to the process of *ijtihād*, which is seen as the primary mechanism through which real-life issues are examined, evaluated, and judged. Along with the theoretical treatment of *ijtihād* in legal theory, several other genres sought to document the actual application of rulings on real-life questions. Two main genres are particularly important: legal responses (*fatāwā*) and court verdicts (*aḥkām*).[3] So, the main question that this chapter raises and seeks to answer is to what extent the concept of custom and its variations, as discussed and constructed in legal theory, were important for the process of legal application, as reflected in the genres of legal responses and court verdicts. I start by illustrating the relationship between custom and *ijtihād*.

## Custom and *Ijtihād*

*Ijtihād* literally denotes expending the effort to carry out a laborious task.[4] Technically it stands for the mujtahid's intensive exercise of his intellectual capability for the purpose of absorbing the rulings of sharīʿah (in general or on a specific issue) to the extent that he feels unable to go any further.[5] The word mujtahid has traditionally been used to describe a jurist who can deduce rulings from the sources directly, without relying on the efforts of another jurist. It is more often used with reference to the pioneering figures or the early founders of legal schools such as Mālik, Abū Ḥanīfah, al-Shāfiʿī, al-Ṭabarī, al-Awzāʿī, and Ibn Abī Laylā. Soon after the consolidation of the major legal schools, a new distinction emerged between an absolute mujtahid and a restricted mujtahid (within a given school). Unlike an absolute mujtahid, a restricted mujtahid is bound by the methods and principles developed by the founder of his school.

The jurists have extensively discussed the conditions that govern the process of *ijtihād* and the qualifications that a competent mujtahid needs to acquire. Knowledge of the customary practice has been repeatedly counted among the prerequisites for an accomplished mujtahid.[6] *Ijtihād* as a legal capacity was considered among the prerequisites for important positions such as the ruler (*khalīfah*), the judge (*qāḍī*), and the jurisconsult (muftī). Soon after the period of the Rightly Guided Caliphs (*al-khulafāʾ al-rāshidūn*),[7] it became clear that it would no longer be realistic to insist on this condition for the post of the caliph. This realization marked the beginning of the dissociation between the political authority and the scholarly/juristic authority. Up until that point, the caliph had enjoyed both types of authority. Gradually, each of these underwent its own development. If the requirement of *ijtihād* was short-lived in the case of the caliph, it continued to be invoked in the cases of the judge and the jurisconsult for much longer, until jurists started to admit that it was difficult for one person to satisfy all the demanding requirements of *ijtihād*.[8]

## Custom and Legal Application between *Fatwā* and *Ḥukm*

Although legal theory and substantive law have been recognized as two separate disciplines, the relationship between them has not always been linear or one-dimensional. The legal process can be seen as a two-dimensional operation that works both deductively from theory to practice but also inductively from practice back to theory. The deductive approach was more frequently used by legal rationalists (theoretical school) and the inductive approach by legal empiricists (applied school). This is best illustrated by the two concepts of analogy (*qiyās*) and juristic preference (*istiḥsān*). In *qiyās*, the jurist starts his analysis by investigating a relevant text-based precedent whose ruling he seeks to extend to a new case. In other words, he moves from the source (theory) to the particular incident (practice).[9] In *istiḥsān*, on the other hand, he reverses the process by starting from the particular incident, analyzing it in light of the specific context. In *istiḥsān*, the conclusion is not supported by a straightforward analogy with the sources. The jurist chooses *istiḥsān* over *qiyās* because a straightforward *qiyās* in a particular situation might result in a conclusion that defeats a higher purpose of the law.[10] A conclusive argument for a case of *istiḥsān*, however, has to be anchored in an alternative piece of evidence that the jurist considers to be more in harmony with the *spirit* of sharīʿah.[11]

Custom has traditionally been one of the most important grounds for the use of *istiḥsān*. The two examples of *ʿarāyā* and *salam* are extremely useful in explaining this dynamic. Both are seen as exceptions to general rules: the exchange of ripe dates for dried dates in the case of *ʿarāyā* and the sale of something non-existent in the case of *salam*. These exceptions were made on the basis of Prophetic aḥādīth and reflected a common practice that the Prophet recognized as valid and therefore *istiḥsān* was used to justify departure from the general rule in these two cases. The question that these two examples (and other similar ones) raised was whether these exceptions were made on the basis of the custom in question or rather on the texts sanctioning such custom. This was the question that inspired the centuries-old debate between the supporters of *istiḥsān* (mostly Ḥanafī and Mālikī) and its critics (mostly Shafiʿī).[12] Most importantly, these two concepts (*qiyās* and *istiḥsān*)demonstrate the dynamic nature of the juristic process in the Islamic legal tradition.

While substantive law was organized thematically to provide the prescriptions of sharīʿah on different subjects (prayer, marriage, sales), it did not provide specific answers to particular real-life incidents (whether the marriage of X and Y is valid). This level of specificity was to be had only through either a legal response (*fatwā*) of a jurisconsult or a verdict (*ḥukm*) of a judge. Eventually legal responses and court verdicts, if they managed to secure enough support, would find their ways into substantive law; they could even be cited as cases that warranted change in legal theory. Again, the example of *istiḥsān* is instructive. It was rooted in the exceptions that were made to rigid or straightforward application of *qiyās*. Eventually, it became an abstract tool in legal theory, a process that was replicated with custom as it became one of the secondary or contested sources. This should explain the consistent, coextensive, and incremental growth of both legal theory and substantive law corpuses over time, admittedly with less creativity in the later stages of the tradition.

In other words, court verdicts (*aḥkām*) and legal responses (*fatāwā*) represented the third and most concrete level in the juristic process after legal theory and substantive law. Substantive law continued to represent the formal (re)statement of the sharīʿah position on the different subjects; it was organized thematically for reference and instruction purposes. Each legal school developed its own version of substantive law (*ʿilm al-madhhab*), which was considered the pinnacle of legal scholarship. Its mastery was a sign of the highest levels of legal competence.[13] Writing a major work of substantive law ensured the author a privileged membership in the exclusive guild of his school's recognized authorities. Within this guild, these recognized authorities formed a successive chain from the school's founder to the current authorities of *al-madhhab*. Gradually the roles undertaken in this three-stage process (legal theory, substantive law, and legal application) became increasingly differentiated; even when combined, the distinctions among these different roles remained recognizable. Because counseling and judgeship represent the most concrete levels of legal scholarship, both the jurisconsult and the judge can provide accurate evaluation of the role of custom in legal application. But if legal responses and court verdicts both seek to address real-life incidents, how do they differ from each other?

The Mālikī jurist Shihāb al-Dīn al-Qarāfī devoted considerable attention to this question in his effort to spell out the differences between the office of the judge and that of the jurisconsult.[14] One of the most important differences that he highlighted was the way the judge and the jurisconsult each reach their conclusions. While the jurisconsult mainly communicates (*yukhbir*) the ruling that he extracts through his examination of the sources, the judge initiates (*yunshiʾ*) that ruling. The judge has the power to initiate the verdict by means of the delegated authority bestowed on him by the Lawgiver (as well as the political authority).[15] The jurisconsult, on the other hand, merely explains his understanding of the intent of the Lawgiver in the issue at hand, which may or may not conform to the actual intent of the Lawgiver.[16] Al-Qarāfī highlighted the crucial role that custom plays in determining the difference between a non-initiating statement (*khabar*) and an initiating statement (*inshāʾ*). The customary practice of a given society not only influences the relationship between specific words (symbols) and their ascribed meanings but also the way or mode in which these meanings are expressed.[17]

Another important difference between a judge and a jurisconsult has to do with the applicability of their decisions. In principle, the considered opinion of a jurisconsult applies automatically to all similar cases, but this is not the case with the verdict of a judge. This difference depends largely on the sources that they rely on for the derivation of their respective decisions. A jurisconsult's ruling relies mainly on the textual sources (Qur'ān, Sunnah, etc.) whose applicability extends to every legally capacitated individual (*mukallaf*), especially those who follow the legal school of the jurisconsult in question. The verdict of a judge, on the other hand, depends on the attending pieces of evidence and arguments (*ḥijāj*) in a particular incident (*ḥādithah juz'iyyah*). These may include witnesses, oaths, and different types of circumstantial evidence (*qarā'in*).[18]

Ibn al-Qayyim (d. AH 751/1350 CE) observed that both the judge and the jurisconsult must combine two types of knowledge that together should allow them to understand not only texts but also the contexts to which they should apply. The first is knowledge of contextual reality (*wāqiʿ*), which should enable them to understand real-life cases. Such knowledge is crucial for verifying the factual details that pertain to the cases they investigate. The second type is knowledge of the textual sources that will enable them to find God's ruling for the questions at hand.[19] Among the prerequisites for either a judge or a jurisconsult, Ibn al-Qayyim counted "knowledge of people" (*maʿrifat al-nās*).[20] This refers to the wisdom that a person gains from dealing with people (of different characters) in a wide variety of situations or circumstances. Litigation can bring out both the best and worst in people; through this direct interaction, jurists gain valuable insights on human nature, which should help them verify the accuracy of the attendant details in each case. Such practical knowledge, however, remains incomplete without extensive familiarity with the customary practices in their regions, hence the famous dictum: legal opinions change depending on change in times, places, circumstances, and customs.[21] The jurists, therefore, have emphasized that mentorship and apprenticeship are integral parts of legal education. Both the judge and the jurisconsult need to acquire not only knowledge of the (theoretical) rulings but also the skill to apply them. Al-Wansharīsī, for example, notes that

> There is no surprise in the excellence of the area of judgeship over the other areas of legal scholarship. The real surprise, however, is (the subtlety involved in) the ability to apply the general rulings of substantive law on the particular cases of reality which has proven to be difficult for many people. You may find an individual who knows, understands, and even teaches many of the legal questions but fails to answer a simple question that a lay

> person may ask him. He may even find himself unable to answer a question about oaths except after great difficulty.[22]

These two types of prerequisite knowledge for both the judge and the jurisconsult are rooted in the indicators that they rely on. The jurists have consistently differentiated between legal (textual) indicators and confirmatory (contextual) indicators.[23] Confirmatory indicators often refer to the fulfillment of conditions or occurrence of causes in correlative rulings (*al-aḥkām al-waḍʿiyyah*).[24] They also refer to the evidentiary indicators used in court such as admission of guilt (*iqrār*) or the testimony of witnesses.

Apart from the issue of the indicators, both the judge and the jurisconsult rely extensively on the common custom in the process of adjusting a general ruling to a particular incident.[25] For example, the application of the punishment for theft requires that the thief must have secretly appropriated the stolen item from its *proper* protected place (*ḥirz*). Valuable items are usually kept in safe places for their protection. A safe or a bank, for example, would be a proper *ḥirz* for cash, jewelry, or documents. Different items have different storage places and common custom determines this relationship between a given item and its proper *ḥirz*. Furthermore, what may be considered *ḥirz* in one region or time might not be considered as such in others. In order for a person to be charged with theft, the judge has to be convinced that he has intentionally and secretly stolen the item in question from its proper *ḥirz*.[26]

## Custom and Judges' Verdicts

One of the main differences between a judge and a jurisconsult is the power of enforcement. Only judges held that power, which depended on the nature and extent of their jurisdiction (*wilāyah*). While some judges were authorized to enforce their verdicts, others were only authorized to initiate them. The application of such verdicts was the responsibility of the governor (*wālī*) or even the caliph in some cases. Ibn Farḥūn observes that the delineation of the judge's responsibilities and the extent of his jurisdiction depended on custom because, following Ibn al-Qayyim, sharīʿah did not provide for such structural or procedural details.

> Know that the criteria used to determine the extent of jurisdictions and whether they are general or specific as well as the responsibilities of their holders are known from the common customary practice because there is no stated limit to that in sharīʿah. The jurisdiction of judgeship in some places or times may (for example) include (what may be included under) the

> jurisdiction of the military. In some other places or times, on the other hand, it may be limited to the rulings of sharīʿah only. Therefore, the jurisdiction of judgeship in each region would follow custom and what it dictates. This is the verified opinion in this question and God Almighty knows best. [27]

This quote is significant for more than one reason. First it illustrates the author's (as well as his sources') understanding of sharīʿah. According to this understanding, sharīʿah consists mainly of a set of general principles that the judge seeks to interpret and relate to the cases that he investigates. Second, these principles do not cover all possible real incidents. Third, if a particular incident is not covered by these general principles, the judge should turn to the other indirect indicators including, among other things, the common customary practice in his region. The scope of custom in this case is not limited to the examination of individual cases but it may include structural aspects pertaining to important institutions such as judgeship and its jurisdiction.[28] Fourth, this quote implies that in principle, such regional customary practice is valid and can be used to justify a verdict as long as it does not violate a higher principle of sharīʿah. Lastly, it shows that judgeship is primarily concerned with purely legal issues (as defined by sharīʿah), though it may occasionally deal with other related questions (e.g., political, military).[29]

Discussions over the scope of the judge's jurisdiction and limits to it are often traced to the different roles that the Prophet undertook throughout his career. Al-Qarāfī, for example, distinguished three main roles that the Prophet assumed.[30] As the political leader of the Muslim state, he wielded the supreme political authority and executive power. In this capacity he led battles, concluded treaties, and executed public punishments (*ḥudūd*). As the supreme jurisconsult, he was the sole interpreter of the texts whose opinions were obligatory for every Muslim. In this capacity he explained the rulings of sharīʿah on the different substantive issues. As the supreme judge, he settled disputes and enforced the different verdicts. To these, we may add the role of the Prophet as a private individual. In this capacity he expressed his personal opinion, which was not considered as binding as the opinions that were associated with the other three roles.[31] Much of the juristic disagreement on the interpretation of texts is rooted in the disagreement over the scope of each of these roles, especially as they pertain to specific incidents or questions. For example, the Prophet is reported to have allowed a wife to spend on the needs of the family, according to the common custom, from her husband's money even without his permission. The license was given because of the husband's failure to discharge his responsibility on his own initiative. The incident shows that the permission given to the wife was governed by two conditions: the first defined its applicability (failure of the husband) and the second regulated its application (according to the common custom). Now, if the Prophet's instruction in this case is considered a ruling of a jurisconsult (muftī), it is possible to extend the same ruling to all similar incidents. If, however, it is considered a verdict of a judge, the permission will be limited to this particular incident.[32] What this example shows is that unlike the opinion of a jurisconsult, the verdict of a judge is not automatically extendable to other similar cases. Yes, it can serve as a legal precedent that the same judge or another one may refer to in the future, but ultimately each case is considered unique in its own right. This again has to do with the different roles that both the jurisconsult and the judge perform and the different types of indicators that they rely on. While the jurisconsult relies on the legal sources of sharīʿah, the judge relies mostly on particular contextual indicators of a particular case as it is presented to him. These contextual indicators are deeply rooted in the common customary practices and depend heavily on them.

The literature on judge's verdicts is replete with references to the importance of the common custom in the construction of these verdicts. Judges are often reminded that they have to be cognizant of this point. For example, Ibn Abī al-Damm (d. AH 642/1244 CE) noted in the introduction to his book that his purpose was to

> provide a collection of the legal procedures as well as the famous verdicts in particular cases that judges have consistently upheld. They should be extremely useful for judges, their assistants (such as secretaries and deputies) and litigants. I also plan to provide some standard examples of a variety of formulae and contracts that are used in our region in this period. Although they do not literally follow those of our predecessors, they fully accord with them in meaning.[33]

This quote clearly shows that many of the authors in this genre saw their primary task to be updating the works of their predecessors to reflect the necessary changes that ensued from changes in the customary practice. This common practice influences the juristic practice in many different ways, most importantly in the area of legal application. Legal application is mainly concerned with addressing real-life incidents, which are part and parcel of the context in which they occur. In comparing their own context with that of their predecessors', the jurists often described the former as more degenerate. This description was used to justify departure from the rigid requirements of legal theory. In a less than perfect reality, judges (and for that matter, jurisconsults) should serve justice by choosing the lesser of the two harms. They should do their best to draw as close as possible to theory without losing sight of the (ever-existing) distance that separates theory from practice.[34] This was clearly evident, for example, in the jurists' insistence on the prerequisite of *ijtihād* for the person who assumes the office of a judge. In the absence of a mujtahid, however, the most qualified should be nominated. This option, although less than perfect, is better than the total suspension of the judicial system.[35]

In the judgeship literature, the role of custom is emphasized in more than one context. From the conditions that a prospective judge has to satisfy to the various aspects of the judicial processes and procedures, references to custom are frequently encountered. For example, a judge is required to know the language of the region(s) under his jurisdiction as well as the different linguistic conventions in which this language is used. This knowledge is indispensable for constructing verdicts and for analyzing the applicability of law to particular cases.[36]

Custom is considered a preponderant factor in cases of competing pieces of evidence. For example, if a judge is confronted with a case for which there are several equally valid proofs, he is to give preference to the proof that is more in line with custom. This argument was particularly important for jurists of the Mālikī school. The Mālikī school placed greater emphasis on the practice (*ʿamal*) of the people of Madīnah. The later Mālikī jurists, however, debated whether *ʿamal* should always remain limited to the customary practice of Madīnah. As we have already seen with other legal concepts, *ʿamal* in the Mālikī school eventually turned into an abstract tool that was used to refer to the local customary practice in general (not only in Madīnah), especially in North Africa and Andalusia.[37] The concept of *ʿamal* as constructed and practiced by later Mālikī jurists used to refer to the choice of a less famous view within the school over the majority or famous view on a given issue because it was more accommodating of a regional customary practice. More particularly, it was used to refer to the judge's choice of this weaker opinion over the stronger opinion and the development of a common understanding about the reasons for such a choice.[38] Not all Mālikī jurists, however, looked favorably on this local practice of *ʿamal*. It did have its critics, who saw it as a sign of weakness in a legal system that was, in turn, the function of a weak political system.[39]

There were several key areas of litigation in which jurists often consulted the local custom. Contractual agreements in general and issues pertaining to personal status in particular are prominent cases in point. For example, common practice determined whether an agent, in a valid sale transaction, was authorized to receive the price or was limited to the negotiation of the deal without its conclusion.[40] Within each field, discipline, or profession there were several standard customs and procedures that insiders commonly accepted, shared, and practiced. The different legal genres—especially in the areas of substantive law and legal application, and even legal theory, to some extent—are replete with references to merchants' custom (*'urf al-tujjār*), artisans' custom (*'urf al-ṣunnā'*), and of course, jurists' custom (*'urf al-fuqahā'*). In this sense we can say that it has been the jurists' custom to distinguish between two main types of custom: general custom (*'urf 'āmm*) and specific custom (*'urf khāṣṣ*).[41] The general custom has a much wider scope because it transcends the boundaries of narrowly defined areas. The specific custom, on the other hand, is shared only by a specific social group that is defined either in terms of professional affiliation or geographical location.[42]

Within the area of contractual agreements, the resolution of marital disputes relied heavily on custom. For example, Ibn Farḥūn observed that if a wife accused her husband of failing to provide for her, the common custom would testify on his behalf because such a claim contradicts social norms.[43] Unless the husband is away or missing, custom indicates that he is more likely to provide for his family due to the implied obligation to do so in the very contract of marriage. The customary indication, however, does not constitute conclusive evidence. A judge would only resort to it either in the absence of a clear proof or in the presence of two (or more) equal proofs.[44] In other words, the judge in this case starts out by assuming the customary indication as presumption to be either confirmed or negated. Similarly, disagreements over furniture or property in post-divorce disputes are to be resolved in accordance with the common customary practice. Since these matters are usually decided on the basis of custom, judges often consulted that originating custom to resolve these types of disputes.

> In this and other similar cases you do not find them say this is what custom dictates or this is what is usually decided in this case. You rather find them say this is what the custom says in the case of such and such in the region of such and such.[45]

Custom therefore was crucial for adjusting legal rulings to different local contexts.[46] The juristic disagreement over these examples and many other similar ones in substantive law is best explained in terms of the relationship between general custom and specific custom even within the framework of the same legal school. The expansion of legal schools in different geographical regions led to the inevitable consequence of regional authorities accommodating the legal thinking of their schools to their own regional contexts. The study of the concept of custom, therefore, enables us to understand not only the legal interschool differences, but also intraschool differences that reflect changes in time (general custom), place (specific custom), or circumstances (general or specific customs).

Custom's role was not limited to the determination of a preponderant piece of evidence; it was important for the evaluation of the claim (*al-daʿwā*) itself. Each claim brought before a judge must be verified. One of the criteria that determines the validity of a claim is non-contradiction with a common customary practice.[47] It is clear from Ibn Farḥūn's discussion of this issue, as well as the examples he used, that the meaning of custom in this context comes close to the meaning of reason or logic. Regarding the relationship between custom (in this sense) and claims in general, there are three types of claims. The first is a claim that contradicts custom and thus becomes inadmissible. A person's claim, for example, that an older person is his son would not be acceptable. The claim that X is the son of Y though Y is younger than X does not stand to reason, logic, or even common sense—let alone common experience—and so it would be ruled out as inadmissible. The second is a claim that is supported by the common practice. For example, a claim against a merchant or an artisan that pertains to a transaction with either of them would be admissible. Common custom supports the fact that people's engagement in business or transactions may result in disagreement or dispute. This customary indication is used to verify a claim (*taṣḥīḥ al-daʿwā*) before it can be brought before a judge. The third type is the neutral claim; common practice neither supports nor negates it. For example, the claim that X owes Y a sum of money is a neutral claim that requires establishment by means of valid evidence.[48]

Since many of the judges' verdicts were based on custom, and since customs tend to change over time or across regions, the jurists often debated the continued authority of these custom-based verdicts. If a given verdict was meant to accommodate a given custom in a specific region at a specific time, upholding the same verdict when or where this given custom no longer applied would defeat the purpose of the legal system. Al-Qarāfī noted:

> Upholding custom-based verdicts after they (the customs) have changed amounts to contradiction to consensus and ignorance of religion. In fact, the ruling regarding anything in sharīʿah that is based on custom would change if the originating custom were to change in order [for the ruling] to cope with the new custom. The application of this principle does not even require the undertaking of a new *ijtihād*. This is a maxim that the jurists collectively upheld and agreed on. We merely follow them [the jurists] in its application without the need for the initiation of a new *ijtihād*. Do not you see that they agreed [on the principle] that in transactions if the [currency

> of the] price was not specified, it would be taken to mean the common one...the same principle applies in issues related to wills, oaths and the rest of the chapters of substantive law that depend on custom...this is not merely the case with the change of custom [in one place over time] but if we move from one place to another where another custom is in place, verdicts and legal opinions should reflect the new custom. Similarly, if one person comes from another region whose custom differs from ours, we shall answer him according to his custom not ours.[49]

A great deal of the judgeship literature is devoted to the ways of establishing evidence (*bayynāt*) before a judge. The word originally signified any means used to reveal truth, but in the judicial context it often referred to witnesses.[50] In principle, a witness is supposed to render a testimony about something that he personally saw or heard.[51] The jurists, however, listed some cases in which a witness can bear witness on the basis of wide circulation (*istifāḍah*). This denotes a type of knowledge that is shared by such a large number of people, especially in a particular region, that it would be inconceivable to assume that they agreed to fabricate it. Although it is based on overwhelming supposition (*ẓann ghālib*), it comes close to certainty. The cases in which testimony may be borne on the basis of *istifāḍah* include the verification of ownership, blood relationships, and death.[52] The concept of *istifāḍah*, as we can see, amounts to a common evidentiary method that legal systems employ in cases involving collective or general knowledge, that is, cases that depend on collective memory.

Authors in the genre of *adab al-qaḍā'* often did not restrict themselves to mere theoretical discussions about judicial processes and procedures. They provided actual verdicts and even recorded some standard forms and formulae that were frequently used in the various areas of transactions. Ibn Abī al-Damm, for example, provided some of these standard forms along with detailed explanations that were meant to adjust these forms to their respective social and historical contexts. In his treatment of a sample sale contract, for example, he specified the type and weight of the currency that should be mentioned. Similarly, he noted the distinctions among the different contracts depending on their subjects.[53] A contract for the sale of an estate, for instance, is different from a contract for the sale of a house, a bathhouse, or a single room. Most importantly, the specifications of these items in terms of the utilities or amenities to be included or excluded should be defined according to the common practice. In contracts, terms (*shurūṭ*) should be specific, detailed, and unequivocal in order to eliminate uncertainty and consequently, minimize chances for disagreement or dispute.[54] The underlying assumption, therefore, is that overlooking the common custom in these cases would defeat the goals of sharīʿah by raising the chances for disagreements and disputes.

## Custom, Jurisconsults' Opinions, and Legal Change

The institution of *iftāʾ* has traditionally been associated with the process of *ijtihād*. *Ijtihād* has often been considered a prerequisite for *iftāʾ*, which is the main function of a mujtahid. A competent muftī is a jurist who is able to explain the position of sharīʿah on a given issue based on his own understanding of the sources. He should be able to make a solid argument for his opinion, a process that often involves the evaluation or even the refutation of all other possible opinions. Therefore, the ability of a jurist who did not attain the rank of *ijtihād* to give valid legal opinions remained questionable at best.

The debate over the non-mujtahid muftī (whether a non-mujtahid can issue a legal opinion) generated three distinct views. The first was the view that it is impermissible for a non-mujtahid to give a legal opinion. In order for a jurist to give considered legal opinions, he needs to possess extensive knowledge of sharīʿah and its sources. The adoption or imitation of the legal opinions of a famous school (*taqlīd*) does not amount to solid independent knowledge. A non-mujtahid jurist has to refer to mujtahid jurists rather than undertake the task of *iftāʾ* himself. The second was the view that he can use his legal opinions just for himself without sharing it with others. The third was the view that a non-mujtahid jurist can offer legal opinions only in the absence of a mujtahid jurist.[55]

Apart from the question of *ijtihād* and its necessity for *iftāʾ*, most of the jurists who dealt with this issue highlighted the muftī's ability to adjust his legal opinion to particular social and cultural settings. Several expressions were often used to convey this notion. For example, awareness of the distinctions among the different regions was consistently counted among the prerequisites for a competent jurisconsult (*an yakūna mushrifan ʿalā ikhtilāf ahl al-amṣār*).[56] Although these expressions can be found in the early works of the Islamic legal tradition, they occur more frequently in the works of the later jurists in the post-classical period. The rapid growth and expansion of the legal tradition during this period raised the urgent need, on the part of the jurists, to adjust the legal thinking of their respective schools to their own settings. These expressions, therefore, are indications of an important and, indeed, continuous process of adjustment.

Similar to the institution of judgeship, *iftāʾ* is not merely concerned with the abstract theoretical knowledge of sharīʿah, but it seeks to relate abstract knowledge to real-life incidents. Sharīʿah informs the decision-making process of each legally-capacitated individual (*mukallaf*). Accordingly, each action that the *mukallaf* undertakes is categorized in terms of the five possible rulings.[57] If the individual is unable to derive the position of sharīʿah on a given issue, he should turn to a competent muftī and ask him (*yastaftī*). The question may have a similar precedent or may be about a novel case (*nāzilah*). In either case, incidents are viewed as originating in a larger context; the muftī is required to examine the cases before him in light of their contexts. Common customary practices constitute an integral part of this larger context, which is why the muftī has to include them in his analysis. Whether or not a case has a similar precedent, the muftī must have knowledge of the common customary practice. If the pertinent case has no precedent, the muftī has to ensure that his analysis accounts for the contemporary customary practice.[58] If, on the other hand, the case has a precedent, the muftī must first study the opinions of his predecessor(s) and evaluate their applicability to the context in question. The process of reexamination would also apply if it was the same muftī who answered the (same) question before.[59]

The gradual consolidation of the legal schools and their transformation into strong legal and social institutions (*madhāhib*) has led to the institutionalization of the process of *iftāʾ* itself. Legal opinions were to be given according to the restrictive framework of particular schools, to the exclusion of those of other schools. For example, the famous Ḥanafī work of Qādikhān opened with an important statement about the method that the muftī should follow:

> The muftī in our time who follows our school (*min aṣḥābinā*) when presented with a question has to follow this order: If there was a reported famous answer on which our predecessors unanimously agreed, he should uphold this answer and should not prefer his own opinion over theirs, even if he was a competent mujtahid because the correct view is more likely to be theirs... He should not trust the opinion of those who disagreed with them and should not accept its evidence because they (our predecessors) knew the indicators and verified the reliable from the unreliable. If, on the other hand, it was a question on which our predecessors disagreed, the muftī would need to investigate further. If along with the opinion of Abū Ḥanīfah there was also the opinion of one of his companions (Abū Yūsuf or Muḥammad Ibn al-Ḥasan al-Shaybānī), the muftī should uphold this opinion for that would often be the opinion that satisfies the conditions and conforms with the verified indicators. If, however, both of Abū Ḥanīfah's companions upheld a different view, he (the muftī) would still need to analyze the situation. If their disagreement was in view of a change

> of period and time (*ʿaṣr wa zamān*)...he should uphold this view because of the change of people's circumstances as it is the case in sharecropping or similar transactions and this has been the consensus among the late jurists. Otherwise, he should choose between their opinions and uphold the preferred view in his judgment.[60]

This opening statement not only explains the method that the Ḥanafī muftī should follow but it also shows jurists' efforts to adjust the theories of their schools to the temporal and spatial variations of their particular social realities. Most importantly, it illustrates the role of the common customary practices in this process of adjustment. Statements such as a disagreement based on (a change of) period and time reveals the jurists' awareness of the implications that such a change involved. Phrases and terms such as *ikhtilāf ʿaṣr wa zamān* or *ʿurf* were therefore important abstract tools that the jurists employed to account for a wide array of factual details that necessitated a change in the constructed rulings of a particular school over time, when they no longer served their objectives.[61] This process of adjustment, however, was to be undertaken within the boundaries of the school and the views of its recognized authorities. This quote illustrates a particular legal trend that supported and encouraged the practice of *taqlīd*[62] over absolute *ijtihād*. According to this understanding, Islamic law was thought of, constructed, and applied only through the lenses of the *madhhab* and its recognized authorities. Needless to say, however, this was not the only trend and the fact that *ijtihād* and its guidelines were included within the main themes of legal theory ensured the continuation of at least the theoretical discussions over *ijtihād*.[63] What is important to note here is that even within this particular trend, which supported and promoted the practice of *taqlīd*, it was through the mechanism of tools such as *ʿurf* that *ijtihād* continued to be practiced, although within the restricted domain of the *madhhab*. This restricted *ijtihād* consisted mainly of certain processes such as verification of a particular view (*tanqīḥ*), choice of a preponderant view (*tarjīḥ*), or extrapolation (*takhrīj*).

Jurists have singled out particular cases for which knowledge of the common customary practice is not a mere condition but a necessary prerequisite. Among these are oaths, admissions, and other cases involving linguistic conventions whose interpretation depended on the common customary practice.[64] For example, words for currencies, such as *dirham* or *dinār*, were used in various regions, but their values differed across them. The jurists, therefore, indicated that their values should be specified whenever they are used. If unspecified, the terms would be taken to refer to the value of the common currency in the particular region in question.[65] Similarly, expressions denoting divorce—both words and the mode in which they are used—differ from one place to another. Ibn Taymiyyah, for example notes:

> Know that the terms that God associated with rulings in the Qur'ān and the sunnah are divided into [three types]: [the first is] what is known and defined by sharī'ah which has been explained by God or His Prophet such as prayer, alms, pilgrimage, belief, Islam, disbelief, and hypocrisy; [the second is] what is known and defined in the language such as sun, moon, sky, earth, earthside, and seaside; [the third is] the one whose definition depends on people's common custom and therefore would change according to these customs such as sale, marriage, collection [of payment], currencies, as well as all other terms for which neither sharī'ah nor language provide a specific definition or limit. The exact definition and measure of these terms [in the third category]would change according to people's common customs.[66]

The example of divorce-related expressions is particularly important. In principle, a divorce becomes irrevocable (*bā'in baynūnah kubrā*) after three separate occasions of revocable divorce (*bā'in baynūnah ṣughrā*).[67] At the event of divorce, the husband is supposed to use the divorce expression (once) and if he fails to reestablish the marital relationship within the prescribed waiting period (*'iddah*),[68] the divorce will become effective.[69] After the waiting period expires, the parties can remarry but with a new marriage contract. The divorce and remarriage can only be repeated twice. After the third incident, the divorce becomes irrevocable, which means that the parties cannot remarry until the wife marries someone else. This condition was meant to deter abuse of the husband's prerogative to initiate divorce. In theory, the power of divorce should be used responsibly and only as a last resort. The jurists debated the question of the triple pronouncement of divorce; this is the case when the husband seeks to combine the three incidents into one by repeating the expressions three times at once. They investigated whether this form would still count as one incident of divorce or three combined incidents. Although the Prophet was reported to have considered this form as a single divorce, the second caliph, 'Umar ibn al-Khaṭṭāb, held the view that it would amount to a triple and therefore irrevocable divorce. He reasoned that since people chose to forfeit a chance that the Lawgiver afforded them, they should suffer the consequences of their choice.[70] Since then, the jurists have debated 'Umar's view and whether what he did was in disagreement with the Prophet or in agreement with the ultimate purpose of the Lawgiver—to discourage abuse of the power to initiate divorce.

Ibn al-Qayyim included this issue among the prominent examples of substantive law whose rulings changed over time in view of change in customary practice. ʿUmar meant to deter irresponsible use of the divorce formula, which was getting increasingly abused. According to Ibn al-Qayyim, this example shows that legal opinions should change according to the changing circumstances. By upholding this principle, the jurist does not seek to change legal rulings *per se*; the jurist should reflect on the intent of the Lawgiver and look for the best way to serve this intent, even if this means changing the rulings themselves. The ruling, therefore, is not a goal in itself, but rather a means to an ultimate goal, achieving the objective of the Lawgiver.[71] In principle, every jurist sees his role as adapting the rules of sharīʿah to the actual context in which he operates. He reflects on the efforts of his predecessors and seeks to distinguish between the unchanging principles of sharīʿah and the constructed rulings that should be adjusted in view of particular spatial or temporal variations. Ibn ʿAbidīn notes:

> Know that legal questions are divided into two main types: what is based on an explicit text on the one hand and what is based on *ijtihād* and opinion on the other. The mujtahid often constructs this latter type according to the customary practice of his time. [This is so much the case that] if such mujtahid were to exist at the time of a new custom, he would change his [initial] opinion to suit this new custom. This is the reason why they counted, among the conditions for *ijtihād*, knowledge of people's customs.[72]

In fact, the entire area of personal status is one of the important sections of Islamic law that can reveal the extent to which the jurists have consistently relied on *ʿurf*. The works of substantive law, and to a larger extent the collections of legal opinions (*fatāwā*), are replete with references to the common practice on issues ranging from the choice of a spouse—criteria to determine suitability (*kafāʾah*), amount and manner of payment of dowry, and respective contributions of the (would-be) spouses and their families—to settling spousal disputes and the rules governing the process of divorce.[73]

The other main areas that reveal the extent to which the jurisconsults relied on custom in the construction of legal opinions were transactions and contractual agreements. For example, in his voluminous *fatāwā* collection, al-Wansharīsī (d. AH 914/1508 CE) included a *fatwā* on the permissibility of borrowing wheat flour by weight. In his famous ḥadīth on the six usurious items (*al-aṣnāf al-ribawiyyah*), the Prophet counts wheat among the items that are measured by volume. Based on this ḥadīth, the majority of jurists concluded that wheat should always be measured by volume.[74] On the other hand, according to the Mālikī view (which is similar to that of Abū Yūsuf), common custom determines whether a certain item is measured by weight or by volume.[75] According to the *fatwā* that al-Wansharīsī cited:

> Knowledge of the exact measurement is known by weight (as it is known by volume). This is what is known to us in the case of flour and it cannot be measured in any other way because sales take place according to the common units of measurements. This would even apply if the common custom disagreed with the custom of sharīʿah. According to our custom, for example, dates cannot be measured by volume although this is the custom of sharīʿah.[76]

According to this view, therefore, the specific units of measurement for the items mentioned in the ḥadīth were not meant to be (let alone remain) prescriptive. Units of measurement were used as common standards to facilitate the exchange of goods and to prevent uncertainty that might result in cheating or exploitation. Whether a particular item was measured by weight or volume was not important as long as such a standard was known, accepted, and upheld as a common means of measurement.[77]

The examples mentioned above do not necessarily indicate that reference to custom in substantive law was limited to the areas of personal status and contractual agreements. As explained in the previous chapter, the use of custom as a measure or scale for estimation, evaluation, or assessment permeates all the chapters of substantive law. This use of custom applies even to the restricted area of devotional deeds. The jurists often reiterate that these devotional deeds fall outside the scope of *ijtihād*. The objective of these deeds is to demonstrate full and unquestioning compliance with the law (*taʿabbud*). But even within this restricted area of devotional deeds, custom was still used to adjust certain aspects of these deeds that were subject to change over time or across different regions. For example, the payment of charity following the month of Ramadān and the determination of the common staple food depends on the customary practice. Similarly, whether such charity is to be paid in kind or in value depends on the common social and juristic customs in particular regions.[78]

To conclude, after surveying the role of custom in the various genres of legal theory in the previous chapters, this chapter illustrated the usage of custom in legal application. There were two modes of legal application, both sharing a common lineage in the process of *ijtihād*. These are the legal opinions of jurisconsults (*fatāwā*) and the verdicts of judges (*aḥkām*). As a sign of the highest degree of legal accomplishment, *ijtihād* was often counted as a prerequisite for the post of a jurisconsult or judge. The definition and scope of *ijtihād*, however, underwent a great deal of modification over time. Nonetheless, the different contextual definitions of *ijtihād* always highlighted the importance of the common custom for the proper implementation of this task. Similarly, as the two institutions of *iftā'* and *qaḍā'* became increasingly differentiated, one of the most important features they continued to share was emphasis on the role of custom in the construction of both legal opinions and verdicts.

# Conclusion

In the Islamic legal tradition, the concept of custom has been associated with the terms of *ʿurf* and *ʿādah*. Each of these two terms had undergone its own development, but at a deeper level they shared the common characteristics of their English counterparts: custom and habit. Although they were occasionally used as synonyms, *ʿurf* was often used to denote a collective custom and *ʿādah* was used to denote an individual habit. Both indicate the recurrence of a certain practice, activity, or action that is not necessarily rationally justified. The fundamental question posed to the Islamic legal system—or any legal system for that matter—is whether the mere recurrence of a certain action constitutes sufficient grounds for its legality. It is often argued that what is important is not the "recurrence" of the action, but rather the "recognition" of this recurrence. Such recognition could be established by judicial decree or other means of institutional ascertainment. In the case of Islamic law, legality is established mainly by agreement, or rather non-contradiction, with the main principles embodied in its founding texts.

The founding texts of Islam, the Qurʾān and the Sunnah of the Prophet, include several direct, indirect, and implied references to the concept of custom. The textual foundations of the concept of custom are often associated with certain passages that contain these two terms and their derivatives. Some jurists, however, referred to other passages that do not contain either of these two terms. These jurists were interested more in the way the texts treated the *concept* of custom rather than the specific terms of *ʿurf* and *ʿādah* . A closer examination of the founding texts shows that the concept of custom is not necessarily antithetical to sharīʿah. After all, sharīʿah did not start from a *tabula rasa*, and it was not meant to. The concept of revelation is not limited to the revealed texts, but these texts presume the instinctive state of *fiṭrah* (purity) into which humans are born. Gradually through social and cultural influences, this inborn purity is obscured. The ultimate objective of sharīʿah is to renew and revive this original state of fiṭrah. In addition to *fiṭrah*, there are also various remnants of the teachings of the earlier prophets that were stored in human collective memory. Many customs and conventions originate in these two sources, and these are the ones that sharīʿah approved and allowed to continue. Therefore, not everything that sharīʿah introduced was completely new to the seventh century Arabian environment. Some of the existing customs were approved and continued while others were condemned and discontinued; this was an attitude that guided jurists' efforts to implement sharīʿah across the different sociohistorical contexts. However, not all the customs that the sharīʿah condemned actually disappeared. Some of these condemned customs, in different sociohistorical contexts, managed to survive and coexist with sharīʿah. The stronger the custom and the more well-established, the harder it was to eliminate completely, hence the constant tension between sharīʿah and custom. The fact that divine revelation, as the ultimate source of religious truth, did not approve all customs indicates that custom in itself cannot be an independent source of legislation. People develop both good and bad customs. Consequently, customs need further validation through rational or legislative ascertainment.

In addition to the textual references in both the Qurʾān and the Sunnah of the Prophet, the early juristic development was shaped by the efforts of the leading authorities of the different regional schools established by the companions of the Prophet. Later, the founders of the famous legal schools, such as those of Abū Ḥanīfah, Mālik Ibn Anas, and al-Shāfiʿī, articulated the teachings of the regional schools. Moreover, the early theological discussions over the concept of *ʿādah* were quite instrumental in the development of the legal concept of *ʿurf*. The works of eminent theologian-jurists, such as al-Bāqillānī, al-Juwaynī, and al-Ghazālī, transported key theological concepts into the juristic discourse. Many Muslim theologians, particularly from the Ashʿarī school, relied on the concept of custom in their treatment of many issues such as causality, human freedom, as well as legal capacity and responsibility. Interestingly, custom was used to provide rational justification for important legal concepts that were conceived as solely text-based, such as *tawātur* and *ijmāʿ*. This was the main distinctive characteristic of the rational or theoretical school of jurisprudence. The applied (mostly Ḥanafī) school, on the other hand, incorporated custom through the two closely related concepts of *qiyās* and *istiḥsān*. Similarly, the Mālikī jurists drew on the well-established concept of the *ʿamal* of the people of Madīnah as first articulated in the *Muwaṭṭaʾ* of Mālik, and later in the subsequent texts that were based on it. The development of the concept until the end of the fifth/eleventh century was characterized by the two approaches of these two schools. Most importantly, these schools reached a general juristic consensus over the four main sources.

In the post fifth/eleventh century period, some jurists started to combine the methods of these two schools. The concept of custom continued to develop beyond the scope of the four main sources, initially through the expansion of *qiyās* and then through the concept of *istidlāl*. With the consolidation of *istidlāl* as a composite category of several secondary sources, custom was itself consolidated as one of these secondary sources.

But the juristic treatment of custom was not limited to the domain of the sources. It was also integrated through a number of hermeneutical procedures such as particularization (*takhṣīṣ*). Particularization was one of the procedures that the jurists adopted to account for a legal exception that could not be subsumed under a general rule of sharīʿah. Such exceptions had to be supported by alternative proofs; custom was used as one of them. This custom-based particularization was not, however, a general rule that was applied without restriction; otherwise, it would subject texts to customs rather than the other way around. The jurists developed several guidelines to ensure that custom remained subject to legislation. For example, in order for a text to be particularized on the basis of a custom, this text must have been grounded in a custom in the first place. The particularization in question becomes, therefore, particularization of a custom by another custom rather than a particularization of a text by a custom.

In addition to the expansion of *qiyās*, the development of *istidlāl* and the various hermeneutical procedures, the concept of custom continued to evolve within the new legal genres that started to emerge from the existing body of legal literature. The two examples of legal maxims and objectives of sharīʿah are cases in point. In legal maxims, for example, many of the usages and applications of custom took the form of general foundational principles. Most importantly, custom was counted among the five cardinal maxims on which the entire system of Islamic law was built. Similarly, within the genre of the objectives of sharīʿah, custom was considered one of the important tools that facilitate the realization of these objectives.

According to al-Shāṭibī, the ultimate objective of sharīʿah is to achieve people's benefits, both in this life and in the afterlife. This ultimate objective is dependent, however, on the assumption of three subsidiary objectives: that sharīʿah is meant to be comprehensible; that it is meant to entail legal stipulations; and that these stipulations are meant to free the individual from the influences of his lower self. Al-Shaṭibī's treatment demonstrates that within this framework of the objectives, custom was incorporated as a structural built-in mechanism to ensure sharīʿah's intelligibility, applicability, and adjustability. The treatment of custom within these two genres—legal maxims and objectives of sharīʿah—represented a significant development of the concept in the post fifth/eleventh century period. Legal maxims articulated the different applications of custom and the objectives of sharīʿah provided the general framework within which the concept should operate. Within these two genres, the jurists sought to place principles such as *maṣlaḥah* and *ʿurf* within a larger hierarchical order that determined the scope of the different sources and governed their relationships with each other.

Tracing the historical development of the concept of custom reveals the organic connection among the various concepts within the Islamic legal tradition. From the beginning, the concept was closely linked with other important concepts such as the Sunnah of the Prophet, the *ʿamal* of the people of Madīnah, *ijmāʿ, istiḥsān, and tawātur*, among many others. But this connection never amounted to confusion. Each of these concepts acquired a unique semantic signification within the Islamic legal culture. Still, the diachronic study of the concept reveals the importance of placing these concepts within particular sociohistorical contexts on the one hand, and particular legal schools on the other. This becomes a necessity in the analysis of the microdebates on major legal concepts such as *qiyās, istidlāl*, or *ʿillah*. Yet, despite these historical inter and intraschool variations both in legal theory and substantive law, it is still possible to trace a common course of development within the general juristic discourse. Similarly, the historical development of the concept of custom demonstrates the organic relationship between legal theory and substantive law. These two systems were concerned more with the theoretical formulations of legal methods and how these methods generated rulings pertaining to different issues than historicizing these formulations in particular contexts. However, the different legal constructions of the concept of custom serve as important indicators of the various sociohistorical contexts that gave rise to these constructions. These constructions become more evident in the realm of legal application, as shown in the literature of legal responses (*fatāwā*) and judgeship (*qaḍāʾ*). These two genres show that the competence of a jurist is not measured solely by sufficient theoretical knowledge of legal methods and rules but, equally importantly, by the way this knowledge applies to real-life cases. Moreover, these two genres demonstrate that sharīʿah is not merely a body of texts or even a set of principles embodied in these texts; it is also a process. Through this process, the jurist constantly constructs reality according to the divine ideals.

In a modern context, one may question the importance of premodern legal theory. In a world where lawmaking is no longer the responsibility of independent jurists, jurisconsults, or mujtahids, but rather undertaken by state legislative bodies, what is the point of discussing *qiyās* or *ijmāʿ*, or even *ʿurf*, for that matter? The underlying assumption behind this question is that premodern legal theories belong to a premodern reality, while a modern reality requires modern legal theories and methods. But still, this question implies that the difference between the premodern and the modern is clear-cut, or even inevitable. Or, it assumes that the transition from the far left end to the far right end of this continuum is inescapable, as is sometimes suggested in modern social science literature. These types of questions, however, tend to obscure the basic concerns that are integral to the human condition irrespective of the question of time. After all, what is law? What is the purpose of lawmaking? How should the law be constructed? Should law be constructed according to a certain moral or philosophical system or should it be completely detached from the latter? What is the relationship between law and religious belief? And more particularly, how does the classical Islamic legal system relate to modern legal theories and methods?

In Muslim societies, legal reform has been the subject of a long and bifurcating debate for the past two centuries. It has been a major battleground between modernity and tradition. On the one hand, some researchers rule out the possibility that classical legal theory can play a significant role in lawmaking in the modern age. On the other hand, other researchers insist that legal reforms should remain within a particular paradigm of the Islamic legal tradition. However, the methods of both groups remain lacking. An efficient legal system has to satisfy at least two main criteria. First, it has to take full cognizance of the reality that it seeks to regulate, availing itself of every effort to avoid simplified and reductionist accounts of this reality. Second, it has to be faithful to its people's historical and cultural background without either idealizing past experiences or being insensitive to other historical and cultural experiences. The question is not whether sharīʿah is an obsolete survival that is doomed to extinction by the all-powerful forces of modernity, or that all legal reforms brought by modernity constitute bad custom (*ʿurf fāsid*) and are destined to be replaced by sharīʿah-compliant laws sometime in the future. If history is any guide, the historical development of the concept of *ʿurf* shows that law is in a constant state of reconstruction and custom is an integral part of the context within which this reconstruction takes place. Moreover, in the Islamic legal tradition, custom and legislation have been irrevocably intertwined; legislation relies on (compatible and approved) custom to ensure its applicability and custom depends on legislation to ensure its legal normativity.

# Notes

## Introduction

1. Custom has often been considered one of the most important sources of law, in addition to legislation, precedent, and equity. See Harold Berman, *Law and Revolution: The Formation of the Western Legal Tradition* (Cambridge: Harvard University Press, 1983), 11. See also, Christoph Kletzer, "Custom and Positivity: An Examination of the Philosophic Ground of the Hegel-Savigny Controversy" in *The Nature of Customary Law*, eds. Amanda Perreau-Saussine and James B. Murphy (Cambridge: Cambridge University Press, 2007), 130–134. Despite the modern misgivings about the legal status of custom, some would argue that custom is at the very foundations of ethical principles, written laws, and philosophical views because they, ultimately, are nothing but reformulations of preexisting customs. See Kletzer, "Custom and Positivity," 1.
2. It may be argued that these legal reforms codified the role of custom in civil law systems but not in Islamic law proper. The fact remains, however, that these civil law systems did not renounce sharīʿah altogether. In fact, sharīʿah was often listed as one of the main sources of these laws. These legal reforms turned sharīʿah from being the sole source of the legal system into one source among others. In the present context, I am mainly concerned with the impact that this development had on the modern reconstructions of the Islamic legal tradition in general and Islamic legal theory in particular.
3. Friedrich M. Müller, preface to "Chips from a German Woodshop" in *Thinking About Religion, A Reader*, ed. Ivan Strenski (Oxford: Blackwell Publishing, 2006), 51.
4. Qurʾān 35:43. In this sense, the concept of custom is closer to the concept of nature or established order than to the concept of a customary practice. I shall elaborate on this point further in chapter 2 and in the conclusion.
5. See, for example, Albert Hourani, *Islam in European Thought* (Cambridge: Cambridge University Press, 1991), 14.

## 1. Custom and Islamic Law in Modern Scholarship

1. Gradually each of these debates inspired many other subdebates. For example, the debate on the origins soon developed into two major debates on the Qurʾān

and Sunnah respectively. As far as the debate on the origins of Islamic law is concerned, more emphasis was placed on the Sunnah rather than the Qur'ān. On the Qur'ān debate see John Wansbrough, *Qur'anic Studies: Sources and Methods of Scriptural Interpretation* (Oxford: Oxford University Press, 1977) and John Burton, *The Collection of the Quran* (Cambridge: Cambridge University Press, 1977). For a recent restatement of the classical Orientalist views see Herbert Berg ed., *Method and Theory in the Study of Islamic Origins* (Leiden: Brill, 2003). For a rebuttal of their argument see Muhammad Mustafa Azami, *The History of the Quranic Text from Revelation to Compilation: A Comparative Study with the Old and New Testament* (Leicester: UK Islamic Academy, 2003). For the Sunnah debate see Ignaz Goldziher, *Muslim Studies* (London: Allen and Unwin, 1967) and Joseph Schacht, *The Origins of Muhammadan Jurisprudence* (Oxford: Clarendon Press, 1959) and *An Introduction to Islamic Law* (Oxford: Clarendon Press, 1964). For a review and rebuttal see Muhammad Mustafa Azami, *On Schacht's Origins of Muhammadan Jurisprudence* (New York: Wiley, 1985); Yasin Dutton, *The Origins of Islamic Law: The Qur'ān, the Muwatta, and the Madinan Amal* (Surrey: Curzon, 1999); Harald Motzki, *The Origins of Islamic Jursprudence: Meccan Fiqh before Classical Schools* (Leiden: Brill, 2002); and Scott Lucas, *Constructive Critics, Hadith Literature and the Articulation of Sunni Islam: The Legacy of the Generation of Ibn Sa'd, Ibn Ma'īn, and Ibn Ḥanbal* (Leiden: Brill, 2004).

2. The term Orientalist scholarship is usually used to refer to the studies of Western scholars, mainly philologists, on the orient and oriental cultures in general and Arab and Muslim cultures in particular. There is already an extensive body of literature, inspired by the work of Edward Said, that analyzes the different aspects of this scholarship. Here I am mainly concerned with the impact of the Western Orientalist scholarship on the construction of the role of custom in the Islamic legal tradition. See, for example, Edward Said, *Orientalism* (New York: Vintage Books, 1979) and Alexander Lyon Macfie, ed., *Orientalism A Reasder* (New York: New York University Press, 2000.
3. This date range is determined based on the sources consulted in the present study.
4. Jacques Waardenburg's treatment of the divide between official or normative and popular religion in the field of Islamic studies provides useful insights on the roots of the problem. This is of great relevance to the issue at hand because as Waardenburg's discussion illustrates, both "customs" and "Islamic law" would mean different things to different people. See Jacques Waardenburg "Official and Popular Religion as a Problem in Islamic Studies," in Jacques Waardenburg et al., *Official and Popular Religion as a Theme in the Study of Religion* (The Hague: Mouton, 1979), 340–368. In this article, Waardenburg's conclusion was that the process of consistent modernization and rationalization associated with the more secular application of Islam would eventually lead to the gradual replacement of both official and popular versions of Islam by a new state of affairs (p. 371). This conclusion is particularly significant because it reveals the type of intellectual projections current at the time of the book's publication. Recently, the author has offered insightful reflections on the evolution of his personal understanding of the subject, as well as the field in the past 50 years. See Waardenburg

*Islam: Historical, Social, and Political Perspectives* (Berlin: Walter de Gruyter, 2002), 1–19 and *Muslims as Actors*, (Berlin: Walter de Gruyter, 2007).

5. There are several scholarly works that review and evaluate the works of the scholars who took part in these debates since their inception. Some of the works I was able to consult are: Stephen Humphreys, *Islamic History: A Framework for Inquiry* (Princeton: Princeton University Press, 1991), 70–103; Norman Calder, *Studies in Early Muslim Jurisprudence* (Oxford: Clarendon Press, 1993), 198–222; Tarif Khalidi, *Arabic Historical Thought in the Classical Period* (New York: Cambridge, 1994), 20–28; Harald Motzki, *The Origins of Islamic Jursprudence: Meccan Fiqh before Classical Schools* (Leiden: Brill, 2002), 2–49; Sherman Jackson, *Islamic Law and the State: The Constitutional Jurisprudence of Shihab al-Din al-Qarafi* (Leiden: Brill, 1996); Ahmad A. Ahmad, *Structural Interrelations of Theory and Practice in Islamic Law : A Study of Six Works of Medieval Islamic Jurisprudence* (Leiden: Brill, 2006); Haim Gerber, *Islamic Law and Culture, 1600–1840* (Leiden: Brill, 1999); and Frank Vogel, "The State of the Field: A Major Advance is Imminent," *The Newsletter of the Islamic Legal Studies Program at Harvard Law School* 11, no. 2 (2006): 1–4.
6. Christiaan Snouck Hurgronje, *Mohammedanism: Lectures on its Origins, its Religious and Political Growth, and Its Present State* (New York: Putnam's Sons, 1916), 22. Goldziher notes: "It is astonishing that foreign cultural influences had an effect on the evolution of this legal method and on various details of its application. Islamic jurisprudence shows undeniable traces of the influence of Roman law both in its methodology and in its particular stipulation." See Ignaz Goldziher, *Introduction to Islamic Theology and Law* (Princeton: Princeton University Press, 1981), 44. See also Goldziher, *Muslim Studies* (London: Allen and Unwin, 1967); Joseph Schacht, "Foreign Elements in Ancient Islamic Law" in *The Formation of Islamic Law*, ed. Wael Hallaq (Burlington: Ashgate/Variorum Publishing Limited, 2004), 60–67; and Joseph Schacht, *An Introduction,* 21, Patricia Crone, *Roman, Provincial and Islamic Law, the Origins of the Islamic Patronate,* (New York: Cambridge, 1987). For a rebuttal of Crone's argument see Wael Hallaq, "The Use and Abuse of Evidence: The Question of Provincial and Roman Influences on Early Islamic Law" *Journal of American Oriental Society* 110, no. 1(1990): 79–91.
7. Christiaan Snouck Hurgronje, *The Achehnese* (Leyden: Brill, 1906).
8. Interest in the "origins issue" has not dissipated. See Wael Hallaq, *The Origins and Evolution of Islamic Law* (New York: Cambridge, 2005), 1–7.
9. G. C. J. J. Van den Bergh, "The Concept of Folk Law in Historical Context: A Brief Outline" in *Folk Law: Essays in the Theory and Practice of Lex Non Scripta,* eds. Alison D. Renteln and Alan Dundes (New York: Garland Publishing, 1994), 17; William Graham, "Traditionalism in Islam: An Essay in Interpretation," *Journal of Interdisciplinary History* 23, no. 3 (1993): 495–522.
10. Alison D. Renteln and Alan Dundes, "What is Folk Law" in *Folk Law,* 3.
11. See, for example, *Encyclopedia of Islam*, 2nd ed. vol. I, s.v. "*Ada*" and vol. X, s.v. "*Urf*."
12. T. O. Beidelman, *W. Robertson Smith and the Sociological Study of Religion* (Chicago: University of Chicago Press, 1974), 6.

13. Jacques Waardenburg, ed., *Classical Approaches to the Study of Religion* (Berlin: de Gruyter, 1999), 150.
14. Ivan Strenski, *Thinking About Religion: An Historical Introduction to Theories of Religion* (Oxford: Blackwell Publishing, 2006), 126.
15. Ibid., 122. It was a common practice among European travelers to dress like the local population and to take up familiar local names in order to ensure ease of movement and to avoid being spotted as outsiders. See, for example, Walter Besant, *The Life and Achievements of Edward Henry Palmer* (London: J. Murray, 1883), 99, 247.
16. See also. *Smith* "A Journey in the Hijaz" in *Lectures and Essays of William Robertson Smith*, eds. John Sutherland Black and George Chrystal (London: A. and C. Black, 1912), 484–597.
17. Ibid., 483.
18. Beidelman, *W. Robertson Smith*, 43. Also see Robert Segal's introduction to the new edition of Smith's *Religion of the Semites* (New Brunswick: Transaction Publishers, 2002).
19. Following his example, James Frazer traced the origins of Christian rituals to heathen and pagan origins. See James Frazer, "William Robertson Smith" in *Thinking About Religion: A Reader*, ed. Ivan Strenski (Oxford: Blackwell Publishing, 2006), 91–96.
20. Beidelman, *W. Robertson Smith*, 29, 49.
21. Goldziher has edited and annotated Smith's *Kinship and Marriage in Early Arabia.*
22. Hurgronje, *Selected Works of C. Snouck Hurgronje,* eds. G. H. Bousquet and J. Schacht (Leiden: Brill, 1957), 5.
23. Hurgronje, *Mekka in the Latter Part of the 19th Century* (Leiden: Brill, 1931), 16.
24. Ibid., 54. See, for example, his account on the practice of grave visitations and celebrations of *Mi'rāj.*
25. Ibid., 249.
26. Hurgronje, *The Achehnese*, 1:356, 363.
27. Ibid., 1:13.
28. Ibid., 2:272.
29. Ibid., 237, 277, and 281.
30. Ibid., 342.
31. Hurgronje, *Mohammedanism,* 41.
32. Ibid., 67, 160.
33. Ibid., 69.
34. Bousquet and Schacht, *Selected Works,* 57.
35. Ibid., 150. See also N. Coulson, *Conflicts and Tensions in Islamic Jurisprudence* (Chicago: University of Chicago Press, 1969), 75–76.
36. Ibid., 133.
37. In his introduction to the English translation of Goldziher's lectures, Bernard Lewis referred to him as "one of the founders of the modern science of Islamics." Ignaz Goldziher, *Introduction to Islamic Theology and Law* (Princeton: Princeton University Press, 1981), ix. Goldziher was nominated to the chair at

Cambridge University in succession to Robertson Smith. He also traveled to the Middle East and spent about seven months in Egypt and Syria.

38. P. Sj. Van Koningsveld, *Scholarship and Friendship in Early Islamwissenschaft: The Letters of C. Snouck Hurgronje to I. Goldziher* (Leiden: Faculteit der Godgeleerdheid, 1985). Also Ignaz Goldziher, *Tagebuch* (Leiden: Brill, 1978).
39. Goldziher, *Introduction to Islamic Theology and Law*, 31.
40. Ibid., 32.
41. Ibid., 33.
42. Goldziher, *Muslim Studies*, 1:2; Goldziher, *Introduction to Islamic Theology and Law*, 36, 231.
43. Ibid., 263.
44. Goldziher, *Muslim Studies*, 1:209–238. and 2:255–341.
45. Ibid., 25.
46. Ibid., 42.
47. Ibid., 75.
48. Ibid., 81.
49. Ibid., 87.
50. Ibid., 88.
51. Ibid., 140.
52. Ibid., 193.
53. Jeanette Wakin, *Remembering Joseph Schacht (1902–1969)* (Cambridge: Islamic Legal Studies Program, Harvard Law School, 2003), 3.
54. Ibid., 2.
55. Ibid.
56. Ibid., 9.
57. Ibid., 11.
58. Ibid., 19.
59. Ibid., 20. The five qualifications, *al-aḥkām al-khamsah,* denote the five designations that Muslim jurists refer to in evaluating a given issue in the light of sharīʿah. According to this sharīʿah framework, any action can be classified as obligatory (*wājib*), recommended (*mustahabb*), permissible (*mubāh*), reprehensible (*makrūh*), or prohibited (*ḥarām*). This point will be treated in more detail in the following chapter.
60. On the origin of the Islamic legal maxims and the exaggerated impact of the non-Arab scholars, see the study of Harald Motzki, in which he analyzed the biographical dictionary of Abu Ishāq al-Shirāzī to determine the ratio of the non-Arab scholars of the first two centuries. Motzki found out that the non-Arabs were a minority among the Islamic scholars. See Harald Motzki, "The Role of Non-Arab Converts in Early Islamic Law," *Islamic Law and Society* 6 (1999): 293–317.
61. Schacht, *An Introduction*, 21.
62. Ibid., 26.
63. Ibid., 27.
64. Ibid., 29.
65. Ibid., 32.
66. Schacht, *Origins*, 242.

67. On this and the other underlying assumptions in Schacht's scholarship, see Wael Hallaq, "The Quest for Origins or Doctrine," *UCLA Journal of Islamic and Near East Law* 2, 1 (2002–2003): 18.
68. Ibid., 71.
69. For more on modern European thought of the theme of religious evolution, see Strenski, *Thinking About Religion;* Daniel Pals, *Eight Theories of Religion* (Oxford: Oxford University Press, 2006); and Jacques Waardenburg, ed., *Classical Approaches to the Study of Religion* (Berlin: de Gruyter, 1999).
70. This attitude is best captured by the English poet Rudyard Kipling in his famous poem entitled "The White Man's Burden."
71. N. J. Coulson, *A History of Islamic Law* (Edinburgh: University Press, 1964), 82. See also the critical review of Schacht in Coulson's book on Joseph Schacht, "Modernism and Traditionalism in a History of Islamic Law," *Middle Eastern Studies* 1, no. 4 (1965): 388–400.
72. Ibid. On this, see also H.A.R. Gibb, *Mohammedanism: An Historical Survey* (Oxford: Oxford University Press , 1980), 60–72.
73. Several recent studies have taken issue with the "tension thesis," pointing out its limitation and inability to explain the proper relationship between theory and practice. See Alan Watson and Khaled Abou El-Fadl "Fox Hunting, Pheasant Shooting, and Comparative Law," *The American Journal of Comparative Law* 48-I (2000): 30–37. Also, Khaled Abou El-Fadl, *Rebellion and Violence in Islamic Law* (Cambridge: Cambridge University Press, 2001), 23–30; Ahmad, *Structural*, 37–45; Gerber, *Islamic Law and Culture*, 1–22; and Aziz Azmeh, "Islamic Legal Theory and the Appropriation of Reality" in *Islamic Law Social and Historical Contexts*, ed. Aziz Azmeh (London: Routledge, 1988), 250–265.
74. Patricia Crone, however, notes that it was invented by another legal scholar (R. Schmidt). See Toby Huff and Wolfgang Schluchter, eds., *Max Weber and Islam* (New Brunswick: Transaction Publishers, 1999), 13.
75. Bryan Turner, *Weber and Islam* (London: Routledge, 1974), 109.
76. Ibid. Weber viewed the development of law in terms of four main stages: "first, charismatic legal revelation through 'legal prophets'; second, empirical creation and finding of law by legal honoratories; third, imposition of law by secular or theocratic powers; fourth and finally, systematic elaboration of law and professionalized administration of justice by persons who have received their legal training in a learned and formally logical manner." Ibid., 110.
77. Coulson, *Conflicts and Tensions,* 40. On this, see also Gerber, *Islamic Law*, 10 and John Makdisi, "Legal Logic and Equity in Islamic Law," *The American Journal of Comparative Law* 33 (1985): 63–66.
78. On the limitations of Weber's understanding of Islam, see Huff and Schluchter, *Max Weber*, 27. See also, John Makdisi, "Formal Rationality in Islamic Law and The Common Law," *Cleveland State Law Review* 34 (1985–1986): 97–112 and Harold Berman, *Law and Revolution,* 548–552.
79. Nabia Abbott, *Studies in Arabic Literary Papyri* (Chicago: University of Chicago Press, 1967), vol. II.
80. In addition to these works, many books were written in other languages, especially Arabic, to refute Schacht's thesis. Since the 1950s, interest in this subject has not died out and every year new books with titles on the authenticity of

Ḥadīth and Sunnah continue to be published. Among the most prominent works in Arabic are, for example, Muṣtafa al-Siba'ī, *al-Sunnah wa makanatuha fī al-Tashrī' al-Islāmī* (Beirut: al-Maktab al-Islamí, 1976); 'Abd al-Ghanī 'Abd al-Khāliq, *Ḥujjiyyat al-Sunnah* (Manṣūrah: Dār al-Wafā', 1997); Muḥammad al-Ghazālī, *al-Sunnah al-Nabawiyah bayna Ahl al-Fiqh wa Ahl al-Ḥadīth* (Cairo: Dār al-Shurūq, 2005).

81. G. H. A. Juynboll, *Muslim Tradition: Studies in Chronology, Provenance, and Authorship in Early Hadith* (Cambridge: Cambridge University Press, 1983). See also, Coulson, *A History*, 69.
82. Humphreys, *Islamic History*, 84. It might be safe to note that Joseph Schacht has become an influential school within the Orientalist tradition. This school still enjoys a large following. Usually this school adopts and defends certain stands on the major debates in the field of Islamic Studies. See, for example, the preface of Ron Shaham, ed., *Law, Custom, and Statute in the Muslim World: Studies in Honor of Aharon Layish* (Leiden: Brill, 2007).
83. Two prominent examples are Motzki, *Origins*, 295, and Dutton, *Origins*. See also, Rif'at Fawzī 'Abd al-Muttalib, *Sahifat Hammām Ibn Munabih 'an Abí Hurayrah Raḍya Allahu 'anhu*, (Cairo: Maktabat al-Khanjí, 1985).
84. Azami, *On Schacht*, and also in *Dirāsāt fi al-Ḥadíth al-Nabawī wa Tarīkh Tadwinihi* (Damascus: al-Maktab al-Islāmī, 1992). See also, Said Ramadan, *Islamic Law: Its Scope and Equity* (London: P. R. Macmillan, 1961).
85. Fazlur Rahman, *Islamic Methodology in History* (Karachi: Central Institute of Islamic Research, 1965), 6.
86. Ibid., 23.
87. Similarly, Ahmad Hasan compares the pre-Shafi'ī meaning of sunnah with the post-Shafi'ī one. Only in the pre-Shāfi'ī period were sunnah and ḥadīth unidentical. In the post-Shāfi'ī period, they became not only identical, but ḥadīth became the carrier of the sunnah (which literally meant the established practice in general, but later was reserved for the established practice of the Prophet). Moreover, in the pre-Shafi'i period, ḥadīth was also used to refer to sayings of the companions and successors. Similarly, Hasan goes to considerable length to refute Schacht's denial of the existence of the term "Sunnah of the Prophet" during the first Hijrī century. He, following Rahman, asserts the existence of the *concept* of the Sunnah of the Prophet (the exemplary conduct of the Prophet that should be emulated by his followers) from the beginning. Hasan notes that "the practice and transmission of ḥadīth after the death of the Prophet went hand in hand. As long as practice was in conformity with the ideal conduct of the Prophet, there was no need for documentation. But when practice grew out of touch with the ideal Sunnah, the need for ḥadīth became more and more acute. This was the reason the early schools emphasized the practice (*'amal*) of the community more than al-Shafi'ī." See Ahmad Hasan, *The Early Development of Islamic Jurisprudence* (Islamabad: Islamic Research Institute, 1970), 86–91.
88. Baber Johansen, "Legal Literature and the Problem of Change: The Case of the Land Rent" in *Islam and Public Law*, ed. Chibli Mallat (London: Graham and Trotman, 1993), 29–31.
89. Rudolph Peters, "Ijtihad and Taqlid in 18th and 19th century Islam," *Die Welt des Islams* 20 (1980): 131–145; Wael Hallaq, "Was the Gate of Ijtihad Closed,"

*International Journal of Middle East Studies* 16 (1984): 3-41. Jackson argued that the institution of *taqlīd* involved as much creativity as *ijtihād* itself, see Jackson, *Islamic Law*, 69–89. Similarly Hallaq notes "it should come as no surprise then that *taqlīd* functioned as a vehicle of legal change to the same extent as *ijtihāad* did, if not more so." See also, Wael Hallaq, *Authority, Continuity, and Change in Islamic Law* (Cambridge: Cambridge University Press, 2001), 239.

90. Baber Johansen, *The Islamic Law on Land Tax and Rent* (London: Croom Helm, 1988). See also, Johansen, "Casuistry between Legal Concept and Social Praxis," *Islamic Law and Society* 2, no. 2 (1995): 135–156; Abraham Udovitch, "Islamic Law and the Social Context of Exchange in the Medieval Middle East," *History and Anthropology* 1 (1985): 445–465.
91. Al-Azmeh, "Islamic Legal Theory and the Appropriation of Reality," 250–261; Johansen, "Legal Literature." Johansen refers to the different genres of *mutūn* (texts), *shurūḥ* (commentaries), *fatāwā* (responses), and *rasā'il* (treatises). Ahmad A. Ahmad points to the less explored genre of *takhrīj* (extrapolation). See Ahmad, *Structural.*
92. Wael Hallaq, "From *Fatawas* to *Furu'*: Growth and Change in Islamic Substantive Law" *Islamic Law and Society* 1(1994): 29–65. See also, Muhammad K. Masud, Brinkley Messick, and David S. Powers, eds., *Islamic Legal Interpretation: Muftis and Their Fatwas* (Cambridge: Harvard University Press, 1996).
93. Galal El-Nahal, *The Judicial Administration of Ottoman Egypt in the Seventeenth Century* (Minneapolis: Bibliotheca Islamica, 1979); Muhammad K. Masud, Rudoloph Peters, and David S. Powers, eds., *Dispensing Justice in Islam: Qadis and their Judgements* (Leiden: Brill, 2006); and Rudolph Peters, "Murder on the Nile: Homicide Trials in 19th Century Egyptian Shari'a Courts," *Die Welt des Islams* 30 (1990): 98–116.
94. Gideon Libson, "On the Development of Custom as a Source of Law in Islamic Law," *Islamic Law and Society* 4 (1997): 133.
95. Muḥamad Ibn Idrīs al-Shāfiʿī, *al-Risālah*, ed., Aḥmad Muḥamad Shākir (Beirut: Dār al-Kutub al-ʿIlmiyyah, n.d.). See, for example, his discussion on the use of the meat of sacrificial animals (235–242), the example of the *salam* transaction (338), and the example of *ʿarāyā* (331). More detailed discussion of these examples and others should follow in the subsequent chapters. In a similar statement on the Ḥanbalī School, Libson observes, "I found no reference to custom in the legal literature of the Ḥanbalī school during the pre-classical and classical periods," 134. The Ḥanbalī jurist Ibn ʿAqīl (513–1119) has dealt extensively with the issue of *ʿurf* in his treatment of *uṣūl* . See in particular his *Kitāb al-Wāḍiḥ fī Uṣūl al-Fiqh*, (Beirut: Muassasat al-Risālah, 1999), Vol. II, 423 and Vol. III, 406. Ibn al-Qayyim is one of the oft-cited authorities on the issue of *ʿurf*, especially his *Iʿlām al-Muwaqiʿīn*. For more on the Ḥanbalī school's treatment of *ʿurf* see ʿĀdil Ibn ʿAbd al-Qādir Qūtah, *al-ʿUrf Ḥujjiyyatuhu wa Atharuhu fī Fiqh al-Muʿāmalāt al-Māliyyah ʿinda al-Ḥanābilah* (Makkah: al-Maktabah al-Makiyyah, 1997).
96. Clearly, the process of abstraction that the later jurists undertook was in principle based on the same examples used by early jurists such as Abū Ḥanīfah, Mālik, and al-Shāfiʿī. In other words, examples such as *ʿarāyā* and *salam* demonstrate the slow development of principles such as *ʿurf* out of prior abstract concepts.

97. In his study on the concept of *ʿamal* in the Mālikī school, Umar Faruq Abd-Allah makes a similar point by noting that "coherent systematic intellectual systems do, in fact, exist and perhaps even come into existence in advance of the terminologies and analytical elaborations that explain those intellectual systems systematically—a further implication of this observation is that studies of intellectual history must search out and define concepts primarily and terms that stand for those concepts secondarily." See Umar Faruq Abd-Allah, "Malik's Concept of *ʿAmal* in the Light of Mālikī Legal Theory" (Ph.D. Diss., University of Chicago, 1978), 12–15.
98. Libson, "On the Development," 138.
99. See Allan Watson and Khaled Abou El-Fadl, "Fox Hunting, Pheasant Shooting, and Comparative Law," *The American Journal of Comparative Law* 48–1(2000): 29. For a concise presentation of the various theories that account for the relationship between law and society, see Alan Watson, *Society and Legal Change* (Philadelphia: Temple University Press, 2001), 1–9.
100. Ibid., 145.
101. See Ibn ʿĀbdīn's detailed discussion of this point in his famous treatise, "*Nashr al-ʿArf fī Binā' baʿḍ al-Aḥkām ʿalā al-ʿUrf*" in *Majmūʿat Rasā'il Ibn ʿĀbidīn* (Beirut: Dār Iḥyā' al-Turāth), 2:116.
102. See Ibn ʿĀbidīn, *Hāshiyat Radd al-Muḥtār ʿalā al-Durr al-Mukhtār, Sharḥ Tanwīr al-Abṣār* (Cairo: Muṣṭafā al-Bābī al-Ḥalabī, 1966), 5:176–7; ʿAlā' al-Dīn Ibn Masʿūd al-Kāsānī, *Kitāb Badā'iʿ al-Ianā'iʿ fi Tartīb al-Sharā'iʿ*(Beirut: Dār al-Kitāb al-ʿArabī, 1974), 5:193–194; ʿAbd al-Raḥmān al-Jazirī, *Kitāb al-Fiqh ʿala al-Madhāhib al-Arbaʿah* (Beirut: Dār al-Kutub al-ʿIlmiyyah, 1990), 2:233. For a detailed discussion on the issue of the operative cause in this Ḥadīth according to different schools, see Ibn al-Qayyim, *Iʿlām al-Muwaqiʿīn ʿan Rabb al-ʿĀlamīn* (Cairo: Dār al-Ḥadith, 2002), 2:413–416 and ʿAbd al-Razzāq al-Sanhurī, *Maṣādir al-Ḥaqq fī al-Fiqh al-Islāmī* (Beirut: Dār Iḥyā' al-Turāth al-ʿArabī, 1997), 3:125–137.
103. Gideon Libson, *Jewish and Islamic Law: A Comparative Study of Custom during the Geonic Period* (Cambridge: Harvard University Press, 2003), 180–181.
104. Ibid.
105. Ibid., viii.
106. Hallaq, *Authority*, 166. Hallaq emphasizes that change did not occur in a passive or unconscious manner, but that "Muslim jurists were acutely aware of both the *occurrence* of, and the *need* for, change in the law" (italics in the original).
107. Ibid., 240.
108. Harold Berman deals extensively with this issue under the concept of a body or system of law that "depended for its vitality on the belief in the ongoing character of law, its capacity for growth over generations and centuries—a belief which is uniquely Western. The body of law survives because it contains a built-in mechanism for organic change." See Berman, *Law and Revolution*, 9. Hallaq's treatment clearly shows that this system of law as outlined by Berman was not restricted to the Western legal tradition but was characteristic of the Islamic legal tradition as well.

109. On the several nuances that the issue of legal change involves and the different "rational" or "causal" theories to explain it, see Waston, *Society and Legal Change*, 1–9.
110. He introduces a four-tier typology that includes the professor (*mudarris*), the judge (*qāḍī*), jurisconsult (muftī), and author-jurist (*muṣannif*). Hallaq argues that legal change was effected mainly through the efforts of the jurisconsult and the author-jurist. Hallaq, *Authority*, 172–173.
111. Ibid., 215–216.
112. In his survey of the idea of "folk law" in the European history, Van den Bergh notes that "with the concept of folk law we acknowledge our plight—knowingly or not—of a binary way of thinking which has haunted the social sciences from their beginning and which perhaps has more to do with a European experience of fundamental social change between roughly speaking, 1750 and 1880, than with social reality elsewhere in the world (status-contract, *Gemeinschaft-Gesellschaft*, *Staat-Volk*, cultural-primitive, pre-industrial-industrial, tribal-urban, etc.)." See G. C. J. J. Van den Bergh, "The Concept of Folk Law in Historical Context: A Brief Outline" in *Folk Law*, 22.
113. Qur'ān 7:199.
114. Hallaq refers to this controversy. See Hallaq, *Authority*, 225.
115. For works in English see, for example, Muḥammad Hāshim Kamālī, *Principles of Islamic Jurisprudence* (Cambridge: Islamic Texts Society, 1991).
116. Zirklī, *al-Aʿlām*, 6:42.
117. Ibn ʿĀbidīn, *Hāshiyat Radd al-Muḥtār.*
118. They were collected and published together in one volume as *Majmūʿat Rasāʾil Ibn ʿĀbidīn*.
119. Published in the above mentioned volume with the title *Nashr al-ʿArf fi Bināʾ baʿḍ al-Aḥkām ʿalā al-ʿUrf.*
120. Gerber, *Islamic Law and Culture*, 9.
121. On the concept of discursive tradition, see Muhammad Qasim Zaman, *The Ulama in Contemporary Islam: Custodians of Change* (Princeton: Princeton University Press, 2002), 6–8 and Talal Asad, *The Idea of an Anthropology of Islam* (Washington, DC: Center for Contemporary Arab Studies, Georgetown University, 1986), 14. On the scholastic method, see Berman, *Law and Revolution*, 131. On the importance of the linguistic practice in the Islamic legal tradition, see Abou El-Fadl, *Rebellion and Violence*, 5.
122. It is interesting to note that one of this committee's members was ʿAlāʾ al-Dīn Ibn ʿĀbidīn the son of Muhammad Amīn Ibn ʿĀbidīn. See Zirkli, *al-A'lām*, 6:42 and ʿAlī Ḥaydar, *Durar al-Ḥukkām Sharḥ Majallat al-Aḥkām* (Beirut: Dār al-Jīl, 1991), 1:13.
123. Schacht, *An Introduction to Islamic Law*, 92; Mustafā Aḥmad al-Zarqa, *al-Madkhal al-Fiqhī al-ʿĀmm* (Damascus: Dār al-Qalam, 1998), 1:235–246. It was applied in Syria, Palestine, Jordan, Iraq, and Libya. Egypt never adopted the *Majallah* and this had to do with its particular historical conditions since the time of Muhammad ʿAlī, who sought to keep Egypt independent of the Ottoman influence. It was at the time of Ismāʿīl (1863–1879) that mixed courts were established in 1875, followed by national courts in 1883. See

'Abd al-Razzaq Sanhūrī, "*al-Qanun al-Madanī al-'Arabī,*" first published by the Cultural Department in the Arab League in 1953, republished in *Islāmiyyāt al-Sanhūrī Bāshā*, ed., Muḥammad 'Imarah (Mansura: Dār al-Wafā', 2006), 2:538 and 1:354.

124. In his study on Islamic legal history, Muḥammad al-Khuḍarī speaks of six main stages. They start with the time of the Prophet, followed by the time of the older companions of the Prophet, the time of the younger companions of the Prophet, from the beginning of the second/eighth century up to mid fifth/eleventh century, the time of the establishment of legal schools up to the fall of Baghdad in the seventh/thirteenth century, and finally from the fall of Baghdad up to the fourteenth/twentieth century. Al-Zarqa follows the scheme of al-Khuḍarī, but he refers to the sixth stage as the period from the fall of Baghdad up to the composition of the *Majallah* in 1286/1870. In addition to that, he adds a seventh stage from the composition of the *Majallah* up to the end of the Second World War 1287/1945 and lastly an eighth stage from that time up to the late 1990s. See Muḥammad Khudarī, *Tarikh al-Tashrī 'al-Islāmī* (Cairo: al-Mañba'ah al-Tijāriyyah al-Kubrā, 1970) and al-Zarqa, *Al-Madkhal*, 1:159–247.

125. Haydar, *Durar*, 1:44–51. Al-Zarqa, *al-Madkhal*, 2:1077–1083.

126. For example, one of the earliest attempts was undertaken by Muḥammad Qadrī Bāshā in *Murshid al-Hayrān ilā Ma'rifat Aḥwāl al-Insān fī al-mu'amalāt al-Shar'iyyah 'alā Madhhab al-Imām Al-A'ẓam Abī Ḥanifah al-Nu'mān mulā'iman li 'Urf al-Diyār al-Miṣriyyah wa Sā'ir al-Umam al-Islāmiyyah* (Cairo: al-Maktabah al-Miṣriyyah, 1919). The subtitle clearly highlights the role of *'urf.*

127. Sanhūrī, "Qanun," 541.

128. 'Abd al-'Azīz al-Khayyaṭ, who was a member of the committee commissioned to write the Jordanian civil code, recorded the details of the Jordanian experience in his book that he wrote on the theory of *'urf.* See 'Abd al-Azīz al-Khayyaṭ, *Naẓariyyat al-'Urf* (Amman: Maktabat al-Aqṣā, 1977), 7–17.

129. See, for example, the proceedings of a seminar on the characteristics of juristic renewal where leading Muslim scholars (Jamāl al-Dīn 'Atiyyah, Tawfīq al-Shāwī, Sayyid Dusūqī, Jamāl Qutb, Alī Jum'ah, Muḥammad 'Imārḥ, Ṭāriq al-Bishrī) took part. See Ḥusnī Muḥammad Naṣr, "Malāmiḥ al-Tajdīd al-Fiqhī" in *Qaḍāyā Islāmiyyah Mu'āṣirah* 9–10 (2000): 82–104.

130. Ṣalāḥ al-Dīn al-Munajjid and Yūsuf al-Khūrī, eds., *Fatāwa al-Imām Muḥammad Rashīd Riḍā* (Beirut: Dār al-Kitāb al-Jadīd, 1971). On issues related to *'urf* and transactions 2:559, and punishment for apostasy 2:576, and clothes and outfits 2:764; 3:866, 868; 4:1564; 5:1829 and family issues 3:1102, and court procedures, 4:1300, 1600. On *maṣlaḥah* and insurance 2:410, and *'urf* 2:558, and al-Tufi 5:1743.

131. Ibid., 1:92.

132. Ibid., 1:172; 2:620; 3:809.

133. Brinkley Messick's account of such transformation in the Yemeni context provides an illustrative example. See Brinkley Messick, *The Calligraphic State: Textual Domination and History in Muslim Society* (Berkeley: University of California Press, 1993), 253–254.

134. See, for example, Muḥammad Saʿīd Ibn ʿAbd al-Raḥmān al-Bānī al-Ḥusaynī, *ʿUmdat al-Taḥqīq fī al-Taqlīd wa al-Talfīq* (Damascus: Dār al-Qādirī, 1997).
135. For example, al-Sanhūrī, *Maṣādir al-Haqq* and Ṣubḥī Maḥmaṣānī, *Falsafat al-Tashrīʿ, al-Islāmī* (Beirut: Dār al-ʿIlm lil-Malāyīn, 1975).
136. Often these studies include introductions that survey the literature and seek to place these works within their historical contexts. See, for example, Ṭāhā Jābir al-ʿAlawānī's edition of al-Rāzī's *al-Maḥṣūl* or Ḥasan Hītū's edition of al-Ghazālī's *al-Mankhūl*.
137. Books on Islamic substantive law continued to be published. The two most famous works are Sayyid Sābiq's *Fiqh al-Sunnah*, which ran into numerous editions and ʿAbd al-Raḥmān al-Jazīrī's *al-Fiqh ʿalā al-Madhāhib al-Arbaʿah.*
138. See ʿAbd al-Qādir ʿAwdah, *al-Tashrīʿ al-Jināʾī al-Islāmī muqāranan bi al-Qānūn al-Waḍʿī* (Cairo: Maktabat Dār al-Turāth, 2003) and Maḥmaṣānī, *Falsafat al-Tashrīʿ*.
139. Among the works of legal theory, the two books of Aḥmad Fahmī Abū Sunna and Muṣṭafā Aḥmad al-Zarqa are probably the most famous ones as far as the subject of custom is concerned. Both were first published in the 1940s and later ran into many editions. Although these two works can be classified as comparative, they focus more on the Ḥanafī school. Some other works focus on particular schools. For example, ʿUmar ʿAbd al-Karīm al-Jīdī, *al-ʿUrf wa al-ʿAmal fī al-Madhhab al-Mālikī wa Mafhūmuhumā ladā ʿUlamāʾal-Maghrib* (Rabāṭ: Ṣundūq Iḥyāʾ al-Turāth al-ʿArabī al-Mushtarak bayna al-Mamlakah al-Maghribiyyah wa al-Imārāt al-ʿArabiyyah al-Muttaḥidah, 1982) focuses on the Mālikī school. Qūtah, *al-ʿUrf Hujjiyyathu wa Atharuhū,* focuses on the Ḥanbalī school. Muṣṭafā Muḥammad Rushdī Muftī, *al-ʿUrf ʿinda al-Usūlyyīn wa Atharuhū fī al-Ahkām al-Fiqhiyyah* (Alexandria: Dār al-Imān, 2006) focuses on some examples from the Shāfiʾī school. Sayyid Ṣāliḥ ʿAwaḍ, *Athar al-ʿUrf fī al-Tashrīʿ al-Islāmī* (Cairo: Dār al-Kitāb al-Jāmiʿī, 1979) does not focus on a particular school. Among the famous modern jurisprudential works, see Muḥammad Abū Zahrah, *Uṣūl al-Fiqh* (Cairo: Dār al-Fikr al-ʿArabī, 2004), 247; ʿAbd al-Wahhāb Khallāf, *Maṣādir al-Tashrīʿ al-Islāmī fīmā lā Naṣṣa fīh* (Kuwait: Dār al-Qalam, 1970); 145–149, and also his *ʿIlm Uṣūl al-Fiqh* (Cairo: Maktabat Dār al-Turāth), 89–91; Khalifah Bābakr al-Ḥasan, *al-Adillah al-Mukhtalaf fīhā ʿinda al-Uṣūliyyīn* (Cairo: Maktabat Wahbah, 1987), 40–47; Muhammad Kamāl al-Dīn Imām, *Uṣūl al-Fiqh al-Islāmī* (Beirut: al-Muʾssassah al-Jāmiʿiyyah lil Dirāsāt wa al-Nashr wa al-Tawzīʿ, 1996), 183–196; Maḥmūd Muḥammad al-Ṭanṭāwī, *Uṣūl al-Fiqh al-Islāmī* (Cairo: Maktabat Wahbah, 2001), 307–313; and Samīr ʿĀliyah, *Niẓām al-Dawlah wa al-Qaḍāʾ wa al-ʿUrf fī al-Islām* (Beirut: al-Muʾssassah al-Jāmiʿiyyah lil Dirāsāt wa al-Nashr wa al-Tawzīʿ, 1997), 391–429. In addition to these general theoretical studies, other studies highlight the role of custom as it relates to particular issues. For example, Ruqayyah Ṭāhā Jābir al-ʿUlwānī, *Athar al-ʿUrf fī Fahm al-Nuṣūṣ, Qaḍāya al-Marʾah Namudhajan* (Damascus: Dār al-Fikr, 2003) and Maḥmūd Muḥammad Shaykh, *al-Mahr fī al-Islām Bayna al-Māḍī wa al-Ḥāḍir: Dirāsah Fiqhiyyah Ijtimāʿiyyah*

(Ṣaydā: al-Maktabah al-ʿAṣriyyah, 2000). Another increasingly popular genre that is relevant to the issue of *ʿurf* includes works on themes such as *ijtihād*, *tajdīd* (renewal), and *iṣlāḥ* (reform). See, for example, Muḥammad ʿAbd al-Raḥmān Marʿashlī, *Ikhtilāf al-Ijtihād wa Taghayyuruhu wa Athar dhālika fī al-Futyā* (Beirut: al-Mu'ssassah al-Jāmiʿiyyah lil Dirāsāt wa al-Nashr wa al-Tawzīʿ, 2003).

## 2. Normative Foundations of the Concept of Custom in the Islamic Legal Tradition

1. For a detailed discussion on this point, see Khaled Abou El-Fadl, *Speaking in God's Name: Islamic Law, Authority and Women* (Oxford: One World, 2006), 23–69.
2. Muḥammad Ibn Aḥmad al-Tamīmī Abū al-ʿArab, *Kitāb al-Miḥan*, ed. Yaḥya Wahīb al-Jabbūrī (Beirut: Dār al-Gharb al-Islāmī, 1983). In this book, al-Tamīmī (d. AH 333/944 CE) surveys the accounts of the early jurists who suffered because of their clash with their contemporary political authorities. See also Khaled Abou El-Fadl, *Rebellion and Violence in Islamic Law* (Cambridge, Cambridge University Press, 2001).
3. See Ibn al-Qayyim, *Iʿlām al-Muwaqqiʿīn*, 1:16 and Schacht, *Introduction*, 5. Schacht argued that Islamic law represents an extreme case of "jurists' law."
4. Works of legal theory often start with an introduction that elaborates on these issues with varying degrees of detail. See, for example, Abū al-Maʿālī ʿAbd al-Malik Ibn ʿAbd Allah al-Juwaynī, *al-Burhān fī Uṣūl al-Fiqh*, ed. ʿAbd al-ʿAẓīm al-Dīb (Mansurah: Dār al-Wafā', 1999), 1:77–130; Abū Ḥāmid Muḥammad Ibn Muḥammad al-Ghazālī, *al-Mustaṣfā min ʿilm al-Uṣūl* (Beirut: Dār al-Fikr, n. d.), 3–55; Fakhr al-Dīn Muḥammad Ibn ʿUmar al-Rāzī, *al-Maḥṣūl fī ʿIlm Uṣūl al-Fiqh*, ed. Tāha Jābir al-ʿAlawānī (Beirut: Muassasat al-Risālah, 1992), 1: 78–81; and Abū Isḥāq Ibrāhīm al-Shāṭibī, *Al-Muwafaqāt fī Uṣul al-Sharīʿah*, ed. ʿAbd Allah Darrāz (Cairo: al-Maktabah al-Tawfiqiyyah, 2003), 1:21–81.
5. The majority of the scholars argued that God is the exclusive Lawgiver and therefore all indicators have to be grounded in the original sources. The Ḥanafī jurists, following the Muʿtazilī and Maturidī schools, argued that reason can be a source of law as well. The roots of the issue pertain to the theological debate on rational bases for beauty (*ḥusn*) and ugliness (*qubḥ*). See Muḥammad Abū Zahrah, *Uṣūl al-Fiqh*, 72.
6. See Abū Zahrah, *Uṣūl al-Fiqh*, 112. Also. for a general introduction to Islamic legal theory in English, see Muḥammad Hāshim Kamālī, *Principles of Islamic Jurisprudence* (Cambridge: Islamic Texts Society, 1991).
7. Ṣubḥī Maḥmaṣānī, *Muqadimah fī Iḥiyā' ʿulūm al-Sharīʿah* (Beirut: Dār al-ʿIlm lil Malāyīn, 1962), 42. For more on the reasons for disagreement among the jurists, see Shāh Waliyullah al-Dahlawī, *Ḥujjat Allah al-Bālighah* (Delhi: Sharikat Amin Delhi, AH 1373), 1:152.
8. Some scholars argued that there is only one type of *aḥkām*, that is, the determinate rulings (*taklifiyyah*). See Shātibī, *al-Muwāfaqāt*, 1:149 and Abū Zahrah,

*Uṣūl al-Fiqh*, 54. For more on this issue, see al-Qarāfī, *al-Furūq*, 1:294; Ṣalāḥ al-Dīn Khalīl Kikaldī al-ʿAlāʾī, *al-Majmūʿ al-Mudhhab fī Qawāʿid al-Madhhab*, ed. Majīd ʿAlī al-ʿUbaydī and Aḥmad Khuḍayr Abbas (Amman: Dār Ammār, 2004) 1:25 and Badr al-Dīn Muḥammad ibn Bahādir ibn ʿAbd Allah al-Zarakshī, *al-Baḥr al-Muḥīṭ fī Uṣūl al-Fiqh*, ed. Muḥammad Muḥammad Tāmir (Beirut: Dār al-Kutub al-ʿIlmiyyah, 2000) 1:98–99.

9. On the issue of finiteness of sources and infiniteness of incidents (*tanāhī al-nuṣūṣ wa ʿadam tanāhī al-waqāʾiʿ*), see al-Juwaynī, *al-Burhān*, vol 2, 1348–1351; Abū al-Walīd Muḥammad Ibn Aḥmad Ibn Rushed, *Bidayat al-Mujtahid wa Nihāyat al-Muqtaṣid* (Cairo: al-Maktabah al-Tawfiqiyyah, n. d.), 1:22.
10. ʿAlī Ibn Saʿīd Ibn Ḥazm, *al-Iḥkām fī Uṣūl al-Aḥkām* (Cairo: Dār al-Ḥadīth, n. d), 8:487.
11. In a famous Ḥadīth, the Prophet is reported to have asked the companion Muʿādh Ibn Jabal, before dispatching him to Yemen, how he would settle disputes. Muʿādh answered that he would look into the Qurʾān, then the sunnah, and if he could not find an answer in these two sources, he would judge on the basis of his own ijtihād. The Prophet is reported to have indicated his approval of the answer of Muʿadh by saying, "Praise be to God who guided the messenger of the messenger of God to what is pleasing to the messenger of God." The Ḥadīth is narrated in the Sunan of Ibn Mājah and the Sunan of Abī Dāwūd. See Ibn al-Qayyim, *Iʿlām al-Muwaqqiʿīn*, 1:162–163. Ibn al-Qayyim supported the *isnād* of the ḥadīth and argued that it belongs to the *mashhūr* category. For an analysis of the *isnād*, see also ʿAbd al-Ghanī ʿAbdal-Khāliq, *Ḥujjiyyat al-Sunnah* (Mansurah: Dār al-Wafāʾ, 1997), 286–287.
12. Abd al-Raḥmān Ibn Khaldūn, *Muqaddimat Ibn Khaldūn*, ed. Ḥāmid ʿAmmār (Cairo: Dār al-Fajr li al-Turāth). According to Ibn Khaldūn, these two disciplines were counted among the "tool-sciences" (*ʿulum al-ālah*), because they were not studied for their own sake but as a preparation for studying other sciences.
13. In his study about the Mālikī concept of *ʿamal*, Abd-Allah points to this connection. He explores later Mālikī theorists and their treatment of the original concept of *ʿamal* in Mālik's *Muwaṭṭaʾ*. See Umar Faruq Abd-Allah, *Malik's Concept of ʿAmal in the Light of Mālikī Legal Theory* (PhD. diss., University of Chicago, 1978), 20.
14. Jamāl al-Dīn Muḥammad Ibn Mukarram Ibn Manẓur, *Lisān al-ʿArab* (Beirut: Dār Ṣādir, 1955), 9:236–243 and Muḥammad Murtaḍā al-Ḥusaynī al-Zubaydī, *Tāj al-ʿArūs min Jawāhir al-Qāmūs*, ed. Muṣtafā Ḥijāzi (Kuwayt: Wizarat al-Iʿlām, 1987), 16:135.
15. Al-Rāghib al-Isfahānī, *Muʿjam Mufradāt Alfāẓ al-Qurʾān* (Beirut: Dār al-Kātib al-ʿArabī, 1972), 343.
16. ʿAlī Ibn Muḥammad al-Sayyid al-Jurjānī, *Kitāb al-Taʿrīfāt* (Cairo: Dār al-Rashād, 1978), 171.
17. Ibn Manẓūr, *Lisān al-ʿArab*, 3:316.
18. Muḥammad Amīn Ibn ʿĀbidīn, "Nashr al-ʿArf fī Bināʾ baʿḍ al-Aḥkām ʿalā al-ʿUrf" in *Majmūʿat Rasāʾil Ibn ʿĀbidīn*, 112; Abū Sunnah, *al-ʿUrf wa al-ʿĀdah* , 31.
19. Ibn ʿĀbidīn, "Nashr al-ʿArf...," 112; al-Jurjānī, *al-Taʿrīfāt*, 171.
20. Abū Sunnah, *al-ʿUrf wa al-ʿĀdah*, 34.

21. Ibid. See also al-Jīdī, *al-ʿUrf wa al-ʿAmal fī al-Madhhab al-Māliki*, 43; al-Zarqā, al-Madkhal al-Fiqhī al-ʿĀmm, 2:872.
22. Isfahānī, *Muʿjam Mufradāt*, 364–365.
23. "By the (winds) sent forth, one after another" Qur'ān 77:1. It is used as a description to *al-mursalāt* (literally, messengers), which is interpreted as "angels" or as "winds." Al-Isfahānī, *Muʿjam Mufradāt*, 343; Abú Jaʿfar Muḥammad Ibn Jarīr al-Tabarī, *Jāmiʿ al-Bayān ʿan Ta'wīl āyy al-Qur'ān* (Cairo: Muṣṭafā al-Bābīal-Ḥalabī, 1954), 29:229.
24. "Between them shall be a veil, and on the heights will be men" Qur'ān 7:46. "The men on the heights will call" 7:48. The word is al-Aʿrāf, which is the name of the entire *surah* (chapter). Tabarī, *Jāmiʿ al-Bayān*, 8:188.
25. "Hold to forgiveness, command *bil ʿurf*, but turn away from the ignorant" Qur'ān 7:199.
26. Ibid. See also Muqātil Ibn Sulaymān, *Tafsīr Muqātil Ibn Sulayman*, ed. ʿAbd Allah Maḥmūd Shiḥātah (Cairo: al-Hay'ah al-Miṣriyyah al-ʿĀmmah lil Kitāb, 1983), 2:81; Tabarī, *Jāmiʿ al-Bayān*, 9:155–156; Abū ʿAbd Allah Muḥammad Ibn Aḥmad al-Anṣārī al-Qurṭubī, *al-Jāmiʿ li Aḥkām al-Qur'ān*, ed. Muḥmmad Ibrāhīm al-Ḥifnāwī and Maḥmūd Ḥāmid ʿUthmān (Cairo: Dār al-Ḥadīth, 1994), 7:330; and Abū Bakr Muḥammad Ibn ʿAbd Allah Ibn al-ʿArabī, *Aḥkām al-Qur'ān*, ed. Muḥammad Bakr Ismāʿīl (Cairo: Dār al-Manār, 2002), 2:331. Ibn al-ʿArabī notes that the word *ʿurf* can refer to four meanings: "The first is *maʿrūf*, the second is the testimony of faith 'there is no god but God,' the third is what is included in sharīʿah, and the fourth is whatever people deem appropriate and regarding which they are unanimous." Al-Qarāfī interprets the word *ʿurf* in this verse as accepted social custom. See Abū al-ʿAbbās Aḥmad ibn Idrīs al-Qarāfī, *Kitāb al-Furūq, Anwā' al-Burūq fī Anwāʿ al-Furūq*, ed. Muḥammad Aḥmad Sirāj and ʿAlī Jumʿah Muḥammad (Cairo: Dār al-Salām, 2001), 3:939, and 4:1213.
27. Maḥmūd Ibn ʿUmar Zamakhsharī, *al-Kashshāf ʿan Ḥaqā'iq Ghawāmiḍ al-Tanzīl wa ʿUyūn al-Aqāwīl fī Wujūh al-Ta'wīl*, ed. Muṣtafā husayn Aḥmad (Qumm: Manshūrāt al-Balāghah, 1992), 2:190, "*al-jamīl min al-afʿāl*"; Abū al-Faḍl Shihāb al-Dīn al-Sayyid Maḥmūd al-Alūsī, *Rūḥ al-Maʿānī fī Tafsīr al-Qur'ān al-ʿAẓīm wa al-Sabʿ al-Mathānī* (Beirut, Dār Iḥyā' al-Turāth al-ʿArabī, 1970), 9:147, "*al-mustaḥsan mina al-afʿāl, fa inna dhalika aqrabu ilā qabul al-nās min ghayr nakīr.*"
28. Muḥammad Ibn ʿUmar Ibn Ḥusayn Al-Rāzī, *Mafātīḥ al-Ghayb* (Cairo: al-Matbaʿah al-Bahiyyah, 1934), 15:96, "*kullu amrin ʿurifa annahu lā budda min al-itiyāni bihi.*"
29. Muḥammad Fu'ād ʿAbd al-Bāqí, *al-Muʿjam al-Mufahras li Alfāẓ al-Qur'ān al-Karīm* (Cairo: Dār al-Ḥadīth, 2001), 562–563.
30. "The mothers shall breastfeed their babies for two years, for whoever desires to complete the term, and the father shall bear the cost of their sustenance and clothing on equitable terms (*bil maʿrūf*), no soul shall have a burden laid on it greater than it can bear" Qur'ān 2:233.
31. Al-Tabarī, *Jāmiʿ al-Bayān*, 2:495. Ibn al-ʿArabī notes that the verse should be interpreted in light of *ʿurf* and *ʿādah*. See Ibn al-ʿArabī, *Aḥkām al-Qur'ān*, 1:246.

32. "There is no blame on you if you divorce women before consummation or the fixation of their dower, but offer them (a suitable gift) the wealthy according to his means and the poor according to his means, a gift of a reasonable amount (*bil maʿrūf*)" "The mothers shall breastfeed their babies for two years, for whoever desires to complete the term, and the father shall bear the cost of their sustenance and clothing on equitable terms (*bil maʿrūf*), no soul shall have a burden laid on it greater than it can bear" Qur'ān 2:236.
33. Ibn al-ʿArabī, 530–538.
34. Muḥammad Fu'ādʿAbd al-Bāqī, *al-Muʿjam al-Mufahras li Alfāẓ al-Qur'ān al-Karīm* (Cairo: Dār al-Ḥadīth, 2001). These are: 3:104, 3:110, 3:114, 7:157, 9:67, 9:71, 9:112, 22:41, and 31:17. See also Toshihiko Izutsu, *Ethico Religious Concepts in the Qur'ān* (Montreal: McGill-Queen's University Press, 2002), 213–217.
35. Such as in verses 2:233, 2:236, and 65:6.
36. See, for example, 2:185, 2:286, 4:28, 22:78, and 65:7.
37. "Believe in God and His Prophet and spend (in charity) out of the (substance) whereof He has made you heirs."
38. "Eat and drink , but waste not for God does not love the wasters."
39. "Make not your hand tied to your neck, nor stretch it forth to its utmost reach so that you become blameworthy and destitute."
40. Similar to the case in the Qur'ān, there is no reference to the word *ʿādah* in the sunnah but reference to the concept of *ʿādah* is frequent both by the derivatives of the word that denote repetition and recurrence. Reference also is very frequent to synonyms of the word especially in different verb forms such as *dāwama*, *ḥāfaẓa* or in conjunction with Arabic modal verbs such as *kāna*.
41. Aḥmad Ibn Ḥanbal, *Musnad al-Imām Aḥmad Ibn Ḥanbal*, ed. Shuʿayb al-Arnā'ūṭ (Beirut: Mu'assasat al-Risālah, 1998), ḥadīth 3600, 6:84.
42. Abū ʿAmr ʿUthmān Ibn al-Ṣalāḥ al-Shahrzūrī, *Muqadimat Ibn al-Ṣalāḥ wa Maḥāsin al-Iṣṭilāḥ*, ed. ʿĀishah ʿAbd al-Raḥmān (Cairo: Dār al-Maʿārif, 1990), 194. In the juristic discourse, the word companion refers to any Muslim who kept the company of the Prophet. The scholars of ḥadīth added that he should have narrated at least one report about the Prophet. See Ibid., 486.
43. For more on the evaluation of the *isnād* of this ḥadīth see Ibn Ḥanbal, *al-Musnad*, 6:84–85 and the commentary of the editors on *isnād*. See also Ibn al-Qayyim, *Iʿlām al-Muwaqqiʿīn*, 1:59; Jalāl al-Dīn ʿAbd al-Raḥmān al-Suyūṭī, *al-Ashbāh wa al-Naẓā'ir fī Qawāʿid wa Furūʿ al-Shāfiʿiyyah* (Cairo: Dār al-Salām, 2004), 221; Ibn Nujaym, *al-Ashbāh wa al-Naẓa'ir*, ed. ʿĀdil Saʿd (Cairo: al-Maktabah al-Tawfiqiyyah, n.d.), 101; Ibn ʿĀbidīn, "*Nashr al-ʿArf*", 113.
44. Ibn Ḥazm deals with this issue in chapter 35 on "the nullification of juristic preference, *istiḥsān*, and deduction, *istinbāṭ*." In his view, even if the ḥadīth was authentic, it would refer to the consensus of Muslims, rather than *istiḥsān*, because the report refers to all Muslims, not just some Muslims. See Ibn Ḥazm, *al-Iḥkām fī Uṣūl*, 2:194. In view of his juristic methodology, Ibn Ḥazm constantly warns against reliance on independent opinion, which is not grounded in the primary texts. For him, such opinion would be more likely to follow arbitrary whims and desires (*taḥakkum* and *tashahhī*), which is condemned by sharīʿah.
45. The scholars of ḥadīth classify the different aḥādīth into *mutawātir* (literally, connected or successive, a report transmitted by such a large number of

reliable transmitters that it would be highly unlikely, if not impossible, that they would agree amongst themselves to lie about the report or fabricate it) and *āḥād* (literally, singular, the other aḥādāth that do not reach the degree of *mutawātir*). The *āḥād* ḥadīith is divided into acceptable, unacceptable, and uncertain—with many subclassifications in each of these categories. The acceptable includes *ṣaḥiḥ* and *ḥasan*, which come next in order to *mutawātir*. The most famous books of ḥadīth are the two books of Bukhārí and Muslim, which include only aḥādīth from the *ṣaḥiḥ* category. For more on the different classifications of ḥadīth, see al-Shahrzūrī, *Muqadimat*.

46. The Qur'ān speaks about the building of Kaʿbah by Prophet Ibrāḥím in a number of verses. See, for example, 2:127 and 14:37.
47. The narrator of the ḥadīth, ʿAbd Allah Ibn ʿUmar, notes that this was the reason the Prophet would not touch the two corners that follow the black stone in the same way he used to do with the other two corners. The black stone is placed in one of the corners of Kaʿbah as a marker for the beginning and the end of the rounds of circumambulation around the Kaʿbah. A corrective measure, instead, was adopted in order to satisfy the requirement of circumambulation by marking the defective side to instruct the pilgrims that this area was originally a part of the Kaʿbah and that they must walk past, not before it. Sulaymān Ibn Khalaf Ibn Saʿd Ibn Ayūb al-Bājī, *al-Muntaqā Sharḥ Muwaṭṭa' al-Imam Mālik* (Cairo: Maṭbaʿat al-Saʿādah, 1983), 2:282.
48. Ibid. See also, Muḥyī al-Dīn Abū Zakariyya Yaḥya Ibn Sharaf al-Nawawī, *Ṣaḥiḥ Muslim bi Sharḥ al-Nawawī* (Cairo: Dār al-Manār, 2003), aḥādīth 1333–1334, 9:439–445.
49. In this report, Hind, the daughter of ʿUtbah son of Rabīʿah asked the Prophet, "Abu Sufiyan is a miserly person, would it be inappropriate for me to take from his money without his knowledge?" The prophet is reported to have replied "take only what is enough for you and for your children *bil maʿrūf*." Hind was the wife of Abū Sufiyān and the mother of Muʿāwiyah, the founder of the Umayyad dynasty. Aḥmad Ibn ʿAli Ibn Ḥajar al-ʿAsqalānī, *Fatḥ al-Bārī bi Sharḥ Ṣaḥiḥ al-Bukhārī* (Cairo: Maktabat al-ʿIlm, 2000), ḥadīth 2211, 4:505. The same ḥadīth is reported with some variations in different chapters in al-Bukhārī's book. See ḥadīth 2460, vol. 5; ḥadīth 3825, vol. 7; aḥādīth 5359, 5364, and 5370, vol. 9; ḥadīth 6642, vol. 11; aḥādīth 7161 and 7180, vol. 13. See also, al-Nawawī, *Ṣaḥiḥ Muslim*, ḥadīth 1714, vol. 12.
50. "*Bāb man ajrā amra al-amṣār ʿala mā yataʿārafūna baynahum.*"
51. Al-ʿAsqalānī, *Fatḥ al-Bārī*, 4:506.
52. Ibid., aḥādīth 2183–2197, vol. 4 and ḥadīth 2380, vol. 5. See also, al-Nawawī, *Ṣaḥiḥ Muslim*, 10:141–145.
53. *Awsuq* (singular, *wasaq*) is a classical unit of measurement. One *wasaq* equals 60 *ṣāʿ*. Each *ṣāʿ* equals 5.33 *arṭāl* (pounds). See *al-Muʿjam al-Wasīṭ* (Cairo: Maktabat al-Shurūq al-Dawliyyah, 2005), 1132.
54. Al-ʿAsqalānī, *Fatḥ al-Bārī*, 4:489.
55. Ibid., 488. This is the only case that Mālīk referred to in his *Muwaṭṭa'*. See al-Bāji, *al-Muntaqā*, 4:224–231. Abū Ḥanīfah was of the opinion that *ʿarāyā* apply only in the case of donation, not sale. See ʿAsqalānī, *Fatḥ al-Bārī*, 4:488.

56. When Ḥakīm Ibn Ḥizām asked about the possibility of selling items that are not (already) in one's possession, the Prophet replied, "Do not sell what you do not own." Ibn Ḥanbal, *Musnad*, aḥādīth 15311–15316, vol. 24., 25–32, See also, Muḥammad Ibn Idrīs al-Shāfiʿī, *al-Risālah*, ed. Ahmad Muḥammad Shākir (Beirut, al-Maktabah al-ʿIlmiyyah, n. d.), 337.
57. Al-ʿAsqalānī, *Fatḥ al-Bārī*, ḥadīth 2240, 4:534. Al-ʿAsqalānī notes that *salam* according to the people of Ḥijāz and *salaf* according to the people of Iraq are synonyms. It is also said that *salaf* means the advance payment of the price and *salam* means the payment of the price in the *majlis* (session where the agreement takes place). Juristically, *salam* means the sale of a deferred but fully described commodity in return for an advance payment (*bayʿu mawṣūfin fī al-dhimmah bi badalin yuʿṭā ʿājilan*). See also Nawawī, *Ṣaḥīḥ Muslim*, 11:220.
58. Ibid.
59. Ibn al-Qayyim (d. AH 751/1350 CE) took issue with this view of *salam* as an exception to the sale of the nonexistent. In the *salam* transaction, he argued, the item is fully described and guaranteed as a debt against the seller (*fī al-dhimmah*). This, in turn, removes it from the area of the nonexistent. For our purposes here, what is important to point out is the socioeconomic context of seventh-century Madinah, and the fact that the report was given in response to a common practice, *ʿurf*, in that society.
60. Nawawī, *Ṣaḥīḥ Muslim*, ḥadīth 2361, 15:474.
61. Ibid., ḥadīth 2362, 475. (*innama ana bashr, idha amartukum bi shay'in min dīnikum fa khudhū bih, wa idha amartukum bi shay'in min ra'yyī fa innama ana bashar*). Ibn Ḥanbal, *Musnad*, ḥadīth 1395, 1399, vol. 3, 15–18 and ḥadīth 24920, vol. 41, 401.
62. Nawawī, *Ṣaḥīḥ Muslim*, ḥadīth 2363, 475. (*antum aʿlamu bi amri dunya-kum*). See also, Ibn Ḥanbal, *Musnad*, ḥadīth 12544, vol. 20, 19.
63. Al-Shirāzī distinguished between two types of the Prophet's actions: those that are done by nature, such as eating, sleeping etc., and those that are done in a religious capacity. Only the latter can be used as normative examples. See Abū Isḥāq Ibrāhīm al-Shirāzī, *Sharḥ al-Lumaʿ*, ed. ʿAbd al-Majīd Turkī (Beirut: Dār al-Gharb al-Islāmī, 1988), 1:545. See also his discussion on the possibility of *ijtihād* at the time of the Prophet, 2:1089. For more on this point, see Ibn Ḥazm, *al-Iḥkām fī Uṣūl al-Aḥkām*, 2:205, 209 and Abū al-ʿAbbas Aḥmad Ibn Idrīs al-Qarāfī, *al-Iḥkām fī Tamyīz al-Fatāwā ʿan al-Aḥkām wa Taṣarrufāt al-Qāḍī wa al-Imām*, ed. ʿAbd al-Fattāḥ Abū Ghuddah (Beirut: Dār al-Bashā'ir al-Islamiyyah, 1995), 106–109; Jamāl al-Dīn ʿAbd al-Raḥīm ibn al-Ḥasan al-Isnawī, *al-Tamhīd fī Takhrīj al-Furūʿ ʿalā al-Uṣūl*, ed. Muḥammad Ḥasan Hītū (Beirut, Muassasat al-Risālah, 1980), 432, 491.
64. Nawawī, *Ṣaḥīḥ Muslim*, ḥadīth 194–196, 306–308, vol. 2; and ʿAsqalānī, *Fatḥ al-Bārī*, ḥadīth 1436, vol. 3; ḥadīth 2220, vol. 4; ḥadīth 2538, vol. 5; and ḥadīth 5992, vol. 10.
65. Abū Bakr Aḥmad Ibn al-Ḥusayn al-Bayhaqī, *al-Sunan al-Kubrā*, ed. Muḥammad ʿAbd al-Qādir ʿAṭā (Beirut: Dār al-Kutub al-ʿIlmiyyah, 1994), ḥadīth 13080, vol. 6, "I have witnessed a pact in the house of ʿAbd Allah Ibn Jadʿān that I would not love to trade for the best of camels and if I were called

to join it after Islam, I would do it." This is the pact known as *Ḥilf al-Fuḍūl.* It was called *Fuḍūl* because it is the plural of *Faḍl*, which happened to be the first name of those who joined it. This pact was formed 20 years before the mission of the Prophet and it was considered the most honorable treaty that the Arabs agreed on. It was reported that one of the Makkan chiefs, Al-ʿĀṣ Ibn Wāʾil, once bought a merchandise from a stranger merchant and refused to pay him. The merchant stood in front of Kaʿbah and called for help. The leaders of Makkah gathered in the house of ʿAbd Allah Ibn Jadʿān and vowed that they would cooperate to help the man until justice was done. They also agreed that they would continue to honor this pact as long as they lived. See Ibn Hishām, *al-Sīrah al-Nabawiyyah*, ed. Suhayl Zakkār (Beirut: Dār al-Fikr, 1992), 1:94. Ismāʿil Ibn ʿUmar Ibn Kathīr, *al-Sirah al-Nabawiyyah* (Cairo: Matbaʿat ʿIsā al-Bābi al-Ḥalabī, 1964), 1:259.

66. Al-ʿAsqalānī, *Fatḥ al-Bārī*, 9:99–100.
67. Ibid. In a famous ḥadīth, the Prophet is reported to have established that lineage is to be established on the basis of a valid marital or possession bond, not on *qiyāfah* (*al-waladu lil-firāsh wa lil ʿāhir al-ḥajar*).
68. On *ribā* and other questionable transactions, see Qurʾānic verses 2:275, 2:282, 3:130, 4:29. There are many aḥādīth that deal with issues such as *ribā* (usury), *gharar* (uncertainty), and deceit (*khidāʿ*).
69. For example, see Qurʾānic verses on the prohibition of unslaughtered animals (5:03) and on wine(5:90 and 5:96).
70. Qurʾān .33:59.
71. Izutsu, *Ethico Religious Concepts*, 22–23.

## 3. From *ʿĀdah* to *ʿUrf*: Theological Foundations of the Concept of Custom as reflected in the Debate over Causality

1. Abū al-Ḥasan ʿAlī Ibn Ismāʿīl al-Ashʿarī, *Maqālāt al-Islamyyīn wa Ikhtilāf al-Muṣallīn*, ed. Muḥammad Muḥyī al-Dín ʿAbd al-Ḥamīd (Beirut: al-Maktabah al-ʿAṣriyyah, 1990), 2:148.
2. Al-Ashʿarī (d. AH 330/941 CE) speaks of five main groups: Shiʿah, Khawārij, Murjiʾah, Muʿtazilah, and finally Aṣḥāb al-Ḥadīth or Ahl al-Sunnah. Al-Shahrstānī (d. AH 548/1153 CE) speaks of six main groups: Muʿtazilah, Jabriyyah, Ṣifātiyyah, Khawārij, Murjiʾah, and Shiʿah. See Abū Al-Fatḥ Muḥammad ʿAbd al-Karīm al-Shahrastānī, *al-Milal wa al-Niḥal*, ed. ʿAbd al-ʿAzīz Muḥammad al-Wakīl (Cairo: Muʾassasat al-Ḥalabī, 1968). Each of these main groups was divided, over time, into many other subgroups. Although these subgroups differed on many details, they still shared the main distinctive characteristics of the main group to which they belonged.
3. Questions related to the imamate or caliphate used to be treated in legal books, but they were occasionally discussed from the theological perspective. It was one of the main issues that led to the emergence of independent sects, such as

al-Khawārij and Shi'ah, who sought to develop their own theology to justify and defend their views. See, for example, al-Ash'arī, *Maqālāt al-Islāmiyyīn*.

4. The jurists also occasionally referred to this concept of custom to corroborate their arguments on the various substantive issues of law. See, for example, al-Shaybānī's reference to people's intrinsic need for necessities of life and how sharī'ah seeks to regulate not only how they should be obtained but also how they should be consumed. See Muḥammad Ibn Aḥmad al-Sarakhsī, *Kitāb al-Kasb*, ed. 'Abd al-Fattāḥ Abū Ghuddah (Ḥalab: Maktab al-Maṭbū'āt al-Islāmiyyah, 1997), 165.
5. 'Abd al-Jabbār Ibn Aḥmad, *Sharḥ al-Usūl al-Khamsah*, ed. Abd al-Karīm 'Uthman (Cairo: Maktabat Wahbah, 1996). These principles are: oneness of God (*tawhīd*), divine justice (*'adl*), promise and warning (*wa'd wa wa'īd*), the status of the sinner (*manzilah bayna al-manzilatayn*), and commanding good and forbidding evil (*al-amr bil-ma'rūf wa al-nahy 'an al-munkar*). On 'Abd al-Jabbār, see Aḥmad Ibn Yaḥyā Ibn al-Murtaḍā, *Kitāb al-Muniyah wa al-Amal fi Sharḥ al-Milal wa al-Niḥal*, ed. Muḥammad Jawād Mashkūr (Beirut: Dār al-Fikr, 1979), 194–195 and Tāj al-Dīn 'Abd al-Wahhāb Ibn al-Subkī, *Ṭabaqāt al-Shāfi'iyyah al-Kubrā*, ed. Mahmūd Muhammad al-Tanāḥī and 'Abd al-Fattaḥ Muḥammad al-Ḥilw (Cairo: 'Isā al-Bābī al-Ḥalabī, 1967), 5:97.
6. On Abū al-Ḥasan al-Ash'arī see Ibn al-Subkī, *Ṭabaqāt*, 3:347–444 and 'Alī Ibn al-Ḥasan Ibn 'Asākir, *Tabiyīn Kadhib al-Muftarī Fimā Nusiba ilā al-Imām Abī al-Ḥasan al-Ash'arī* (Beirut: Dār al-Kitāb al-'Arabī, 1979).
7. 'Abd al-Qāhir Ibn Ṭāhir Ibn Muḥammad al-Baghdādī, *Kitāb al-Farq bayna al-Firaq wa Bayān al-Firqah al-Nājiyah Minhum*, ed. Muḥammad Badr (Cairo: Matba'at al-Ma'ārif, 1910), 300. Muḥammad Zāhid al-Kawtharī, in the introduction to Ibn 'Asākir's *Tabiyīn*, 19.
8. The Mu'tazilī views have been recently regenerated due to the discovery and publication of some of their important works and due to the adoption of their views by some prominent modern reformers.
9. 'Alī Sāmī al-Nashshār, *Manāhij al-Baḥth 'inda Mufakirī al-Islām* (Cairo: Dār al-Ma'ārif, 1967), 158. See also, Muḥammad 'Ābid al-Jābrī, *Binyat al-'Aql al-'Arabī* (Beirut: Markaz Dirasāt al-Waḥdah al-'Arabiyyah, 1996), 202.
10. Abū al-Ḥasan 'Abd al-Jabbār, *Al-Mughnī fi Abwāb al-Tawḥīd wa al-'Adl* (Cairo: al-Dār al-Miṣriyyah lil Ta'līf wa al-Tarjamah wa al-Nashr, 1965).
11. Ibid., 4:42.
12. Abū al-Ṭayyib Muḥammad al-Baqillānī, *Kitāb al-Tamhīd*, ed. Richard Yusuf Macarthi (Beirut: al-Maktabah al-Sharqiyyah, 1957), 266–279. On Baqillānī, see Ibn 'Asākir, *Tabiyīn*, 217–231.
13. 'Abd al-Jabbār, *Mughnī*, 4:42 and *Sharḥ Al-Usūl*, 251. See also, al-Ash'arī, *Maqalāt*, 1:289.
14. Ibid., 4:51, 122, 139, 142 and 6:166. In his review of the debate on causality among Muslim theologians (*Mutakallimūn*), Wolfson identifies three main positions. The first, which he ascribes to "most of the *Mutakallimūn*, both orthodox and Mu'tazilites," holds that God is the direct cause of every event in the world and that there is no causal connection between these events. The second is that of Naẓẓām, which holds that the world is governed by the laws of causality that have been placed in it by God at the time of creation.

These laws operate under God's supervision and they remain subject to his will. The third is the position of Muʿammar, which holds that the world is governed by the laws of causality, which although originally created by God, operate independently without his supervision and they are not subject to his will. See Harry Austryn Wolfson, *The Philosophy of Kalam* (Cambridge: Harvard University Press, 1976), 575 and Wael Hallaq, *Law and Legal Theory in Classical and Medieval Islam* (Brookfield: Variorum, 1994), 437. Al-Ashʿarī mentions that most Muʿtazilī theologians uphold causality, except Al-Jubāʾī who held that causes don't have to lead to effects. See al-Ashʿarī, *Maqalāt*, 2:97. Wolfson relates the theological concept of custom to the Aristotelian framework in which " 'custom' is contrasted with 'nature' where nature refers to that which is always; custom to that which is often." Ibid., 545–546. ʿAbd al-Jabbār makes frequent references to this distinction.

15. ʿAbd al-Jabbār, *Mughnī*, 4:79.
16. Baqillānī, *Tamhīd*, 9–10.
17. Abū al-Maʿālī al-Juwaynī, *Kitāb al-Irshād ilā Qawāṭiʿ al-Adillah fi Usūl al-Iʿtiqād*, ed. Muḥammad Yūsuf Mūsā and ʿAli ʿAbd al-Munʿim ʿAbd al-Ḥamīd (Cairo: Maktabat al-Khānjī, 2002), 173, 180. On Juwaynī, see Ibn al-Subkī, *Ṭabaqāt*, 5:165–222 and Ibn ʿAsākir, *Tabiyīn*, 278–287.
18. ʿAbd al-Jabbār, *Mughnī*, 86, 122.
19. Ibid., 42, 122, 86, 142, passim.
20. Baqillānī, *Tamhīd*, 9–11.
21. Abd al-Jabbār, *Sharḥ Al-Usul*, 53.
22. Baqillāānī, *Tamhīd*, 286–295; Juwaynī, *Irshād*, 187.
23. This is a more literal interpretation of a verse in the Qurʾān that reads "and Allah has created you and what you do" (37:96).
24. ʿAbd al-Jabbār, *Mughnī*, 8:3. Ashʿarī, *Maqalāt*, 1:298. Al-Ashʿarī mentions that the Muʿtazilī theologians were divided into three groups. The first said there is no difference between the doer and the creator, but the word *creator* cannot be used for humans. The second group said creator refers to the one who acts indepdendently with no tool or limb (*la bi ālah wala jāriḥa*), which is impossible for humans. The third said that creation refers to will-based action, whether it is performed by God or humans.
25. Tāj al-Dīn Ibn al-Subkī notes that the difference between *creation* and *acquisition* is nominal and that al-Ashʿarī chose the latter mainly because it was the word used in the Qurʾān. He also notes that the late Ashʿarites' view is very similar to that of the Muʿtazilites. See Ibn al-Subkī, *Ṭabaqāt*, 3:386.
26. Al-Ashʿarī offers several definitions for generated action, which include: the action whose cause is initiated by one person but its effects are experienced by another; the action whose cause is initiated but can no longer be controlled; the action that is derived from another action; or the action that is either done by mistake or that is not willful. See al-Ashʿarī, *Maqālāt*, 2:92–93. These definitions tend to overlap and most of the examples used in the literature refer to one or more of these definitions, such as the downward movement of a rock after it was pushed down a slope or the pain/swelling that follows a strike.
27. ʿAbd al-Jabbār, *Mughnī*, 9:37. ʿAbd al-Jabbār deals with this issue in detail in the ninth volume of *al-Mughnī*. There are several varying views even within

the Muʿtazilī school as reflected in the work of ʿAbd al-Jabbār and also al-Ashʿarī, but still a common denominator can be found. Most of the Muʿtazilī theologians uphold the view that the actor is responsible for both the direct and indirect effects of the action caused by him. See al-Ashʿarī, *Maqalāt*, 2:86–92.

28. Baqillānī, *Tamhīd*, 296; Juwaynī, *Irshād*, 230.
29. Baqillāanī, *Tamihīd*, 300–301.
30. ʿAbd al-Jabbār, *Mughnī*, 9:22. See also his argument on the issue of rise and fall of prices and his refutation of the customs-based view, 11:56. Similarly, Ibn Ḥazm launched a severe attack on the Ashʿarī theologians for confusing custom with nature and for their denial of intrinsic properties (*ṭabāʾiʿ*). He noted that the denial of intrinsic properties in things amounts to nothing but sheer sophistry. See Ibn Ḥazm, *al-Fiṣal fī al-Milal wa al-Ahwāʾ wa al-Niḥal* (Cairo: Maktabat Muḥammad Ṣubayḥ, 1965), 5:84–86.
31. ʿAbd al-Jabbār, *Mughnī*, 15:202 and *Sharḥ al-Uṣūl*, 571; Baqillānī, *Tamhīd*, 132; Juwaynī, *Irshād*, 331; ʿAbd al-Karīm al-Shahrastanī, *Nihayat al-Iqdām fī ʿIlm al-Kalām*, ed. Alfrid Jiyum (Baghdad: Maktabat al-Muthannā, 1964), 421.
32. Although both the Muʿtazilī and the Ashʿarī theologians agreed on the occurrence of miracles through the agency of prophets, they disagreed on many other details. For example, while the Ashʿarī theologians differentiate between miracles that prophets can produce (*muʿjizāt)* and supernatural events that pious individuals can produce (*karamāt),* the Muʿtazilites recognize only the former. See ʿAbd al-Jabbār, *Mughnī*, 15:242 and Juwaynī, *Irshād*, 318.
33. On al-Ghazālī, see Ibn al-Subkī, *Ṭabaqāt*, 6:191–389 and Ibn ʿAsākir, *Tabiyīn*, 291–307.
34. Abū Ḥamid al-Ghazālī, *Tahāfut al-Falāsifah*, ed. Muḥammad al-Saʿīd Muḥammad (Cairo: al-Maktabah al-Tawfiqiyyah, 2003), 27. For an English translation, see Michael Marmura, *The Incoherence of the Philosophers* (Provo: Brigham Young University Press, 1997), 9.
35. On Ibn Rushd, see Ibrahīm Ibn ʿAlī Ibn Farhūn, *al-Dībāj al-Mudhahhab fī Maʿrifat Aʿyān ʿUlamāʾ al-Madhhab*, ed. Muḥammad al-Aḥmadī Abū al-Nūr (Cairo: Dār al-Turāth, 1975), 2:257–259.
36. Ibn Khaldūn, *Muqadimah*, 612; Muḥammad ʿĀbid al-Jābrī, *Tahāfut al-Tahāfut, Intiṣāran lil Rūḥ al-ʿIlmiyyah wa Taʾsīsan li Akhlaqiyyāt al-Ḥiwār* (Beirut: Markaz Dirasāt al-Waḥdah al-ʿArabiyyah, 1998), 20–35.
37. Abū Ḥamid al-Ghazālī, *al-Munqidh min al-Ḍalāl*, ed. ʿAbd al-Ḥalīm Maḥmūd (Cairo: Dār al-Kutub al-Ḥadīthah, 1974). For an English translation, see Montgomery Watt, *The Faith and Practice of Al-Ghazali* (Oxford: Oneworld Publications, 2000).
38. Al-Ghazālī, *Tahāfut*, 168.
39. Ibid., 167. This is sometimes referred to as religious occasionalism. See Marmura, *The Incoherence of the Philosophers,* xxiv. See also, Majid Fakhry, *Islamic Occasionalism and its Critique by Averroes and Aquinas* (London: George Allen & Unwin, 1958), 9. Fakhry defines occasionalism as "the belief in the exclusive efficacy of God, of whose direct intervention the events of nature are alleged to be the overt manifestation or 'occasion'."

40. "*Al-Iqtiranu bayna mā yuʿtaqadu fi al-ʿādati sababan wa bayna mā yuʿtaqadu musababan laysa ḍaruriyan ʿindanā.*" Al-Ghazālī, *Tahāfut*, 168.
41. Marmura, *The Incoherence of the Philosophers*, 170.
42. Al-Ghazālī, *Tahāfut*, 168. Bargeron points out the similarity between the two terms *fī taqdīr Allah* and *fī al-maqdūr* that al-Ghazālī used and their equivalents in the late medieval Christian scholastic tradition: *de potentia ordinata* and *de potentia absoluta*. The former was used to refer to the "de facto order established by God and the way in which God has chosen, in the past, to operate within the contingent order outside of himself," and the latter used to refer to "the total divine capacity to act, subject only to the limit imposed by the principle of non-contradiction." See Carol Bargeron, "Re-thinking Necessity (*al-Darūra*) in al-Ghazālī's Understanding of Physical Causation," *Theology and Science*, 5–1 (2007): 21–33 and Bargeron, *The Concept of Causality in Abu Hāmid Muhammad Al-Ghazālī's Tahafut Al-Flāsifah* (PhD diss., University of Wisconsin-Madison, 1978), 218 and 334.
43. Students of Islamic intellectual history identify al-Juwaynī as the founder of this contingency theory, which was advocated as an alternative to the classical Ash'arī theory of the creation of the world. Ibn Rushd, *Manāhij al-Adillah fī ʿAqā'id al-Millah*, ed Mahmūd Qāsim (Cairo: Maktabat al-Anglo al-Miṣriyyah, 1964), 137. The classical Ashʿarī theory is based on the concept of essences (*jawāhir*) and accidents (*aʿrāḍ*). According to it, since essences cannot be separated from accidents, and since accidents are created, then what cannot be separated from accidents is also created. Al-Juwaynī's alternative theory states, first, that the world and whatever it contains is contingent (*jā'iz*), and, second, whatever is contingent is created. These two premises lead to the conclusion that the world is created. See Ibn Rushd's critique of the two Ashʿarī theories, *Manāhij*,144. Ibn Rushd introduces another theory, which he describes as more in line with sharī'ah. This theory is based on two main proofs: providence (*ʿināyah*) and invention (*ikhtirāʿ*). The contingency theory has led to another famous theory also ascribed to al-Juwaynī called *takhṣīṣ* (particularization). It provides that the contingent is dependent on an agent and the agent must possess the will by means of which he chooses one contingent over other possible contingents; these two premises lead to the conclusion that the object of the will is created. It is also used to prove the free will of the eternal creator of the world. Also on the relationship between this notion of *takhṣīṣ* and al-Ghazālī's theory of causality, see Bargeron, *The Concept of Causality*, 224.
44. Al-Ghāzalī, *Tāhāfut*, 169.
45. Ibid., 170.
46. "Then let each of us allow the possibility of there being in front of him ferocious beasts, raging fires, high mountains, or enemies ready with their weapons [to kill him], but [also the possibility] that he does not see them because God does not create for him [vision of them]. And if someone leaves a book in the house, let him allow as possible its change on his returning home into a beardless slave boy—intelligent, busy with his tasks—or into an animal; or if he leaves a boy in his house, let him allow the possibility of his changing into a dog; or [again] if he leaves ashes, [let him allow] the possibility of its

changing into musk; and let him allow the possibility of stone changing into gold and gold into stone. If asked about any of this, he ought to say: 'I do not know what is at the house at present. All I know is that I have left a book in the house, which is perhaps now a horse that has defiled the library with its urine and its dung, and that I have left in the house a jar of water which may well have turned into an apple tree.' Indeed if [such a person] looks at a human being he has seen only now and is asked whether such a human is a creature that was born, let him hesitate and let him say that it is not impossible that some fruit in the marketplace has changed into a human , namely this human—for God has power over every possible thing, and this thing is possible." Quotation from Marmura, *The Incoherence of the Philosophers,* 174.

47. Al-Ghazālī, *Tahāfut*, 171.
48. "*Fahādhihi ʿulūmun yakhluquha Allāhu taʿālā bimajārī al-ʿādāti ("yuʿrafu bihā wujudu"* in Marmura's text, 181; *"naʾrifu biha wujuda"* in al-Ghazālī's *Tahāfut*, 176"*) aḥadi qismayy al-imkāni walā yatabayyanu bihi istihālatu al-qismi al-thānī.*"
49. Ibn Rushd, *Tahāfut Al-Tahāfut*, 505.
50. Ibid., 507. Ibn Rushd refers to the Qur'ānic verse 27:62, "No change will you find in the practice of Allah," and 35:43,"No change will you find in Allah's way, no turning off will you find in Allah's way." Translation has been slightly modified from that of Abdullah Yusuf Ali, *The Meaning of the Holy Qur'ān* (Brentwood: Amana Corporation, 1991). In both verses the word *sunnah* means "way, manner, or practice."
51. Ibn Rushd uses the word *sunnah* to refer to the Aristotelian concept of nature which stands for "that which is permanent." See Wolfson, *The Philosophy*, 545 and Bargeron, *The Concept of Causality*, 334.
52. *Wa imma an takuna ʿādatan lana fī al-ḥukmi ʿalā al-mawjūdati fa inna hādhihi al-ʿādati laysat shayʾan ākthara min fiʿli al-ʿaqli alladhi yaqtaḍihi tabʿuhu wa bihi ṣara al-ʿaqlu ʿaqlan.*
53. Ibn Rushd, *Tahāfut Al-Tahāfut*, 508.
54. Ibid., 505.
55. Ibid., 508. "*lā yanbaghī ann yushakka fī anna hādhhi al-mawjudāt qad yafʿalu baʿḍuha baʿḍan wa min baʿḍ, wa annaha laysat muktafiyah bi anfusiha fī hadha al-fiʿl bal bi fāʿilin min khārijn fiʿluhu sharṭun fī fiʿlihā bal fī wujudihā faḍlan ʿan fiʾlihā.*" Ibn Rushd does not go any further but comments that this is the worthiest point that philosophy seeks to investigate, "*wa ashrafu mā tafḥaṣu ʿanhu al-falsafatu huwa hādha al-maʿnā.*"
56. Al-Ghazālī, *Tahāfut*, 172. Again the example that al-Ghazālī refers to is the incident of Prophet Ibrāhīm when he was thrown into fire: "*wahua anna nusalimu anna al-nāra khuliqat khilqatan idha lāqāhā qutnatāni mutamāthilatāni ahraqathuma wa lam nufarriq baynahuma idha tamāthalatā min kulli wajhin walākin maʿa hādha nujawwizu ann yulqā nabiyyun fī al-nāri falā yahtariqu imma bitaghiyīr ṣifati al-nāri aww bi taghiyīri ṣifati al-nabiyy ʿalayhi al-salam.*"
57. "*fahuwa nazarun fī wajh al-iqtirān, lā fī nafs al-iqtirān, falyufham dhalik.*" See Al-Ghazālī, *Miʾyār Al-ʿIlm*, ed. Sulaymān Duniyā (Cairo: Dār Al-Maʿārif, 1961), 190–191. See also, Bargeron, *The Concept of Causality*, 261.

58. Ibid., 173. Al-Ghazālī uses this argument in many of his other works. See his treatise "*Iljām al-ʿAwamm ʿan ʿIlm al-Kalām*" in *Majmuʿat Rasāʾil al-Imām al-Ghazālī*, ed. Ibrāhīm Amin Muḥammad (Cairo: al-Maktabah al-Tawfiqiyyah, n. d.), 364–365.
59. In many of his writings, al-Ghazālī is mainly concerned with refuting the views of the Bāṭiniyyah, which is clear in his *Tahāfut al-Falāsifah*, *al-Munqidh min al-Ḍalāl* and many of his treatises such as "*al-Qisṭāṣ al-Mustaqīm*" and "*Qanūn al-Taʾwīl*" (both in *Majmuʿat Rasāʾil*, 194–228 and 623–630, respectively).
60. Al-Ghazālī, *Qanūn*, 626.
61. Al-Ghazālī, *Qisṭās*, 228.
62. Ibn Rushd, *Tahāfut al-Tahāfut*, 500, 510.
63. Nashshar, *Manāhij al-Baḥth*, 165.
64. Fakhry, *Islamic Occasionalism*, 124.
65. Ibn Khaldūn, *Muqadimat Ibn Khaldūn*, 548; Abū Zahrah, *Uṣūl Al-Fiqh*, 20.
66. Ibn Khaldūn, *Muqadimat Ibn Khaldūn*, 549. Ibn Khaldūn notes that the four books are Al-Juwaynī's *Burhān*, al-Ghazālī's *al-Mustaṣfā*, ʿAbd al-Jabbār's *al-ʿUmad*, and al-Baṣrī's *al-Muʿtamad*.
67. Al-Juwaynī, *al-Burhān fī Uṣūl al-Fiqh*, 77. The book deals with many themes that are normally treated in the books of theology such as *taklīf*, sources of knowledge and criteria for *ḥusn* (beauty) and *qubḥ* (ugliness). See also his *Al-Talkhīṣ fī Uṣūl Al-Fiqh*, ed. Muḥammad Ḥasan Ismāʿīl (Beirut: Dār Al-Kutub Al-ʿIlmiyyah, 2003).
68. Similarly, Al-Ghazālī opens his *Mustaṣfā* with a long methodological introduction that deals with issues of pure logic. *Al-Mustaṣfā* is said to represent an important turning point in which Aristotelian logic infiltrated jurisprudence. Abū Ḥāmid al-Ghazālī, *al-Mustaṣfā*, 1:10–55.
69. Ibid., 116.
70. Al-Juwaynī, *al-Irshād*, 324–331. He even uses the same examples in both books.

## 4. Custom between the Theoretical School and the Applied School

1. Wael Hallaq, *The Origins and Evolution of Islamic Law*, 102, 103. In this study, Hallaq slightly modifies the dominant Western view that the prophetic sunnah was a later development that involved the legal, cultural, and political practice projected backwards to the Prophet. Hallaq notes that this later-constructed sunnah was not completely devoid of authentic religious elements. These elements represented the early Muslims' religious experience during the first Islamic century in addition to the pre-Islamic Arabic cultural practices that were appropriated by the all-inclusive Sunnah of the Prophet.
2. Hallaq, *Origins*, 108–109.
3. These are the works of al-Bukhārī (d. 256/870), Muslim (d. 261/875), Abū Dāwūd (d. 275/888), al-Nasāʾī (d. 303/915), al-Tirmidhī (d. 279/892),

and Ibn Mājah (d. 273/886), in addition to the *Musnad* of Aḥmad Ibn Ḥanbal(d. 241/855).

4. Other collections from the same period (first half of the second Islamic century) include those of Ibn Jurayj in Makkah; Ḥammad Ibn Salama, al-Rabīʿ Ibn Ṣabiḥ, and Saʿīd Ibn Abi ʿArūba in Baṣrah; Sufiyan al-Thawrī in Kufah; al-Awzāʿī in al-Shām; Hushaym in Wāsiṭ; Maʿmar in Yemen; Jarīr Ibn ʿAbd al-Ḥamīd in al-Rayy; and Ibn al-Mubarak in Khurasān. See Jalāl al-Dīn ʿAbd al-Raḥmān al-Suyūṭī, *Tanwīr al-Ḥawālik Sharḥ Muwaṭṭaʾ al-Imām Mālik* (Cairo: al-Maktabah al-Tijāriyyah al-Kubrā, 1969), 1:6–7 and Muḥmmad Fuʾād ʿAbd al-Bāqī, *al-Muwaṭṭaʾ li Imām al-Aʾimmah wa ʿĀlim al-Madīnah Mālik Ibn Anas* (Cairo: Dār Iḥiyāʾ al-Kutub al-ʿArabiyah, n.d), iv. Dutton also mentions Ibn Isḥāq, Ibn Abi Dhiʾb, Ibn ʿUyayna, Abū ʿAwāna, and Shuʿba Ibn al-Ḥajjāj. See Dutton, *The Origins of Islamic Law*, 187. For more details on this see Muḥammad Muṣṭafa Aʿẓamī, *Dirāsāt fī al-Ḥadīth al-Nabawī* (Beirut: al-Maktab al-Islāmī, 1992), 1:71–83. See also Hammam Ibn Munabbih, *Ṣaḥifat Hammām Ibn Munabbih ʿan Abī Hurayrah*, ed. Rifʿat Fawzī ʿAbd al-Muṭṭalib (Cairo: Maktabat al-Khanji, 1985). According to Ibn Saʿd, Hammam Ibn Munabbih died in 101/719.

5. It is a ḥadīth reported by a successor (the generation following the companions of the Prophet) without mentioning the companion who heard it from the Prophet. See Ibn al-Ṣalāḥ al-Shahrazūrī, *Muqaddimat Ibn al-Ṣalāḥ*, 202. On the comparison between these two types see, for example, Abū al-Ḥusayn Muḥammad Ibn ʿAlī al-Baṣrī, *Kitāb al-Muʿtamad fī Uṣūl al-Fiqh*, eds. Muḥammad Ḥamid Allah and Ḥasan Ḥanafī (Damascus: al-Maʿhad al-ʿIlmī al- Faransī li al-Dirāsāt al-ʿArabiyyah, 1964–1965), 2:677.

6. It is a ḥadīth with a complete chain of transmitters. See Ibn al-Ṣalāḥ al-Shahrazūrī, *Muqaddimat Ibn al-Ṣalāḥ*, 190.

7. On Malik's cautious and meticulous approach in collecting *al-Muwaṭṭaʾ*, see Abū al-Faḍl ʿIyāḍ Ibn Musa, *Tartīb al-Madārik wa Taqrīb al-Masālik li Maʿrifat Aʿlām Madhhab Malik*, ed. Aḥmad Bakīr Maḥmūd (Beirut: Maktabat al-Ḥayah, 1967), 1:123 and Ibrāhīm Ibn ʿAlī Ibn Farḥūn, *al-Dibāj al-Mudhhab,* 1:119.

8. Dutton, *Origins*, 17.

9. In a number of publications, Hallaq took issue with the classical view that Shāfiʿī's *Risālah* was the first formulation of Islamic legal theory. He notes that *al-Risālah,* due to its novel approach, was not well received among the contemporaries of Shāfiʿī. *Al-Risālah*, however, remains the earliest attempt to formulate a systematic and comprehensive legal theory. See Wael Hallaq, "Was al-Shāfiʿī the Master Architect of Islamic Jurisprudence?" *International Journal of Middle East Studies*, 25 (1993): 578–605. See also, Norman Calder, *Studies in Early Muslim Jurisprudence*, 241. For a recent review of the scholarship on the *Risālah* of al-Shāfiʿī and reevaluation of the attempts to cast doubt on his authorship of it, see Joseph Lowry, *Early Islamic Legal Theory: The Risāla of Muḥammad ibn Idrīs al-Shāfiʿī* (Leiden: Brill, 2007), 15. Lowry, however, reviews the different opinions without making a determination either for or against any specific view.

10. Al-Suyūṭī, *Tanwīr al-Ḥawālik*, 5–8.

11. Two of the most important studies on this theme are Abd-Allah, *Malik's Concept*, and Dutton, *Origins*. For illustrative examples for the use of *ʿurf* in the various substantive issues according to the Mālikī school, one can refer to the famous *Mudawwanah* by Saḥnūn (d. 240/854), especially the chapters on transactions. See Abū Saʿīd al-Barādhiʿī, *al-Tahdhīb fī Ikhtiṣār al-Mudawwanah*, ed. Muḥammad al-Amīn Walad Muḥammad Sālim bin al-Shaykh (Dubai: Dār al-Buḥūth lil-Dirāsāt al-Islāmiyyah wa Iḥyāʾ al-Turāth, 2002), on the expiation for oaths, 2:105; on the estimation of *mahr*, 2:198: on disagreement between spouses, 2:222; and on the various transactions such as sales, leases, inheritance, and trusts, 3–4 passim.
12. Qurʾān 14:1, 13:44, 16:89, and 42:52. See al-Shāfiʿī, *al-Risālah*, 20.
13. For a detailed exposition of al-Shāfiʿī's view on this, see his *Kitāb al-Umm*, ed. Aḥmad Badr al-Dīn Hassūn(Beirut: Dār Qutaybah, 1996), 10:7–75.
14. Ibid., 22.
15. Ibid., 24. This particular example was probably the foundation of the Shāfiʿī position on the question of *ijtihād*.
16. Ibid., 39.
17. Ibid., 477, 512.
18. See reference to this ḥadīth in chapter 3.
19. The classic example of juristic analogical reasoning is the prohibition of wine, which is mentioned in the Qurʾān. The operative cause for such prohibition was identified as intoxication. A valid *qiyās* consists of four main components: original case (*aṣl*), in this case wine; secondary case (*farʿ*), which may be any intoxicating substance that is not mentioned in the texts; common operative cause (*ʿillah*), in this case intoxication; and finally, ruling (*ḥukm*), in which the new case follows the original case. This would be prohibition in the present example.
20. Al-Shāfiʿī, *al-Risālah*, 40.
21. See, for example, how al-Juwaynī follows this basic structure in his *al-Burhān* and his frequent references to *al-Risālah*. Al-Juwaynī, *al-Burhān*, 1:165.
22. Muḥammad Ibn ʿUmar Al-Rāzī, *Manāqib al-Shāfiʿī*, ed. Aḥmad Ḥijāzī al-Saqqā (Cairo: Maktabat al-Kulliyyāt al-Azhariyyah, 1986), 156. Al-Rāzī compares al-Shāfiʿī to both Aristotle and al-Khalīl Ibn Aḥmad al-Farāhīdī, the founder of *al-ʿarūḍ* (Arabic prosody). See also Abū Bakr Aḥmad Ibn al-Ḥusayn al-Bayhaqī, *Manāqib al-Shāfiʿī*, ed. al-Sayyid Aḥmad Ṣaqr (Cairo: Dār al-Turāth, 1971), 1:368; Nashshār, *Manāhij al-Baḥth*, 66.
23. Al-Shāfiʿī, al-*Risālah*, 222 passim.
24. Ibid., 20.
25. It was in his major work on substantive law, *al-Umm*, that al-Shāfiʿī made frequent direct references to the concept of *ʿurf*. See al-Shāfiʿī, *Kitāb al-Umm*, 3:21 on the interpretation of financial ability, which is a prerequisite for the performance of the pilgrimage; 3:8 on the interpretation of the proper right of option in a sale contract; 3:18 on the concept of linguistic practice and its role in business transactions; 3:170 on *ʿarāyā*; 3:290 on *salam*; 5:195, 230 on dowry and the concept of the equal dowry (*mahr al-mithl)*; 5:295–297, 302, 364 on expenditure (*nafaqah*) and marital financial rights and obligations;

7:645 on compensations (*ḍamān*); 8:419, 423 on expiations (*kaffārāt*); and 8:449, 472 on the interpretation of oaths (*aymān*).

26. Ibid., 8:236. In his commentary on this and other similar cases, al-Shāṭibī observed that proper understanding of the Qur'ān and the Sunnah of the Prophet requires knowledge of the common customary practices of the Arabs at the time of the Prophet. See al-Shāṭibī, *al-Muwāfaqāt*, 3:299.
27. Al-Shāfiʿī, *al-Risālah*, 238.
28. Ibid., 240. In his commentary on al-Shāfiʿī's text, Shākir notes that this example shows the difference between the different actions of the Prophet that derive from the different roles that he assumed. The Prophet gave the command forbidding Muslims to save the meat for more than three days by means of his capacity as a leader of the Muslim community rather than as a Prophet conveying revelation, because the Prophet explained that he gave the command for a particular reason and when it no longer existed, the command expired. See Ibid., 242. See also al-Shāfiʿī's references to the cases of built-in toilets, 292–296; *ʿarāyā*, 331–335; and salam, 335–242. See also the discussion on these issues above (in chapter 3).
29. See, for example, ʿAlā' al-Dīn ʿAbd al-ʿAzīz Ibn Aḥmad al-Bukhārī, *Kashf al-Asrār ʿan Uṣūl Fakhr al-Islām al-Bazdawī*, ed. Muḥammad al-Muʿtaṣim bi Allah al-Baghdādī (Beirut: Dār al-Kitāb al-ʿArabī, 1997), 4:10–13. See also a vindication of the concept and meaning of *istiḥsān* against the Shāfiʿī's severe criticism of it in Abū Bakr Aḥmad Ibn ʿAlī al-Jaṣāṣ al-Rāzī, *Uṣūl al-Jaṣāṣ al-Musammā al-Fuṣūl fī al-Uṣūl*, ed. Muḥammad Muḥammad Tāmir (Beirut: Dār al-Kutub al-ʿIlmiyyah, 2000), 2:340.
30. Ibn Khaldūn, *al-Muqaddimah*, 548 and Muhamad Abū Zahra, *Uṣul Al-Fiqh*, 18.
31. Al-Shāfiʿī, *al-Risālah*, 42–49.
32. Al-Baṣrī, *Kitāb al-Muʿtamad fī Uṣūl al-Fiqh*, 1:16.
33. Ibid.
34. Ibid., 27.
35. The Qur'ān refers to this meaning in verses 6:38 and 11:6.
36. Al-Baṣrī, *al-Muʿtamad*, 1:28.
37. Abū Isḥāq Ibrāhīm Al-Shīrāzī, *Sharḥ al-Lumaʿ*, 1:180. See also al-Juwaynī's discussion on the possibility of the change of literal meanings either by sharīʿah or by convention. He was of the opinion that both sharīʿah and convention can add to or modify the literal meaning rather than completely change it. See *al-Burhān fī Uṣūl al-Fiqh*, ed. ʿAbd al-ʿAẓīm al-Dīb (Cairo: Dār al-Anṣār, 1980), 1:174–177. In another discussion, he cites the disagreement between al-Shāfiʿī—who denied the possibility that conventional meaning may change the literal meaning—and Abū Ḥanífah—who approved of it. See Ibid., 446. See also, al-Ghazālī, *al-Mustaṣfā*, 1:325–326. As will become clearer later, these legal debates on the role and significance of a particular meaning could have serious legal implications. For example, there is the famous case of disagreement between the Shāfiʿī school and the Ḥanafī school on the interpretation of the word *ṭaʿām* (food) in the ḥadīth that forbids usurious transactions. While the former limited the word to wheat because it was the common referent of *al-ṭaʿām*, the latter held that the literal meaning of

*al-ṭaʿām* is not restricted to wheat and even if it became known by custom to be as such, it is a post-Prophetic custom and therefore cannot limit the scope of the text. See, for example, al-Shirāzī, *Sharḥ al-Lumaʿ*, 1:180.

38. Al-Shirāzī notes that meanings are determined by four factors: *ʿurf al-Lughah* (linguistic convention), *ʿurf al-sharʿ* (legal convention), *ʿurf al-istiʿmāl* (customary convention), and *qiyās* (analogy). See al-Shirāzī, *Sharḥ al-Lumaʿ*, 1:176–190.
39. Al-Shāfiʿī, al-*Risālah*, 53.
40. Ibid., 56 passim.
41. Al-Baṣrī, *al-Muʿtamad*, 1:301.
42. Ibid.
43. Al-Shirāzī, *Sharḥ al-Lumaʿ*, 1:391. See also, al-Juwaynī, *al-Burhān*, 1:446.
44. For more on the classification of the *āḥād* type, see Ibn al-Ṣalāḥ al-Shahrazūrī, *Muqadimat Ibn al-Ṣalāḥ*.
45. Al-Shirāzī, *Sharḥ al-Lumaʿ*, 2:570–574.
46. See also, Ibid., 679.
47. Al-Juwaynī, *al-Burhān*, 1:568.
48. Ibid. See also, al-Baṣrī, *al-Muʿtamad*, 2:551.
49. Al-Juwaynī, *al-Burhān*, 1:580.
50. Ibid., 574–576.
51. Ibid., 582.
52. Ibid., 146. Appeal to *ʿurf* is consistently made throughout his other discussions. See, for example, on the establishment of miracles, 153; on the veracity of the Prophet, 154; passim.
53. Al-Baṣrī, *al-Muʿtamad*, 2:674–688; al-Shirāzī, *Sharḥ al-Lumaʿ*, 2:653; al-Juwaynī, *al-Burhān,* 1:583–586.
54. Al-Shirāzī, *Sharḥ al-Lumaʿ*, 2:654.
55. Al-Juwaynī, *al-Burhān*, 1:596. "*Kullu khabarin yukhālifuhū ḥukma al-ʿurfi fa huwa kadhibun*"
56. Ibid., 1:679.
57. Ibid., 678.
58. Ibid., 680–683.
59. For an overview of the issue, see Wael Hallaq, *Law and Legal Theory in Classical and Medieval Islam*, 437. For a discussion on the theme of *ijmāʿ* in general, see Al-Shirāzī, *Sharḥ al-Lumaʿ*, 2:665–751.
60. Al-Shirāzī, *Sharḥ al-Lumaʿ*, 2:682. See also, Abū Zayd Ibn ʿUmar Ibn ʿĪsā al-Dabbūsī, *Taqwīm al-Adillah fī Uṣūl al-Fiqh*, ed. Khalīl Muḥyī al-Dīn al-Mays (Beirut: Dār al-Kutub al-ʿIlmiyyah, 2001), 31. Al-Dabbūsī mentioned four types of *ijmāʿ*: the consensus of the companions, the consensus of some and the silence of others, the consensus of the people of a given generation on a new issue, and the consensus on one of the issues on which the early generations(*salaf*) disagreed. He also spoke of four different views on the authority of *ijmāʿ*: every generation, the companions, the people of Madinah, descendants of the Prophet, or the early generations. He chose the first view.
61. See, on this point, Wael Hallaq, *A History of Islamic Legal Theories*, 104.
62. For more details on this point and whether, after being formed, an *ijmāʿ* can be revoked by a subsequent generation, see al-Baṣrī, *al-Muʿtamad*, 2:495–497.

63. Modern scholars have also discussed the possibility of using *ijmāʿ* as an *initiative* consensus building mechanism in the form of learned councils or scholarly conferences.
64. Al-Juwaynī, *Ghiyāth al-Umam fī Iltiyāth al-Ẓulam*, eds. Mustafā Ḥilmī and Fu'ād ʿAbd al-Munʿim Aḥmad (Alexandria: Dār al-Daʿwah, 1979), 73.
65. For an exposition of these texts, see al-Shirazī, *Sharḥ al-Lumaʿ*, 2:665–751, especially 682 and al-Baṣrī, *al-Muʿtamad*, 2:458–479.
66. Al-Juwaynī, *al-Burhān*, 1:678; *al-Talkhīṣ fī Uṣūl al-Fiqh*, 367; and al-Shirazī, *Sharḥ al-Lumaʿ*, 2:683.
67. Al-Juwaynī, *al-Burhān*, 1:682.
68. Al-Shirazī, *Sharḥ al-Lumaʿ*, 2:1036.
69. Al-Juwaynī, *al-Burhān*, 2:1332; *Ghiyāth al-Umam*, 257, 267; and al-Baṣrī, *al-Muʿtamad*, 2:929–933.
70. Later jurists speak about *tanqīḥ al-manaṭ* and *taḥqīq al-manāṭ*. We will deal with these concepts in more detail in the following chapters. See also, Juwaynī, *Ghiyāth al-Umam*, 208.
71. Al-Juwaynī, *Ghiyāth al-Umam*. Al-Juwaynī is considered among the jurists who developed a sharīʿah-based political discourse, along with al-Māwardī and Ibn al-Farrā'. Representatives of other political discourses in the Islamic tradition included political philosophers, such as al-Kindī, al-Fārābī and Ibn Sinā on the one hand, and administrative assistants and advisers, such as Ibn al-Muqaffaʿ, al-Jāḥiẓ, and al-Ṭarṭūshī on the other. See, Ibid., 4.
72. Ibid., 192, 269.
73. Ibid., 62.
74. Ibid., 69.
75. Ibid., 70.
76. Ibid., 73. (*fa aqūlu: madāru al-kalāmi fī ithbāti al-ijmāʿi ʿalā al-ʿurfi wa iṭṭirādihi, wa bayāni istiḥālati jarayānihi ḥā'idan ʿan ma'lūfihi wa muʿtādihi*).
77. Ibid., 75.
78. The jurists have been accused of legitimizing the status quo by siding with whoever was able to wield power. Such an accusation, however, fails to recognize the higher juristic concern for preserving order. For more on this, see Abou El-Fadl, *Rebellion and Violence in Islamic Law.*
79. Ibid., 87.
80. Ibid., 97.
81. Ibid., 139.
82. Ibid., 212.
83. Ibid., 107.
84. Ibid., 113.
85. Ibid., 176.
86. Ibid., 246.
87. Abū al-Ḥasan al-Karkhī, *Risālah fī al-Uṣūl*, ed. Zakariyā ʿAlī Yusuf (Cairo: Zakariyyah ʿAlī Yusuf, 1970), 112, published together with *Ta'sīs al-Naẓar* of al-Dabbūsī.
88. Al-Isnawī, *al-Tamhīd fī Takhrīj al-Furūʿ ʿalā al-Uṣūl*, 194.
89. I am grateful to Professor Abou El-Fadl for his clarification of this point.

90. Al-Dabbūsī, *Ta'sīs al-Nazar*, 8.
91. Ibid., 10
92. Ibid., 37.
93. Ibid., 56.
94. Ibid., 107.
95. "*lā yajuzu liman ista'hala an yakūna ḥākiman aw muftiyan an yaḥkuma walā yuftī illa min jihati khabarin lazimin wa dhālika al-kitābu thumma al-sunnatu aww mā qālahu ahlu al-ʿilmi lā yakhtalifuna fihi aww qiyasin ʿalā baʿḍi hādhā.*" See al-Shafiʿī, *Kitāb al-Umm*, 10:119.
96. Al-Rāzī, *Uṣūl al-Jaṣāṣ*, 2:340; Bukhārī, *Kashf al-Asrār*, 4:7; and al-Dabbūsī, *Taqwīm al-Adillah*, 404.
97. Ibid., 343. Here, al-Jaṣāṣ refers to the Qurā'nic verses 2:233 and 2:236 that invoke the concept of *maʿrūf* in the determination of the proper amount of expenditure. See above chapter 2, See also, Abū Bakr Muḥammad Ibn Aḥmad Ibn Abi Sahl al-Sarakhsī, *Uṣūl al-Sarakhṣī*, ed. Abū al-Wafa al-Afghānī( Beirut: Dār al-Kutub al-ʿIlmiyyah, 1993), 2:200.
98. Traditionally, *istiḥsān* has been closely connected with *qiyās*, for the former was for the most part a substitution of one *qiyās* by another due to consideration of stronger evidence—hence the other name of *istiḥsān* as *qiyās khafī* (hidden analogical reasoning). See al-Bukhārī, *Kashf al-Asrār*, 4:8.
99. Ibid., 344.
100. Ibid., 348. The punishment for highway robbery is mentioned in the Qur'ān in 5:33. See Abou El-Fadl, *Rebellion and Violence in Islamic Law*.
101. As mentioned earlier, there are four main components of a valid qiyās: source (*aṣl*), derivative (*farʿ*), operative cause (*ʿillah*), and ruling (*ḥukm*). The general principle is that the third and fourth components are concomitantly connected with each other (*al-ḥukm yadūr maʿa al-ʿillah wujūdan wa ʿadaman*). If one of them exists the other follows, and vice versa. In this form of *istiḥsān*, however, although the operative cause exists, the ruling does not follow because of another "stronger" consideration. As al-Jaṣāṣ explains, one of these considerations is *ʿurf*. As will be shown, this was a controversial issue within the Ḥanafí school and many Ḥanafí jurists did not follow this line of reasoning.
102. Ibid., 351–355.
103. Ibid., 354–355.
104. See al-Bukhārī, *Kashf al-Asrār*, 4:71 and al-Sarakhsī, *Uṣūl al-Sarakhṣī*, 2:208.
105. Al-Bukhārī, *Kashf al-Asrār*, 4:12.
106. Al-Sarakhsī, *Usūl*, 2:200.
107. Al-Bukhārī, *Kashf al-Asrār*, 4:10; Al-Sarakhsī, *Usūl*, 2:202. The examples given for text-based *istiḥsān* is the case of *salam* and the lease contract, *ijārah*. The example given for the consensus-based *istiḥsān* is *istiṣnāʿ*. It is interesting to note that this example was used sometimes to refer to consensus (*ijmāʿ*) (Bazdawī and Sarakhsī) and sometimes to refer to *ʿurf* (al-Jaṣāṣ). The example given for necessity is purification of utensils and wells: according to *qiyās*, if they are impacted by impurity they are never purified, but according

to *istiḥsān*, they are purified as long as the impact of impurity can no longer be detected.

108. See also al-Dabbūsī, *Taqwīm al-Adillah*, 405–406. For more on this case, see al-Sarakhsī, *Kitāb al-Mabsūṭ* (Beirut: Dār al-Maʿrifah, 1978), 13:29. *Al-Mabsūṭ* of al-Sarakhsī is considered one of the most authoritative sources of substantive law according to the Ḥanafī school. It is replete with references to *ʿurf*, which permeate his discussions of many issues especially in the area of transactions. See, for example, 5:180–198 for the role of the common practice on the issue of expenditure (*nafaqah*) and the determination of the proper amount thereof, 14:2 on the issue of currency exchange (*ṣarf*), 14:31 on the issue of loan (*qirāḍ*), and 15:130 on the issue of leasing houses (*ijārah*). See also, Muḥammad Ibn al-Ḥasan al-Shaybānī, *Kitāb al-Aṣl*, ed. Abū al-Wafā al-Afghānī (Hyderabad: Majlis Dāʾirat al-Maʿārif al-ʿUthmāniyyah, 1971), 3:222 on the determination of the expiation for oaths, 3:258 on the determination of the breaking of oaths. See also al-Sarakhsī, *Kitāb al-Kasb*, 181.
109. For more on these classifications of *istiḥsān*, see al-Bukhārī, *Kashf al-Asrār*, 4:21 and al-Sarakhsī, *Uṣūl*, 2:206.

## 5. The Expansion of Legal Theory

1. The most vocal opponent of this hierarchy, especially as far as *qiyās* is concerned, was Ibn Ḥazm. See his *al-Iḥkām fī Uṣūl al-Aḥkām*, 2:368. See also, al-Ghazālī's criticism of the deniers of *qiyās* in *al-Mustaṣfā*, 2:234; al-Dabbūsī, *Taqwīm al-Adillah*, 277; Manṣūr Ibn Muḥammad Ibn ʿAbd al-Jabbār Ibn al-Samʿānī, *Qawāṭiʿ al-Adillah fī al-Uṣūl* (Beirut: Dār al-Kutub al-ʿIlmiyyah, 1997), 2:72–101. For a list of the arguments against *qiyās* and their counter arguments, see Tāj al-Dín ʿAbd al-Wahhāb Ibn ʿAlí Ibn al-Subkí, *Rafʿ al-Ḥājib ʿan Mukhtaṣar Ibn al-Ḥājib*, ed. ʿAlī Muḥammad Muʿawwaḍ and ʿĀdil Aḥmad ʿAbd al-Mawjūd (Beirut: ʿĀlam al-Kutub, 1999), 4: 418–479. The Jaʿfarī Shīʿī jurists were the other major group that did not subscribe to this structure. Instead of *qiyās*, they listed reason (*ʿaql*).
2. See, for example, al-Juwaynī, *al-Burhān*, 2:743; al-Samʿānī, *Qawāṭiʿ al-Adillah*, 2:68; al-Ghazālī, *al-Mustaṣfā*, 2:228; al-Rāzī, *al-Maḥṣūl fī ʿIlm Uṣūl*, 5:5; Sayf al-Dīn ʿAlī Ibn Abi ʿAlī Ibn Muḥammad al-Āmidī, *al-Iḥkām fī Uṣūl al-Aḥkām* (Beirut: Dār al-Fikr, 1996), 3:124; Badr al-Dīn Muḥammad Ibn Bahādir Ibn ʿAbd Allah al-Zarakshī, *al-Baḥr al-Muḥīṭ fī Uṣūl al-Fiqh*, ed. Muḥammad Muḥammad Tāmir (Beirut: Dār al-Kutub al-ʿIlmiyyah, 2000), 4:3.
3. Al-Rāzī, *al-Maḥṣūl*, 5:353. See also, Jamāl al-Dīn ʿAbd al-Raḥīm Ibn al-Ḥasan al-Isnawī, *Nihāyat al-Sawl fī Sharḥ Minhāj al-Wuṣūl ilā ʿIlm al-Uṣūl*, ed. Shaʿbān Muḥammad Ismāʿíl (Beirut: Dār Ibn Ḥazm, 1999), 2:832 and al-Shirāzī, *Sharḥ al-Lumaʿ*, 2:797.
4. Shihāb al-Dīn Aḥmad Ibn Idrīs al-Qarāfī, *Sharḥ Tanqīḥ al-Fuṣūl*, ed. Tāha ʿAbd al-Raʾūf Saʿd (Cairo, Maktabat al-Kullliyyat al-Azhariyyah, 1973), 408.
5. Ibn al-ʿArabī, *Aḥkām al-Qurʾān*, 1:246–7, 4:280–281.

6. For the different classifications of *qiyās*, see, for example, al-Ghazālī, *al-Mustaṣfā*, 2:310; Ibn al-Samʿānī, *Qawāṭiʿ al-Adillah*, 2:126; al-Āmidī, *al-Iḥkām*, 4:207; and al-Zarakshī, *al-Baḥr al-Muḥīṭ*, 4:33.
7. Al-Ghazālī, *al-Mustaṣfā*, 2: 231 and al-Zarakshī, *al-Baḥr al-Muḥīṭ*, 4:227.
8. Al-Ghazālī, *al-Mustaṣfā*, 2:288; al-Rāzī, *al-Maḥṣūl*, 5:229, 334; al-Āmidī, *al-Iḥkām*, 3:204.
9. See al-Juwaynī, *al-Burhān*, 1:91–92; al-Ghazālī, *al-Mustaṣfā*, 1:56–57; al-Qarāfī, *Sharḥ Tanqīḥ al-Fuṣūl*, 88–94; and Muḥammad Ibn Aḥmad Ibn Juzayy, *Taqrīb al-Wuṣūl ilā ʿIlm al-Uṣūl*, ed. ʿAbd Allah Muḥammad al-Jabbūrī (Amman: Dār al-Nafā'is, 2002), 92; Najm al-Dīn Sulaymān Ibn ʿAbd al-Qawī al-Ṭūfī, *Sharḥ Mukhtaṣar al-Rawḍah*, ed. ʿAbd Allah Ibn ʿAbd al-Muḥsin al-Turkī (Beirut: Mu'ssasat al-Risālāh, 1987), 3: 403; ʿAbd al-Qawī al-Ṭūfī, *Dar' al-Qawl al-Qabīḥ bi al-Taḥsīn wa al-Taqbīḥ*, ed. Ayman Maḥmūd Shiḥādah (Riyadh: Markaz al-Malik Fayṣal lil Buḥūth wa al-Dirāṣāt al-Islāmiyyah, 2005), 83; and Ibn al-Subkī, *Rafʿ al-Ḥajib ʿan Mukhtaṣar Ibn al-Ḥājib*, 1:447. On the difference between the Shāfiʿī school and the Ḥanafī school on this issue, see al-Zanjānī, *Takhrīj al-Furūʿ ʿalā al-Uṣūl*, 244.
10. Al-Zarakshī, *al-Baḥr al-Muḥīṭ*, 4:186.
11. For more on these debates, see al-Samʿānī, *Qawāṭiʿ al-Adillah*, 2:185–198.
12. See also, Muḥammad Muṣṭafā Shalabī, *Taʿlīl al-Aḥkām* (Beirut: Dār al-Nahḍah al-ʿArabiyah, 1981), 97, 114 and Muḥammad Saʿīd Ramaḍān al-Būṭī, *Ḍawābiṭ al-Maṣlaḥah fī al-Sharīʿah al-Islāmiyyah* (Damascus: Dār al-Fikr, 2005), 99.
13. Shalabī, *Taʿlīl*, 94.
14. Asʿad ʿAbd al-Ghanī al-Kafrāwī, *al-Istidlāl ʿInda al-Uṣūliyyīn* (Cairo: Dār al-Salām, 2005), 105, and ʿAbd al-ʿAẓīm al-Dīb, *Fiqh Imām al-Ḥaramayn ʿAbd Al-Malik Ibn ʿAbd Allāh al-Juwaynī* (Mansurah: Dār al-Wafā', 1988), 262.
15. Al-Juwaynī, *al-Burhan*, 2:1113, "*maʿnā mushʿir bi al-ḥukm munāsib lahū fīmā yaqtaḍīh al-fikr al-ʿaqlī min ghayr wujdan aṣl muttafaq ʿalayh wa al-taʿlīl al-manṣūb jārin fīh.*"
16. Al-Zarakshī, *al-Baḥr*, 4:377.
17. Al-Juwaynī, *al-Burhan*, 2:1114.
18. See also, Ibn al-Samʿānī, *Qawātiʿ al-Adillah*, 2:259. Ibn al-Samʿānī follows the argument of al-Juwaynī almost verbatim, but he adds a criterion to distinguish *istidlāl*, which could be referred to as the non-contradiction criterion. If the meaning that the jurist pursues in constructing a given ruling is not contradicted by a definitive text, it can be construed as a valid *istidlāl*, 261–267. See also, al-Ghazālī, *al-Mankhūl*, 453–475. Al-Ghazālī referred to it as *istidlāl mursal* (unrestricted) to distinguish it from regular *qiyās*. In his comment on this point, al-Qarāfī argued that closer examination would reveal that the use of the concept of *maṣlaḥah mursalah* (public interest) was not limited to the Mālikī school; it could be found in all other schools as well. See Qarāfī, *Sharḥ Tanqīḥ al-Fuṣūl*, 446.
19. Ibid.
20. Ibid., 1116.

21. Ibid., 1332.
22. Al-Āmidī, *al-Iḥkām*, 1: 112; al-Zarakshī, *al-Baḥr al-Muḥīṭ*, 1:18.
23. Al-Āmidī, *Iḥkām*, 4: 282.
24. Ibid., 287.
25. For a clear example of this usage of *istidlāl*, see Najm al-Dīn al-Ṭūfī, *ʿAlam al-Jadhal fī ʿIlm al-Jadal*, ed. Wolfhart Heinrichs (Wiesbaden: Franz Steiner Verlag, 1987). Al-Ṭūfī, following the juristic practice, distinguished between the general and the technical meanings of *istidlāl*. The former simply means establishing a ruling on the basis of a *dalīl* (indicator/evidence). The indicator may be rational, sensory, *sharʿī*, or a combination of more than one of these, 39–81. The latter refers to the set of rational/logical principles that the jurist uses in the absence of an agreed upon source. He listed 15 examples of these principles, 82–91.
26. Ibn al-Subkī, *Rafʿal-Ḥājib*, 4:480; Maḥmūd Ibn ʿAbd al-Raḥmān al-Iṣbahānī, *Bayān al-Mukhtaṣar, Sharḥ Mukhtaṣar Ibn al-Ḥājib fī Uṣūl al-Fiqh*, ed. ʿAlī Jumʿah Muḥammad (Cairo: Dār al-Salām, 2004), 2:792.
27. This correlation (*talāzum*) could be between two positive rulings, e.g., the person who can execute a divorce can also execute a *ẓihār* (an oath that suspends the marital relationship); between two negative rulings, e.g., if *wuḍu'* (ablution) is valid without intention, so will be *tayammum* (dry ablution with sand); between a positive ruling and a negative ruling, e.g., whatever is permissible cannot be forbidden; and finally between a negative ruling and a positive ruling, e.g., whatever is not permissible is forbidden.
28. On the question of whether the Prophet was following the laws of the earlier prophets before his mission, the jurists were divided into three groups. One group held that he was, but they disagreed whether it was Noah, Abraham, Moses, or Jesus. The second group held that he was not. The third group chose suspension of judgment. Similarly, the jurists disagreed whether the Prophet upheld the earlier laws that were not abrogated by the sharīʿah. See Isbahānī, *Sharḥ al-Mukhtaṣar*, 2:798.
29. Ibn al-Subkī, *Rafʿ al-Ḥājib*, 4:482. See also his *Jamʿ al-Jawāmiʿ* (Beirut: Dār Ibn Ḥazm, 2005), 57; Badr al-Dīn Muḥammad Ibn Bahādir al-Zarakshī, *Tashnīf al-Masāmiʿ bi Jamʿ al-Jawāmiʿ*, ed. al-Ḥusaynī Ibn ʿUmar (Beirut: Dār al-Kutub al-ʿIlmiyyah, 2000), 2:139; and Aḥmad Ibn ʿAbd al-Raḥmān Ibn Mūsā Ḥalūlū, *Kitāb al-Ḍiyā' al-Lāmiʿ Sharḥ Jamʿ al-Jawāmiʿ*, ed. Nādī Faraj al-ʿAṭṭār (Cairo: Marka Ibn al-ʿAṭṭār li al-Turāth, 2004), 2:435.
30. For more about the definition and the types of *istidlāl*, see Kafrāwī, *al-Istidlāl ʿInd al-Uṣuliyyīn*, op. cit.
31. Al-Qarāfī, *Sharḥ Tanqīḥ al-Fuṣūl*, 445. These were the Qur'ān, the Sunnah, consensus, consensus of the people of Madinah, *qiyās*, the opinion of the companions, public interest, presumption of continuity (*istiṣḥāb*), original innocence (*barā'ah aṣliyyah*), customs (*ʿawā'id*), induction (*istiqrā'*), blocking the means (*sadd al-dharā'iʿ*), *istidlāl*, juristic preference (*istiḥsān*), choosing the lesser alternative (*al-akhdh bi al-akhaff*), infallibility (*ʿiṣmah*), the consensus of the people of Kufah, the consensus of the family of the Prophet, and the consensus of the four caliphs. It is clear that al-Qarāfī's list of sources is a combination of conventional sources and general legal principles. These

two categories would be differentiated with the emergence of the genres of *qawā'id*.

32. Ibid., 454.
33. Ibn Juzayy, *Taqrīb al-Wuṣūl*, 101.
34. Ibn Juzayy's list is almost identical with al-Qarāafī's with the exception that he added the special consensus of the ten "leading" companions.
35. Al-Ṭūfī, *Sharḥ Mukhtaṣar al-Rawḍah*, 3:147.
36. Ibid., 150. See also, al-Zarakshī, *al-Baḥr al-Muḥīṭ*, 4:327. Al-Zarakshī listed six types of *istiṣḥāb* (presumption of continuity). The first is the one whose presence or continuation is proved either by reason or sharī'ah, such as the claim to ownership, which is to be accepted as long as it is not disproved. The second is the presumption of the original negation known by reason in rulings of sharī'ah, such as the negation of a sixth obligatory prayer. The third is the presumption of the establishment of a ruling on the basis of rational proof, which was advocated by al-Mu'tazilah and opposed by the majority. The former held that rulings can be known by means of reason even before sharī'ah. The latter held that rulings can only be known by sharī'ah. The fourth is the presumption of the general ruling unless it is either particularized or abrogated. The fifth is the presumption of the ruling of *ijmā'* in the case of disagreement. The sixth is considered the opposite of the standard meaning of *istiṣḥāb* in which the present is presumed to follow the past. In this case, however, the past is presumed to follow the ruling of the present. See Ibid., 330–336. In his vindication of *istiṣḥāb*, al-Rāzī invoked *'urf* along with religion and sharī'ah. See *al-Maḥṣūl*, 6:121 and Ḥalūlū, *Kitāb al-Ḍiyā' al-Lāmi'*, 2:441.
37. See, for example, his reference to it as one of the main sources, al-Zarakshī, *al-Baḥr al-Muḥīṭ*, 1:18; as a synonym of *qiyās*, 4:9; as a synonym of *munāsabah*, 4:186; and as a synonym of *tanqīḥ al-manāṭ* 4:227.
38. See, for example, Baber Johansen, "Casuistry Between Legal Concept and Social Praxis,"
39. Muḥmmad Ibn Muḥammad Ibn Amir al-Ḥājj, *al-Taqrīr wa al-Taḥbīr 'alā al-Taḥrīr fī ūṣūl al-Fiqh*, ed. 'Abd Allah Maḥmūd Muḥammad (Beirut: Dār al-Kutub al'Ilmiyyah, 1999), 1:340.
40. Al-Qarāfī, *Sharḥ Tanqīḥ al-Fuṣūl*, 212. See also, al-Qarāfī, *al-'Iqd al-Manẓūm fi al-Khuṣūṣ wa al-'Ūmūm*, ed. 'Alī Muḥammad Mu'awwaḍ and 'Adil Aḥmad 'Abd al-Mawjūd (Beirut: Dār al-Kutub al-'Ilmiyyah, 2001), 738.
41. Al-Qarāfī, *Sharḥ Tanqīḥ al-Fuṣūl*, 740.
42. Literally, *dābbah* refers to any walking animal, *ghā'iṭ* to the low spot of ground, and *khalā'* to empty or isolated space.
43. Al-Qarāfī, *Sharḥ Tanqīḥ al-Fuṣūl*, 739. See also, al-Qarāfī, *Kitāb al-Furūq*, 1:307 and al-Ghazālī, *al-Mustaṣfā*, 1:345–346.
44. 'Abd al-'Alyy Muḥammad Ibn Niẓām al-Dīn al-Anṣārī, *Fawātiḥ al-Raḥamūt*, 1:345 (printed together with al-Ghazālī's *Mustaṣfā*). See also, Isnawī, *Nihayat al-Sawl*, 1:534; Ibn Amir al-Ḥājj, *al-Taqrir;* and Ibn 'Ābidīn, "*Risālat Nashr al-'Ārf*" in *Majmu'at Rasā'il ibn 'Ābidīn*, 112–113.
45. Ibid. See also, Zarakshī, *al-Baḥr*, 2:521.
46. Ibid.

47. Al-Rāzī, *al-Maḥṣūl*, 3:131–132.
48. Ibid.
49. Ibid. See also, al-Qarāfī, *al-ʿIqd al-Manẓūm*, 737. Al-Qarāfī was influenced by al-Rāzī's treatment of the issue of particularization.
50. See, for example, Al-Rāzī, *al-Maḥṣūl*, 3:27.
51. Ibid., 3:75.
52. Ibn al-Subkī, *Rafʿ al-Ḥājib*, 3:301 and Al-Ghazālī, *al-Mustaṣfā*, 2:99.
53. Al-Qarāfī, *al-ʿIqd al-Manẓūm*, 672. Al-Isnawī divides the particularizing proofs into lexical and nonlexical. The latter include intention, *sharʿī* convention, and customary convention. See al-Isnawī, *al-Tamhīd*, 374.
54. Ibid., 737.
55. Ibid., 672.
56. Ibid., 743. Al-Qarāfī notes that he reviewed 36 works of *uṣūl* on this point. All of them, except al-Āmidī, agreed that only linguistic conventions can particularize general texts. He even cites some Ḥanafī sources that share the same view. See also al-Ghazālī, *al-Mustaṣfā*, 2:112.
57. Ibn al-Subkī, *Rafʿ al-Ḥājib*, 3:345 and al-Zarakshī, *al-Baḥr*, 2:521–522.
58. For more about *salam* and *ʿarāyā*, see chapters 2 and 4.
59. Abū Sunnah, *al-ʿUrf*, 113. For more on this point see chapters 1, 2, and 4.
60. Al-Qarāfī, *Sharḥ Tanqīḥ al-Fuṣūl*, 212; *al-ʿIqd al-Manẓūm*, 742; *al-Furūq*, 1:310.
61. See also, al-Zarakshī, *al-Baḥr*, 2:523.
62. Abū Sunnah takes issue with al-Qarāfī's view and confirms the standard Ḥanafī view of upholding practical customs as a valid particularizing proof. See Abū Sunnah, *al-ʿUrf*, 219. The Ḥanafī jurists compare the general statement (*al-ʿāmm*) to the unqualified statement (*muṭlaq*) which can be particularized by the practical custom. The argument goes that if practical custom can qualify the unqualified, it can also particularize the general. The example given is the case of a person who speaks of meat in a province that usually identifies meat with mutton (because it is the common type of meat consumed in this province). In this case, meat will be understood as mutton. The majority view, however, differentiated between the unqualified and the general because equating them would amount to linguistic analogy, which is considered invalid. See Ibn al-Subkī, *Rafʿ al-Ḥājib*, 3:347–348. The Ḥanafī jurists still rebutted the majority criticism by noting that equating the general with the unqualified is not the result of a linguistic but rather an inductive analogy, which proves their similarity. See al-Anṣārī, *Fawātiḥ al-Raḥamūt*, 1:345. See also, al-ʿAlāʾī, *al-Majmuʿʿ al-Mudhhab*, 1:106–109. On the debate over linguistic analogy, see al-Isnawī, *al-Tamhīd*, 454 and al-Zanjānī, *Takhrīj*, 344.

## 6. Custom and Legal Maxims: *al-Qawāʿid al-Fiqhiyyah*

1. Al-Zarqā, *al-Madkhal al-Fiqhī al-ʿĀmm*, 1:235–246; Al-Sanhūrī, "*al-Qanūn al-Madanī al-ʿArabī*" in Muḥammad ʿImārah, *Islāmiyyāt al-Sanhūrī Bāshā*, 2:538 and 1:354; and Joseph Schacht, *An Introduction to Islamic Law*, 92.

2. Haydar, *Durar*, 1:44–51; al-Zarqā, *al-Madkhal*, 2:1077–1083; al-Zarqā, *Sharḥ*, 219–243.
3. ʿAlī Ḥaydar, *Durar al-Ḥukkām Sharḥ Majallat al-Aḥkām*, 1:13.
4. Aḥmad Muḥammad al-Zarqā, *Sharḥ al-Qawāʿid al-Fiqhiyyah* (Damascus: Dār al-Qalam, 2001).
5. ʿAlī Aḥmad al-Nadwī, *al-Qawāʿid al-Fiqhiyah* (Damascus: Dār al-Qalam, 2004), 87.
6. In his study on Islamic legal history, Muḥammad al-Khuḍarī speaks of six main stages that shaped the development of the entire legal tradition. They start with the time of the Prophet, followed by the time of the older companions of the Prophet, the time of the younger companions of the Prophet (from the beginning of the second/eighth century to the mid fifth/eleventh century), the time of the establishment of legal schools up to the fall of Baghdad in the seventh/thirteenth century, and finally from the fall of Baghdad up to the fourteenth/twentieth century. Al-Zarqā follows the scheme of al-Khuḍarī but he refers to the sixth stage as the period from the fall of Baghdad up to the composition of the *Majallah* in 1286/1870. In addition to that he adds a seventh stage from the composition of the *Majallah* up to the end of the Second World War in 1287/1945, and lastly an eighth stage from that time up to the end of the twentieth century. See Muḥammad al-Khuḍarī, *Tārikh al-Tashrīʿ al-Islāmī*, 159–247.
7. Qur'ān 2: 185.
8. Qur'ān 2: 173.
9. Qur'ān 2: 286.
10. Qur'ān 22: 78.
11. Qur'ān 35: 18.
12. al-ʿAsqalānī, *Fatḥ al-Bārī*, 1:5.
13. Ibn Ḥanbal, *al-Musnad*, 3:249, 19:149, 20:23.
14. Al-Suyūṭī, *Tanwīr al-Ḥawālik*, 2:122 and Ibn Ḥanbal, *al-Musnad*, 5:55.
15. Abū Dāwūd Sulaymān Ibn al-Ashʿath al-Sijistānī al-Azdī, *Sunan Abī Dāwūd*, ed. Muḥammad Muḥyī al-Dīn ʿAbd al-Ḥamīd (Beirut: Dār Iḥyā' al-Sunnah al-Nabawiyah, 1970), 3:304. After the death of the Prophet, the reports of his companions and successors represented another source of legal maxims. The most famous example is the letter of ʿUmar I to Abū Mūsā al-Ashʿarī on adjudication procedures as recorded in Ibn al-Qayyim, *Iʿlām al-Muwaqqiʿīn ʿan Rabb al-ʿĀlamīn*, 1:75 and al-Suyūṭī, *al-Ashbāh*, 58. The period covering the first three centuries of Islamic history constitutes the formative period of the Islamic tradition. As far as the legal aspect of the tradition is concerned, the major schools were founded and the four surviving ones were consolidated. The major works that shaped the future of the tradition were written during this period. For the Ḥanafī school, this includes the six major works that constitute the foundation of the Ḥanafi legal corpus (*ẓāhir al-riwāyah*) that were written by Muḥammad Ibn al-Ḥasan al-Shaybānī, as well as other early works such as *Kitāb al-Kharāj* of Abū Yūsuf. For the Mālikī school, this includes *al-Muwaṭṭa'* of Imam Mālik as well as *al-Mudawwanah* of Saḥnūn. For the Shāfiʿī school, this includes *al-Risālah* and *al-Umm* of al-Shāfiʿī. In

addition to the legal works, the major collections of Prophetic reports were collected and many commentaries on them were composed. Some researchers attempted to survey these early works and look for the roots of legal maxims in them. See, for example, al-Nadwī, *al-Qawāʿid*, 94, Nūr al-Dīn Mukhtār al-Khādimī, *ʿIlm al-Qawāʿid al-Sharʿiyyah* (Riyadh: Maktabat al-Rushd, 2005), 118–130. For more on the early formative period, see chapter 2 on the normative foundations of *ʿurf.*

16. See, for example, Muḥammad al-Rūqī, *al-Qawāʿid al-Fiqhiyyah min khilāl Kitāb al-Ishrāf li al-Qāḍī ʿAbd al-Wahhab al-Baghdādī* (Dubayy: Dār al-Buḥūth lil Dirāsāt al-Islāmiyyah wa Iḥyāʾ al-Turāth, 2003), 251.
17. Al-Karkhī's treatise, published together with al-Dabbūsī's *Taʾsīs al-Naẓar*, 110–120.
18. Tāj al-Dīn ʿAbd al-Wahhab Ibn al-Subkī, *al-Ashbāh wa al-Naẓāʾir*, ed. ʿĀdil Aḥmad ʿAbd al-Mawjūd and ʿAlī Muḥammad ʿAwaḍ (Beirut: Dār al-Kutub al-ʿIlmiyyah, 1991),1:12. Ibn al-Subkī, *Tabaqāt al-Shāfiʿiyyah al-Kubrā*, 4:356–365.
19. Al-Suyūṭī, al-Ashbāh wa al-Naẓāʾir, 63.
20. ʿIzz al-Dīn ʿAbd al-ʿAzīz ibn ʿAbd al-Salam, *al-Qawāʿid al-Kubrā al-Mawsūm bi Qawāʿid al-Aḥkām fī Iṣlāḥ al-Anām*, ed. Nazīh Hammad and Uthman Ḍamīriyyah (Damascus: Dār al-Qalam, 2000).
21. Some use the word *ikhtaraʿa* (invented). See Ṣalāḥ al-Dín Khalīl Kikaldī al-ʿAlāʾī, *al-Majmūʿ al-Mudhhab fī Qawāʿid al-Madhhab*, eds. Majīd ʿAlī al-ʿUbaydī and Aḥmad Khuḍayr Abbas (Amman: Dār Ammār, 2004), 1:13 and Ibn al-Subkī, *al-Ashbāh wa al-Naẓāʾir*, 1:6.
22. For a useful introduction to the genre in English, see Wolfhart Heinrichs "*Qawāʿid* as a Genre of Legal Literature," in *Studies in Islamic Legal Theory*, ed. Bernard Weiss (Leiden: Brill, 2002), 365–384. Unlike the approach adopted here, Heinrichs includes *maqāṣid* within the Qawāʿid genre.
23. Ibn ʿAbd al-Salām, *al-Qawāʿid*, 1:13 and passim. See also, al-ʿAlāʾī, *al-Majmūʿ*, 1:14.
24. Ibid.
25. In fact, the jurists often describe the different substantive rulings as speculative (*ẓanniyyah*) rather than definitive (*qaṭʿiyyah*). This particular description of the rulings as speculative has always had consequences on various debates over important issues such as *ijtihād* and its foundations. See al-Isnawī, *al-Tamhīd fī Takhrīj al-Furūʿ ʿalā al-Uṣūl*, 47–51.
26. Ibn ʿAbd al-Salām, *al-Qawāʿid*, 1:6–7, 309.
27. Ibid., 2:238–243.
28. Ibid., 1:9.
29. Ibid., 1:11 and 2:130.
30. Ibid., 1:14.
31. Ibid., 1:7.
32. Ibid., 2:260.
33. Ibid., 2:126–130.
34. Ibid., 2:97 and al-Qarāfī, *Sharḥ Tanqīḥ al-Fuṣūl*, 445–454.
35. Ibid.

36. Obviously, there was no standard classification of these indicators. While Ibn ʿAbd al-Salām used two types (legal and confirmatory), al-ʿAlāʾī used three (legal, confirmatory, and evidentiary). Al-Qarāfī initially followed his teacher Ibn ʿAbd al-Salām and included evidentiary indicators under the confirmatory indicators. He divided the confirmatory indicators into definitive indicators and speculative indicators. The definitive confirmatory indicators refer to the causes of rulings (e.g.,times of prayer, seeing of new moon for the beginning of months, etc.). Speculative confirmatory indicators refer to evidentiary indicators used mainly in court. See *Sharḥ Tanqīḥ al-Fuṣūl*, 454. In *al-Furūq*, however, he referred to the speculative confirmatory indicators separately as arguments (*ḥijāj*). See *al-Furūq*, 1:251–252.
37. Al-ʿAlāʾī, *al-Majmūʿ*, 1:160.
38. Ibid., 162.
39. Ṣadr al-Dīn Ibn al-Wakīl, *al-Ashbāh wa al-Naẓāʾir*, ed. Aḥmad Ibn Muḥammad al-ʿAnqarī and ʿAdil Ibn ʿAbd Allah al-Shuwaykh (Riyadh: Maktabat al-Rushd, 1993).
40. Al-ʿAlāʾī, *al-Majmūʿ*, 1:12.
41. Ibid., 2:225.
42. Al-Qarāfī, *al-Furūq*, 3:1070–1073.
43. Ibid., 2:226–227.
44. Ibid.
45. Ibid., 2:244.
46. Ibid., 2:232.
47. Ibid., 2:231.
48. Ibn al-Qayyim, *Iʿlām al-Muwaqqiʿīn,* 1:605.
49. Ibid.
50. Ibid., 2:311.
51. Modern commentators also divide legal maxims into general principles that pertain to different themes and general questions of the law, on the one hand, and specific maxims that pertain to one theme or one question only, on the other. The latter is sometimes referred to as *ḍābiṭ*. See al-Nadwī, *al-Qawāʿid al-Fiqhiyyah*, 46.
52. Al-Qarāfī, *al-Furūq*, 1:70–71.
53. Ibn al-Wakīl, *al-Ashbāh wa al-Naẓaʾir*, 1:140. Some jurists divide meanings into two main categories: real and allegorical. The former is in turn divided into three subcategories: linguistic, *sharʿī*, and customary. See al-Zarakshī, *al-Manthūr fī al-Qawāʿid*, 2:109, 117; al-Suyūṭī, *al-Ashbāh wa al-Naẓaʾir*, 226; and Shihāb al-Dīn Maḥmūd Ibn Aḥmad al-Zanjānī, *Takhrīj al-Furūʿ ʿalā al-Uṣūl*, ed. Muḥammad Adīb Ṣāliḥ (Beirut: Muʾssasat al-Risālah, 1979), 123.
54. Al-Isnawī, *al-Tamhīd,* 230.
55. Ibid., 1:141.
56. Ibid., 1:150 and al-Qarāfī, *al-Furūq*, 1:125–132.
57. Al-Qarāfī, *al-Furūq*, 1:126.
58. *Khiyār al-majlis* (literally, the option of the session) denotes the freedom to revoke the transaction as long as the parties remain in the session, which

means that they haven't yet concluded the transaction. The Shāfiʿī, and the Ḥanbalī jurists consider it an implicit condition in a valid contract of sale; the Ḥanafī jurists approve it if the parties agree on it; and the Mālikī jurists don't recognize it at all. See Muwaffaq al-Dīn ʿAbd Allah Ibn Aḥmad Ibn Muḥammad Ibn Qudāmah, *al-Mughnī* (Beirut: Dār al-Kutub al-ʿIlmiyyah, n.d.), 4:6; al-Jazīrī, *Kitāb al-Fiqh ʿalā al-Madhāhib al-Arbaʿah*, 2:154; and al-Zarakshī, *al-Manthūr fī al-Qawāʿid*, 1:355. As al-Zanjānī points out, this is one of the examples that reveal the difference between the Shāfiʿī school and the Ḥanafī school over reliance on singular aḥādīth in rulings that pertain to the oft-repeated, often unavoidable, incidents, *mā taʿummu bihi al-balwā*. Only the Shāfiʿī school accepted a singular ḥadīth in this case. Al-Zanjānī, *Takhrīj*, 66.

59. Ibn Qudāmah, *al-Mughnī*, 4:85 and al-Jazīrī, *Kitāb al-Fiqh*, 2:172.
60. Ibn al-Wakīl, *al-Ashbāh wa al-Naẓā'ir*, 1, 141–142, 156–161.
61. These terms should be known or estimated because they affect a woman's capacity to perform certain devotional deeds such as prayer, fasting, and pilgrimage.
62. Al-ʿAlā'ī, *al-Majmūʿ*, 1:141; Ibn al-Subkī, *al-Ashbāh wa al-Naẓā'ir*, 1:51; Ibn al-Qayyim, *Iʿlām al-Muwaqqiʿīn*, 1:605; al-Zarakshī, *al-Manthūr fī al-Qawāʿid*, 2:118; al-Suyūṭī, *al-Ashbāh wa al-Naẓā'ir*, 235; and Isnawī, *al-Tamhīd*, 224.
63. Al-Zarakshī, *al-Ashbāh*, 2:100 and al-Suyūṭī, *al-Ashbāh*, 224. Other questions included the relationship between the different types of meanings (*sharʿī*, linguistic, customary, and allegorical), especially in cases of ambiguity or conflict; the distinction between the general custom and the specific custom; and the distinction between antecedent, concurrent, and subsequent customs.
64. Al-Qarāfī, *al-Furūq*, 1:71.
65. The jurists debated the question of meaning or signification and its association with words. While some argued that this relationship is intrinsic (*dhātiyyah*), others argued that it is conventional (*waḍʿiyyah*). The latter again were divided on the origin of this convention and whether it is divine or human. Another view held that the origin of the linguistic convention is partly divine and partly human. See al-Rāzī, *al-Maḥṣūl*, 1: 181 and al-Isnawī, *al-Tamhīd*, 131.
66. For more on this point, see al-Qarāfī, *al-Furūq*, 1:92–105 and also his *al-Iḥkām fī Tamyīz al-Fatāwā min al-Aḥkām*, 75–77. See also, Isnawī, *al-Tamhīd*, 137, 198.
67. Al-Qarāfī, *al-Furūq*, 1:126.
68. Complete customary transformation is achieved by immediate recognition of the customary meaning whenever the expression in question is used without the need for additional circumstantial evidence. See al-Qarāfī, *al-Furūq*, 3:831.
69. He noted that the same ruling applies to many other cases, such as currencies and the evaluation of expenditure. He observed that during his time it was customary for the witness to use only the present tense as he would begin by a phrase such as "I bear witness that..." Conversely, a seller would only use the past tense as in a statement such as "I sold you..." Al-Qarāfī asserted

that these formulae are custom-based and that it is important for jurists to be aware of different customs of the different regions. See al-Qarāfī, *al-Furūq*, 1:138, 176. In a telling passage he noted "the legal responses, *fatāwā*, should always be adjusted according to this rule: whatever was added by the customary practice, should be added and whatever was cancelled by the customary practice, should be cancelled. One should not forever adhere to what is written in the books. If a person from a region other than yours asked you, you should not give him the answer that is suitable for your locality but you should ask him about the customary practice of his region and answer him accordingly... This is the right approach because blind adherence to the written views amounts to misguidance in religion, ignorance of the approaches of the learned as well as the early (followed) generations. " Al-Qarāfī, *al-Furūq*, 1:314.

70. Ibn al-Subkī, *Tabaqāt al-Shāfiʿiyyah al-Kubrā*, 4:356–365. The anecdote goes that when al-Marwarrūdhī was told that the Ḥanafī jurist Abū Tāhir al-Dabbās summed up the basics of the Ḥanafī school into 17 foundational principles, he said that the basics of the Shāfiʿī school are summed up into only four. See al-ʿAlāʾī, *al-Majmūʿ*, 1:34; Ibn al-Subkī, *al-Ashbāh*, 1:12; al-Suyūṭī, *al-Ashbāh*. These four principles are: certainty cannot be removed by doubt (*al-yaqīn lā yazūl bi al-shakk*), difficulty brings forth ease (*al-mashaqqah tajlib al-taysīr*), harm should be removed (*al-ḍarar yuzāl*), and custom should be acknowledged (*taḥkīm al-ʿādah wa al-rujūʿ ilayhā*). Al-ʿAlāʾī observed that a fifth one was added: matters should be judged on the basis of their intended objectives (*al-ūmūr bi maqāṣidihā*).
71. Al-ʿAlāʾī, *al-Majmūʿ*, 1:137.
72. After al-ʿAlāʾī, Ibn al-Subkī, al-Suyūṭī, and Ibn Nujaym have adopted the same classification scheme. While both al-ʿAlāʾī and al-Suyūṭī refer to custom as the fifth maxim, Ibn al-Subkī refers to it as the fourth maxim and Ibn Nujaym refers to it as the sixth maxim. See Ibn al-Subkī, *al-Ashbāh*, 1:50; al-Suyūṭī, *al-Ashbāh*, 221: and Ibn Nujaym, *al-Ashbāh*, 101.
73. "We did send messengers before you and gave them wives and children, it was never the part of a messenger to bring a sign except as Allah permitted." There are similar other passages such as 6:8, 17:94, and 25:7.
74. Abū Dāwūd al-Sijstānī, *Sunan Abi Dāwūd*, 3:243.
75. Ibid., 3:296.
76. Al-ʿAlāʾī, *al-Majmūʿ*, 1:140.
77. Some jurists followed other schemes. For example, al-Zarakshī arranged the maxims alphabetically and Ibn Rajab arranged them according to the different chapters of substantive law. See al-Zarakshī, *al-Durr al-Manthūr* and ʿAbd al-Raḥmān al-Baghdādī Ibn Rajab, *al-Qawāʿid fī al-Fiqh al-Musammā Taqrīr al-Qawāʿid wa Taḥrīr al-Fawāʾid* (Beirut: Bayt al-Afkār al-Dawliyah, 2004). Although occasionally the literature of legal maxims would deal with jurisprudential questions, it mostly addressed substantive issues. See also Ahmad Ibn Taymiyah, *al-Qawāʿid al-Nūrāniyyah al-Fiqhiyyah*, ed. Muḥammad Ḥāmid al-Fiqī (Cairo: Matbaʿat al-Sunnah al-Muḥammadiyyah, 1951).

## 7. Custom and the Objectives of Sharīʿah: *Maqāṣid al-Sharīʿah*

1. Qur'ān 2:183.
2. Qur'ān 2:179.
3. Al-Shāṭibī, *al-Muwāfqāt fī Uṣūl al-Sharīʿah.*
4. Al-Shāfiʿī, *al-Risālah*, 560.
5. Al-Juwaynī, *al-Burhān*, 2:923.
6. Al-Ghazālī, *al-Mustaṣfā*, 1:286.
7. Ibid., 1:287.
8. For more details on this point, see Shalabī, *Taʿlīl al-Aḥkām*, 239.
9. Al-Zarakshī, *al-Baḥr al-Muḥīṭ*, 4:377.
10. Al-Shāṭibī, *al-Muwāfqāt*, 1:22.
11. Ibid., 1:25.
12. Ibid., 2:26.
13. On this point, see Abū Naṣr al-Fārābī, *Iḥṣā' al-ʿUlūm*, ed. Osman Amine (Cairo: Maktabat al-Anglo, 1968), 132–133.
14. Al-Juwaynī, *al-Burhān*, 1:580, 682. See also, chapter 4.
15. Al-Shāṭibī, *al-Muwāfqāt*, 1:41–42. Al-Shāṭibī uses the term "meaning induction" (*istiqrā' maʿnawī*), which is not dependent on one particular indicator but is supported by a body of multiple indicators. It is such meaning induction that furnished the knowledge about the generosity of Ḥātim and the bravery of ʿAlī. These two attributes are not known by one single report but by many different reports that together indicate certain knowledge by means of induction.
16. Ibn ʿAbd al-Salām, *al-Qawāʿid al-al-Kubrā*, 1:14.
17. Al-Shāṭibī, *al-Muwāfaqāt*, 2:33.
18. Ibid., 2:26.
19. Ibid., 2:21.
20. Al-Shāṭibī differentiates between the constitutive intent (*al-qaṣd al-takwīnī*) of a benefit, which often entails an accompanying incidental harm(s) on the one hand, and the legislative intent (*al-qaṣd al-tashrīʿī*) that seeks to identify the outweighing beneficiary elements within a particular order or entity. He often uses the example of a physician who, in administering bitter medicine, does not intend to torture the patient with its bitter taste but to benefit him with its healing effect. Al-Shāṭibī, *al-Muwāfaqāt*, 2:24.
21. Al-Shāṭibī, *al-Muwāfaqāt*, 2:23.
22. Al-Shāṭibī, *al-Muwāfaqāt*, 2:31–32. As noted earlier, this world is considered a prelude to the afterlife because worldly benefits are often mixed and relative. Real benefits (as defined by sharīʿah) are not always coextensive with desired benefits (as perceived by the self). The former may sometimes entail an element of inconvenience for trial. Sharīʿah meant to subject the individual through *taklīf* to the demands of the law rather than to personal desires.
23. This is clearly shown in al-Shāṭibī's, treatment of several issue in *al-Muwāfaqāt* such as causality, 1:152, 158 and moral epistemology, 2:36, 147,

283, in addition to his frequent mention of al-Ghazālī, whom he cited probably more than anyone else. See *al-Muwāfaqāt* 1:94, 103, 185, 239; 2:12, 94, 126, 182, and 249.

24. Ibn ʿAbd al-Salām, *al-Qawāʿid*, 1:13.
25. Al-Shāṭibī, *al-Muwāfaqāt*, 2:39–40.
26. Al-Shāṭibī, *al-Muwāfaqāt*, 2:4–8.
27. Al-Shāṭibī, *al-Muwāfaqāt*, 2:20.
28. Some jurists added honor to the list of the five fundamentals and others put life before religion. See Al-Shāṭibī, *al-Muwāfaqāt*, 2:8.
29. Al-Ghazālī also used this distinction between rituals and customs in his famous *Iḥyāʾ ʿulūm al-Dīn* (Revivification of Religious Knowledge), which he divided into four parts: rituals (*ʿibādāt*), customs (*ʿādāt*), delivering acts (*munjiyat*), and destructive acts (*muhlikāt*).
30. For example, a prerequisite for a valid prayer is completion of ablution (*wuḍūʾ*). A proper ablution involves the washing of hands, face, arms, head, and feet in a specific manner and order combined with the correct intention. The mere washing of these body parts without the proper intention does not amount to a proper ablution. Al-Shāṭibī, *al-Muwāfaqāt*, 2:183 and Ibn ʿAbd al-Salām, *al-Qawāʿid al-Kubrā*, 1:311.
31. Al-Shāṭibī, *al-Muwāfaqāt*, 2:256.
32. Ibid., 2:257.
33. Ibid., 2:260.
34. Ibid.,2:150, 166, and 339.
35. The jurists debated the validity of deeds of worship that have multiple intentions, as is the case in this example. While some maintained the intention must be completely devoid of worldly considerations, others held that as long as the primary objective is otherworldly, it will still be valid. Al-Shāṭibī, *al-Muwāfaqāt*, 2:187.
36. Al-Shāṭibī, *al-Muwāfaqāt*, 2:332. Al-Shāṭibī differentiates between the two extremes of the Zahirī school and the Bāṭinī school. The former held that the will of the Legislator is exclusively known from the texts and that is why they disapproved of *qiyās*. The latter held that the will of the Legislator cannot be known from the texts, but it is known only through the infallible imam.
37. Al-Shāṭibī, *al-Muwāfaqāt*, 2:334.
38. Ibid., 2:336.
39. Ibid., 2:271.
40. See also, Ibn ʿAbd al-Salām, *al-Qawāʿid al-Kubrā*, 1:219.
41. Al-*Shāṭibī*, *al-Muwāfaqāt*, 1:238–239. See also, al-Ghaẓālī, *al-Mustaṣfā*, 1:94.
42. Al-Shāṭibī, *al-Muwāfqāt*, 2:7–9.
43. Ibd., 2:54. Muslims believe that the language and the style of the Qurʾān prove its divine origin, for although written in Arabic, it is believed to be inimitable. The Qurʾān in more than one occasion challenges its listeners to produce similar passages. It is believed that the challenge has never been met. See Qurʾān 2:23, 10:38, and 11:13. see also Al-Shāṭibī, *al-Muwāfqāt*, 2:48.

44. Al-Shāfiʿī, *al-Risālah*, 42–50.
45. Al-Shāṭibī, *al-Muwāfqāt,* 2:58,74. Al-Shāṭibī emphasized the notion of the "illiterate nation" (*al-ummah al-ummiyyah*) to indicate that sharīʿah was constructed in simple terms in order to remain accessible and comprehensible even to those who are illiterate. The Prophet himself is believed to have been illiterate. Despite the Prophet's illiteracy and lack of prior education or training, he communicated a text that the most learned found incomparable.
46. Al-Shāṭibī, *al-Muwāfqāt,* 2:77.
47. Al-Shāṭibī, *al-Muwāfqāt,* 3:325.
48. Al-Shāṭibī, *al-Muwāfqāt,* 2:60.
49. The example of Prophet Ibrāhīm (Abraham) was specifically important. The rituals of the pilgrimage were connected with his legacy. Al-Shāṭibī, *al-Muwāfqāt,* 2:79.
50. Al-Shāṭibī, *al-Muwāfqāt,* 2:65.
51. Ibid., 2:78–9.
52. Ibid., 2:92.
53. Ibid., 2:101.
54. Ibid., 2:103.
55. Ibid., 2:105.
56. Ibid., 2:144.
57. Ibid., 2:145.
58. Ibid., 2:147.
59. Ibid., 2:241.
60. Ibid., 2:241.
61. Ibid., 2:242.
62. See also, al-Juwaynī, *al-Burhān*, 2:947.
63. Al-Shāṭibī, *al-Muwāfqāt,* 4:74. For more on *taḥqīq al-manāṭ,* see chapter 5.
64. Al-Shāṭibī, *al-Muwāfqāt,* 2:143.
65. Ibid., 1:159.
66. Ibid., 1:149.
67. Al-Shāṭibī will modify this opinion. See note 72 below.
68. Al-Shāṭibī, *al-Muwāfqāt,* Ibid., 1:158.
69. Ibid., 1:161.
70. Ibid., 1:163,168.
71. Ibid., 1:169.
72. Qur'ān 37:96, 39:62.
73. Qur'ān 5:32.
74. Al-Shāṭibī, *al-Muwāfqāt,* 1:171.
75. Ibid., 1:188.
76. Ibid., 1:173.
77. Ibid., 1:183–190.
78. For more on the theory of contingency, please refer to chapter 3.

## 8. CUSTOM, LEGAL APPLICATION, AND THE CONSTRUCTION OF REALITY

1. See Abou El-Fadl, *Rebellion and Violence*, 29.
2. For example, al-Ghazālī divided his famous *al-Mustaṣfā* into four main parts, each part addressing one of the main areas of *uṣūl al-fiqh*: rulings (*aḥkām*), sources (*maṣādir*), means of extracting rulings, and qualifications of the person who should undertake the process. This final part has traditionally been designated to *ijtihād*, which was devoted to the theoretical discussions dealing with *ijtihād*, including new or novel cases that are not covered by the texts, as well as the guidelines that the mujtahid should refer to when performing ijtihād. This was the general format already in place even before al-Ghazālī, especially in the Shāfiʿī rational school of jurisprudence as evident in the works of al-Baṣrī, al-Shirāzī and al-Juwaynī. Al-Ghazālī helped further consolidate this archetypal format, which most legal theorists since his time have adopted.
3. So far we have used the word ruling (*ḥukm*) to refer to *al-ḥukm al-sharʿī al-taklīfī* and its five divisions: prohibited (*ḥarām*), disliked (*makrūh*), permissible (*mubāḥ*), recommended (*mustaḥabb*), and obligatory (*wājib*). In this chapter, however, the word refers mainly, to a judge's verdict.
4. "*Badhl al-majhūd wa istifrāgh al-wūsʿ fī fiʿl min al-afʿāl wa lā yustaʿmal illā fīmā fīhī kulfah wa jahd.*" See al-Ghazālī, *al-Mustaṣfā*, 2:350.
5. "*Badhl al-mujtahid wusʿahu fī ṭalab al-ʿilm bi aḥkām al-sharīʿah wa al-ijtihād al-tāmm an yabdhula al-wusʿa fī al-ṭalab bi ḥaythu yaḥussu min nafsihi bi al-ʿajzi ʿan mazīdi ṭalab.*" Ibid.; al-Rāzī, *al-Maḥṣūl*, 6:6; and al-Zarakshī, *al-Baḥr*, 4:488.
6. Al-Rāzī, *al-Maḥṣūl*, 6:21 and al-Zarakshī, *al-Baḥr*, 4:492.
7. This is the term used to refer to the first four caliphs after the death of the Prophet: Abū Bakr, Umar ibn al-Khattāb, ʿUthmān ibn ʿAffān, and ʿAlī ibn Abī Tālib.
8. Some jurists continued to insist on the condition of *ijtihād* for these posts. See. for example. Jalāl al-Dīn ʿAbd al-Raḥmān Ibn Abī Bakr al-Suyūṭī, *Kitāb al-Radd ʿalā man Akhlada ilā al-Arā wa Jahila anna al-Ijtihād fī Kulli ʿAṣr Farḍ*, ed. Khalīl al-Mays (Beirut: Dār al-Kutub al-ʿIlmiyyah, 1983), 82–93. Similarly, al-Bājī saw that the judge must attain the rank of *ijtihād*. See Abū al-Walīd Sulaymān Ibn Khalaf al-Bājī, *Fuṣūl al-Aḥkām wa bayān mā Maḍā ʿalayhi al-ʿamal ʿinda al-Fuqahā' wa al-Ḥukkām*, ed. Muḥammad Abū al-Ajfān (Tunis: al-Dār al-ʿArabiyyah lil Kitāb, 1985), 129. Shihāb al-Dīn Ibrāhīm Ibn ʿAbd Allāh Ibn Abī al-Damm, *Kitāb Adab al-Qaḍā' aw al-Durar al-Manẓūmāt fī al-Aqḍiyah wa al-Ḥukūmāt*, ed. Muḥammad ʿAbd al-Qādir ʿAṭā (Beirut: Dār al-Kutib al-ʿIlmiyyah, 1987), 37. Some jurists observed that *ijtihād* is a prerequisite for a jurisconsult but not necessarily for a judge. See Abū al-Walīd Ibrāhīm Muḥammad Ibn Abī al-Faḍl Ibn al-Shiḥnah, *Lisān al-Ḥukkām fī Maʿrifat al-Aḥkām* (Beirut: Dār al-Fikr, 1982), 218 (published together with ʿAlā' al-Dīn ʿAlī Ibn Khalīl al-Ṭarābulsī's *Muʿīn al-Ḥukkām fīmā Yataradad*

*bayna al-Khiṣmayn min al-Aḥkām*). See also, Burhān al-Dīn Ibrāhīm Ibn ʿAlī Ibn Abī al-Qāsim Ibn Muḥammad Ibn Farḥūn, *Tabṣirat al-Ḥukkām fī al-Aqḍiyah wa Manāhij al-Aḥkām* (Cairo: Maktabat al-Kulliyyāt al-Azhariyyah, 1986), 1:68; Ibn al-Qayyim, *Iʿlām al-Muwaqqiʿīn*, 2:442–443; al-Māwardī, *al-Aḥkām al-Sulṭāniyyah*, 130; Abū Yaʿlā al-Farrāʾ, *al-Aḥkām al-Sulṭāniyyah*, 80; and Abū Zakariyyā Yaḥyā Ibn Sharaf al-Nawawī, *Ādāb al-Fatwā wa al-Muftī wa al-Mustaftī*, ed. Bassām ʿAbd al-Wahhāb al-Jābī (Damascus: Dār al-Fikr, 1988), 24.

9. It is no wonder, therefore, to see that al-Shafiʿī emphasized the role of *qiyās* so much that he equated it with *ijtihād*. Al-Shāfiʿī's main concern was to provide a theoretical framework to organize the hitherto unstructured legal process. Legal analogy seemed ideal for maintaining this structure.
10. This is the reason legal scholars often compare the concept of *istiḥsān* to the concept of equity in the common law tradition. In fact, it is often translated as equity. For a detailed discussion of this point, see Makdisi, "Legal Logic and Equity in Islamic Law," *The American Journal of Comparative Law* 33, no. 1 (1985): 70.
11. This is the reason *istiḥsān* is sometimes referred to as the subtle analogy (*qiyās khafyy*). The most famous (and most cited) example that illustrates this dynamic is the contract of *istiṣnāʿ*. For a detailed discussion of this type of transaction and several concrete examples of it, which also highlight the role of *ʿurf*, see Ibn ʿĀbidin "*Nashr al-ʿArf*."
12. For more on *istiḥsān*, see chapter 4. For a useful summary of the *istiḥsān* debate in general and custom-based *istiḥsān* in particular, see al-Zarakshī, *al-Baḥr al-Muḥīṭ*, 4:386–396. Al-Zarakshī listed different meanings of *istiḥsān* depending on its particular foundation: a ḥadīth, an opinion of a companion, a common custom, a subtle piece of evidence (*maʿnā khafyy*), or a personal preference of the jurist. Most later jurists explain that al-Shāfiʿī's vehement condemnation is specifically directed at the *istiḥsān* that is based on the personal preference of the jurist. Interestingly, the Ḥanafī jurists themselves deny this type of *istiḥsān*, hence the famous explanation that the disagreement is only nominal. See also, Ibn al-Subkī, *Rafʿ al-Hājib*, 4:524. Al-Rāzī, however, insisted that the disagreement is not nominal, but is based on the other debate on the particularization of the operative cause (*takhṣīṣ al-ʿillah*). See *al-Maḥṣūl*, 6:128.
13. Ibn Abī al-Damm, *Kitāb Adab al-Qaḍāʾ*, 14.
14. Al-Qarāfī, *al-Iḥkām fī Tamyīz al-Fatāwā min al-Aḥkām*, 99.
15. Al-Qarāfī takes issue with the traditional view of why the judge's verdict is binding. According to this view a judge's verdict has to be binding in order to eliminate disputes (*ḥukm al-ḥākim yarfaʿ al-khilāf*). Al-Qarāfī, however, argues that a judge has a delegated authority from the Lawgiver to choose one opinion in cases of disagreement. A judge's choice functions as a text from the Lawgiver in this particular question. As such, it represents a particular indicator (*dalīl khāss*) that takes precedence over a general indicator in cases of disagreement. See al-Qarāfī, *al-Iḥkām*, 80–81.
16. Al-Qarāfī, *al-Furūq*, 1:135–138, (*al-ḥākim mulzim wa al-muftī mukhbir*). For the Ḥanafī and the Shafiʿī views, see al-Zanjānī, *Takhrīj*, 372.

17. See Jackson, *Islamic Law and the State,* 177. For more on custom, *khabar*, and *inshā'*, see chapter 6.
18. Custom in the sense of individual habit, *'ādah*, is also used as circumstantial evidence, especially in case of doubt or in discretionary judgments. For example, a person's habit, character, and history are used to corroborate or negate a particular claim. See Shalabī, *T'līl al-Aḥkām*, 79–80.
19. Ibn al-Qayyim, *I'lām al-Muwaqqi'īn*, 1:77.
20. Ibn al-Qayyim observed that Aḥmad Ibn Ḥanbal is reported to have determined several prerequisites for a jurisconsult, including proper intention, specialized knowledge, competence, moral character, financial sufficiency, and knowledge of people. See *I'lām al-Muwaqqi'īn*, 2:444.
21. Ibn al-Qayyim, *I'lām al-Muwaqqi'īn*, 2:448–449. Similarly, al-Wansharīsī differentiated between the understanding of judgeship/legal opinions (*fiqh al-qaḍā'/ al-futyā*) and the science of judgeship/legal opinions (*'ilm al-qaḍā'/ al-futyā*). The former refers to (theoretical) knowledge of the rulings, which are the subject matter of both judgeship and legal opinions. The latter, however, is the ability to apply the theoretical knowledge of the rulings to particular contextualized cases. See Aḥmad Ibn Yaḥyā al-Wansharīsī, *Kitāb al-Wilāyāt*, ed. Henri Bruno et al (Rabat: Moncho, 1937), 17.
22. Al-Wansharīsī, *Kitāb al-Wilāyāt*, 16–17. See also, Ibn 'Ābidīn, "*Nashr al-'Arf fī binā' ba'ḍ al-Aḥkām 'alā al-'Urf*" in *Majmū'at Rasā'il Ibn 'Ābidīn*, 127 and Ibn 'Ābidīn "*Sharḥ al-Manẓūmah al-Musammāh 'Uqūd Rasm al-Muftī*" in *Majmū'at Rasā'il Ibn 'Ābidīn*, 16, 46.
23. Ibn 'Abd al-Salām, *al-Qawā'id*, 2:97; al-Qarāfī, *Sharḥ Tanqīḥ al-Fuṣūl*, 445–454; al-'Alā'ī, *al-Majmū'*, 1:160; al-Qarāfī, *al-Furūq*, 1:251–252. For more on this point, see chapters 5 and 6.
24. For example, the five daily prayers are obligatory but their performance is made dependent on their respective times (causes).
25. Al-Suyūṭī, *Kitāb al-Radd 'alā man Akhlada ilā al-Arḍ*, 179.
26. There are many other examples that, similar to the case of *ḥirz*, depend for their interpretation on the common practice. This includes, for example, separation between a seller and a buyer in the case of a sale transaction (*tafarruq*). The concept of *tafarruq* is particularly important in the Shāfi'í school according to which as long as both the seller and the buyer did not separate, any of them can revoke the transaction based on *khyār al-majlis*. According to the Shāfi'ī jurists, what constitutes *tafarruq* depends on the common custom. The jurists observe that in the absence of a clear indication both in sharī'ah and in language, such indication is to be derived from the common custom (*Kul mā warada bihī al-shar'u muṭlaqan walā ḍābiṭa fīhī walā fī al-lughati, yuḥakkamu fīhī al-'urf*). See, for more examples, al-Zarakshī, *al-Manthūr fī al-Qawā'id*, 2: 118.
27. Ibn Farḥūn, *Tabṣirat al-Ḥukkām*, 1:18 ("*I'lam anna 'umūm al-wilayāt wa khuṣūṣahā wa mā yastafīduhū al-mutawallī bi al-wilāyah yutalaqqā min al-alfāẓ wa al-aḥwāl wa al-'urf, wa laysa li dhālika ḥadd fī al-shar' faqadd yadkhul fī wilāyat al-qaḍā' fī ba'ā al-amkinah wa fī ba'ā al-azminah mā yadkhul fī wilāyat al-ḥarb wa qad takūn fī ba'ḍ al-amkinah wa al-azminah qāṣirah 'alā al-aḥkām al-shar'iyyah faqaṭ, fa yustafad min wilāyat al-qaḍā' fī kull quṭr mā jarat bihī al-'ādah wa iqtaḍāh al-'urf wa hādhā huwa al-taḥqīq fī hādhihī

*al-mas'alah wa Allah subḥānahū wa ta'ālā a'lam.*") See also, 2:146; al-Qarāfī, *al-Iḥkām*, 166; and Ibn al-Qayyim, *al-Ṭuruq al-Ḥukmiyyah fī al-Siyāsah al-Shar'iyyah* (Cairo: Dār al-Ḥadīth, 2002), 202.

28. For example, the general jurisdiction of judgeship may involve several particular jurisdictions. Each of these particular jurisdictions addresses specific areas such as marriage/divorce contracts or orphan affairs. See Ibn Farḥūn, *Tabṣirat al-Ḥukkām*, 20.
29. The jurists disagreed on the question of determining the scope of the judge's jurisdiction and whether it includes purely political issues. See Ibn Farḥūn, *Tabṣirat al-Ḥukkām*, 2:146–155.
30. Al-Qarāfī, *al-Iḥkām*, 109; al-'Alā'ī, *al-Majmū'*, 2:422; Ibn Farḥūn, *Tabṣirat al-Ḥukkām*, 1:22; al-Māwardī, *al-Aḥkām al-Sulṭāniyyah*, 146; and Abū Ya'lā al-Farrā', *al-Aḥkām al-Sulṭāniyyah*, 91.
31. See, for example, the discussion about the incident of the pollination of palm trees in chapter 2. On the different roles of the Prophet, see al-Qarāfī, *al-Furūq*, 1:346; Ibn al-Wakīl, *al-Ashbāh wa al-Naẓā'ir*, 1:87; *al-'Alā'ī, al-Majmū' al-Mudhhab*, 1:422.;
32. Al-Qarāfī, *al-Iḥkām*, 112.
33. Ibn Abī al-Damm, *Kitāb Adab al-Qaḍā'*, 14–15.
34. Ibn Farḥūn, *Tabṣirat al-Ḥukkām*, 2:154 and Ibn 'Ābidīn, *Nashr al-'Arf fī binā' ba'd al-Aḥkām 'alā al-'Urf*," 140.
35. Al-Suyūṭī, *Kitāb al-Radd 'alā man Akhlada ilā al-Arḍ*, 87.
36. Ibn Farḥūn, *Tabṣirat al-Ḥukkām*, 1:29.
37. Ibid., 1:64–69. Al-Bājī's work in particular offers many examples of how judges used *'amal* to choose from a number of competing views. See al-Bājī, *Fuṣūl al-Aḥkam*, 32 (on testimony), 135 and passim (on writing of verdicts).
38. Al-Jīdī, *al-'Urf wa al-'Amal fī al-Madhhab al-Mālikī*, 342.
39. Ibid., 343–349. Al-Shāṭibī went to great length to explain the difference between a custom and innovation (*bid'ah*). He defined *bid'ah* as "an invented way in religion which resembles the way defined by sharí'ah and which is meant to express exaggerated obedience to God." According to this definition the condemned innovation falls mainly in the area of devotional deeds*'(ibādāt)*. See *al-I'tiṣām*, 27–28.
40. Ibn Farḥūn, *Tabṣirat al-Ḥukkām*, 1:162.
41. Ibn 'Ābidīn, "*Nashr al-'Arf fī binā' ba'ḍ al-Aḥkām 'alā al-'Urf*," 15. There are also many other similar expressions, such as *'urf al-muftīn* and *sunnat al-balad*. See, Ibn al-Ṣalāḥ, *Adab*, 111, 117 and al-Bājī, *Fuṣūl al-Aḥkam*, 193.
42. For example, in his fatāwā, Ibn 'Abd al-Salām answers a question about the meaning of the phrase "the people of the (considered) custom (*ahl al-'urf*) and whether the people here refers to people in general or to the scholars exclusively." Ibn 'Abd al-Salām's answer was, "The word custom can be used to refer to the general custom of the public (*'urf al-'āmmah*) as it is the case with currencies and values, to the general linguistic convention (*'urf al-lughah*), to the common juristic convention (*'urf al-fuqahā'*) such as the words and phrases that the jurists often use, to the customary or conventional expressions (*ta'āruf al-'āmmah*), and finally to the sharí'ah convention such as the

cases of dry ablution (*tayammum*), prayer, alms, and pilgrimage." See ʿIzz al-Dīn ʿAbd al-ʿAzīz Ibn ʿAbd al-Salām, *al-Fatāwā al-Mawṣiliyyah*, ed. Iād Khālid al-Ṭabbāʿ (Damascus: Dār al-Fikr, 1999), 29 and also ʿIzz al-Dīn Ibn ʿAbd al-Salām, *Fatāwā Shaykh al-Islām ʿIzz al-Dīn Ibn ʿAbd al-Salām*, ed. Muḥammad Jumʿah Kurdī (Beirut: Mu'ssasat al-Risālah, 1996), 380.

43. The distinction between the claimant (*al-muddaʿī*) and the defendant (*al-muddaʿā ʿalayhi*) was again one of the questions that the jurists debated and one that was also determined, partially, by reference to the common customary practice. Al-Qarāfī noted that the claimant is the one whose argument contradicts either a norm (*aṣl*) or a custom (*ʿurf*). Conversely, the defendant is the one whose argument accords either with a norm or a custom. See Ibn Farḥūn, *Tabṣirat al-Ḥukkām*, 1:140–143 and Ibn ʿAbidín, "*Nashr al-ʿArf fī bināʾ baʿḍ al-Aḥkām ʿalā al-ʿUrf*," 125.
44. Ibn Farḥūn compares the views of the Mālikī school and the Shāfiʿī school. According to the Mālikī school, the judge gives precedence to the husband's denial because of the indication of the common custom. According to the Shāfiʿī view, the judge gives precedence to the wife's claim because the husband's failure to provide for his wife should be the norm to be assumed until the opposite is proven. See Ibn Farḥūn, *Tabṣirat al-Ḥukkām*, 1:141.
45. Ibn Farḥūn, *Tabṣirat al-Ḥukkām*, 1:69 and Ibn al-Shiḥnah, *Lisān al-Ḥukkām*, 238.
46. For many other examples in which custom is used as a preponderating factor, see Ibn Farḥūn, *Tabṣirat al-Ḥukkām*, 1:382–385 and 2:67–69.
47. Ibn Farḥūn, *Tabṣirat al-Ḥukkām*, 1:148. Ibn Farḥūn listed five main criteria for the validity of claims. The first is that it should be known or specified. A person cannot, for example, claim that X owes him "something." The second is that the claim must involve such a right that if the defendant were to admit it, he or she would be under obligation to render it. This excludes non-obligatory agreements such as gifts, for example. The third is that it must involve a valid or a sound purpose. This excludes, for example, the request of an indicted person to have the judge take oath that he was not unfair to the indicted person. The fourth is that it must be emphatic. This excludes, for example, a person's claim about something that he or she "thinks" to be right. The fifth is that the claim must not contradict the common customary practice. See Ibn Farḥūn, *Tabṣirat al-Ḥukkām*, 1:145–148.
48. Ibn Farḥūn, *Tabṣirat al-Ḥukkām*, 1:149.
49. Al-Qarāfī, *al-Iḥkām*, 218–219, 232. Similarly, Ibn Farḥūn, following al-Qarāfī, commented on one form of *murābaḥah* that became obsolete due to a change in custom: "As for today, this is not understood from custom and people in their markets do not deal with each other according to it. Therefore, there is no standard custom (in this case)... Legal opinions, therefore should not be (blindly) extracted from books because they (the books) do not reflect the change in custom." See Ibn Farḥūn, *Tabṣirat al-Ḥukkām*, 2:76. *Murābaḥah* stands for a transaction in which the seller informs the buyer the original price paid for the sold item and agrees on a profit the seller will take in addition to that original price. See al-Bājī, *Fuṣūl al-Aḥkām*, 242.

50. Ibn al-Qayyim, *I'lām al-Muwaqqi'īn*, 1:78–79 and Ibn 'Abd al-Salām, *al-Qawā'id al-Kubrā*, 2:102.
51. Ibn Abī al-Damm, *Kitāb Adab al-Qaḍā'*, 267.
52. Ibid., 269 and al-Bājī, *Fuṣūl al-Aḥkām*, 145. Ibn al-Shiḥnah added marriage and court judgments. See Ibn al-Shiḥnah, *Lisān al-Ḥukkām*, 241.
53. Ibn Abī al-Damm, *Kitāb Adab al-Qaḍā'*, 369–389.
54. Ibid., 376; for the role of custom on lease in general and lease of endowed property, 408; hiring 414–415; registration forms, 428; calculation/estimation of expenses, 458; child support and custody, 545. See also, Ibn al-Shiḥnah, *Lisān al-Ḥukkām*, 237.
55. Ibn al-Qayyim, *I'lām al-Muwaqqi'īn*, 1:44. Ibn al-Ṣalāḥ differentiates between the independent muftī and the dependent muftī. See Abū 'Amr 'Uthmān Ibn al-Ṣalāḥ al-Shahrazūrī, *Adab al-Fatwā wa Shurūṭ al-Muftī wa Ṣifat al-Mustaftī wa Aḥkāmuh wa Kayfiyat al-Fatwā wa al-Istiftā'*, ed. Rif'at Fawzī 'Abd al-Muṭṭalib (Cairo: al-Hay'ah al-Miṣriyyah al-'Ammah li al-Kitāb, 1998), 41–57; Ibn al-Subkī, *Raf' al-Ḥājib*, 4:601 and al-Zarakshī, *al-Baḥr al-Muḥīṭ*, 4:586. On the different types of jurists and their ranks, see Ibn 'Ābidīn "*Sharḥ al-Manẓūmah al-Musammāh 'Uqūd Rasm al-Muftī*" in *Majmū'at Rasā'il Ibn 'Ābidīn*, 11.
56. Al-Qayyim , 1:45.
57. Prohibited (*ḥarām*), reprehensible (*makrūh*), permissible (*mubāḥ*), recommended (*mustaḥabb*), and obligatory (*wājib*).
58. Ibn al-Ṣalāḥ, *Adab al-Fatwā*, 42.
59. According to Ibn al-Ṣalāḥ, the jurist can give the same answer if he finds no difference between the new case and the older one. Some observed that the jurist has to reexamine the case. See Ibn al-Ṣalāḥ, *Adab al-Fatwā*, 84; Ibn al-Subkī, *Raf' al-Ḥājib*, 4: 596; and al-Isnawī, *al-Tamhīd*, 509. Al-Rāzī observed that the reexamination is a sign of the muftī's attainment of the rank of *ijtihād*. See *al-Maḥṣūl*, 6:69; al-Zarakshī, *al-Baḥr*, 4:582; and al-Nawawī, *Ādāb al-Muftī*, 43.
60. Fakhr al-Dīn Ḥasan Ibn Manṣūr al-Uzjandī, *Fatāwā Qāḍikhān* (in the margin of *al-Fatāwā al-Hindiyyah*) (Beirut: Dār al-Ma'rifah, 1973), 2. See also, al-Kāsānī, *Badā'i' al-Ṣanā'i'*, 7:5.
61. Ibn 'Ābidīn notes, "If you said that custom changes from time to time and consequently if a new custom emerges that was not in existence before, would it be possible for the muftī to change the recorded opinion (*al-manṣūṣ*) of the recognized authorities to cope with the new custom? I would say yes. The late jurists (*al-muta'khkhirūn*) changed these recorded opinions on the examples above mainly due to the emergence of a new custom after the time of these early authorities. The muftī, therefore, should consider the new custom for the interpretation of linguistic conventions and also for the rulings that the [earlier] muftī constructed on the basis of his contemporary custom and which later changed into a new one provided that the [later] muftī is qualified to give considered opinions based on careful consideration of the principles of sharī'ah. He should be able to differentiate between customs that may influence the construction of rulings and others that may not. This is the reason the early jurists (*mutaqaddimūn*) stipulated that a muftī must have attained the rank of

*ijtihād*. Although this requirement has become infeasible in our time, the muftī is still required to know legal questions by their conditions and restrictions. The [early] jurists did not always mention these points in detail depending on the assumption that the [learned] reader would be able to understand the missing details which depend on the particular contemporary custom. Therefore, it has been emphasized that...even if the individual memorized all the books of our school, he would not be able to give considered opinions unless he was trained under a competent jurist because the answers to many questions are constructed on the basis of contemporary customs that do not conflict with sharīʿah." Ibn ʿĀbidīn "*Sharḥ al-Manẓūmah al-Musammāh ʿUqūd Rasm al-Muftī*," 45–46.

62. *Taqlīd* stands for the unreflective imitation and unquestioned following of a particular legal school in its entirety.
63. For more on this, see al-Suyūṭī, *Kitāb al-Radd ʿalā man Akhlada ilā al-Arḍ*, 67. On *taqlīd* and *talfīq*, see al-Ḥusaynī, *ʿUmdat al-Taḥqīq fī al-Taqlīd wa al-Talfīq*, 1997.
64. Ibid., 77. See also, Ibn al-Qayyim, *Iʿlām al-Muwaqqiʿīn*, 2:466; al-Zarakshī, *al-Manthūr fī al-Qawāʿid*, 2:99; and al-Nawawī, *Ādāb al-Fatwā*, 40. Some jurists differentiated between unspecified currencies in new contracts on the one hand and unspecified currencies in formal claims before a judge on the other. In the case of new contracts it can be interpreted according to the common custom because contracts are initiated in the present while the common custom is being upheld. Claims, on the other hand, pertain to former transactions which might be associated with a different (previous) customary practice. See Ibid., 101.
65. Ibn ʿAbidīn, "*Nashr al-ʿArf fī binā' baʿḍ al-Aḥkām ʿalā al-ʿUrf*," 117–119, 122. Ibn ʿAbidīn explained that custom applies as long as there is only one currency in circulation. If there were more than one currency in circulation, the failure of the contract to specify one of them would, in all likelihood, result in disagreement and even dispute.
66. Taqyy al-Dīn Aḥmad Ibn ʿAbd al-Ḥalīm Ibn ʿAbd al-Salām IbnTaymiyyah, *Majmūʿ Fatāwā Shaykh al-Islām Aḥmad Ibn Taymiyyah*, ed. ʿAbd al-Raḥmān Ibn Muḥammad Ibn Qāsim al-ʿAṣimī (Cairo: Maktabat Ibn Taymiyyah, 1970), 19:235.
67. This ruling is based on a clear text in the Qur'ān: "A divorce is only permissible twice, after that the parties should either hold together on equitable terms or separate with kindness." Verse 2:229.
68. *ʿIddah* is the waiting period that a woman observes after the dissolution of the marital bond. The main purpose of this waiting period is to verify whether there is pregnancy as a result of the dissolved marriage. There are three types of *ʿiddah:* the first is the one observed by a widow, which is four months and ten days. The second is the one observed by the divorcee, which is the duration of three menstrual periods. The third is the one observed by a pregnant woman, which extends for the duration of her pregnancy.
69. The waiting period extends for three consecutive menstruation periods. This is again based on a clear text in the Qur'ān, verse2:228.
70. Ibn al-Qayyim, *Iʿlām al-Muwaqqiʿīn*, 2:25. The overwhelming majority of the jurists held the view that the triple divorce nullifies marriage and renders

it irrevocable. Ibn Taymiyyah, on the other hand, held the view that it only counts as one pronouncement. See Ibn Qudāmah, al-Mughnī, 8:407 and Abū Zakariyyā Yaḥyā Ibn Sharaf al-Nawawī, *al-Manthūrāt fī 'Uyūn al-masā'il al-Muhimmāt*, ed. Muḥammad Raḥmat Allah al-Nadwī (Beirut: al-Maktab al-Islāmī, 2001), 214.

71. Ibn al-Qayyim, *I'lām al-Muwaqqi'īn*, 2:30. Ibn al-Qayyim gave nine different examples that illustrate the change of legal opinions following changing circumstances. In his treatment of these nine examples he sought to highlight the guidelines that govern the application of this principle. The first example is about the principle of commanding the good and forbidding the evil. Ibn al-Qayyim concluded that if the elimination of an evil results in a greater evil, the lesser evil takes priority over the greater evil. The second and third examples discuss the suspension of public punishments (*ḥudūd*) in war time. The fourth example discusses the possibility of giving the charity of breaking the fast (*ṣadaqat al-fiṭr*) according to the common staple food. The fifth example discusses the famous ḥadīth of *al-muṣarrāh* (an animal that was left intentionally unmilked to lure potential buyers by giving the impression that it produces more milk than the average). The sixth example discusses the permissibility of circumambulation around the Ka'bah for a woman during the menstrual period. The seventh example discusses the issue of three combined pronouncements of divorce. The eighth example discusses the payment of the dowry. See Ibid., 2: 5–76. Ibn al-Qayyim has also invoked *'urf* in many other examples in the area of contractual transactions. See Ibid., 1: 606–607.

72. Ibn 'Ābidīn, *Nashr al-'Arf fī binā' ba'ḍ al-Aḥkām 'alā al-'Urf*, 123. Ibn 'Ābidīn gives many examples of cases whose rulings changed over time in view of changing customs. They include the paying for teaching Qur'ān, the insufficiency of the presumed uprightness of witnesses, the interpretation of particular expressions that are related to oaths, among many others. See Ibid., 123–125, 131. See also, Ibn 'Ābidīn *Sharḥ al-Manẓūmah al-Musammāh 'Uqūd Rasm al-Muftī*, 44–45.

73. See, for example, Aḥmad Ibn Yaḥyā al-Wansharīsī, *al-Mi'yār al-Mu'rib wa al-Jāmi' al-Mughrib 'an Fatāwā Ahl Ifrīqiyah wa al-Andalus wa al-Maghrib*, ed. Muḥammad Ḥijjī (Rabaṭ: Wazārat al-Awqāf wa al-Shu'ūn al-Islāmiyyah, 1981), 3:18 on the estimation of the period of the absence of a spouse (especially the husband) that will allow the other spouse to deal with issues such as divorce or inheritance; on marital expenses 3:28, 36, 44, 46; on bridal furniture 3:46 and passim; on custody, breastfeeding and other related issues 4:21, 25, 39, and passim; on bridal gifts 9:180–181. See also, al-Shaykh Niẓām, *al-Fatāwā al-Hindiyyah*, 1:291, 328 and passim. See Ibn Qudāmah, *al-Mughnī*, 7: 377, 391; 9:230 and passim; 12:225. See also, al-Kāsānī, *Badā'i' al-Ṣanā'i'*, 2:308, 309, 320 and 4:23.

74. Ibn 'Abidīn, *Nashr al-'Arf fī binā' ba'ḍ al-Aḥkām 'alā al-'Urf*, 116.

75. Ibn Rushd, *Bidayat al-Mujtahid wa Nihāyat al-Muqtaṣid*, 2:231. The famous six usurious items are gold, silver, wheat, barley, dates, and salt. They were the ones mentioned in this famous ḥadīth: "(when) gold is traded for gold, (it has to be) an equal measure for an equal measure and hand by hand—the

surplus will be usury, silver is traded for silver an equal measure for an equal measure and hand by hand—the surplus will be usury, wheat is traded for wheat, an equal measure for an equal measure and hand by hand—the surplus will be usury, salt is traded for salt, an equal measure for an equal measure and hand by hand—the surplus will be usury, barley is traded for barley, an equal measure for an equal measure and hand by hand—the surplus will be usury, dates are traded for dates, an equal measure for an equal measure and hand by hand—the surplus will be usury." Obviously, the immediate exchange of equal amounts of the same kind does not involve any gain. The ḥadīth was meant to prevent exchange of certain amounts of these kinds for larger/smaller amounts of its kind based on a difference in quality (e.g., one pound of dates of a better quality for two pounds of dates of a lesser quality). Ultimately, the ḥadīth aimed to rule out any possibility of exploitation, but also to regulate trade of these items that are considered staple food. The ḥadīth also discourages preferential treatment of items of the same kind, for that often opens the door for extravagance and wasteful consumption. Only the Ẓāhirī school limited the scope of usury to these six items. The other schools had their own explanation of the operative cause for the prohibition of these particular items and therefore they had different opinions on what can or cannot be included among these "usurious items." The Ḥanafī school, for example, reasoned that these items were singled out because they were measured either by weight, in the case of gold and silver (*mawzūn*), or volume, in the case of the rest (*makīl*), and therefore any item that is measured by weight or volume will also be included even if it was not expressly mentioned in the ḥadīth. The Shāfiʿī school reasoned that these items were singled out because they were considered either standard prices, in the case of gold and silver (*thaman*), or edible items (*maṭʿūm*), and therefore any item that meets these criteria will also be included even if it was not expressly mentioned. The Mālikī school reasoned that they were singled out because, similar to the Shāfiʿī school in the case of gold and silver, they are standard prices. In the case of the other items they are staple food (*qūt*), which is usually stored for long-term consumption (*muddakhar*). Consequently, according to the Mālikī school, any item that meets these criteria will be included even if it was not expressly mentioned in the ḥadīth. For more details on this and on the distinctions between surplus usury (*ribā al-faḍl*) and deferred usury (*ribā al-nasīʾah*), see al-Sanhūrī, *Maṣādir al-Ḥaqq fī al-Fiqh al-Islāmī*, part 3 2:124–137.

76. Al-Wansharīsī, *al-Miʿyār*, 5:20.
77. For example, see al-Wansharīsī, *al-Miʿyār*, on the value of currencies 5:46, 56; amenities of rented houses 5:86; estimation of prices 5:91, 96, 106; estimation of fees 5:154. See also, Ibn ʿĀbidīn, *Nashr al-ʿArf fī binā' baʿḍ al-Aḥkām ʿalā al-ʿUrf*, 134. There are many other prominent examples of transactions whose rulings were either constructed or amended in view of custom. For the contract of sale which entails a condition of redemption (*bayʿ al-wafā'*), see *al-Fatāwā al-Hindiyyah*, 3:208–209. For the different forms of sharecropping (*musāqāh*, *muzāraʿah*, and *mukhābarah*), see al-Nawawī, *Ṣaḥīḥ Muslim bi Sharḥ al-Nawawī*, 5:part 10, 160. For the different options in contracts

(*khiyār*), see Shams al-Dīn Muḥammad Ibn Muḥamad al-Khaṭīb al-Shirbīnī, *Mughnī al-Muḥtāj ilā Maʿrifat Maʿānī alfāẓ al-Mihāj*, ed. ʿAlī Muḥammad Muʿawwaḍ and ʿĀdil Aḥmad ʿAbd al-Mawjūd (Beirut: Dār al-Kutub al-ʿIlmiyyah, 1994), 2:160. Covering the entire range of transactions and contractual agreements in the major works of substantive law or legal responses would definitely fall beyond the scope of the present context. Surveying the full extent of the concept of custom would require more focused attention on the treatment of the concept within the framework of particular schools or even particular works. See, for example, ʿAbd al-ʿAzīz al-Khayyāṭ, *Naẓariyyat al-ʿUrf*, 108–127; al-Sayyid Ṣāliḥ ʿAwaḍ, *Athar al-ʿUrf fī al-Tashrīʿ al-Islāmī* (Cairo: Dār al-Kitāb al-Jāmiʿī, 1981), 244–251; Muftī, *al-ʿUrf ʿinda al-Uṣūliyyīn wa Atharuhu fī al-Aḥkām al-Fiqhiyyah*, 151–181; and Qūtah, *al-ʿUrf*, 2:992.

78. See, for example, *al-Fatāwā al-Hindiyyah*, for the estimation of the menstrual period, 1:39–40; for the payment of the charity following the month of Ramadān according to the common staple food, 191–192; for fasting and the swallowing of insignificant pieces of food, 208.

# Bibliography

## Arabic Sources


ʿAbd al-Bāqī, Muḥammad Fu'ād. *al-Muʿjam al-Mufahras li Alfāẓ al-Qur'ān al-Karīm*. Cairo: Dār al-Ḥadīth, 2001.

ʿAbd al-Jabbār, Abū al-Ḥasan. *Al-Mughnī fī Abwāb al-Tawḥīd wa al-ʿAdl*. Cairo: al-Dār al-Miṣriyyah lil Ta'līf wa al-Tarjamah wa al-Nashr, 1965.

ʿAbd al-Khāliq, ʿAbd al-Ghanī. *Ḥujjiyyat al-Sunnah*. Manṣūrah: Dār al-Wafā', 1997.

Abu Dāwūd al-Sijistānī, Sulaymān Ibn al-Ashʿath al-Azdī. *Sunan Abī Dāwūd*, ed. Muḥammad Muḥyī al-Dīn ʿAbd al-Ḥamīd, Dār Iḥyā' al-Sunnah al-Nabawiyah. Beirut: Dār Iḥyā' al-Sunnah al-Nabawiyah,1970.

Abū Sunnah, Aḥmad Fahmī. *al-ʿUrf wa al-ʿĀdah fī Naẓar al-Fuqahā'*. Cairo: Dār al-Baṣā'ir, 2004.

Abū Zahrah, Muḥammad. *Uṣūl al-Fiqh*. Cairo: Dār Al-Fikr al-ʿArabī, 2004.

ʿAlā'ī, Ṣalāḥ al-Dīn Khalīl Kikaldī. *al-Majmūʿ al-Mudhhab fī Qawāʿid al-Madhhab*, ed. Majīd ʿAlī al-ʿUbaydī and Aḥmad Khuḍayr Abbas. Amman: Dār Ammār, 2004.

ʿĀliyah, Samīr. *Niẓām al-Dawlah wa al-Qaḍā' wa al-ʿUrf fī al-Islām*. Beirut: al-Mu'assasah al-Jāmiʿiyyah lil Dirāsāt wa al-Nashr wa al-Tawzīʿ, 1997.

ʿĀlimkīr, Abū al-Muẓaffar Muḥyī al-Dīn Muḥammad Urangzīb. *al-Fatāwā al-Hindiyyah*. Beirut: Dār al-Maʿrifah, 1973.

Āmidī, Sayf al-Dīn ʿAlī Ibn Abi ʿAlī Ibn Muḥammad. *al-Iḥkām fī Uṣūl al-Aḥkām*, Beirut: Dār al-Fikr, 1996.

Anṣārī, Abd al-ʿAlyy Muḥammad Ibn Niẓām al-Dīn. *Fawātiḥ al-Raḥamūt*. (printed together with al-Ghazālī's *Mustaṣfā*).

Ashʿarī, Abu al-Ḥasan ʿAlī Ibn Ismāʿīl. *Maqālāt al-Islamyyīn wa Ikhtilāf al-Muṣallīn*, ed. Muḥammad Muḥyī al-Dīn ʿAbd al-Ḥamīd. Beirut: al-Maktabah al-ʿAṣriyyah, 1990.

ʿAsqalānī, Aḥmad Ibn ʿAli Ibn Ḥajar. *Fatḥ al-Bārī bi Sharḥ Ṣaḥiḥ al-Bukhārī*. Cairo: Maktabat al-ʿIlm, 2000.

ʿAwaḍ, al-Sayyid Ṣāliḥ. *Athar al-ʿUrf fī al-Tashrīʿ al-Islāmī*. Cairo: Dār al-Kitāb al-Jāmiʿī, 1981.

ʿAwdah, ʿAbd al-Qādir. *al-Tashrī' al-Jinā'i al-Islāmī muqāranan bi al-Qānūn al-Waḍʿī*. Cairo: Maktabat Dār al-Turāth, 2003.

A'ẓamī, Muḥammad Muṣṭafa. *Dirāsāt fī al-Ḥadīth al-Nabawī.* Beirut: al-Maktab al-Islāmī, 1992.

Baghdādī, 'Abd al-Qāhir Ibn Ṭāhir Ibn Muḥammad. *Kitāb al-Farq bayna al-Firaq wa Bayān al-Firqah al-Nājiyah Minhum*, ed. Muḥammad Badr. Cairo: Matba'at al-Ma'ārif, 1910.

Bājī, Sulaymān Ibn Khalaf Ibn Sa'd Ibn Ayyúb. *al-Muntaqā Sharḥ Muwaṭṭa' al-Imam Mālik.* Cairo: Maṭba'at al-Sa'ādah, 1983.

———. *Fuṣūl al-Aḥkām wa bayān mā Maḍā 'alayhi al-'Amal 'inda al-Fuqahā' wa al-Ḥukkām*, ed. Muḥammad Abū al-Ajfān. Tunis: al-Dār al-'Arabiyyah lil Kitāb, 1985.

Baqillānī, Abū al-Ṭayyib Muḥammad. *Kitāb al-Tamhīd*, ed. Richard Yusuf Macarthi. Beirut: al-Maktabah al-Sharqiyyah, 1957.

Barādhi'ī, Abū Sa'īd. *al-Tahdhīb fī Ikhtiṣār al-Mudawwanah*, ed. Muḥammad al-Amīn Walad Muḥammad Sālim bin al-Shaykh. Dubayy: Dār al-Buḥūth lil Dirāsāt al-Islāmiyyah wa Iḥyā' al-Turāth, 2002.

Baṣrī, Abū al-Ḥusayn Muḥammad Ibn 'Alī. *Kitāb al-Mu'tamad fī Uṣūl al-Fiqh*, ed. Muḥammad Ḥamid Allah and Ḥasan Ḥanafī. Damascus: al-Ma'had al-'Ilmī a l-Faransī lil Dirāsāt al-'Arabiyyah, 1964–1965.

Bayhaqī, Abu Bakr Aḥmad Ibn al-Ḥusayn. *al-Sunan al-Kubrā*, ed. Muḥammad 'Abd al-Qādir 'Aṭā. Beirūt: Dār al-Kutub al-'Ilmiyyah, 1994.

———. *Manāqib al-Shāfi'ī*, ed. al-Sayyid Aḥmad Ṣaqr. Cairo: Dār al-Turāth, 1971.

Bukhārī, 'Alā' al-Dīn 'Abd al-'Azīz Ibn Aḥmad. *Kashf al-Asrār 'an Uṣūl Fakhr al-Islām al-Bazdawī*, ed. Muḥammad al-Mu'taṣim bi Allah al-Baghdādī. Beirut: Dār al-Kitāb al-*'Arabī*, 1997.

Būṭī, Muḥammad Sa'īd Ramaḍān. *Ḍawābiṭ al-Maṣlaḥah fī al-Sharī'ah al-Islāmiyyah.* Damascus: Dār al-Fikr, 2005.

Dabbūsī, Abu Zayd Ibn 'Umar Ibn 'Īsā. *Taqwīm al-Adillah fī Uṣūl al-Fiqh*, ed. Khalīl Muḥyī al-Dīn al-Mays. Beirut: Dār al-Kutub al-'Ilmiyyah, 2001.

———. *Ta'sīs al-Naẓar*, ed. Zakariyah 'Alī Yusuf. Cairo: Zakariyyah 'Alī Yūsuf, 1972.

Dahlawī, Shāh Waliyullah. *Ḥujjat Allah al-Bālighah.* Delhi: Sharikat Amin Delhi, 1373 A.H.

Dīb 'Abd al-'Aẓīm. *Fiqh Imām al-Ḥaramayn 'Abd Al-Malik Ibn 'Abd Allāh al-Juwaynī.* Manṣūrah: Dār al-Wafā', 1988.

Fārābī, Abū Naṣr. *Iḥṣā' al-'Ulūm*, ed. Osman Amine. Cairo: Maktabat al-Anglo, 1968.

Farrā', Abū Ya'lā Muḥammad Ibn al-Ḥusayn. *al-Aḥkām al-Sulṭāniyyah.* Cairo: Maktabat al-Qur'ān, n.d.

Ghazālī, Muḥammad. *al-Sunnah al-Nabawiyah bayna Ahl al-Fiqh wa Ahl al-Ḥadith.* Cairo: Dār al-Shurūq, 2005.

Ghazālī, Abu Ḥamid Muḥammad Ibn Muḥammad. *Tahāfut al-Falāsifah*, ed. Muḥammad Al-Sa'īd Muḥammad. Cairo: al-Maktabah al-Tawfiqiyyah, 2003.

———. *Mi'yār Al-'Ilm*, ed. Sulaymān Duniyā . Cairo: Dār Al-Ma'ārif, 1961.

———. *al-Munqidh min al-Ḍalāl*, ed. 'Abd al-Ḥaliīm Maḥmūd. Cairo: Dār al-Kutub al-Ḥadīthah, 1974.

———. Ghazālī, Abu Ḥāmid Muḥammad Ibn Muḥammad. *al-Mustaṣfā min ʿilm al-Uṣūl*. Beirut: Dār al-Fikr, n.d.

———. Ghazālī, Abu Ḥāmid Muḥammad Ibn Muḥammad. *Iḥyāʾ ʿulūm al-Dīn*. Cairo: al-Maktabah al-Tijāriyyah al-Kubrā, n.d.

———. Ghazālī, Abu Ḥāmid Muḥammad Ibn Muḥammad. *Majmuʿat Rasāʾil al-Imām al-Ghazālī*, ed. Ibrāhīm Amin Muḥammad. Cairo: al-Maktabah al-Tawfiqiyyah, n.d.

Ḥalūlū, Aḥmad Ibn ʿAbd al-Raḥmān Ibn Mūsā. *Kitāb al-Ḍiyāʾ al-Lāmiʿ Sharḥ Jamʿ al-Jawāmiʿ*, ed. Nādī Faraj al-ʿAṭṭār. Cairo: Markaz Ibn al-ʿAṭṭār lil Turāth, 2004.

Ḥasan, Khalifah Bābakr. *al-Adillah al-Mukhtalaf fīhā ʿinda al-Uṣūliyyīn*. Cairo: Maktabat Wahbah, 1987.

Ḥaydar, ʿAlī. *Durar al-Ḥukkām Sharḥ Majallat al-Aḥkām*. Beirut: Dār al-Jīl, 1991.

Ḥusaynī , Muḥammad Saʿīd Ibn ʿAbd al-Raḥmān al-Bānī. *ʿUmdat al-Taḥqīq fī al-Taqlīd wa al-Talfīq*. Damascus: Dār al-Qādirī, 1997.

Ibn ʿAbd al-Salam, ʿIzz al-Dīn ʿAbd al-ʿAzīz. *al-Qawāʿid al-Kubrā al-Mawsūm bi Qawāʿid al-Aḥkām fī Iṣlāḥ al-Anām*, ed. Nazīh Hammad and Uthman Ḍamīriyyah. Damascus: Dār al-Qalam, 2000.

———. ʿIzz al-Dīn ʿAbd al-ʿAzīz. *al-Fatāwā al-Mawṣiliyyah*, ed. Iād Khālid al-Ṭabbāʿ. Damascus: Dār al-Fikr, 1999.

———. ʿIzz al-Dīn ʿAbd al-ʿAzīz. *Fatāwā Shaykh al-Islām ʿIzz al-Dīn Ibn ʿAbd al-Salām*, ed. Muḥammad Jumʿah Kurdī. Beirut: Muʾssasat al-Risālah, 1996.

Ibn Abī al-Damm, Shihāb al-Dīn Ibrāhīm Ibn ʿAbd Allāh. *Kitāb Adab al-Qaḍāʾ aw al-Durar al-Manẓūmāt fī al-Aqḍiyah wa al-Ḥukūmāt*, ed. Muḥammad ʿAbd al-Qādir ʿAṭā. Beirut: Dār al-Kutib alʿIlmiyyah, 1987.

Ibn ʿĀbidīn, Muḥammad Amīn. *Hāshiyat Radd al-Muḥtār ʿalā al-Durr al-Mukhtār, Sharḥ Tanwīr al-Abṣār*. Cairo: Mustafa al-Babī al-Ḥalabī, 1966.

———. *Majmūʿat Rasāʾil Ibn ʿĀbidīn*. Beirut: Dār Iḥyāʾ al-Turāth n.d.

Ibn Amir al-Ḥājj, Muḥmmad Ibn Muḥammad. *al-Taqrīr wa al-Taḥbīr ʿalā al-Taḥrīr fī ūṣūl al-Fiqh*, ed. ʿAbd Allah Maḥmūd Muḥammad. Beirut: Dār al-Kutub alʿIlmiyyah, 1999.

Ibn ʿAqīl, Abū al-Wafāʾ ʿAlī. *Kitāb al-Waḍiḥ fī Usūl al-Fiqh*. Beirut: Muassasat al-Risālah, 1999.

Ibn al-ʿArabī, Abu Bakr Muḥammad Ibn ʿAbd Allah. *Aḥkām al-Qurʾān*, ed. Muḥammad Bakr Ismāʿīl. Cairo: Dār al-Manār, 2002.

Ibn ʿAsākir, ʿAlī Ibn al-Ḥasan. *Tabiyīn Kadhib al-Muftarī Fimā Nusiba ilā al-Imām Abī al-Ḥasan al-Ashʿarī*. Beirut: Dār al-Kitāb al-ʿArabī, 1979.

Ibn Farḥūn, Burhān al-Dīn Ibrāhīm Ibn ʿAlī Ibn Abī al-Qāsim Ibn Muḥammad. *al-Dībāj al-Mudhahhab fī Maʿrifat Aʿyān ʿUlamāʾ al-Madhhab*, ed. Muḥammad al-Aḥmadī Abu al-Nūr. Cairo: Dār al-Turāth, 1975.

———. *Tabṣirat al-Ḥukkām fī al-Aqḍiyah wa Manāhij al-Aḥkām*. Cairo: Maktabat al-Kulliyyāt al-Azhariyyah, 1986.

Ibn Ḥanbal, Aḥmad. *Musnad al-Imām Aḥmad Ibn Ḥanbal*, ed. Shuʿayb al-Arnāʾūṭ, Beirut: Muʾassasat al-Risālah, 1998.

Ibn Ḥazm, ʿAlī Ibn Saʿīd. *al-Iḥkām fī Uṣūl al-Aḥkām*. Cairo: Dār al-Ḥadīth, n.d.

———. *al-Fiṣal fī al-Milal wa al-Ahwā' wa al-Niḥal*. Cairo: Maktabat Muḥammad Ṣubayḥ, 1965.

Ibn Hishām. *al-Sīrah al-Nabawiyyah*, ed. Suhayl Zakkār. Beirūt: Dār al-Fikr, 1992.

Ibn Juzayy, Muḥammad Ibn Aḥmad. *Taqrīb al-Wuṣūl ilā ʿIlm al-Uṣūl*, ed. ʿAbd Allah Muḥammad al-Jabbūrī. Amman: Dār al-Nafā'is, 2002.

Ibn Kathīr, Ismāʿil Ibn ʿUmar. *al-Sirah al-Nabawiyyah*. Cairo: Matbaʿat ʿIsā al-Bābi al-Ḥalabī, 1964.

Al-Khādimī, Nūr al-Dīn Mukhtār. *ʿIlm al-Qawāʿid al-Sharʿiyyah*. al-Riyaḍ: Maktabat al-Rushd, 2005.

Ibn Khaldūn, ʿAbd al-Rahmān. *Muqadimat Ibn Khaldūn*, ed. Ḥamid Aḥmad Al-Ṭahir. Cairo: Dār Al-Fajr lil Turāth, 2004.

Ibn Manẓur, Jamāl al-Dīn Muḥammad Ibn Mukarram. *Lisān al-ʿArab*. Beirūt: Dār Ṣādir, 1955.

Ibn Munabbih, Hammam. *Ṣaḥifat Hammām Ibn Munabbih ʿan Abī Hurayrah*, ed. Rifʿat Fawzī ʿAbd al-Muṭṭalib. Cairo: Maktabat al-Khanji, 1985.

Ibn al-Murtaḍā, Aḥmad Ibn Yaḥyā. *Kitāb al-Muniyah wa al-Amal fī Sharḥ al-Milal wa al-Niḥal*, ed. Muḥammad Jawād Mashkūr. Beirut: Dār al-Fikr, 1979.

Ibn Nujaym, Zayn al-ʿĀbidīn Ibn Ibrāhīm. *al-Ashbāh wa al-Naẓā'ir ʿalā Madhhab Abī Ḥanīfah al-Nuʿmān*. Cairo: al-Maktabah al-Tawfiqiyyah, n.d.

Ibn al-Qayyim, Muḥammad Ibn Abi Bakr Ibn Ayyūb. *Iʿlām al-Muwaqiʿīn ʿan Rabb al-ʿĀlamīn*. Cairo: Dār al-Ḥadith, 2002.

———. *al-Ṭuruq al-Ḥukmiyyah fī al-Siyāsah al-Sharʿiyyah*. Cairo: Dār al-Ḥadīth, 2002

Ibn Qudāmah, Muwaffaq al-Dīn ʿAbd Allah Ibn Aḥmad Ibn Muḥammad. *al-Mughnī*. Beirut: Dār al-Kutub al-ʿIlmiyyah, n.d.

Ibn Rajab, ʿAbd al-Raḥmān al-Baghdādī. *al-Qawāʿid fī al-Fiqh al-Musammā Taqrīr al-Qawāʿid wa Taḥrīr al-Fawā'id*. Beirut: Bayt al-Afkār al-Dawliyah, 2004.

Ibn Rushed, Abu al-Walīd Muḥammad Ibn Aḥmad. *Bidayat al-Mujtahid wa Nihāyat al-Muqtaṣid*. Cairo: al-Maktabah al-Tawfiqiyyah, n.d.

Ibn Rushd, Abu al-Walīd Muḥammad Ibn Aḥmad. *Manāhij al-Adillah fī ʿAqā'id al-Millah*, ed. Mahmūd Qāsim. Cairo: Maktabat al-Anglo al-Miṣriyyah, 1964.

Ibn al-Ṣalāḥ al-Shahrazūrī, Abū ʿAmr ʿUthmān. *Muqadimat Ibn al-Ṣalāḥ*, ed. ʿĀishah ʿAbd al-Raḥmān, Cairo: Dār al-Maʿārif, 1990.

Ibn al-Ṣalāḥ al-Shahrazūrī, Abū ʿAmr ʿUthmān. *Adab al-Fatwā wa Shurūṭ al-Muftī wa Ṣifat al-Mustaftī wa Aḥkāmuh wa Kayfiyat al-Fatwā wa al-Istiftā'*, ed. Rifʿat Fawzī ʿAbd al-Muṭṭalib, Cairo: al-Hay'ah al-Miṣriyyah al-ʿAmmah lil Kitāb, 1998.

Ibn al-Samʿānī, Manṣūr Ibn Muḥammad Ibn ʿAbd al-Jabbār. *Qawāṭiʿ al-Adillah fī al-Uṣūl*. Beirut: Dār al-Kutub al-ʿIlmiyyah, 1997.

Ibn al-Shiḥnah, Abū al-Walīd Ibrāhīm Muḥammad Ibn Abī al-Faḍl. *Lisān al-Ḥukkām fī Maʿrifat al-Aḥkām*. Beirut: Dār al-Fikr, 1982. (published together with al-Ṭarābulsī, ʿAlāʾ al-Dīn ʿAlī Ibn Khalīl *Muʿīn al-Ḥukkām fīmā Yataradad bayna al-Khiṣmayn min al-Aḥkām*).

Ibn al-Subkī, Tāj al-Dīn ʿAbd al-Wahhāb. *Ṭabaqāt al-Shāfiʿiyyah al-Kubrā*, ed. Mahmūd Muhammad al-Tanāḥī and ʿAbd al-Fattaḥ Muḥammad al-Ḥilw. Cairo: ʿIsā al-Bābī al-Ḥalabī, 1967.

Ibn al-Subkī, Tāj al-Dīn ʿAbd al-Wahhāb Ibn ʿAlī. *Rafʿ al-Ḥājib ʿan Mukhtaṣar Ibn al-Ḥājib*, ed. ʿAlī Muḥammad Muʿawwaḍ and ʿĀdil Aḥmad ʿAbd al-Mawjūd. Beirut: ʿĀlam al-Kutub, 1999.

Ibn al-Subkī, Tāj al-Dīn ʿAbd al-Wahhāb Ibn ʿAlī. *al-Ashbāh wa al-Naẓāʾir*, ed. ʿĀdil Aḥmad ʿAbd al-Mawjūd and ʿAlī Muḥammad ʿAwaḍ. Beirut: Dār al-Kutub al-ʿIlmiyyah, 1991.

Ibn al-Subkī, Tāj al-Dīn ʿAbd al-Wahhāb Ibn ʿAlī. *Jamʿ al-Jawāmiʿ*. Beirut: Dār Ibn Ḥazm, 2005.

Ibn Sulaymān, Muqātil. *Tafsīr Muqātil Ibn Sulayman*, ed. ʿAbd Allah Maḥmūd Shiḥātah. Cairo: al-Hayʾah al-Miṣriyyah al-ʿĀmmah li a- Kitāb, 1983.

IbnTaymiyyah, Taqyy al-Dīn Aḥmad Ibn ʿAbd al-Ḥalīm Ibn ʿAbd al-Salām. *Majmūʿ Fatāwā Shaykh al-Islām Aḥmad Ibn Taymiyyah*, ed. ʿAbd al-Raḥmān Ibn Muḥammad Ibn Qāsim al-ʿAṣimī. Cairo: Maktabat Ibn Taymiyyah, 1970.

———. *al-Qawāʿid al-Nūrāniyyah al-Fiqhiyyah*, ed. Muḥammad Ḥāmid al-Fiqī. Cairo: Matbaʿat al-Sunnah al-Muḥammadiyyah, 1951.

Ibn al-Wakīl, Ṣadr al-Dīn. *al-Ashbāh wa al-Naẓāʾir*, ed. Aḥmad Ibn Muḥammad al-ʿAnqarī and ʿAdil Ibn ʿAbd Allah al-Shuwaykh. al-Riyāḍ: Maktabat al-Rushd, 1993.

Imām, Muhammad Kamāl al-Dīn. *Uṣūl al-Fiqh al-Islāmī*. Beirut: al-Muʾassasah al-Jāmiʿiyyah lil Dirāsāt wa al-Nashr wa al-Tawzīʿ, 1996.

ʿImarah, Muḥammad. *Islāmiyyāt al-Sanhūrī Bāshā*. Mansura: Dār al-Wafāʾ, 2006.

Iṣbahānī, Maḥmūd Ibn ʿAbd al-Raḥmān. *Bayān al-Mukhtaṣar, Sharḥ Mukhtaṣar Ibn al-Ḥājib fī Uṣūl al-Fiqh*, ed. ʿAlī Jumʿah Muḥammad. Cairo: Dār al-Salām, 2004.

Isfahānī, al-Rāghib. *Muʿjam Mufradāt Alfāẓ al-Qurʾān*. Beirut: Dār al-Kātib al-ʿArabī, 1972.

Isnawī, Jamāl al-Dīn ʿAbd al-Raḥīm Ibn al-Ḥasan. *al-Tamhīd fī Takhrīj al-Furūʿ ʿalā al-Uṣūl*, ed. Muḥammad Ḥasan Hītū. Beirut: Muʾassasat al-Risālah, 1980.

Isnawī, Jamāl al-Dīn ʿAbd al-Raḥīm Ibn al-Ḥasan. *Nihāyat al-Sawl fī Sharḥ Minhāj al-Wuṣūl ilā ʿIlm al-Uṣūl*, ed. Shaʿbān Muḥammad Ismāʿīl. Beirut: Dār Ibn Ḥazm, 1999.

ʿIyāḍ, Abu al-Faḍl ʿIyāḍ Ibn Musa. *Tartīb al-Madārik wa Taqrīb al-Masālik li Maʿrifat Aʿlām Madhhab Malik*, ed. Aḥmad Bakīr Maḥmūd. Beirut: Maktabat al-Ḥayah, 1967

Jābrī, Muḥammad ʿĀbid. *Binyat al-ʿAql al-ʿArabī*. Beirut: Markaz Dirasāt al-Waḥdah al-ʿArabiyyah, 1996.

Jābrī, Muḥammad ʿĀbid. *Tahāfut al-Tahāfut, Intiṣāran lil Rūḥ al-ʿIlmiyyah wa Ta'sīsan li Akhlaqiyyāt al-Ḥiwār*. Beirut: Markaz Dirasāt al-Waḥdah al-ʿArabiyyah, 1998.

Jazirī, ʿAbd Al-Raḥmān. *Kitāb al-Fiqh ʿala al-Madhāhib al-Arbaʿah*. Beirut: Dār al-Kutub al-ʿIlmiyyah, 1990.

Jīdī, ʿUmar ʿAbd al-Karīm. *al-ʿUrf wa al-ʿAmal fī al-Madhhab al-Mālikī wa Mafhūmuhumā ladā ʿUlamā' al-Maghrib*. Rabāṭ: al-Lajnah al-Mushtarakah lil Nashr wa Iḥiyā' al-Turāth, 1982.

Jurjānī, ʿAlī Ibn Muḥammad al-Sayyid. *Kitāb al-Taʿrīfāt*. Cairo: Dār al-Rashād, 1978.

Juwaynī, Abu al-Maʿālī ʿAbd al-Malik Ibn ʿAbd Allah. *al-Burhān fī Uṣūl al-Fiqh*, ed. ʿAbd al-ʿAẓīm al-Dīb. Cairo: Dār al-Anṣār, 1980.

———. *Kitāb al-Irshād ilā Qawāṭiʿ al-Adillah fī Uṣūl al-Iʿtiqād*, ed. Muḥammad Yūsuf Mūsā and ʿAli ʿAbd al-Munʿim ʿAbd al-Ḥamīd. Cairo: Maktabat al-Khānjī, 2002.

———. *al-Talkhīṣ fī Usūl Al-Fiqh*, ed. Muḥammad Ḥasan Ismāʿīl. Beirut: Dār Al-Kutub Al-ʿIlmiyyah, 2003.

———. *Ghiyāth al-Umam fī Iltiyāth al-Ẓulam*, ed. Mustafā Ḥilmī and Fu'ād ʿAbd al-Munʿim Aḥmad. Alexandria: Dār al-Daʿwah, 1979.

Kafrāwī, Asʿad ʿAbd al-Ghanī. *al-Istidlāl ʿInda al-Uṣūliyyīn*. Cairo: Dār al-Salām, 2005.

Karkhī, Abu al-Ḥasan. *Risalah fī al-Uṣūl*, Cairo: Zakariyā ʿAlī Yusuf, 1972. (published together with *Ta'sīs al-Naóar* of al-Dabbúsí).

Kāsānī, ʿAlā' al-Dīn Ibn Masʿūd. *Kitāb Badā'iʿ al-Ṣanā'iʿ fi Tartīb al-Sharā'iʿ*. Beirut: Dār al-Kitāb al-ʿArabī, 1974.

Khallāf, ʿAbd al-Wahhāb. *Maṣādir al-Tashrīʿ al-Islāmī fimā lā Naṣṣa fīh*. Kuwait: Dār al-Qalam, 1970.

Khaṭīb al-Shirbīnī, Shams al-Dīn Muḥammad Ibn Muḥamad. *Mughnī al-Muḥtāj ilā Maʿrifat Maʿānī alfāẓ al-Mihāj*, ed. ʿAlī Muḥammad Muʿawwaā and ʿĀdil Aḥmad ʿAbd al-Mawjūd. Beirūt: Dār al-Kutub al-ʿIlmiyyah, 1994.

Khayyaṭ, ʿAbd al-Azīz. *Naẓariyyat al-ʿUrf*. Amman: Maktabat al-Aqṣā, 1977.

Khudarī, Muḥammad. *Tarikh al-Tashrīʿ al-Islāmī*. Cairo: al-Matbaʿah al-Tijāriyyah al-Kubrā, 1970.

Maḥmaṣānī, Ṣubḥī. *Falsafat al-Tashrīʿ, al-Islāmī*. Beirut: Dār al-ʿIlm lil Malāyīn, 1975.

———. *Muqadimah fī Iḥiyā' ʿulūm al-Sharīʿah*. Beirūt: Dār al-ʿIlm li al-Malāyīn, 1962.

Marʿashlī, Muḥammad ʿAbd al-Raḥmān. *Ikhtilāf al-Ijtihād wa Taghayyuruhu wa Athar dhālika fī al-Futyā*. Beirut: al-Mu'ssassah al-Jāmiʿiyyah l-al-Dirāsāt wa al-Nashr wa al-Tawzīʿ, 2003.

Māwardī, ʿAlī Ibn Muḥammad. *al-Aḥkām al-Sulṭāniyyah*. Cairo: al-Maktabah al-Tawfīqiyyah, n. d.

Muftī, Muṣṭafā Muḥammad Rushdī. *al-ʿUrf ʿinda al-Usūlyyīn wa Atharuhū fī al-Ahkām al-Fiqhiyyah*. Alexandria: Dār al-Imān, 2006.

Nadwī, ʿAlī Aḥmad, *al-Qawāʿid al-Fiqhiyah*. Damascus: Dār al-Qalam, 2004.

Nashshār, ʿAlī Sāmī, *Manāhij al-Baḥth ʿinda Mufakirī al-Islām*. Cairo, Dār al-Maʿārif, 1967.

Nawawī, Muḥyī al-Dīn Abu Zakariyya Yaḥya Ibn Sharaf, *Ṣaḥiḥ Muslim bi Sharḥ al-Nawawī*. Cairo: Dār al-Manār, 2003.

———. *al-Manthūrāt fī ʿUyūn al-masāʾil al-Muhimmāt*, ed. Muḥammad Raḥmat Allah al-Nadwī. Beirut: al-Maktab al-Islāmī, 2001.

———. *Ādāb al-Fatwā wa al-Muftī wa al-Mustaftī*, ed. Bassām ʿAbd al-Wahhāb al-Jābī. Damascus: Dār al-Fikr, 1988.

Qarāfī, Abu al-ʿAbbas Aḥmad Ibn Idrīs, *al-Iḥkām fī Tamyīz al-Fatāwā ʿan al-Aḥkām wa Taṣarrufāt al-Qāḍī wa al-Imām*, ed. ʿAbd al-Fattāḥ Abū Ghuddah. Beirūt: Dār al-Bashāʾir al-Islamiyyah, 1995.

———. *al-ʿIqd al-Manẓūm fī al-Khuṣūṣ wa al-ʿŪmūm*, ed. ʿAlī Muḥammad Muʿawwaḍ and ʿAdil Aḥmad ʿAbd al-Mawjūd. Beirut: Dār al-Kutub al-ʿIlmiyyah, 2001.

Qarāfī, Abu al-ʿAbbas Aḥmad Ibn Idrīs, *Kitāb al-Furūq, Anwāʾ al-Burūq fī Anwāʾ al-Furūq*, ed. Muḥammad Aḥmad Sirāj and ʿAlī Jumʿah Muḥammad. Cairo: Dār al-Salām, 2001.

———. *Sharḥ Tanqīḥ al-Fuṣūl*, ed. Ṭāhā ʿAbd al-Raʾūf Saʿd. Cairo: Maktabat al-Kulliyyāt al-Azhariyyah, 1973.

Qurṭubī, Abu ʿAbd Allah Muḥammad Ibn Aḥmad al-Anṣārī, *al-Jāmiʿ li Aḥkām al-Qurʾān*, ed. Muḥmmad Ibrāhīm al-Ḥifnāwī and Maḥmūd Ḥāmid ʿUthmān. Cairo: Dār al-Ḥadīth, 1994.

Qutah, ʿAdil Ibn ʿAbd al-Qādir, *al-ʿUrf Ḥujjiyyatuhu wa Atharuhu fī Fiqh al-Muʿāmalāt al-Māliyyah ʿinda al-Ḥanābilah*. Makkah: al-Maktabah al-Makiyyah, 1997.

Rāzī, Fakhr al-Dīn Muḥammad Ibn ʿUmar, *al-Maḥṣūl fī ʿIlm Uṣūl al-Fiqh*, ed. Tāha Jābir al-ʿAlawānī. Beirūt: Muassasat al-Risālah, 1992.

Rāzī, Fakhr al-Dīn Muḥammad Ibn ʿUmar Ibn Ḥusayn, *Mafātiḥ al-Ghayb*. Cairo: al-Matbaʿah al-Bahiyyah, 1934.

Rāzī, Muḥammad Ibn ʿUmar, *Manāqib al-Shāfiʿī*, ed. Aḥmad Ḥijāzī al-Saqqā. Cairo: Maktabat al-Kulliyyāt al-Azhariyyah, 1986.

Rāzī, Abū Bakr Aḥmad Ibn ʿAlī al-Jaṣāṣ, *Uṣūl al-Jaṣāṣ al-Musammā al-Fuṣūl fī al-Uṣūl*, ed. Muḥammad Muḥammad Tāmir. Beirut: Dār al-Kutub al-ʿIlmiyyah, 2000.

Riḍā, Muḥammad Rashīd, *Fatāwa al-Imām Muḥammad Rashīd Riḍā*, ed. Ṣalāḥ al-Dīn Al-Munajjid and Yūsuf al-Khūrī ed. Beirut: Dār al-Kitāb al-Jadīd, 1971.

Rūqī, Muḥammad. *al-Qawāʿid al-Fiqhiyyah min khilāl Kitāb al-Ishrāf lil Qāḍī ʿAbd al-Wahhab al-Baghdādī*. Dubayy: Dār al-Buḥūth lil Dirāsāt al-Islāmiyyah wa Iḥyāʾ al-Turāth, 2003.

Sābiq, Sayyid. *Fiqh al-Sunnah*. Beirut: al-Maktabah al-ʿAṣriyyah, 1999.

Sanhurī, ʿAbd al-Razzāq. *Maṣādir al-Ḥaqq fī al-Fiqh al-Islāmī*. Beirut: Dār Iḥyāʾ al-Turāth al-ʿArabī, 1997.

Sarakhsī, Abu Bakr Muḥammad Ibn Aḥmad Ibn Abi Sahl. *Kitāb al-Kasb*, ed. ʿAbd al-Fattāḥ Abū Ghuddah, Ḥalab, Damascus: Maktab al-Maṭbūʿāt al-Islāmiyyah, 1997.

Sarakhsī, Abu Bakr Muḥammad Ibn Aḥmad Ibn Abi Sahl. *Uṣūl al-Sarakhṣī*, ed. Abu al-Wafa al-Afghānī. Beirut: Dār al-Kutub al-ʿIlmiyyah, 1993.

———. *Kitāb al-Mabsūṭ*. Beirut: Dār al-Maʿrifah, 1978.

—— Shāfiʿī, Muḥamad Ibn Idrīs. *al-Risālah*, Ed. Aḥmad Muḥamad Shākir. Beirut: Dār al-Kutub al-ʿIlmiyyah, n.d.

———. *Kitāb al-Umm*, ed. Aḥmad Badr al-Dīn Hassūn. Beirut: Dār Qutaybah, 1996.

Shahrastānī, Abu Al-Fatḥ Muḥammad ʿAbd al-Karīm. *Nihayat al-Iqdām fī ʿIlm al-Kalām*, ed. Alfred Giyum. Baghdād: Maktabat al-Muthannā, 1964.

———. *al-Milal wa al-Niḥal*, ed. ʿAbd al-ʿAzīz Muḥammad al-Wakīl. Cairo: Muʾassasat al-Ḥalabī, 1968.

Shalabī, Muḥammad Muṣtafā. *Taʿlīl al-Aḥkām*. Beirut: Dār al-Nahḍah al-ʿArabiyah, 1981.

Shāṭibī, Abu Isḥāq Ibrāhīm. *Al-Muwafaqāt fī Uṣul al-Sharīʿah*, ed. ʿAbd Allah Darrāz. Cairo: al-Maktabah al-Tawfiqiyyah, 2003.

Shaybānī, Muḥammad Ibn al-Ḥasan. *Kitāb al-Aṣl*, ed. Abu al-Wafā al-Afghānī. Ḥaydarābād: Majlis Dāʾirat al-Maʿārif al-ʿUthmāniyyah, 1971.

Shirāzī, Abu Isḥāq Ibrāhīm. *Sharḥ al-Lumaʿ*, ed. ʿAbd al-Majīd Turkī. Beirut: Dār al-Gharb al-Islāmī, 1988.

Sibaʿī, Muṣtafa. *al-Sunnah wa makanatuha fī al-Tashrīʿ al-Islāmī*. Beirut: al-Maktab al-Islamī, 1976.

Suyūṭī, Jalāl al-Dīn ʿAbd al-Raḥmān. *al-Ashbāh wa al-Naẓāʾir fī Qawāʿid wa Furūʿ al-Shāfiʿiyyah*, ed. Muḥammad Muḥammad Tāmir and Ḥāfiẓ ʿĀshūr Ḥāfiẓ. Cairo: Dār al-Salām, 2004.

———. *Tanwīr al-Ḥawālik Shaḥ Muwaṭṭaʾ al-Imām Mālik*. Cairo: al-Maktabah al-Tijāriyyah, 1969.

———. *Kitāb al-Radd ʿalā man Akhlada ilā al-Arḍ wa Jahila anna al-Ijtihād fī Kulli ʿAṣr Farḍ*, ed. Khalīl al-Mays. Beirut: Dār al-Kutub al-ʿIlmiyyah, 1983.

Tabarī, Abu Jaʿfar Muḥammad Ibn Jarīr. *Jāmiʿ al-Bayān ʿan Taʾwīl āyy al-Qurʾān*. Cairo: Muṣṭafā al-Bābī al-Ḥalabī, 1954.

Tamīmī, Abū al-ʿArab Muḥammad Ibn Aḥmad. *Kitāb al-Miḥan*, ed. Yaḥya Wahīb al-Jabbūrī. Beirūt: Dār al-Gharb al-Islāmī, 1983.

Ṭanṭāwī, Maḥmūd Muḥammad. *Uṣūl al-Fiqh al-Islāmī*. Cairo: Maktabat Wahbah, 2001.

Ṭarābulsī, ʿAlāʾ al-Dīn ʿAlī Ibn Khalīl. *Muʿīn al-Ḥukkām fīmā Yataradad bayna al-Khiṣmayn min al-Aḥkām*. Beirut: Dār al-Fikr, 1982.

Ṭūfī, Najm al-Dīn Sulaymān Ibn ʿAbd al-Qawī. *Sharḥ Mukhtaṣar al-Rawḍah*, ed. ʿAbd Allah Ibn ʿAbd al-Muḥsin al-Turkī. Beirut: Muʾssasat al-Risālah, 1987.

———. *Darʾ al-Qawl al-Qabīḥ bi al-Taḥsīn wa al-Taqbīḥ*, ed. Ayman Maḥmūd Shiḥādah. Riyāḍ: Markaz al-Malik Fayṣal lil Buḥūth wa al-Dirāṣāt al-Islāmiyyah, 2005.

Ṭūfī, Najm al-Dīn Sulaymān Ibn ʿAbd al-Qawī. *ʿAlam al-Jadhal fī ʿIlm al-Jadal*, ed. Wolfhart Heinrichs.Wiesbaden: Franz Steiner Verlag, 1987.

Uzjandī, Fakhr al-Dīn Ḥasan Ibn Manṣūr. *Fatāwā Qāḍikhān*, (in the margin of *al-Fatāwā al-Hindiyyah*). Beirut: Dār al-Maʿrifah, 1973.

Wansharīsī, Aḥmad Ibn Yaḥyā. *al-Miʿyār al-Muʿrib wa al-Jāmiʿ al-Mughrib ʿan Fatāwā Ahl Ifrīqiyah wa al-Andalus wa al-Maghrib*, ed. Muḥammad Ḥijjī. Rabāṭ: Wazārat al-Awqāf wa al-Shuʾūn al-Islāmiyyah, 1981.

———. *Kitāb al-Wilāyāt*, ed. Henri Bruno et al. Rabat: Moncho, 1937.

Zamakhsharī, Maḥmūd Ibn ʿUmar. *al-Kashshāf ʿan Ḥaqāʾiq Ghawāmiḍ al-Tanzīl wa ʿUyūn al-āqāwīl fī Wujūh al-Taʾwīl*, ed. Muṣṭafā husayn Aḥmad. Qumm: Manshūrāt al-Balāghah, 1992.

Zanjānī, Shihāb al-Dīn Maḥmūd Ibn Aḥmad. *Takhrīj al-Furūʿ ʿalā al-Uṣūl*, ed. Muḥammad Adīb Ṣāliḥ. Beirut: Muʾssasat al-Risālah, 1979.

Zarakshī, Badr al-Dīn Muḥammad Ibn Bahādir Ibn ʿAbd Allah. *al-Baḥr al-Muḥīṭ fī Uṣūl al-Fiqh*, ed. Muḥammad Muḥammad Tāmir. Beirut: Dār al-Kutub al-ʿIlmiyyah, 2000.

———. *Tashnīf al-Masāmiʿ bi Jamʿ al-Jawāmiʿ*, ed. al-Ḥusaynī Ibn ʿUmar. Beirut: Dār al-Kutub al-ʿIlmiyyah, 2000.

Zarakshī, Badr al-Dīn Muḥammad Ibn Bahādir Ibn ʿAbd Allah. *al-Manthūr fī al-Qawāʿid*. Beirut: Dār al-Kutub al-ʿIlmiyyah, 2000.

Zarqā, Aḥmad Muḥammad. *Sharḥ al-Qawāʿid al-Fiqhiyyah*. Damascus: Dār al-Qalam, 2001.

Zarqa, Mustafā Aḥmad. *al-Madkhal al-Fiqhī al-ʿĀmm*. Damascus: Dār al-Qalam, 1998.

Ziriklī, Khayr al-Dīn. *al-Aʿlām*. Beirut: Dār al-ʿIlm lil Malāyīn, 1979.

Zubaydī, Muḥammad Murtaḍā al-Ḥusaynī. *Tāj al-ʿArūs min Jawāhir al-Qāmūs*, ed. Muṣṭafā Ḥijāzi. Kuwayt: Wizarat al-Iʿlām, 1987.

## ENGLISH SOURCES

Abbott, Nabia. *Studies in Arabic Literary Papyri*. Chicago: University of Chicago Press, 1967.

Abd-Allah, Umar Faruq. "Malik's Concept of ʿamal in the light of Malikī Legal Theory." Ph.D. diss., University of Chicago, 1978

Abou El-Fadl, Khaled. *Rebellion and Violence in Islamic Law*. Cambridge: Cambridge University Press, 2001.

———. *Speaking in God's Name, Islamic Law, Authority and Women*. Oxford: One World, 2006.

Ahmad, Ahmad Atif. *Structural interrelations of theory and practice in Islamic law: a study of six works of medieval Islamic jurisprudence*. Leiden: Brill, 2006.

Ali, Abdullah Yusuf. *The Meaning of the Holy Qurʾān*. Brentwood: Amana Corporation, 1991.

Asad, Talal. *The Idea of an Anthropology of Islam*. Washington D. C.: Center for Contemporary Arab Studies, Georgetown University, 1986.

Azami, Muhammad Mustafa. *The History of the Quranic Text: From Revelation to Compilation a Comparative Study with the Old and New Testament*. Leicester: UK Islamic Academy, 2003

———. *On Schacht's Origins of Muhammadan Jurisprudence*. New York: Wiley, 1985.

Azmeh, Aziz. *Islamic Law Social and Historical Contexts*. London: Routledge, 1988

Berman, Harold. *Law and Revolution, the Formation of the Western Legal Tradition*. Cambridge: Harvard University Press, 1983.

Besant, Walter. *The Life and Achievements of Edward Henry Palmer*, London: J. Murray, 1883.

Beidelman, T. O. *W. Robertson Smith and the Sociological Study of Religion*. Chicago: University of Chicago Press, 1974.

Berg, Herbert, ed. *Method and Theory in the Study of Islamic Origins*. Leiden: Brill, 2003.

Bargeron, Carol. "Re-thinking Necessity (*al-Ḍarūra*) in al-Ghazālī's Understanding of Physical Causation," *Theology and Science*, 5, no. 1 (2007).

———. "The Concept of Causality in Abu Hāmid Muhammad Al-Ghazālī's Tahafut Al-Flāsifah," Ph.D. diss., University of Wisconsin-Madison, 1978.

Burton, John. *The Collection of the Quran*. Cambridge: Cambridge University Press, 1977.

Calder, Norman. *Studies in Early Muslim Jurisprudence*. Oxford: Clarendon Press, 1993.

Coulson, Noel. *Conflicts and Tensions in Islamic Jurisprudence*. Chicago: University of Chicago Press, 1969.

———. *A History of Islamic Law*. Edinburgh: Edinburgh University Press, 1964.

Crone, Patricia. *Roman, Provincial and Islamic Law, the Origin of the Islamic Patronate*. Cambridge: Cambridge University Press, 1987.

Dutton, Yasin. *The Origins of Islamic Law: The Quran, The Muwatta, and the Madinan Amal*. Surrey: Curzon, 1999.

Fakhry, Majid. *Islamic Occasionalim and its Critique by Averroes and Aquinas*, London: George Allen & Unwin, 1958.

Frazer, James. "William Robertson Smith." In *Thinking about Religion a Reader*, edited by Ivan Strenski, 91–96. Oxford: Blackwell Publishing, 2006.

Gerber, Haim. *Islamic Law and Culture, 1600–1840*. Leiden: Brill, 1999.

Gibb, H. A. R. *Mohammedanism,an Historical Survey*. Oxford: Oxford University Press, 1980.

Goldziher, Ignaz. *Muslim Studies*. London: Allen and Unwin, 1967.

———. *Introduction to Islamic Theology and law*. Princeton: Princeton University Press, 1981.

———. *Tagebuch*. Leiden: Brill, 1978.

Graham, William. "Traditionalism in Islam: An Essay in Interpretation" *Journal of Interdisciplinary History* 23, no. 3 (1993): 495–522.

Hallaq, Wael. "Was the Gate of Ijtihad Closed," *International Journal of Middle East Studies* 16 (1984): 3–41.

———. "Was al-Shāfiʿī the Master Architect of Islamic Jurisprudence," *International Journal of Middle East Studies*, 25 (1993): 578–605.

———. "From *Fatawas* to *Furu'*: Growth and Change in Islamic Substantive Law" *Islamic Law and Society* 1(1994): 29–65.

———, ed. *The Formation of Islamic Law*. Burlington: Ashgate/Variorum Publishing Limited, 2004.

———. "The Use and Abuse of Evidence: The Question of Provincial and Roman Influences on Early Islamic Law" *Journal of American Oriental Society*, 110, no. 1(1990): 79–91.

———. *Law and Legal Theory in Classical and Medieval Islam*. Brookfield: Variorum, 1994.

———. *Authority, Continuity, and Change in Islamic Law*. Cambridge: Cambridge University Press, 2001.

———. "The Quest for Origins or Doctrine" *UCLA Journal of Islamic and Near East Law* 2, no. 1 (2002–2003).

———. *The Origins and Evolution of Islamic Law*. Cambridge: Cambridge University Press, 2005.

Hasan, Ahmad. *The Early Development of Islamic Jurisprudence*. Islamabad: Islamic Research Institute, 1970.

Heinrichs, Wolfhart. "Qawāʿid as a Genre of Legal Literature." in *Studies in Islamic Legal Theory*, edited by Bernard Weiss. Leiden: Brill, 2002.

Hourani, Albert. *Islam in European Thought*. Cambridge: Cambridge University Press, 1991.

Humphreys, Stephen. *Islamic History A Framework for Inquiry*. Princeton: Princeton University Press, 1991.

Huff, Toby and Wolfgang Schluchter ed. *Max Weber and Islam*. New Brunswick: Transaction Publishers, 1999.

Hurgronje, Christiaan Snouck. *Mohammedanism Lectures on its Origins, its Religious and Political Growth, and its Present State*. New York: Putnam's sons, 1916.

———. *The Achehnese*. Leyden: Brill, 1906.

———. *Mekka in the Latter Part of the 19th Century*. Leiden: Brill, 1931.

———. *Selected Works of C. Snouck Hurgronje*. Edited by G. H. Bousquet and J. Schacht. Leiden: Brill, 1957.

Izutsu, Toshihiko. *Ethico Religious Concepts in the Qur'ān*. Montreal: McGill-Queen's University Press, 2002.

Kamālī, Muḥammad Hāshim. *Principles of Islamic Jurisprudence*. Cambridge: Islamic Texts Society, 1991.

Lucas, Scott. *Constructive Critics, Hadith Literature and the Articulation of Sunni Islam: The Legacy of the Generation of Ibn Saʿd, Ibn Maʿīn, and Ibn Ḥanbal*. Leiden: Brill, 2004.

Johansen, Baber. "Casuistry between Legal Concept and Social Praxis." *Islamic Law and Society*, 2, no. 2 (1995): 135–156

———. *Contingency in a Sacred Law: Legal and Ethical Norms in Muslim Fiqh*. Leiden: Brill, 1999.

———. *The Islamic Law on Land Tax and Rent*. London: Croom Helm, 1988.

Jackson, Sherman. *Islamic Law and the State: The Constitutional Jurisprudence of Shihab Al-Din Al-Qarafi*. Leiden: Brill, 1996.

Juynboll, G. H. A. *Muslim Tradition: Studies in Chronology, Provenance, and authorship in Early Hadith*. Cambridge: Cambridge University Press, 1983.

Khalidi, Tarif. *Arabic Historical Thought in the Classical Period*. Cambridge: Cambridge University Press, 1994.

Kamālī, Muḥammad Hāshim. *Principles of Islamic Jurisprudence*. Cambridge: Islamic Texts Society, 1991.

Kletzer, Christoph. "Custom and Positivity: an examination of the Philosophic ground of the Hegel-Savigny Controversy" in *The Nature of Customary*

*Law*, edited by Amanda Perreau-Saussine and James B. Murphy, 125–148. Cambridge: Cambridge University Press, 2007.

Libson, Gideon. "on the Development of Custom as a Source of Law in Islamic Law." *Islamic Law and Society* 4, no. 2(1997): 131–155.

———. *Jewish and Islamic Law a Comparative Study of Custom during the Geonic Period*. Cambridge: Harvard University Press, 2003.

Lowry, Joseph. *Early Islamic Legal Theory, the Risāla of Muḥammad Ibn Idrīs al-Shāfiʿī*. Leiden: Brill, 2007.

Makdisi, John. "Legal Logic and Equity in Islamic Law" *The American Journal of Comparative Law* 33, no. 1 (1985): 63–92.

———. "Formal Rationality in Islamic Law and The Common Law" *Cleveland State Law Review* 34 (1985–1986): 97–112.

Mallat, Chibli ed. *Islam and Public Law*. London: Graham and Trotman, 1993.

Marmura, Michael. *The Incoherence of the Philosophers*. Provo, Utah: Brighan Young University Press, 1997.

Masud, Muhammad K., Brinkley Messick, and David S. Powers, ed. *Islamic Legal Interpretation: Muftis and their Fatwas*. Cambridge: Harvard University Press, 1996.

Masud, Muhammad K., Rudoloph Peters, and David S. Powers, ed., *Dispensing Justice in Islam, Qadis and their Judgements*. Leiden: Brill, 2006.

Masud, Muhammad Khalid. *Shāṭibī's Philosophy of Islamic Law*. Kuala Lumpur: Islamic Book Trust, 2000.

Messick, Brinkley. *The Calligraphic State, Textual Domination and History in Muslim Society*. Berkeley: University of California Press, 1993.

Motzki, Harald. *The Origins of Islamic Jursprudence Meccan Fiqh before Classical Schools*. Leiden: Brill, 2002.

Müller, Friedrich Max. "Preface to *Chips from a German Woodshop*" in *Thinking about Religion, a Reader*, edited by Ivan Strenski, 49–53. Oxford: Blackwell Publishing, 2006.

El-Nahal, Galal. *The Judicial Administration of Ottoman Egypt in the Seventeenth Century*. Minneapolis: Bibliotheca Islamica, 1979.

Peters, Rudolph. "Ijtihad and Taqlid in 18th and 19th century Islam." *Die Welt des Islams* 20 (1980): 131–145.

———. "Murder on the Nile, Homicide Trials in 19th Century Egyptian Shari'a Courts." *Die Welt des Islams* 30 (1990): 98–116.

Rahman, Fazlur. *Islamic Methodology in History*. Karachi: Central Institute of Islamic Research, 1965.

Ramadan, Said. *Islamic Law Its Scope and Equity*. London: P. R. Macmillan, 1961.

Schacht, Joseph. *The Origins of Muhammadan Jurisprudence*. Oxford: Clarendon Press, 1959.

———. *An Introduction to Islamic Law*. Oxford: Clarendon Press, 1964.

———. "Modernism and Traditionalism in a History of Islamic Law." *Middle Eastern Studies* 1, no. 4 (1965): 388–400.

Shaham, Ron ed. *Law Customs, and Statue in the Muslim World, Studies in honor of Aharon Layish*. Leiden: Brill, 2007.

Smith, William Robertson. *Kinship and Marriage in Early Arabia*. London: Darf Publishers LTD, 1990.

———. *Religion of the Semites*. New Brunswick: Transaction Publishers, 2002.

———. *Lectures and Essays of William Robertson Smith*. Edited by John Sutherland. London: A. and C. Black, 1912.

Strenski, Ivan. *Thinking about Religion, an Historical Introduction to Theories of religion*. Oxford: Blackwell Publishing, 2006.

———. *Thinking about Religion, a Reader*. Oxford: Blackwell Publishing, 2006.

Turner, Bryan. *Weber and Islam*. London: Routledge, 1974.

Udovitch, Abraham. "Islamic Law and the Social Context of Exchange in the Medieval Middle East." *History and Anthropology* 1 (1985): 445–465

Van den Bergh, G. C. J. J. "The Concept of Folk Law in Historical Context: A Brief Outline" in *Folk Law, Essays in the Theory and Practice of Lex Non Scripta*. Edited by Alison D. Renteln and Alan Dundes. New York: Garland Publishing, 1994.

Van Koningsveld, P. S. j. *Scholarship and Friendship in Early Islamwissenschaft, the Letters of C. Snouck Hurgronje to I. Goldziher*. Leiden: Faculteit der Godgeleerdheid, 1985.

Vogel, Frank. "The State of the Field: A Major Advance is Imminent." *The Newsletter of The Islamic Legal Studies Program at Harvard Law School* 11, no. 2 ( 2006): 1–4.

Vrijhof, Pieter H. and Jacques Waardenburg ed. *Official and Popular Religion*. The Hague: Mouton, 1979.

Wakin, Jeanette. *Remembering Joseph Schacht (1902–1969)*. Cambridge: Islamic Legal Studies Program, Harvard Law School, 2003.

Waardenburg, Jacques ed. *Classical Approaches to the Study of Religion*. Berlin: Walter de Gruyter, 1999.

———. *Islam, Historical, Social, and Political Perspectives*. Berlin: Walter de Gruyter, 2002.

———. *Muslims as Actors*. Berlin: Walter de Gruyter, 2007.

Wansbrough, John. *Quranic Studies: Sources and Methods of Scriptural Interpretation*. Oxford: Oxford University Press, 1977.

Watson, Alan and Khaled Abou El-Fadl. "Fox Hunting, Pheasant Shooting, and Comparative Law." The *American Journal of Comparative Law* 48, no. 1(2000):1–37.

Waston, Alan. *Society and Legal Change*. Philadelphia: Temple University Press, 2001.

Watt, Montgomery. *The Faith and Practice of Al-Ghazali*. Oxford: Oneworld Publications, 2000.

Wolfson, Harry Austryn. *The Philosophy of Kalam*. Cambridge: Harvard University Press, 1976.

Zaman, Muhammad Qasim. *The Ulama in Contemporary Islam, Custodians of Change*. Princeton: Priceton University Press, 2002.

# Index

Made in the USA
Monee, IL
15 September 2026

63215534R00149